Perspectives on Human Suffering

Jeff Malpas • Norelle Lickiss
Editors

Perspectives on Human Suffering

Springer

Editors
Jeff Malpas
School of Philosophy
University of Tasmania
Private Bag 41
Hobart Tasmania
Australia
e-mail: jeff.malpas@utas.edu.au

Norelle Lickiss
School of Philosophy
University of Tasmania
Private Bag 41
Hobart Tasmania
Australia
e-mail: n.lickiss@sydney.edu.au

ISBN 978-94-007-2794-6 e-ISBN 978-94-007-2795-3
DOI 10.1007/978-94-007-2795-3
Springer Dordrecht Heidelberg London New York

Library of Congress Control Number: 2011946259

Printed on acid-free paper

Springer is part of Springer Science+Business Media (www.springer.com)

Foreword

His Excellency, the Honourable Peter Underwood AC, Governor of Tasmania

The philosopher Thomas Hobbes, in his 1651 treatise *Leviathan* written during the English Civil War, famously concluded that without the protection of political society people's lives would be 'solitary, poor, nasty, brutish, and short'. The bluntness of the statement reinforces the reality that governance by laws reduces individual and collective suffering. It is equally the case that medical treatment reduces suffering. Arguably therefore these two great pillars of civilization—the legal and the medical—exist in their sophistication substantially because of human suffering. Hence to examine the phenomenon is to examine considerably more than pain and anguish; a feat ably achieved in *Perspectives on Human Suffering*.

The task is complex, ranging as it must from overarching philosophical considerations (of which the progenitor may be the frequently invoked 'The Book of Job'), through great ravages caused by nature and war, to the vicarious suffering experienced by a carer or loved one empathizing with a single sufferer. As suggested by one contributor, suffering 'raises fundamental questions to which all our disciplines offer but a partial answer'. Furthermore, 'tracing the history of suffering is an immense task'. Who would have thought that such an apparently base condition could be so vexatious and elusive?

Definitions of suffering are offered throughout the book. Collectively they take into account the innumerable ways that one can 'suffer', be that physically, psychologically, spiritually or in some combination of these. An agreed generic definition seems to be this: 'A state of severe distress associated with events that threaten the intactness of the person [as a person]'. This is a description of suffering as a personal phenomenon, and it is accepted that suffering is overwhelmingly realized as an individual experience. Even so, one person's severe distress might not be another's. The language of suffering, as befitting the subject and its investigation in a philosophical treatise, is sensitive and requires handling with care. To take another example, 'illness' is defined in these pages as 'a deficit of well-being', which seems uncomfortably bland, yet is entirely accurate. (It would however be a brave contributor to any debate about suffering, and thankfully there is none here, describing with equal accuracy a torturer as engaging with the tortured in a negatively physical manner for a desired outcome.)

Not surprisingly suffering has always been a key component of religious thought. Whether caused by 'an act of God', accident, disease, infamous human behaviour or something else altogether, the question is invoked: why must the innocent and the righteous suffer? Consider these as answers: we suffer in this life because of sins in a previous life; suffering in this life will lead to reward in the next life; Christ suffered for our sins; suffering is proof that there is no divine benevolent being. These are foundational matters underpinning the great religions; surely another indication of the overbearing influence of suffering on humanity.

The contributors to *Perspectives on Human Suffering* write with considerable authority, in a range of disciplines, the latter evidenced by the division of the work into three discrete sections, which themselves are somewhat multi-faceted. The contributors also represent a truly international viewpoint, an essential feature when considering the meaning and purpose of a book such as this one. Editors Jeff Malpas and Norelle Lickiss, following on their editorship of *Perspectives on Human Dignity*, have ensured that impressive intellect and variety is brought to bear upon this difficult subject. Indeed, the very act of pondering the meaning and modes of suffering and then writing about it cannot be easy.

Perspectives on Human Suffering makes an important contribution to contemporary thinking about mortality and morality, be it in a small hospital ward or in the Security Council of the United Nations. We can individually desire not to suffer, but can never be immune from it. We therefore need to continually strive to increase our understanding of this fundamental aspect of our being, in order to be able to deal with suffering—for ourselves, and for our fellow human beings where we can.

Acknowledgements

The idea of conversation that underpins this volume has its physical realization in a series of interdisciplinary colloquia that have been held at the University of Tasmania in Hobart, Tasmania, more or less every two years since 2004 (now known as the W. D. Joske Interdisciplinary Colloquium), and that have focused on human dignity, human suffering, human hope, and, in 2012, on human presence. The physical event is the counterpart to the printed volume, but only in the sense that the one provides the impetus and inspiration for the other. The Colloquium series has its own dynamic and its own outcomes that are very different from those of a published work, while the list of contributors to *Perspectives on Human Suffering* only partially matches the list of participants in the corresponding Colloquium. Nevertheless, since this volume would not have occurred without the Colloquium, we would like both to acknowledge and to thank those who have been participated in those meetings, who have provided support for them, and who have contributed to in a range of other ways to their success.

In particular, we wish to thank the University of Tasmania, including both the School of Philosophy and the Office of Events and Protocol (especially Amanda Wojtowicz); Jane Frankin Hall; Mundipharma Australia; Sydney University and the Sydney Institute for Palliative Medicine. We are also grateful to the family of the late Prof W. D. Joske for ensuring that the Colloquium will continue into the future.

More specific to the volume itself, we are grateful to Maja de Keijzer at Springer (as well as Fritz Schmuhl) for supporting our proposal to publish a sequel to *Perspectives on Human Dignity*. Thanks go to Maja and her team for their work in getting the volume into press—edited volumes such as this are complex and sometimes difficult beasts, and to have an understanding and supportive editor makes an enormous difference. We thank the Governor of Tasmania, the Honourable Peter Underwood, for providing a Foreword to the volume. We are also extremely grateful to our contributors for providing us with the material without which this volume would not exist, and for their willingness to take part in the conversation.

Finally, Prof Jeff Malpas's work on this volume has been undertaken as part of an Australian Research Council Professorial Fellowship, and we gratefully acknowledge this support.

Contents

Notes on Contributors

Andrew Benjamin is Professor of Philosophical Aesthetics at Monash University, Melbourne. His most recent books include *Of Jews and Animals* (2010) and *Place, Commonality and Judgment: Continental Philosophy and the Ancient Greeks* (2010).

Dougal Blyth is Senior Lecturer in Classics and Ancient History at the University of Auckland. His most recent articles have been on Cicero (*Classical Journal*, 2010) and Menander (*Antichthon* 2008). He is a co-editor (with Dirk Baltzly and Harold Tarrant) of *Power and Pleasure, Virtues and Vices* (*Prudentia* Supplement 2001) and author of other articles and book chapters on Aristophanes, Plato and Aristotle.

Andrew Brennan is Professor of Philosophy and Pro-Vice Chancellor (Graduate Research) at LaTrobe University in Melbourne. His most recent publications include *Understanding Environmental Philosophy* (2010) and *Logic: Key Concepts* (2005).

Frank Brennan is a Palliative Care Physician. He has an interest in all aspects of Palliative Care, including its interface with the law and humanities. In 2009 he published *Standing on the Platform–Stories and Reflections From Palliative Care*. He is also a lawyer and has written extensively on the human rights dimensions of pain management and Palliative Care.

Gaetano Chiurazzi is Professor of Philosophy at the University of Turin. He is the editor of the journal *Tropos* and his most recent books include *Teorias del Juricio* (2009) and *Modalität und Existenz* (2005).

Jack Coulehan is Emeritus Professor of Medicine and Senior Fellow of the Center for Medical Humanities, Compassionate Care, and Bioethics at Stony Brook University. His most recent books include *The Medical Interview: Mastering Skills for Clinical Practice* (F. A. Davis, 2005) and *Primary Care: Poems by Physicians* (University of Iowa, 2006).

Grant Gillett is a qualified neurosurgeon and practiced until 2006. He is now a Professor of Medical Ethics at the Bioethics Centre of the Medical School, at the University of Otago, New Zealand, and a fellow of the Royal Society. He is author of *The Mind and its Discontents* (2009), *Subjectivity and Being Somebody: human identity and neuroethics* (2008), *Bioethics in the clinic: Hippocratic reflections* (2004) and over 250 articles in philosophy, bioethics, the philosophy of psychiatry and neuroscience.

Guy Green was the Chief Justice and then the Governor of Tasmania. Amongst other offices he is Chairman of Trustees, Tasmanian Museum and Art Gallery. Recent publications include 'Governors, Democracy and the Rule of Law' (2006), 'Human Dignity and the Law' (2007), and 'Skepticism in Science' (2008).

Edith Hall was, until recently Research Professor at Royal Holloway University of London. She is now Professor of Classics at King's college London. Her most recent books are Th*e Return of Ulysses: a Cultural History of Homer's Odyssey* (Johns Hopkins, 2008), *Greek Tragedy: Suffering under the Sun* (Oxford, 2010) and *India, Greece and Rome 1757–2007* (Institute of Classical Studies, 2010).

Matthew Hamilton is a 5th year medical student at Otago University New Zealand. Moving through medical training his interest is in the complex power relations between patient, doctor and medical system.

Wayne Hudson is Professor of Humanities in the School of Philosophy at the University of Tasmania and Research Professor in the Centre for Public and Contextual Theology at Charles Sturt University, Canberra. His most recent publications include *The English Deists: Studies in Early Enlightenment* (London: Pickering and Chatto, 2009) and *Enlightenment and Modernity: The English Deists and Reform* (London:Pickering and Chatto, 2009) and he is now finishing a monograph on *Post-secular Enlightenment*.

Norelle Lickiss is Clinical Professor (Medicine) at the University of Sydney and Consultant Emeritus at the Royal Prince Alfred Hospital, Sydney, and Royal Hospital for Women, Sydney; she is also Honorary Research Professor in School of Philosophy, University of Tasmania. Her career has been focussed on the exercise of clinical medicine and medical education. She was consultant and visiting professor concerning cancer pain relief and other aspects of palliative medicine in several regions, notably China and Iran. Her most recent publications include 'The Human Experience of Illness' and 'The Physician' (in *Palliative Medicine*, ed Walsh et al. Elsevier, 2008).

Norva Y. S . Lo is Lecturer in Philosophy at La Trobe University. She publishes also in the name of 'Y. S. Lo'. She has published on topics in metaethics, environmental philosophy, and David Hume. Some of her recent publications include: 'Is Hume Inconsistent—Motivation and Morals' (2009); and *Understanding Environmental Philosophy* (2010).

Elizabeth A. Lobb is an Associate Professor of Palliative Care at Calvary Health Care Sydney. She has 21 years' experience as a bereavement counsellor. Her current research is on the role of uncertainty in patients with incurable cancer.

Michael Mack is Reader in Medical Humanities in the Department of English Studies of the Centre for Medical Humanities, University of Durham. His most recent books are *German Idealism and the Jew* (University of Chicago Press, 2003), and *Spinoza and the Specters of Modernity* (Continuum, 2010).

Jeff Malpas is Research Professor in Philosophy at the University of Tasmania and Distinguished Visiting Professor at LaTrobe University. His most recent books include *Heidegger's Topology* (MIT, 2006), *Dialogues with Davidson* (MIT, 2011) *The Place of Landscape* (MIT, 2011), *Consequences of Hermeneutics* (Northwestern, 2010).

Ross Mellick is a Neurologist at the Institute of Neurological Sciences at the Prince of Wales Hospital, University of New South Wales, Sydney. He has a PhD in experimental neurobiology from University of London. His most recent essay was 'The Neurology of Laughter' (*Australian Financial Review*, Literary Section, 2008).

Thaddeus Metz is Research Professor and Head in the Department of Philosophy at the University of Johannesburg. He has published some 70 scholarly papers on topics in moral, political and legal philosophy. Most of his research has addressed three major areas: the African ethic of *ubuntu*, Kantian justice and the meaning of life, with a book on the latter topic forthcoming from Oxford University Press.

Peta Jones Pellach is Director of Educational Activities for the Elijah Interfaith Institute, an international organization based in Jerusalem, where she conducts training in interreligious dialogue. She is a scholar of Judaism and recently completed a paper on 'Human Rights, Religion and Gender—A Jewish Perspective' for the Australian Human Rights Commission.

Daryl Pullman is Professor of Medical Ethics in the Faculty of Medicine at Memorial University, Newfoundland, Canada. He has published on topics in research ethics, ethics and ageing, privacy and access to health information, and issues related to genetic research and therapy, and has a continuing philosophical interest in the concept of human dignity and its foundational role in moral epistemology.

Samuel Cuff Snow is completing his Masters in Critical Theory at Monash University. He wrote his Honours thesis on the hermeneutical debate between Gadamer and Derrida, and studied for that year at Freie Universität Berlin. He is currently researching the relationship between subjectivity and suffering in European philosophy. This is his first publication.

Peter Sutton is Affiliate Professor at the University of Adelaide and the South Australian Museum. He has worked with Aboriginal people since 1969. His latest book is *The Politics of Suffering: Indigenous Australia and the End of the Liberal Consensus* (2009).

Norchaya Talib is Professor in the Faculty of Law at the University of Malaya, Malaysia. She is an editor of *Medicine and Law* and author of *Physician-Assisted Death in Malaysia* and *Law of Torts in Malaysia.* She has a keen interest in the integration of different disciplines and how law may play a role in enhancing the welfare of the community.

Nicholas Tarling is Emeritus Professor of History at the University of Auckland, New Zealand. He is the author of some 36 books of which the most recent are *Southeast Asia and the Great Powers* (2010), and *Britain and the Neutralisation of Laos* (2011).

Lucy Tatman is Coordinator of Gender Studies in the School of Philosophy at the University of Tasmania. She is the author of *Numinous Subjects*.

Paul Turner is an Honorary Lecturer in Paediatric Allergy and Immunology at the University of Sydney, and is currently working as a Clinical Lecturer at Great Ormond Street Hospital for Children in London, UK. He has an ongoing interest in Theodicy, having been involved in the symptom care of terminally-ill children in the past, and is a teacher in adult education within the Jewish community.

Mary L. S. Vachon is a psychotherapist in private practice, Professor in the Department of Psychiatry and Dalla Lana School of Public Health at the University of Toronto and Clinical Consultant at Wellspring. She has written the chapter on the Emotional Care of the Dying Person for the four editions of *The Oxford Textbook of Palliative Medicine* and writes the chapters on occupational stress and burnout in many international textbooks on palliative, supportive care and psycho-oncology.

Chapter 1
Introduction: Human Suffering

Jeff Malpas and Norelle Lickiss

The fact of suffering, whether in the catastrophic form that extends across entire communities—cruelly exemplified, as we write this Introduction, by the distressing famine that now threatens hundreds of thousands of people in conflict-riven Somalia—or the suffering that focuses on just one person as a result of individual illness or misfortune, is so closely bound to the character of human life, that it seems we cannot address the question of what it is to be human without also attending to the question of what it is to suffer, of how suffering is to be understood, and of what suffering calls for by way of response. Suffering ought thus to be a fundamental concern regardless of whether we are now suffering, regardless of whether we have suffered in the past, regardless of whether we will do so, or think we will do so, in the future.

To attend to suffering, to recognize the fact of suffering, to respond to the suffering around us, is simply to attend to the fact our own humanity; and so to ignore it, to fail to respond to its call, is also a failure to face up to the character of our own being. In this respect, given the ethical imperative that suffering and the response to suffering surely carries with it, one might also argue that to attend to suffering is to attend to the fundamentally ethical character of the human. The human situation is always an ethical situation, so that to be human is already to be given over to the ethical, and it is the fact of suffering that ought to bring this home to us in an especially exemplary and incontrovertible fashion. It is perhaps with suffering that we are first brought to face our own humanity, as well as the humanity of those around us, and so are brought to face the essentially ethical dimension in which human being essentially moves.

The focus of the volume on specifically *human* suffering, as well as on the connection between suffering and human being, is not intended to imply any denial of

J. Malpas (✉)
School of Philosophy, University of Tasmania, Hobart 7001, Tasmania, Australia

Department of Philosophy, LaTrobe University, Bundoora 3086, Victoria, Australia
e-mail: jeff.malpas@utas.edu.au

N. Lickiss
School of Philosophy, University of Tasmania, Hobart 7001, Tasmania, Australia

Sydney Medical School, University of Sydney, Sydney 2006, NSW, Australia
e-mail: norelle.lickiss@gmail.com

J. Malpas, N. Lickiss (eds.), *Perspectives on Human Suffering*,
DOI 10.1007/978-94-007-2795-3_1, © Springer Science+Business Media B.V. 2012

the distress that may be experienced by non-human animals. Indeed, the violation of (or failure to respect) the dignity of non-human animals or the deliberate inflicting of distress upon them (no matter the larger purpose that may be served) is properly understood as itself a failure in our own humanity—which is why it is correctly termed 'inhumane'. Whether the distress experienced by non-human animals is itself to be termed 'suffering' is a complex question. Here we have chosen to refer to animal 'distress' rather than 'suffering' largely because of the way in which, throughout most of the essays that make up this volume, 'suffering' is understood, in the sense championed by Cassell (1982), as involving a sense of impending personal disintegration, that is distinct from pain or distress taken alone, and that is not immediately translatable (which is not to say that it cannot be so translated) into terms appropriate to the being of non-human animals. There are, however, a number of reasons why one might favor a broader use of the term 'suffering', even while remaining attentive to Cassell's characterization: since suffering does carry such a strong ethical component, the refusal to allow the term to be applied beyond the human may actually serve to encourage and support inhumane and unethical behavior in relation to non-human animals, and even perhaps to those members of the human community who may have difficulty in articulating their suffering to others or who may be inappropriately viewed as somehow having a diminished sense of their own being as persons. Thus, while we will continue to talk specifically about *human* suffering, this usage should be understood against the larger background that is also important here.

The focus on the human, as well as the ethical, is one of the central themes that unites this volume, on *human suffering*, with its predecessor, on *human dignity* (Malpas and Lickiss 2006), as it also unites almost all of the essays contained in the two volumes. Yet although the concern with the human character and significance of suffering is a constant throughout this volume, the range of perspectives that are encompassed also reflects the complexity and variability that is to be found within the phenomenon of suffering itself. It should thus not be surprising, that, in spite of the fact that many of the contributors to this volume take Cassell's characterization of suffering as their starting-point, their explorations take them in many different directions. The complexity and variability of suffering reflects the complexity and variability of human life itself. Of course, the plurality of perspectives that are evident here is also a function of the plurality of disciplines that the volume encompasses. Like the previous volume on dignity, *Perspectives on Human Suffering* is explicitly interdisciplinary in its approach, even while it acknowledges the importance of also drawing upon the strengths of deep disciplinary expertise. It thus includes essays by philosophers, medical practitioners and researchers, anthropologists, historians, lawyers, Judaic and literary scholars. Suffering, like dignity, and like the concept of the human, cannot belong solely to one discipline or one perspective alone.

One of the aims of this volume, and of its predecessor, is to open up a broader conversation than is usual between medicine and other disciplines—a conversation oriented around a set of essentially philosophical questions that is nevertheless not restricted by the standard disciplinary frameworks of philosophy itself or, indeed, of medicine. Too often, the treatment of philosophical issues within medicine or of medical issues within philosophy depends on a relatively weak engagement with the human issues at stake, frequently tending towards an almost legalistic discourse built around a narrow range of biomedical concepts, and typically drawing on a relatively narrow ranges of sources and experiences. This volume, again reflecting an approach continuous with the previous work, presents an alternative discourse that emphasizes a much broader set of concerns—concerns that run through almost all of the essays here, no matter their disciplinary origin—as they center on the character of the human, and as they also implicate literature, art, history, and other dimensions of human experience and existence. In this respect, while the volume can be seen as arguing for a broader interdisciplinary engagement in medicine that would also be more genuinely humanistic, it also aims to present a form of philosophical engagement that is equally expansive and inclusive in character and approach. The idea of the philosophical as exemplified in this volume is thus one oriented by a set of existential and phenomenological concerns as much as by any desire for conceptual precision and analytical rigor.

The idea of conversation that underpins this broader engagement is itself grounded in a conception of the project of inquiry and understanding as always shaped through linguistic encounter and articulation—even though it also encompasses more than just the linguistic as narrowly construed. To speak in ways that are adequate to suffering is always a challenge—the danger is that one's words, no matter how eloquent, will always seem to fall short of what is undergone, to be incapable of meeting the needs of the one who suffers. Sometimes we can do no more than stand as witnesses, and yet even then silence is itself meaningful only in the light of a deliberate forbearance from speech. In this respect, language pervades our lives, our actions, and our experiences even when it may appear to be absent. The significance of language in the attempt to engage with suffering is evident in many of the essays contained here—and nowhere more so than in the centrality given by so many contributors to literary and poetic sources in their discussions. Here suffering is able, as Frank Brennan puts it, to find 'a voice',[1] and not only that, but to find a voice that is itself reflects the concrete singularity that, as Malpas argues, is so central to suffering in its relation to the human.[2]

The volume divides into three main sections (although the division is not to be construed as strict or precise): *Philosophical considerations; Humanities approaches; Legal, medical, and therapeutic contexts*.

The essays that make up the first part of the volume are the most explicitly philosophical in the materials on which they draw and in the nature of their approach: Malpas addresses the relation between suffering, temporality, and the self, asking to what extent there can be a proper response to suffering within the realm of the political; Chiurazzi takes up ideas from Nietzsche and others to explore the connection between suffering and knowledge; Benjamin and Snow use Kierkegaard and Levinas to explore the way suffering is connected to the ethical understood in essentially relational terms (the emphasis on relationality being a theme that emerges in

[1] See Brennan, 'Suffering Seeks a Voice', Chap. 20.

[2] See Malpas, 'Suffering, Compassion, and the Possibility of a Humane Politics', Chap. 2.

a number of contributions); Tatman undertakes a phenomenological exploration of the logic of suffering, laying bare some of the problematic associations that seem to have accrued to the idea of suffering within western culture; Metz examines the ways in which suffering appears from a non-western, and specifically, African philosophical perspective; Mack uses Žižek and Arendt to take up the encounter with suffering as that occurs in literature and the arts suggesting ways in which these can provide ways better to understand, and perhaps even to ameliorate, suffering; Brennan and Lo use the focus on suffering as a starting point to examine what is surely a crucial counterpart to suffering, namely, forgiveness.

The second group of essays are more disparate in the perspectives they encompass although all of them are strongly oriented towards historical considerations, whether of the ancient or the more recent past. Pellach takes up the archetypal figure of Job, exploring the way Job's suffering is understood from within the tradition of Talmudic commentary, while also considering some of its wider implications; positioning himself explicitly as an historian, Tarling addresses suffering as it appears in the life and work or artists, especially musicians, as well as in the life of the nation; Turner, echoing some of Pellach's concerns, examines the response to suffering as articulated within Jewish thought and culture; Blyth discusses the response to suffering within the tradition of classical thought, notably as exemplified in Cicero; Hall continues the classical theme, though with a focus on tragedy more so than philosophy, through consideration of the suffering figure of Philoctetes; Hudson looks to place suffering within a temporal-historical frame, emphasizing the way the experience and understanding of suffering is affected by changing social and cultural frameworks; Sutton examines an instance of the politicization of suffering as that occurs in health policy affecting Aboriginal Australians.

In the final, and largest, section, the focus is on matters legal and medical, although once again philosophical concerns, and literary and historical engagement, are never far away: Green explores the way suffering appears in the criminal law, and may even arise as a consequence of the operation of the criminal justice system itself; Talib considers the treatment of suffering as handled in civil law and the award of damages; Coulehan addresses suffering as it arises in medical practice, arguing for the importance of 'compassionate solidarity' in the physicians' response to suffering, but also exploring the possibilities for the relief of suffering through 'symbolic healing'; Lickiss gives closer attention to the concept of person that is at the heart of Cassell's concept of suffering, thereby also arguing for the importance of that concept (along with the commitment to the relief of suffering) to clinical practice in medicine; Brennan argues for the importance of giving a voice to suffering and provides some striking examples of the way such a voice can be heard; Pullman, like many of the contributors, takes up the connection between suffering and the person, but does so in a way that gives particular attention to the way both are shaped by the technologies in which they are embedded; drawing on lessons from Lacanian theory, Hamilton and Gillett examine the way the relief of suffering, and the process of healing, are themselves tied to processes of personal integration and signification; Lobb examines that particular form of suffering, 'complicated grief', that arises in the wake of bereavement; Vachon examines the effect of being witness to suffering on caregivers, and the manner in which this may be addressed for the benefit of patients as well as caregivers; Mellick brings together neurology and literature to explore the way suffering may be illuminated by reference to the underlying physical structure of the brain.

The human pattern is so complex and the human canvas so immense, that no volume of essays can do adequate justice to the issues surrounding any aspect of human being, let alone the complexities of human suffering. Moreover, like any conversation, the one enacted here has its own idiosyncrasies, its own preoccupations, its own elisions and omissions. There are many instances and forms of suffering that receive little or no sustained consideration in these pages: the use of suffering as an instrument of power, whether through torture or through other forms of control and subjugation; the experience of suffering that arises through the burden of impossible decision or the destruction of deeply-held commitments and ideals; the often silent suffering of those in situations of isolation and deprivation whether caused by economic or social circumstance or psychological impairment. There is too little consideration of the enormous suffering that arises through war, famine, commercial exploitation, and the continuing legacies of slavery, colonialism and other forms of past and present injustice. There are many disciplinary, as well as cultural and religious perspectives that the volume does not properly encompass. There is little by way of the ethnographic exploration of suffering; the aesthetic response to suffering outside of the literary and the poetic is barely touched upon; suffering as it might be addressed in sociological terms is largely absent. Some notable exceptions notwithstanding, the compass of many of the discussions remains tied to what might well be thought of as a predominantly 'western' or 'European' perspective, and although one might argue that there are currents of Christian and Buddhist thinking that run through many of the contributions, the explicit discussion of suffering within religious contexts is largely restricted to the Judaic (perhaps not surprisingly given the way in which the experience of the Holocaust looms so large here).

Yet the threads that run through this volume, even though they are indeed tied to a particular set of experiences and contexts (and often reflect accidental circumstances of the volume's production), nevertheless run beyond the specificities and contingencies of this volume alone. The richness of a conversation, and its capacity to contribute to understanding, is not exhausted merely by what is said or, indeed, by what is written. A genuine conversation opens up the subject matter that is addressed as well as opening up the participants to that subject matter. In this respect one might say that the real aim of a volume such as this is merely to open up a larger space of discourse to which it can only ever be a partial contribution. Even more than this, however, a genuine conversation also brings to the fore its own character as an encounter in which we are opened up to ourselves and to one another. What appears at the heart of conversation is the fact of human presence and encounter—significantly, it is this same human presence and encounter that suffering, understood not only as something undergone but as that to which we must respond, brings to the fore.

Bibliography

Cassell, E.J. 1982. The nature of suffering and the goals of medicine. *New England Journal of Medicine* 306:639–645.

Malpas, Jeff, and Norelle Lickiss (eds.). 2006. *Perspectives on human dignity*. Dordrecht: Springer.

Part I
Philosophical Considerations

Chapter 2
Suffering, Compassion, and the Possibility of a Humane Politics

Jeff Malpas

> *I merely wanted to express that anguish I feel every day when faced with the prostituting of words, the slandered victims, the smug justification of oppression, the insane admiration of force.*
> *Albert Camus, Resistance, Rebellion and Death*

The issue of human suffering is one that I will approach here through three questions: (1) What is the relation between suffering and temporality; (2) What is the relation between suffering and the singularity of the person, and (3) What is the relation between suffering and a humane politics? These questions are not arbitrary, since not only are they interconnected in ways that I hope will become evident as my discussion proceeds, but they also concern the relation between suffering and human being, and it is this issue that seems to me to be central here. The focus on this relation is not meant to suggest that humanity *requires* suffering, which is true at least to the extent that being human requires the *capacity* to suffer (and perhaps simply having that capacity will make some degree of suffering inevitable), nor that only human beings can suffer (which is manifestly false[1]), but rather that coming

---

[1] That non-human animals can suffer seems clear even if their suffering is not, in all respects, identical to human suffering. One might argue, in fact, that there is a distinction between suffering and mere pain or discomfort that holds in the case of adult human experience, but that does not hold in the case of the experience of non-human animals or human infants. The suffering of animals is an issue that I do not address in the discussion below, although it undoubtedly introduces further complications for any attempt to articulate an ethical and political stance that is indeed attentive to the fact of suffering. In particular, one of the questions that my account here immediately raises is whether the *refusal* of suffering must also entail a refusal of the suffering *of non-human animals*, and if so, what the implications of this would be (would it not imply the alignment of the position outlined here with some of the stronger animal rights positions?) While I agree that this is an important and pressing issue, it is not one that I have time properly to address here.

J. Malpas (✉)
School of Philosophy, University of Tasmania, Hobart 7001, Tasmania, Australia

Department of Philosophy, LaTrobe University, Bundoora 3086, Victoria, Australia
e-mail: jeff.malpas@utas.edu

J. Malpas, N. Lickiss (eds.), *Perspectives on Human Suffering*,
DOI 10.1007/978-94-007-2795-3_2, © Springer Science+Business Media B.V. 2012

to a proper recognition of the human, and maintaining a sense of that recognition, is fundamentally tied to a proper recognition of the nature and reality of *human* suffering, and that this is what also supports the possibility of any properly ethical stance or indeed an ethical, which is to say also, a humane, politics. In this respect, the relation between human suffering and human being directs our attention to the centrality of *compassion* as an essential element in what it is to be human, and so also in any proper response to the human.

Suffering and Temporality

> So it is that Tasmania has never come to terms with its past. That past has the stature of a dark family secret – quite literally a dark family secret – the half-brother bogeyman boarded up out of sight in the attic. He/it is shame for our bastard birth as a prison for the unwanted dregs of the British slums and our subsequent legacy of depravity hard upon vileness, brutality fast upon atrocity. He/it is institutionalized sodomist rape, its echoes clearly audible in the hysteria that surrounded the 1990s debate about the legal status of sodomy. He/it is the unbearable legacy of brutal dispossession and the near-complete genocide of those whose land this was. He/it is a weight of guilt that could not be borne. (Hay 2002, p. 29)

Tasmania is a large island (about the size of Switzerland) that lies off the south-east coast of Australia, and was first known to Europeans as Van Dieman's Land. Tasmania has had a dark and difficult history. Its settlement by Europeans in the first half of the nineteenth century, settlement based in the island's role as a place of banishment and exile, was accompanied by the destruction of the original Aboriginal population as a direct consequence of that settlement. The convict industry that was the mainstay of the island's early development included a system of harsh and often brutal treatment that led to misery and death for many. Not only have subsequent public debates within the island often been determined by the ever-present spectre of the past (including, for instance, the debate about the legalization of sodomy referred to by the Tasmanian essayist, geographer, and poet Pete Hay in the passage quoted above), but those spectres seemed to return with a vengeance when, in 1996, at the site of the main convict settlement at Port Arthur (which had become a set of 'picturesque' ruins popular for picnics and family outings), 35 people were shot dead and 37 injured in a single horrendous killing spree—the Port Arthur Massacre.[2]

Hay argues that the failure to acknowledge the suffering that has taken place in the island—the denial of the past and the refusal of memory—has also contributed to a loss of meaning for Tasmanians. Such a loss of meaning takes the form of an inability to shape a proper sense of one's own identity and place in the world or to reconstitute a sense of self that allows an adequate recognition of what has gone before as well as a genuine capacity to act productively in the face of what is to come. Here *recognition of suffering* appears as the key to the constitution of meaning, and to a proper sense of history and futurity. Yet might time itself, or perhaps better, the

[2] The man was Martin Bryant, later condemned to life imprisonment in Hobart's Risdon jail.

sense of lived time at issue in the idea of history (time as worked out in concrete places and lives), stand in a special relation to suffering? Can there be suffering, *human* suffering, without time, without memory, without history?

In the now-classic definition advanced by Eric Cassell, suffering is said to be 'a state of severe distress associated with events that threaten the intactness of the person' (Cassell 1982, p. 639). As he emphasizes elsewhere, 'What is threatened or injured [in suffering] is the intactness of the person as a person' (Cassell 2004, p. 274). Suffering is thus not to be simply identified with physical pain, nor, Cassell argues, can it be understood on the basis of any bifurcation of the human into different domains, bodily and mental, natural and cultural, physical and spiritual. The notion of the person encompasses all of these, and cannot be decomposed into them—it is a concept of personhood as essentially *holistic*.

The emphasis in Cassell's definition on suffering as a form of distress that is directly related to one's sense of personhood, itself suggests a connection to the idea of memory, time, and history, since the person would seem to be formed precisely through the working out of time in relation to place and to person, through a sense of history, both personal and communal. In fact, Cassell himself makes a direct connection to time, writing that 'it follows, then, that suffering has a temporal element. For a situation to be a source of suffering, it must influence the person's perception of future events'[3]—events, one might add, that relate to that person, and their capacity to remain intact as a person, hence it is not time alone that is at issue here, but time as it is involved in a genuine sense of the personal, and as it contributes to the formation of the person. Moreover, while Cassell emphasizes the future here, neither is it the case that what is implicated is only *futural* time. To have a grasp of the future is to have a grasp of the past, as well as the present, and this, indeed, is what it is to have a grasp of time. Futurity is thus bound up with memory, as well as with current activity and affectivity.

In this respect, and although he himself does not develop the point in this way, Cassell's reference to time suggests an immediate connection with contemporary narrative accounts of personhood, particularly as worked out in the work of such as Paul Ricoeur (1992). Indeed, while Ricoeur does not specifically address the issue of human suffering, his account of personhood almost exactly dovetails with that to be found in Cassell. Similarly holistic in orientation, and refusing the dichotomies of conventional philosophical analyses, Ricoeur understands human persons as formed through the complex interweaving of elements that occurs primarily in and through narrative—and narrative itself cannot be divorced from the temporal and the historical. The formation of personhood is thus the formation of a sense of self, of the sense of a life, as that is shaped in the constant formation and reformation of accounts of past and future. Something like such an account may also be seen to be invoked in Hay's comments above—although in his case, the connection at issue encompasses, not only the relation between the temporal and the personal, but also the way in which collective identity and community, with which the personal is itself implicated, has an essentially temporal element, such that the collective

[3] Cassell (2004, p. 35).

suppression of memory may create problems for the collective ability to act in the present and project into the future, as well as for the personal.

Narrative accounts of personhood typically emphasize the relational character of the person. Not only does this mean that persons are constituted through the relating of the parts of a life, but also that the life of the person is itself formed through the relating of persons, and the relating of persons to the entities and events that surround them and with which they are already engaged. One of the ways in which this idea can be expressed is in the form of an emphasis on the character of persons, and of human lives, as formed always in and through the places in which persons are shaped and in which human lives are lived. Since places themselves carry within them a strongly narrative structure—places are not static containers, but are instead dynamic openings of action and movement—so the complex holistic and relational character of personhood is mirrored in the complexity of place. Indeed, the relation between person and place can be seen to exemplify the same holistic and dynamic character: places are shaped by human interaction with them, while human lives are shaped by those places. There is no absolute priority to place over person or person over place, and each can be understood only as worked out in relation to the other (Malpas 1999).

The relationality of the person, and the essential interconnection of personal life with a larger inter-personal and worldly context, means that we can never completely separate ourselves from those around us, nor indeed from the places in which we find ourselves and the entities and events in those places. If we are to think about this in temporal terms, we might say that what this means is that the experience of temporality, and perhaps the very idea of time (bound up as it is, in human terms, with structures of narrativity that give form and content to both past and future), is never an experience separated from the experience of the world, or from the engagement with others. Temporality, properly understood (which means understood as more than merely the passage of a series of discrete moments), always takes us to a greater or lesser extent outside of ourselves, always connects us to frameworks of meaning that implicate ourselves with others as they also differentiate us from others—that give us a sense of identity and commonality, that give a place and orientation to our lives—but in so doing also enable our lives as such.

On this account, even our own suffering can never be completely removed from the suffering of others. Not only does our suffering implicate others, but the suffering of others also implicates us. At least, this is so just insofar as meaning can be attached to such suffering, and insofar as the experience of suffering forces us to attend to the meaningful character of our lives, and to the interdependence of our lives with others. There is a reverse side to this, however, in that if, as in Cassell's characterization, human suffering is indeed to be understood as occurring in the face of a threat to the intactness of the person, then suffering must also threaten the very relationality that is constitutive of persons—both the internal relationality of the person and the integrally connected relationality of the person to the wider context in which the life of the person is formed and shaped. The experience of suffering can thus be characterized, not only in terms of the experience of an imminent breakdown in one's sense of personhood, but more than this, as the experience of an imminent breakdown in one's sense of the world.

Suffering is always borne by the singular individual, but that does not mean that it remains the individual's alone. The singularity of suffering is thus not incompatible with the temporality of suffering according to which suffering, while directly connected with the sense of personhood, always implicates more than just the individual who suffers. What I have referred to as the temporality of suffering is itself tied to the way in which suffering, while it threatens the intactness of the person, is also tied to the character of the person as formed through the complex narratives that connect persons to themselves, to other persons, and to the world. Suffering threatens just that connectedness. The connectedness of persons does not, however, entail a dissolution of the person into mere connections or relations. The person remains, but their being as a person is not given only through the way in which they are differentiated from other persons through the qualities or properties that pertain to them—there are no such qualities or properties that mark us out as somehow unique in relation to others, since such qualities or properties are themselves constituted in and through our relations with others.

If we recognize the temporality of suffering, then we must also recognize the way in which suffering extends beyond the individual. The recognition of suffering, and the experience of compassion (which is not to experience the *same* suffering as the one who suffers, although it may entail a suffering *with*), are correlative with one another. Thus while suffering may threaten the integrity of the self, the recognition of suffering is also a recognition of the being of others, and so opens up the possibility of a felt relation with others (which is true compassion). Suffering may be singular, but compassion, with which it is conjoined, is always double.

Yet if suffering threatens a breakdown in the intactness of the person, then the refusal to recognize the suffering of others represents a double threat: it is a refusal to acknowledge the persons who bear that suffering, and a refusal to recognize them as persons (no matter how implicit that refusal might be), but in addition, it is a refusal to recognize our own connectedness to those persons, and so is a refusal of our own personhood, our own being human, as it is formed in and by that relation. Where the suffering at issue is a suffering with which we are ourselves implicated, even if the implication is historically mediated through our common belonging to a place, then the refusal at issue is a refusal of our own identity, and so also has the potential to compromise our own being as persons. This is why, in Hay's account, the attitude Tasmanians take to their past, and to the past suffering that has left its marks on the island, is intimately tied to the way in which Tasmanians engage with themselves, and so with their own sense of personhood, with their own being as human. Put in terms of the temporal (which is more than a matter of time alone), we might say that recognizing the temporality of suffering, which is tied to the very recognition of suffering as suffering, is also to open oneself, in varying degrees, to the sufferings of others.

Suffering and the Singularity of the Person

> The fifth paragraph of chapter four in the 'Sanhedrin' of the Mishnah declares that, for the Justice of God, he who kills a single man destroys the world; if there is no plurality, he who annihilated all men would be no more guilty than the primitive and solitary Cain, which is orthodox, nor more universal in his destruction, which can be magic. I believe that is true. The tumultuous general catastrophes – fires, wars, epidemics – are but a single sorrow, illusorily multiplied in many mirrors. That is Bernard Shaw's judgment when he states (*Guide to Socialism*, 86) that what one person can suffer is the maximum that can be suffered on earth. If one person dies of starvation, he will suffer all the starvation that has been or will be. If ten thousand other persons die with him, he will not be ten thousand times hungrier nor will he suffer ten thousand times longer. There is no point in being overwhelmed by the appalling total of human suffering; such a total does not exist. Neither poverty nor pain is accumulable. (Borges 1964, p. 178)

The idea for which Borges argues in the above passage appears in many different places (and not only those that Borges himself catalogues). It is an idea that need not be taken to diminish the horror of suffering on a mass scale, but can rather be taken to direct attention to the *singularity* of suffering. The way this appears in Borges is, of course, that there can be no more suffering for the many than there can be for the one, but perhaps another way of putting the point is to say that there cannot be suffering of the many *without* the suffering of the one. Suffering is always borne by individual human beings, and to recognize suffering is to recognize the suffering of individuals, and not merely of the mass. Suffering, we may say, is always *singular*.

Could we conceive of suffering that was not the suffering of an individual? To say that we can conceive of the sufferings of a society, a nation, or of a people is not necessarily to say that we can therefore conceive of a mode of suffering that is other than the suffering of individuals. Indeed, very often to talk in this way is already to presuppose the idea of a common mode of identity, shared *among individuals*, that enables each of them, to a greater or lesser extent, to understand their own identity as bound up with that of the larger whole to which they take themselves to belong, and to understand the trials that may afflict the many as also, therefore, a burden borne by each individual. To talk of the suffering of a society, a nation, or a people may thus be taken not as an alternative mode of suffering, but as one of the ways in which *individuals* may suffer—through the harms that befall the larger communities to which they belong.

To emphasize the singularity of suffering is not the same as merely adopting a generalized individualism as against some form of collectivism. What is at issue here is not a question concerning a choice of ontologies, but instead concerns the character of suffering as itself directly related to the very character of human being, to the character of personhood, to the being of the self. Just as it is the integrity of the person or the self that is threatened in the face of suffering, so it is also the person or the self—*this one*—that suffers. One might argue that the singularity of suffering is a specific instance of the singularity, perhaps even the uniqueness, of the person. Uniqueness, however, is almost certainly the wrong term to use here, since it is all too readily associated with ideas of a uniqueness given in some special quality or set of qualities, in a uniqueness of personality or character. For the most part, human beings are not so different from one another, and it is hard to see why we should focus merely on some abstract concept of the 'unique' as that which marks out persons as persons. The singularity of the person does not derive from anything that belongs to one person over another—it is, in fact, more a point of commonality than of simple difference. Instead, singularity belongs to the very nature of personhood so that to be a person is to be singular, while singularity is, one might say, most fully realized in the person. This is why suffering, as distinct from almost any of the other affections or activities of human being, is itself singular in character, since it is in suffering that the being of the person, the intactness of the self, is itself directly threatened—the singularity of suffering is a direct correlate to the absolute singularity of personal being.[4]

One of the most powerful, although also perhaps the most difficult, evocations of personhood in English literature is to be found in the famous passage in Shakespeare's Merchant of Venice (Shakespeare 2007) in which Shylock challenges his Christian persecutors:

> I am a Jew. Hath not a Jew eyes? Hath not a Jew hands, organs, dimensions, senses, affections, passions? Fed with the same food, hurt with the same weapons, subject to the same diseases, healed by the same means, warmed and cooled by the same winter and summer, as a Christian is? If you tickle us, do we not laugh? If you prick us, do we not bleed? And if you wrong us, shall we not revenge? (*Merchant of Venice*, Act 3, Scene 1)

On the one hand Shylock can here be seen to be drawing attention to a set of attributes that belong to Jews, of whom Shylock is one, and that they also share with Christians—the possession of certain bodily parts, certain capacities, dispositions, dependencies and vulnerabilities. On the other hand, the power of this passage derives from the fact that it is not some faceless representative, even if of a particular religion and culture, who speaks here, but *this singular human being*, who draws attention, to his own singular capacity *to suffer*, and in bringing attention to this, to his own singular being *as a person*, and so as one whose being can never completely be taken up under any of the appellations that may be applied to him, whether as Jew or Christian. In his own standing before us as this one who suffers, Shylock also makes a demand on us for a recognition of that suffering, and for a recognition of his own being as one who, when his suffering is unrecognized, may seek to impose suffering on others—the latter being itself an expression of the relationality of personhood in a manner as unlooked-for, at least to modern eyes, as it is awful.

The singularity of suffering is not incompatible with the temporality of suffering that was evident in the discussion above. The temporality of suffering is tied

[4] While the connection is not made explicit in the text, the account of personhood that is presented here clearly resonates with the account of the ethical relation to be found in the work of Emmanuel Levinas—particularly in its emphasis on the singularity of the ethical relation and its character as given in the face-to-face encounter with another—see, for instance, Levinas (1969). Although there are important features of the Levinasian account that are replicated here, there are also aspects of Levinas' approach that I would contest—particularly his emphasis on the ethical relation as preceding anything ontological. In fact, on the account sketched here, and also I would argue in Levinas' own account (in spite of his own claims to the contrary), the ethical and the ontological converge: ethics is ontology and any adequate ontology is also an ethics.

to the way in which suffering, while it threatens the intactness of the person, is also tied to the character of the person as formed through the complex narratives that connect persons to themselves, to other persons, and to the world. Suffering threatens just that connectedness. Yet the connectedness of persons does not imply that persons are nothing but concatenations of connections or relations. Persons are constituted through the complex relations in which they participate, and yet it is precisely through such relationality that persons emerge as single entities—as beings who have a sense of their own being as persons, and not merely as persons in some generic sense, but as persons for whom their being as persons matters to them. It is thus that suffering emerges as a possible mode of such being—suffering is what occurs in the face of an imminent threat to one's being as a person, and so also to one's own singularity.

What I have been calling the 'temporality' of personhood thus encompasses a sense of the person as both relational *and* singular. Similarly, while suffering is always borne by the individual, suffering does not remain the individual's alone. As was already evident in the discussion above, once we recognize the temporality of suffering, then we must also recognize the way in which suffering extends beyond the individual. To have a sense of personhood cannot only be to have a sense of oneself as a person, but requires, instead, a sense of participation and involvement with other persons. But recognizing others as person also means recognizing their singularity as persons, and their capacity to suffer as persons. Moreover, the singularity of suffering and of personhood means that the recognition of suffering is not a recognition merely of some set of objectively specifiable responses. Recognition of suffering must involve a recognition, a felt sense even, of the singularity of the one who suffers, and so the singularity of that suffering. Suffering and compassion are thus, as I noted above, essentially conjoined.

If suffering is always singular, then when we look to the suffering of the many, presented not in terms of the suffering of any single individual, but only in the suffering of a population, in the suffering of numbers, it may well be that such suffering will no longer present itself to us as suffering. This is not because such a mode of presentation lacks the same emotional impact—even though it may well be less emotionally confronting—but rather that there is no suffering in numbers alone, only in those who suffer. Who suffers is not a number, not a population, but a singular human being—even when there are many such. Borges tells us that 'there is no point in being overwhelmed by the appalling total of human suffering'. Not only is there no point, but to be overwhelmed in that way is to lose one's own sense of the suffering that is at issue—it is to be overwhelmed by a multiplicity that does not itself reflect the genuine suffering undergone. If we wish to avoid the reality of suffering, if we do not wish to be moved to recognize our own implication in such suffering, then perhaps we need do no more than turn our attention away from the individual and on to the mass, the population, the number. It is perhaps for this reason that we can remain relatively insensitive to the suffering of a million no less than of a thousand or a hundred. For when we look at suffering in this way, the real fact of suffering all but disappears. Not only, then, is suffering not increased through the multiplication of those who suffer, but suffering is also removed from us, rendered in a form that no longer makes the same demands upon us, perhaps no longer gives rise to the same compassion.

Suffering and a Humane Politics

> The end of the movement of absurdity, or rebellion etc, and consequently the end of the contemporary world, is compassion in the original meaning of the word, that is to say, in the last analysis, love and poetry. (Camus 1966, p. 103)

Albert Camus' politics and ethics of rebellion—an ethics and politics that emerges at its strongest in his writing after the end of the Second World War, and especially in his writings on the Algerian situation—is an ethics based on a simple idea: the absolute refusal of human suffering. Already this idea is clear in a passage from *The Plague* in which Camus presents his own unequivocal answer to the question that appears in Dostoyevsky's *The Brothers Karamazov*: can any amount of good be justified if it depends on the suffering of one innocent human being? Camus describes a scene in which the novel's main protagonist, the doctor Rieux, has just attended the tortured death from plague of a young girl. When the priest who is with him offers what is intended to be the consoling advice that the divine order that allows the girl's death and suffering cannot be understood but must simply be loved, Rieux angrily replies: 'I've a very different idea of love. And until my dying day I shall refuse to love a scheme of things in which children are put to torture' (Camus 1960, p. 178).

The response that Rieux, and through him, Camus, makes here can be seen, not only to be based on the conception of human suffering as an absolute evil, one that is not able to be mitigated even by the role it may play in some larger divine order, but as also embodying a recognition of the singular character of suffering. If suffering is not multiplied by the multiplication of those who suffer, then neither is suffering reduced by the reduction of those who suffer—not even if the suffering at issue is reduced from the suffering of an entire world to the suffering of a single child. Rieux's refusal of what is put to him by the priest should not be construed as directed only against suffering as it might be taken to be ordained by God. It is as much a rejection of any order that issues from human beings as from the divine. 'I shall refuse to love a scheme of things in which children are put to torture', Rieux says, and when we read this in conjunction with Camus' explorations elsewhere, we know that this means a refusal willingly to go along with any ordering of the world in which suffering is not itself refused and in which it is not struggled against. Camus' philosophy of rebellion is thus above all a rebellion *against suffering*—a rebellion against our own suffering and against the suffering we may impose on others—a rebellion in which Camus rejects the roles both of victim and of executioner.[5]

If what Camus refuses is indeed any scheme of things 'in which children are put to torture', then what he refuses is the very scheme of things that we find in the con-

[5] See Camus (2005) written shortly after the end of the Second World War, and originally published in 1946 in the Resistance newspaper *Combat*.

temporary world. The scheme of things that operates in the world in which we now live is indeed one that involves the torture of children, as well as of adults, even if it is a torture enacted, not only through violence and war, but through poverty, starvation, exploitation, and disease. It is, moreover, a torture that is a direct consequence of decisions and policies taken by politicians and governments around the world—a torture in which we are ourselves implicated through our participation in an economic and social order that not only allows, but is often predicated upon, the existence of inequality and injustice (one need only think of the use of child labour to produce goods for Western markets to see to what extent this is so). In this respect, the use of torture as an instrument in the so-called 'war against terror' by nations such as the United States and the United Kingdom can be seen as an expression of a deeper willingness to use suffering as an instrument of policy, as an instrument of governance, a deeper willingness to participate in a scheme of things in which what matters is not the singularity of the person, but the generalized interest of the nation, the financial elite, the government of the day, the globalized corporation.

The singularity of suffering is directly tied to the singular character of personal, which is to say, human being. Camus' refusal of suffering can thus also be seen to rest on a recognition of the singularity of the human, and to itself constitute an assertion of the human—an assertion, even, of the *dignity* of the human (Malpas 2007).[6] Yet the position that Camus exemplifies here, a position to which we seem to be led by precisely the reasoning set out in the pages above, also seems to present us with an impossible situation. On the one hand, the singularity of suffering means that suffering can never allow of being quantified across persons—can never allow of the possibility of balancing the suffering of one individual against the diminution of suffering among some greater mass of individuals. Moreover, to treat suffering only in terms of the suffering of the mass is already to overlook the genuine character of suffering, is already to turn away from suffering, and so also, to turn away from a genuine recognition of the human. On the other hand, it seems to be precisely in the nature of that mode of decision-making associated with the governmental and the political that it should not concern itself with the single individual, but only with the collective, the group, the mass. Thus, within even liberal, democratic polities, decision-making routinely deploys utilitarian calculations that allow suffering to appear only in terms of the statistics that characterize a population, while such quantified levels of suffering are considered merely as elements within larger calculative frames.

On the face of it, the conclusion to which are driven here is that the idea of a genuinely human politics, a genuinely humane mode of government, is truly a chimera, since it would require stitching together two radically different modes of engagement with the world and with the fact of human suffering. It would seem to require a mode of politics, a mode of government, that acknowledges the singular-

[6] On the nature of dignity, and the manner of its relation to concepts of the human, as well as to the relational understanding developed here, see the discussions contained in the volume to which this is a successor, Malpas and Lickiss (2007) including my own essay in that volume, 'Human Dignity and Human Being'.

ity of human being, and yet is also geared to that which goes beyond the singular, that pertains to the collective, and to the mass; a mode of politics, a mode of government, that refuses to allow the quantification of human suffering as one of the methods and instruments of operation, and yet nevertheless continues to operate at the level of the quantified and the generic.[7]

It may well be that the difficulty that appears here is one that is fundamental to any politics and to any mode of government. Yet it would surely be a mistake to therefore consign politics and the practice of government to the realm of the inhumane, if for no other reason than that it would itself constitute an acceptance of a form of inhumanity. Camus' position is not one that draws back from political engagement, even if it is an engagement that often remains purely critical. At the very least, what has to be recognized is the danger that is always present within a purely political or governmental frame—the danger that such a frame will lead us away from the realities of human life and suffering, to an obscuring of the singular nature of the human, and so to a mode of operation that may well turn out to be a denial of the human.

More than just this, however, any mode of political or governmental practice that aspires to retain a sense of the human and potentially humane character of such practice must always remain open and responsive to the challenge that can be made on the basis of the singular character of the human, and that constantly confronts the anonymity of the political and the governmental with the singular reality of the sufferings of individuals. Such responsiveness to the fact of suffering need not imply that we can always exercise a power sufficient to relieve suffering—but it does imply a refusal simply to accept it, and a need constantly to find ways to address it. In this respect, it is not the need to judge fairly between different interests, or to find just means to allocate finite resources that gives rise to inhumanity, but rather the development of systems of political and governmental decision-making and modes of administrative organization that operate according to what is effectively a *calculus* of human suffering in which suffering becomes almost an *instrument* of policy.

There must always exist a tension within modes of political and governmental operation between their grounding in the realities of human life, and so in the singu-

[7] One might argue, in addition, that the insistence on the refusal of suffering of the sort found in Camus can never be satisfied—is not to live already to be enmeshed in a system that involves suffering as an inevitable part of it?—and enjoins us to do what cannot be done. The refusal of suffering cannot mean, however, that we are committed to the attempt to eradicate every instance of suffering by our own efforts nor can it mean that we should refuse our own lives (rather as Schopenhauer, but not Camus, argued that the only properly ethical course available was the suicide of the ascetic who simply ceases to will the means to live). Not only would such courses of action fail to achieve their ends, but they are more likely to contribute to suffering rather than diminish it. What the refusal of suffering requires, more than anything else, is a willingness to take seriously the singularity of our own lives, as well as the singularity of those whose lives connect with our own, and to act in ways that are attentive to that singularity, within the capacities available to us and in a way that accords with our own situation. Camus' own position is one that stands against excess—whether the excess of the one who does nothing or of the one who attempts to do everything. What is absolutely refused is the turning away from the singular, the concrete and the lived that is the necessary accompaniment of all forms of excess.

larity of the human, and the demands of their ever-widening spheres of operation, as well as the collective interest that they appear to serve. The danger of our contemporary situation is that this tension has been exacerbated almost to breaking point by the increasing dominance of modes of organization and decision-making that belong to a technology of governance based around the quantifiable, the measurable, and the manipulable.[8] Within this frame the very singularity of the human, and of human suffering, seems indeed almost completely to have disappeared. Nowhere is this more evident than in the transformation, within all manner of public and private institutions, of singular individuals, into customers, clients, consumers—even the vocabulary of the citizen has now become one that transforms us from acting, deliberating persons, into elements within a system of electoral obligation and civic accountability.[9]

I began this discussion with the observation that the refusal to recognize suffering may contribute to a loss of identity, to a loss of a proper sense of the past as well as the future, to a loss of a proper sense of our own humanity. The refusal to recognize suffering, which is always a refusal to recognize the singularity of suffering, is thus not some form of particular and limited blindness that affects only a part of our functioning as human beings, but is instead corrupting of the singular relationality that is itself determinative of who and what we are. To the extent that contemporary modes of politics and governance embody such a refusal of suffering within their very modes of operation, then to that same extent they also function as corrupting of any proper sense of the human, as cutting us off from an ability to engage with ourselves, with others, and with the world. The challenge, then, and it is a challenge whose answer will always remain difficult and perhaps even obscure, is to find ways in which the machinery of contemporary life, a machinery that seems itself to include human suffering as part of its very mechanism, can be redirected, reconfigured, redesigned so as to enable the human to reappear within it, to enable a properly humane politics, to enable a politics in which suffering is not accepted, but constantly and steadfastly refused. Such a conclusion may well be viewed as a nothing more than a naïve idealism that is incapable of facing up to the pragmatic realities of things. But one can have too little idealism as well as too much. If the

[8] The tension that is evident here is apparent in many aspects of contemporary organizations, and particularly organizations whose primary concern is human welfare—organizations concerned with matters of social welfare, health, and education. It is significant that not only does this tension have an impact on those whose welfare is supposed to be the focus of such organizations, but also on those who work within the organizations in question. Thus Thomas R. Cole and Nathan Carlin, for instance, have written of 'the suffering of physicians' as this arises due to the way in which medical practitioners increasingly find themselves unable to live up to the ideals and obligations of their profession because of the limits imposed by the organizational situations in which they find themselves—see Cole and Carlin (2009). The 'dehumanization' of medicine to which Cole and Carlin refer is, I would argue, directly linked to the inability of contemporary medical policy and modes of organization to respond to the singularity of suffering.

[9] The work of Michel Foucault provides us with a detailed elaboration of the rise of what he referred to as 'bio-power'—a shift in the character of governmental operation towards the management not of individuals, but of populations, a shift made possible because of the rise of new actuarial practices and managerial techniques. See, for instance, Foucault (1976).

demands of the pragmatic are indeed such as to require that we give up a capacity for human responsiveness, then the cost of such pragmatism is surely more than we should ever be willing to pay.

Bibliography

Borges, Jorge Luis. 1964. *Other Inquisitions*. Trans. R.L.C. Simms. Austin: University of Texas Press.

Camus, Albert. 1966. *Carnets 1942–1951*. Trans. P. Thody. London: Hamish Hamilton.

Camus, Albert. 1960. *The Plague*. Trans: S. Gilbert. Penguin, Harmondsworth.

Camus, Albert. 2005. *Neither Victims nor Executioners: An Ethic Superior to Murder*. Trans. M. Dwight. Wipf & Stock, Eugene.

Cassell, E.J. 2004. *The nature of suffering and the goals of medicine*, 2nd edn. New York: Oxford University Press.

Cassell, E.J. 1982. The nature of suffering and the goals of medicine. *New England Journal of Medicine* 306: 639–645.

Cole, Thomas R., and Nathan Carlin. 2009. The suffering of physicians. *The Lancet* 374: 1414–1415.

Foucault, Michel. 1976. *The history of sexuality, vol. 1: The will to knowledge*. London: Penguin.

Hay, Pete. 2002. *Vandiemonian essays*. Hobart: Walleah Press.

Levinas, Emmanuel. 1969. *Totality and Infinity: An Essay on Exteriority*. Trans. A. Lingis. Duquesne University Press, Pittsburgh.

Malpas, Jeff. 2007. Human dignity and human being. In *Perspectives on Human Dignity*, eds Jeff Malpas and Norelle Lickiss. Dordrecht: Springer.

Malpas, Jeff. 1999. *Place and experience*. Cambridge: Cambridge University Press.

Ricoeur, Paul. 1992. *Oneself as Another*. Trans. K. Blamey. University of Chicago Press, Chicago.

Shakespeare, William. 2007. *Complete Works* (*The RSC Shakespeare*), eds Jonathan Bate and Eric Rasmussen. Basingstoke: Macmillan.

Chapter 3
Pathei Mathos: The Political-Cognitive Value of Suffering

Gaetano Chiurazzi

Suffering opens up the path that leads to the truth.
Alice Miller, Dein gerettetes Leben. Wege zur Befreiung

Principle of Reality and Principle of Coercion

Suffering is knowledge. I assume this sentence as a leitmotiv, as a *basso continuo* or a mantra, for my text—a theme that I will repeat with the awareness that no comment will ever be able to explicate it fully.

The sentence 'suffering is knowledge' should itself be understood as a primitive truth, a sort of unanalysable archi-gnosis. The primitiveness of this truth means that it is not a logical truth or a content of thought, but a physical and bodily truth. Suffering is primarily a physical phenomenon. This physicality makes it difficult to ascribe a cognitive content to suffering, since truth and knowledge are matters of thought. The fact that there can be a physical knowledge of which suffering is evidence is difficult to comprehend, yet suffering is something that pertains to our own lives. It also pertains to our relation to the world in which we live. In respect of the latter, suffering can be seen as a symptom of the primitive character of that relation, and as one of the initial modes of knowledge of the world within which the organism finds itself, and of which it is aware, even at the cellular level. 'Aware' might sound inadequate here, yet, if consciousness is negation—as a reflexive tradition has taught us to think (something as will be discussed further, in relation to the thought of Hegel, below)—there is no reason why its first form, its early manifestation, cannot be found just in that physical negation represented by suffering. It is thus possible to claim that every cell in an organism *knows*, and that this knowledge is the source of its life, without which it could not survive even for one minute. Living without pain, without suffering, in a fully anaesthetized way, is all but impossible. A rare genetic disease, Congenital Insensitivity to Pain with Anhidrosis (CIPA),

G. Chiurazzi (✉)
Faculty of Letters and Philosophy, University of Turin, Turin, Italy
e-mail: gaetano.chiurazzi@unito.it

J. Malpas, N. Lickiss (eds.), *Perspectives on Human Suffering*,
DOI 10.1007/978-94-007-2795-3_3, © Springer Science+Business Media B.V. 2012

causes a complete insensitivity to pain, and so gives rise to a mortal danger: those who are affected by it can suffer injuries, serious illnesses or an accident without being aware of it. It is thus that suffering can be understood as knowledge on a very fundamental level. It carries truth: about oneself, about the world, and about one's own relation to the world.

On a philosophical level, the latter truth was often conceived as knowledge of a limit: suffering reveals finitude. It is an experience well described in Greek tragedy, and revived, within an infinitizing logic, by the Hegelian theory of experience. According to Hegel, experience is moved by a negativity that shakes every previous expectation, inducing an overturning of the consciousness that ends up in sceptical despair. However, this negativity is redeemed in the totality of this process, where the whole sum of that which appears as 'non-knowledge' assumes a positive value, becoming 'absolute knowledge'—just as in Greek tragedy, according to Nietzsche's interpretation, the tragic figures taken together become 'the bacchanalian revel, where not a member is sober' (Hegel 1970a, p. 46).

The revel that appears here consists in the fluidification of all limits, so that the negative moments are at the same time moments that dissolve, i.e. are raised up (*aufgehoben*). The bacchanalian revel, in which the Dionysian dimension of the tragedy of experience finds its complete fulfilment, is the realization of the ideality of the finite, of its inconsistency: idealism is actually the recognition that the finite is not real[1]. This is the content of absolute knowledge: the *pathei mathos* of experience leads to the knowledge of one's own non-finitude as a consciousness that knows (namely, denies, at a superior level) its own negativity. In his conception of experience Hegel renews the spirit of Greek tragedy: but the final triumphalist element constitutes also the real dividing line, separating the tragic nature of the Hegelian *pathei mathos* from the Greek, specifically from that which can be found in the work of the father of Greek tragedy, Aeschylus.

According to Aeschylus, through the experience of suffering men learn their own limit: suffering is a consequence of their *hybris*, namely of their pretention to get over the limit imposed by nature. Suffering is then a punishment, a chastisement, through which gods let men know their fault. It aims at restoring a broken balance, at bringing back justice. The consequence of this juridical, even punitive and revengeful conception of suffering (which seems a constant of Greek thought, perhaps even of Western culture in general, whose germinal meaning emerges already in the interpretation of the first known fragment of philosophical thought, the 'Saying' of Anaximander[2]) is a certain self-knowledge completely opposed to absolute knowledge. It is not a form of knowledge in which every limit is annulled, but a knowledge that takes the form of a knowledge of one's own limit. Experience is in this case the experience of one's own finitude.

[1] 'The proposition that the finite is ideal constitutes idealism. The idealism of philosophy consists in nothing else than in recognising that the finite has no veritable being.' (Hegel 1970b, p. 172)

[2] As given in Simplicius: "And the source of coming-to-be for existing things is that into which destruction, too, happens, 'according to necessity; for they pay penalty and retribution to each other for their injustice according to the assessment of Time'", in Kirk et al. (1983, p. 117).

Hans-Georg Gadamer, in opposition to Hegel, has condensed his own conception of experience in the idea expressed by the Aeschylean *pathei mathos*:[3]

> What a man has to learn through suffering is not this or that particular thing, but insight into the limitations of humanity, into the absoluteness of the barrier that separates man from the divine [...] Real experience is that whereby man becomes aware of his finiteness. (Gadamer 2004, p. 351)

Gadamer's conception of the experience of finitude is not far from Freud's theorization of the conflict between the principle of pleasure (desire) and the principle of reality, as a conflict between the subjective will and the instances of an over-subjective order: actually, according to Gadamer, in the authentic experience:

> ...all dogmatism, which proceeds from the soaring desires of the human heart, reaches an absolute barrier. Experience teaches us to acknowledge the real. The genuine result of experience, then—as for all desire to know—is to know what is. But 'what is', here, is not this or that thing, but 'what cannot be destroyed' (Ranke). (Gadamer 2004, p. 351)

This Gadamerian 'realism' sets as a goal of suffering the overcoming of one's own narcissisms in favour of a principle of reality, ultimately a matter of the recognition of human historicity and the acknowledgment of finitude. To what extent this 'realism' ends up by excessively solidifying the historical reality, trespassing on a form of conservatism, is a political problem, which puts Gadamer at the centre of the debate with the Frankfurt School.[4]

That there is a cognitive value of suffering is an idea that is not universally accepted: according to the Stoics, for instance, the perfect knowledge requires rather apatheia, that is the absence of suffering, which is seen as something that impedes or makes knowledge confused. But here it is not a question of a subjective disposition: the thesis I want to argue is on the contrary that suffering reveals always something, it brings about an awareness of a limit, which functions as principle of reality. Moreover, because of the *nature* of the limit, of its necessary or contingent determination, this awareness takes ethical-political connotations. This idea has been well expressed by Michel Foucault in his 1984 conference *What is Enlightenment?* Foucault remarks first of all that the critical inquiry is always a reflection on *limits*, but this task can be understood in two different ways:

> ...if the Kantian question was that of knowing what limits knowledge has to renounce transgressing, it seems to me that the critical question today has to be turned back into a positive one: in what is given to us as universal, necessary, obligatory, what place is occupied by whatever is singular, contingent, and the product of arbitrary constraints? The point, in brief, is to transform the critique conducted in the form of necessary limitation into a practical critique that takes the form of a possible transgression. (Foucault 1984, p. 45)

---

[3] Aeschylus, *Agamemnon*, line 177, in Aeschylus (2009)

[4] See Apel (1971). Against the charge of political conservativism we should remember that according to both Gadamer and Heidegger, acknowledging finitude means at the same time acknowledging the radical historicity and contingency of existence, and then the transformability of every human construction.

According to Foucault, *contemporary* critique aims at discovering not the necessary and insurmountable limits of knowledge, but those that *can* (and indeed *should*, because—we must not forget it—critique has a clear and unavoidable ethical motive) be overcome, after being recognised as *contingent*. The ethical motive of critique is justified on the basis of its ontological background, i.e. the acknowledgement of the contingency of limit, of which suffering is a symptom: suffering can produce a knowledge *of* limit (*that* there is a limit) and a knowledge *on* the limit (its necessary or contingent nature); a knowledge of 'reality', linked up with the very idea of life, without which life itself would be in danger, i.e. a knowledge of the physical dimension of suffering, of pain; and a knowledge of coercion, that makes the physical suffering shade off into the psychical and spiritual dimension. Part of the unavoidable task of critique, and of every process of liberation, is not the anaesthetization, but the clear awareness of suffering.

Nietzsche: Between Forgetfulness and the *apologia* of Suffering

To forget suffering: so Nietzsche understands liberation. The human envy towards the animal is due to the 'natural' capability of the latter to forget immediately what it does and feels, above all pain—since memory is pain. At a point in *On the Genealogy of Morals*, where he questions the genesis of memory, by asking 'how does the human animal form a memory?,' Nietzsche refers this origin back to pain:

> 'Someone brands something, so that it remains in memory: only what does not stop hurting, remains in memory'—this is an axiom of the most ancient (and unfortunately also more long-lived) psychology on Earth.... It has never happened without blood, martyrdoms, sacrifices, when man believed necessary making a memory. (Nietzsche 1999a)

An impression would not produce by itself any memory—for Nietzsche, this is the condition of the animal life, 'enchained' to its *hic et nunc*. The pure *aisthesis* has thus the paradoxical advantage of being *anaesthetic* to pain, of impeding and removing the suffering, which is a cause—but also an effect: the effect, for Nietzsche, of the 'history-illness'—of memory. Linked to suffering are the dimension and the awareness of the past: the passivity of suffering is correlative to the passivity of the past, of what cannot but be suffered. Man became such, ceasing to be an animal, when he learned 'to understand a word 'there was', the password by which struggle, suffering and tedium get close to the man so as to remind him what at the very end his existence is—something imperfect, which can never be fulfilled' (Nietzsche 1999b). To understand the past as past is for Nietzsche the origin of suffering.

The way Nietzsche considers suffering suggests a movement beyond the condition of passivity in which man lives—a liberation from the past in the form of the forgetfulness in which, somehow mythically (do animals not remember the sufferings they go through?), he thinks animal live,[5] or an intensification of the activity,

[5] About this 'mythicization' of the animal by Nietzsche see Lemm (2009, p. 88): 'Nietzsche's approach to the animals is not that of a scientist who desires to know about the animals, but that of a

that is of the will to power, which in the human being (because of the residual passivity which persists in him) is still not completely unfolded. From this point of view, the 'active forgetfulness' (*aktive Vergesslichkeit*) is nothing else that the attempt of the *Übermensch* to restore the animal condition on a level beyond the human being. From the perspective of the will to power, suffering—and the past in general—can only be *wanted*: 'To redeem what is past, and to transform every 'It was' into 'Thus would I have it!'—that only do I call redemption!' (Nietzsche 1999c) The lightness of forgetfulness gives way to the greatest weight: the voluntary affirmation-acceptation of the eternal recurrence of the same. In this transfiguring vision of humankind, suffering takes for Nietzsche another function: since it cannot be forgotten, it becomes the 'hothouse' of a new human form of being—the *Übermensch.*

If it is not possible to remove suffering (to suppose that it can be removed is, according Nietzsche, the mistake of those political systems that let themselves move and be moved by compassion for 'social poverty', and by the consequent desire for its elimination), then it will be necessary to conceive it as a moulding force, as a formative discipline. Nietzsche exalts therefore the 'formative discipline of suffering, of the *great* suffering', (Nietzsche 1999d, § 225) against every softening and weakening, which have always political roots. The democratic movement, in particular, as the heir of the Christian spirit, shares with the 'anarchic baying of hounds' and the 'silly philosophrasters and fraternity zealots, who are called socialists, and wish the "free society,"' the unanimous pitying cry against world suffering, the 'mortal hate against the pain in general, because of their almost feminine inability to watch, to *let* one suffer' (Nietzsche 1999d, § 202).

For Nietzsche, then, suffering is something that must be either forgotten or wanted. It has no relation with *knowing* and is not a *political* problem. At most, suffering selects, in a Darwinian way, the men, by splitting them into weak and strong, depending on their capability to be moulded by it. The couple weak-strong is nothing but the expression, on an energetic level, of the chemical dialectic of action-reaction (which imbues, from *On the Genealogy of Morals*, a great part of Nietzschean thought). Moral formations are actually a result of reactive processes, and the moral itself is the precipitate of a reaction between heterogeneous chemical forces. The strong elements are the active ones; the weak are instead the reactive, whose counteraction gives birth to the moral domain. For Nietzsche there is not, in fact, a moral of the strong—morality is always and only a reactive construction of the weak, a result of a *ressentiment* tending to contrast and to reduce the affirmative and positive forces. However important, from a biological point of view, the reactive sentiments may be, they are certainly less significant than the 'properly *active* affections, as the lust for power, the lust for possession and the like' (Nietzsche 1972, § 11).

The Hobbesian background within which Nietzsche inscribes the question of violence, of exploitation and suffering, suggests that, far from being radical, the genealogical method turns out eventually as a factual endorsement of the right of the strongest. Life *is* violence, and every political solution tending to a limitation of

poet who imagines the life of the animals, whose thoughts on the animals are imaginary, illusory, and fantastic rather than scientific, rational, and true.'

violence is nothing else than an exceptional state, a partial restriction of the will to power: '*in itself* to offend, to do violence, to exploit, to annihilate cannot be naturally 'illegitimate', since life is fulfilled *essentially*, that is in its basic functions, by offending, doing violence, exploiting, annihilating, and cannot in any way be thought without this character' (Nietzsche 1972, § 11). If there is something historical, then this is, according to Nietzsche, the momentary suspension of violence by means of the law: what is historical is the law, not the struggle between the wills. *On the Genealogy of Morals*, as the subtitle states, is a polemics (*Streitschrift*), and not only in the sense that it debates against the common conceptions of the moral, but above all because it is a writing about the polemic character of life, turning the *polemos* into the profound essence of existence. Life is will to power, and therefore a fight between the strong and the weak.

In Nietzsche's understanding of suffering there is, in conclusion, no political significance—since there is no cognitive significance that could otherwise reveal that 'principle of coercion' that shows the contingency of violence. Actually, the one who sees and understands suffering is forced to feel pity for the sufferer; his attempt to bring relief is the immediate political repercussion of such a comprehension. But the 'weak', for Nietzsche, are not the living effect of political causes of suffering. Through their suffering they attest only their poverty and subjective incapacity: compassion towards them is only a compassion for "poverty', for the 'society', for its sick and its wretches, for the depraved and for originally shattered individuals, such as those who are lying on the ground in front of us,' it is the compassion for the 'class of snarling, oppressed, seditious slaves, craving for the domination—they call it 'liberty' (Nietzsche 1999d, § 225)'. Nietzsche shows no feeling of solidarity for this humanity; he does not criticize social poverty.

At the Origin of Suffering: The Pain of Misrecognition

The will to power affirms itself by *not willing* to see the huge load of suffering that it produces in the world: it rises above suffering and builds its absolute positivity on the basis of this 'non-will'. The 'will not to remember' of the *aktive Vergesslichkeit* is more deeply grounded on a 'non-will to see', and above all on a 'non-will to understand' the *political* meaning of suffering. The question is then to what extent Nietzschean genealogy is really a critique. If the critique, as Foucault wrote, works by pointing out the *contingent* conditions that determine us to be what we are (this is the sense of the Foucaultian expression 'ontology of actuality'), then we cannot say that Nietzsche achieves a real critique. Nietzsche addresses the *mechanism*—or the *reactive process*—that has produced certain functions, specifically the moral habits, but he does not question the conditions of this process. The *essence* of life is and remains for Nietzsche violence, domination, and exploitation. By making suffering apolitical, Nietzsche, through his doctrine of the *Übermensch*, crystallizes violence in a biological fact.

We must not hope to find in Nietzsche a *critical* analysis of the origin of violence and suffering, namely of the 'chains'. The 'masters of suspicion', Nietzsche and Marx, have opposite views of the political implications of suffering: for Nietzsche, suffering is and remains a symptom of weakness; for Marx, instead, it is a symptom of an exploitation that one has to become aware of, beyond any ideologisation—or anaesthetisation—of the real. According to Marx—as well as to a long-lasting tradition to which he himself belongs to, a tradition that ranges from gnosticism to Heidegger[6]—suffering has a cognitive value. By this I mean that suffering should not be considered as a mere biological fact, but as a sign that hints at something else, as something which is not biological. Suffering is a sign of violence, and violence is always more than a natural matter. This means that the concept of 'violence' can never qualify something natural. It has always an ethical connotation, by which we distinguish pain from suffering. In this sense, suffering is a protestation that reveals, negatively, the possibility of the freedom.

By crossing swords with the Hegelian Left's leading exponents, themselves concerned with the problem of human emancipation, rather than finding the possibility of emancipation in the enlightened, democratic-bourgeois consciousness, Marx opted to concentrate on the 'suffering humanity'(Marx 1964a, p. 342), the proletariat as social group oppressed by 'universal sufferings' (Marx 1964c, p. 390). Only by looking at the 'vale of tears', by taking up the fact of suffering, would it have become possible to change the whole ideological superstructure, the capitalistic system grounded on the domain of the strongest. In Marx's opinion 'exploitation' is not the natural consequence of the polemical character of life but the *contingent* origin of suffering: it is the right ethical denomination for the economical relation 'surplus labour–surplus value'. This also explains, in contrast with Nietzsche, Marx's evaluation of religion. Religion is not a mere consolatory and reactive product of petty and bungled souls, but the denunciation of human suffering and constitutes an indirect awareness of such suffering (Marx 1964b, pp. 347–377). The emancipatory impulse not only refuses to shrink from the concreteness of suffering—neither can it accept the virtualization of the real, nor the aesthetization and anaesthetization of suffering that accompanies it.

In producing an awareness of suffering, the Marxian theory of exploitation shows the *contingent*—i.e. historical—character of the struggle, as well as the contingency of its cause, namely, the domination of a few over the others. While Nietzsche looks at the consequences of the chains—the *ressentiment*—only to condemn them

[6] Voegelin (1959) pointed out some Gnostic elements in Marxian political theory (the alienation, the perfectivism, the eschatology etc.), but what is completely unconvincing in his reconstruction is the idea that Marxism is founded on an uncritical knowledge, which moreover would unite it to the Nietzschean doctrine of the Overman (is really the Overman basically characterised by knowledge?) and even to Nazism. The main point of gnosticism, however, is neither the 'irrational' nor the 'aristocratic' nature of knowledge, but the general idea that liberation can come only from knowledge. We need knowledge, in order to free ourselves, and under given conditions knowledge is even the most democratic concept. So, if Marxism is after all not a science, it is also true that there is no Marxism without science.

as sign of a reactive attitude[7], Marx realizes that it is only by removing the chains that emancipation can be reached: 'proletarians have nothing to lose but their chains'(Marx and Engels 1964).

The relation between suffering and struggle takes two opposite shapes in Marx and Nietzsche. In Marx the cause of suffering is not a struggle, but vice versa it is suffering that generates and justifies the struggle. Class struggle—like every struggle in general—is not for Marx the insurmountable logic of history, it is not the *essence* of human life, but a historical fact; we could say with an apparently oxymoric expression that it is a 'historical necessity', the necessity of which arises from the human desire to realize freedom as its very essence. The knowledge and awareness of suffering is the first step of a critique of these conditions. With Axel Honneth, the Marxian thought of the Frankfurt School has come to conclude the *consequent* and *not primary* character of the struggle. Hegel's limit was to consider the struggle for recognition as an atemporal figure of the spirit, while it is rather a historical fact, which follows the failure of recognition.

In the *Phenomenology of Spirit*, the description of the encounter between self-consciousnesses is tainted by a basic abstractness, since a secondary situation, the confrontation between two adults, is assumed as a model: and women and children do not fall within the figures of the spirit.[8] Although the adult-child relationship is not considered by Hegel to be a 'spiritual' relationship, it is much more primitive than the struggle between two adults. Axel Honneth, by bringing recognition back to an empirical basis, i.e. to a social psychology that takes into consideration also the early years of growth in the relationship between the child and the mother (as studied by Donald W. Winnicott and Jessica Benjamin), has shown the 'artificiality'—i.e. the derivativeness—of the Hegelian master-slave figure described in the *Phenomenology of Spirit*. In its ideality, this figure hides the empirical ground from which it arises, namely the fact that its ground is a previous and deeper misrecognition, occurred during childhood: the 'presupposition of a successful growth of the 'I' is a certain sequence of forms of mutual recognition whose lack… is conveyed to the subjects through the experience of a misrecognition, which urges them to a struggle for recognition' (Honneth 1994, p. 112).

Thus struggle is not a primitive fact but the reactive outcome of maltreatments, violence, mortifications, exclusions, humiliations, and affronts that can mark negatively the child's growth. Its logic—as struggle for recognition—is prescribed by the consciousness that the fulfilment of oneself can be achieved only through the realization of the other. It is a necessarily holistic logic, under which nobody is truly free without the others being free, so that to desire one's own liberty means

---

[7] "Of course, as I said, a good temperament would be necessary—a secure, mild, and basically cheerful soul; such a disposition would not need to be on guard for tricks and sudden explosions, and its expressions would have neither a growling tone nor sullenness – those familiar bothersome traits of old dogs and men who have lain a long time chained up." (Nietzsche 1999e, p. 34)

[8] Women and children do not belong to the history of spirit, at most they belong to a natural history of the moral: so by Nietzsche the ethical principle (*neminem laede, immo omnes, quantum potes, juva*), on which Schopenhauer thought all people could agree, is only a 'children's and old silly women's chatter' (see Nietzsche (1999d, § 186)).

intrinsically to desire other people's liberty.[9] In this way, the struggle for one's own liberty is always and also a struggle for other people's liberty, and vice versa.

Struggle is possible—and even needed—because the process of recognition has failed when it could have been fulfilled through love; since misrecognition leads to inevitable suffering, the desire of liberation expresses itself in reactive, and even destructive forms. Since the knowledge of suffering—in both its forms, as 'principle of reality' and 'principle of coercion'—is the ground of political activity, there is no wonder that totalitarianism, which always requires a certain 'unconsciousness' of its real domination, needs suffering to become unconscious and a denial of any subjective 'feeling unwell'. This aim, deliberately pursued in modern society by the aesthetic drives of cultural industry, is surreptitiously present also in some religious conceptions of suffering. Considering suffering as an experience of fault produces a subtle coercion, the efficacy of which is directly proportional to the repression of suffering that can be induced in this way. This phenomenon can be expressed by the following logical argument: since I suffer I am guilty; then, in order to not to feel guilty and feel 'adequate', comfortable in the world where I live, it is better if I remove suffering. This argument contains a form of blackmail, a violence as effective and powerful as subtle, on which many educational systems and many cultures (more than we can imagine) are founded. We can detect here the micrologic (to use a Foucaultian word) principle of every totalitarianism. Totalitarianism presupposes such a 'principle of coercion'—the possible repression of suffering, but which leads a political organism to its own anaesthetization, to a sort of induced, artificial 'insensitivity to pain', that is as destructive to the system of the social as physical insensitivity is to the biological. Unlike physical suffering, however, psychological suffering can be denied and inhibited with the greatest ease. Contrary to what Nietzsche believes, only humans can repress even the knowledge of their own suffering (this is perhaps the most auto-destructive sign of human liberty), and build a totalitarian repression of suffering. In this, the human stands in contrast to the animal, for whom suffering, or its onset, instinctively triggers off a reactive behaviour whether for fight or flight. The awareness of psychical suffering is even more important than the awareness of physical suffering, because on it depends the 'ethical-political' survival of the individual—as Axel Honneth, in his debate with Hobbes and Hegel, has shown very clearly.[10] As the animal knows well, the essence of 'taming', as we can call the coercive pseudo-education in which the micrologic principle of totalitarianism consists, is not to teach *through* suffering, but to cause the *forgetfulness* of suffering undergone (Miller 2004, 2007).[11]

---

[9] On this topic see. Chiurazzi (2007).

[10] A. Honneth, *Kampf um Anerkennung,* cit., Chap. I.

[11] This is what the psychotherapist Alice Miller has, in a very upsetting way, tried to show: according to Miller, violence which adults commit is nothing but the reaction to a violence they suffered as children and they are made unaware of. In texts such as *Die Revolte des Körpers* (2004) and *Dein gerettetes Leben. Wege zur Befreiung* (2007), Alice Miller shows that the most destructive side of the violence, which we suffered as children, is not in the violence as such, but in the repression of suffering that its 'educational' justification involves: an impossible repression, because suffering remains on a somatic level, like a physical memory, and this is why it can always reactivate the awareness of its origin, presupposition of every real liberation.

Bibliography

Aeschylus. 2009. *Oresteia: Agamemnon, Libation-Bearers, Eumenides*, Loeb classical library. Trans. A.H. Sommerstein. Harvard: Harvard University Press.

Apel, Karl-Otto, Claus v. Bormann, Rüdiger Bubner, Hans-Georg Gadamer, Hans-Joachim Giegel, and Jürgen Habermas. 1971. *Hermeneutik und Ideologiekritik.* Frankfurt a. M.: Suhrkamp.

Chiurazzi, Gaetano. 2007. L'olismo della libertà. Interazione e indipendenza nella figura hegeliana del signore e del servo. *Annuario Filosofico* 23:291–307. Milano: Mursia.

Foucault, Michel. 1984. What is enlightenment? In *The Foucault reader,* ed. Paul Rabinow. New York: Pantheon Books.

Gadamer, Hans-Georg. 2004. *Truth and Method.* Trans. J. Weinsheimer and D.G. Marshall. London: Continuum.

Hegel, G. W. F. 1970a. *Phänomenologie des Geistes.* In *Werke*, vol. 3, eds. E. Moldenhauer and K. M. Michel. Frankfurt a. M.: Suhrkamp.

Hegel, G. W. F. 1970b. *Wissenshaft der Logik.* In *Werke*, vol. 5, eds. E. Moldenhauer and K. M. Michel. Frankfurt a. M.: Suhrkamp.

Honneth, Axel. 1994. *Kampf um Anerkennung. Zur moralischen Grammatik sozialer Konflikte.* Frankfurt a. M.: Suhrkamp.

Kirk, G. S., J. E. Raven, and M. Schofield. 1983. *The presocratic philosophers*, 2nd edn. Cambridge: University Press.

Lemm, V. 2009. *Nietzsche's animal philosophy: Culture, politics, and the animality of the human being.* New York: Fordham University Press.

Marx, Karl. 1964a. *Briefe aus den 'Deutsch-Französischen Jahrbüchern'*. In *Werke*, vol. 1. Berlin: Dietz. (*Brief an Ruge*, May 1843)

Marx, Karl. 1964b. *Zur Judenfrage.* In *Werke*, vol. 1. Berlin: Dietz.

Marx, Karl. 1964c. *Zur Kritik des Hegelschen Staatsrecht. Einleitung.* In *Werke*, vol. 1. Berlin: Dietz.

Marx, Karl, and Friedrich Engels. 1957–1968. *Marx-Engels Werke*, 39 vols. Berlin: Dietz.

Marx, Karl, and Friedrich Engels. 1964. *Manifest der Kommunstischen Partei.* In *Werke*, vol. 4. Berlin: Dietz.Miller, Alice. 2004. *Die Revolte des Körpers.* Frankfurt a. M.: Suhrkamp.

Miller, Alice. 2007. *Dein gerettetes Leben. Wege zur Befreiung.* Frankfurt a. M.: Suhrkamp.

Nietzsche, Friedrich. 1972. *Zur Genealogie der Moral*, vol. II, § 11. Oxford: Blackwell.

Nietzsche, Friedrich. 1999. *Kritische Studienausgabe*, 15 vols. Berlin: de Gruyter.

Nietzsche, Friedrich. 1999a. *Zur Genealogie der Moral.* In *Kritische Studienausgabe*, vol. 5, II, § 3. Berlin: de Gruyter.

Nietzsche, Friedrich. 1999b. Vom Nutzen und Nachteil der Historie für das Leben. In *Kritische Studienausgabe: Unzeitgemässe Betrachtungen,* vol. 1, § 1. Berlin: de Gruyter.

Nietzsche, Friedrich. 1999c. *Also sprach Zarathustra. In Kritische Studienausgabe: Von der Erlösung*, vol. 4. Berlin: de Gruyter.

Nietzsche, Friedrich. 1999d. *Jenseits von Gut und Böse.* In *Kritische Studienausgabe*, vol. 5. Berlin: de Gruyter.

Nietzsche, Friedrich. 1999e. *Menschliches, Allzumenschliches.* In *Kritische Studienausgabe*, vol. 2. Berlin: de Gruyter.

Voegelin, Eric. 1959. *Wissenschaft, Politik und Gnosis.* Munich: Kösel.

Chapter 4
Economies of Suffering: Kierkegaard and Levinas

Andrew Benjamin and Samuel Cuff Snow

Introduction

Suffering has a palpable presence. The ubiquity of suffering—both its everydayness as well as its inescapable exigency—makes demands. The philosophical questions arising from the acuity of suffering's presence concern the complex relationship between the demands that suffering makes and the conception of subjectivization to which it gives rise. (Subjectivization pertains, here, to the different conception of the subject who suffers.) The fact that suffering makes demands necessitates that part of any philosophical approach to this *topos* be structured by the development of an economy of suffering. Economies will differ. However, the use of the term 'economy' is intended to underscore the presence of agents (subjects) constructed by, and thus held within, a dynamic set of relations. Those relations are structured, in this instance, by how suffering is understood. One dominant economy of suffering defines it in terms of a logic of utility. As such suffering acquires the meaning it has as an after effect of the operative presence of this logic. Within this setting the meaning of suffering is located in a relation in which the constituting element is external, and therefore indifferent, to the actuality of suffering. In contrast to the posited link between suffering and utility there is the possibility of accounting for suffering where the account would be based on the refusal to attribute to suffering any form of utility. A different economy would be at work and thus a different conception of subjectivization would be present. Two of the most critically sustained engagements with the parameters of a topos of suffering are found in writings of Søren Kierkegaard and Emmanuel Levinas. What is found are two divergent economies of suffering. Their difference mirrors the distinction adumbrated above in relation to different logics of utility.

Kierkegaard, in his *Christian Discourses* and *Purity of Heart is to Will One Thing*, among other texts, defines suffering through its relation to Eternity, a relation which structures the subject such that through suffering it is allowed to prove

A. Benjamin (✉)
Monash University, Clayton VIC 3168, Australia
e-mail: andrew.benjamin@monash.edu.au

J. Malpas, N. Lickiss (eds.), *Perspectives on Human Suffering*,
DOI 10.1007/978-94-007-2795-3_4, © Springer Science+Business Media B.V. 2012

its faith and reach eternal salvation. By connecting the moment of suffering to a subsequent moment of Eternity, the former is necessarily subsumed under the faithful path to the latter. In this way, suffering denotes a means to an (eternal) end, functioning along the lines of a logic of utility. (Kierkegaard's position will be explored in the first section, 'Useful Suffering'.) Primarily in his seminal essay 'Useless Suffering', Levinas provides an economy of suffering that emerges underneath a logic of utility, demonstrating the way in which such a logic undermines itself in the face of the suffering Other. With Levinas, it is no longer possible to maintain a conception of suffering that reduces suffering to an individual exercise of self-mastery; this would be in reality a disavowal of the primordial relationality underpinning human being. The divergence that unfolds between the two authors importantly indicates the divide between a conception of care that, on the one side, focuses on subordinating suffering to a constant that is always external to it—e.g. guilt, sin—and which positions the subject as an isolated individual, and, on the other, one that provides room for living out and living with suffering.

Useful Suffering

The commonplace approach to suffering is directed by the question—'why?' Such questioning locates suffering within a structure of utility by assuming, in the first instance, the inherent viability of the question and thus, in the second, the necessity that there be an answer. The question of suffering, suffering as a question—thus suffering positioned within that economy in which the 'why?' is assumed to have genuine interrogative force, requires an answer. The answer can be in two forms: either it provides a reason for suffering, or it explains suffering as occurring without a defined reason. That is, the presence of suffering has no particular reason, rather it is simply part of human life. In the first case, suffering is comprehended within a framework that understands suffering through something other than suffering itself; namely its cause, end, *telos*, or use. In the second case, suffering is viewed as a fundamental part of existence and in that way serves as a possible explanation of what life could entail. Evidently, arguing the absurdity of suffering as an answer to the question 'why?' still operates according to the same logic of utility. This logic permits a concept of suffering that either will serve a particular purpose, or positions suffering in relation to the single individual—positioning as subjectivization—whose reality is to suffer.

Instantiations of such a logic of utility, in particular those which posit a certain reason for suffering, include arguments grounded on guilt, justice, retribution, redemption, salvation, grace, fate, *telos* (to name just a few). Recourse to such terminology posits suffering as a means to an end. Wrongdoing leads to the assigning of guilt, which translates to suffering, either at the hands of therefore justified retribution, punishment, or 'bad conscience'. As Levinas writes, '[i]s not fear of punishment the beginning of wisdom? Do people not have the idea that suffering, undergone as punishment, regenerates the enemies of society and humankind?'

(Levinas 1998). Connected with guilt, suffering can be explained as a means to an end, a *telos*. That is, following a logic of guilt, suffering occurs for a reason. Even more strongly, suffering occurs for a certain purpose. Moreover, those who bear affliction, enduring what is required as they move towards redemption, are provided precisely through their suffering with the way to salvation. Even in a non-spiritual register, following a teleological reading, it can be understood as a marker of ill-health; not only does an individual's physical pain manifest the weakness in need of care and treatment, 'social discontent awakens a useful attention to the health of the collective body' (Levinas 1998, p. 95). Central to the above and any responses to suffering that provide an answer to the question 'why?' is the positioning of suffering as a means to an end and thus its articulation within a logic of utility. In the case that suffering is interpreted as absurd, it is nevertheless construed as a necessary illumination of wrongdoing. As mentioned above, such a 'service of suffering' opens itself to a more general argument, which understands suffering as a necessary part of existence; a certain degree of Bad, Evil, suffering, is the condition of understanding Good. In this light, any conceptual approach to suffering in response to the question 'why?' is evidently interwoven with, even contained within, a logic of utility.

Kierkegaard wrote extensively on suffering. His interpretation of 'temporal suffering' and 'active suffering', in relation to a concept of the 'Good' and 'eternal victory', espouses a paradigmatic teleological reading of suffering; which is another instantiation of a logic of utility. In short, it is distinguished between useful and useless suffering.[1] Suffering is a necessary component of what Kierkegaard terms 'willing for the Good' (Kierkegaard 1948, p. 121). If one suffers within the pursuit of the highest Good, the pursuit of a faithful relation to Eternity, the suffering endured is the pathway to eternal victory; it is useful. Indeed, those who pass through suffering in this way are not real sufferers at all, rather active persons. In his *Christian Discourses*, Kierkegaard writes:

> The one time of suffering is a passing through that leaves no mark at all upon the soul, or, even more glorious, it is a passing through that completely cleanses the soul, and as a result the purity becomes the mark the passing through leaves behind. But just as gold is purified in the fire, so the soul is purified in sufferings. (Kierkegaard 1997, p. 102)

In this work, and others that will be explored, the argument that the 'soul is purified' rather than marked through suffering is maintained consistently. It is worth noting that the purification of the soul decidedly evokes Christo-theological teachings on suffering.[2] The question of Kierkegaard's connection to the Church and religiosity is by no

---

[1] See the comments below on Kierkegaard's affinity with Christian teachings on suffering.

[2] For example, John Paul II (1984) outlined the parameters for understanding the way that God bore suffering as His Son, imbuing suffering with a structure of His gift, Love, and eventual salvation: 'Human suffering has reached its culmination in the Passion of the Christ… it has entered into a completely new dimension and a new order: *it has been linked to love*… which creates Good, drawing it out by means of suffering' (John Paul 1982, Part IV). As John Paul II sees in suffering the 'price of Redemption', so Kierkegaard announces man's victory 'on the day of suffering.' Furthermore, the distinction drawn by Kierkegaard between *real* and *useless* suffering and suffering as a step to eternal victory is latent in the Pope's words: 'Man 'perishes' when he loses 'eternal life'. The opposite of salvation is not, therefore, only temporal suffering, any kind of suffering,

means simple. One of his primary concerns was to challenge Church dogma, while instilling through his writings a deep sense of both the absolute distance that separates human beings from God and the absolute importance, necessity, and redemptive power, of faith. The central point here is that the Christo-theological exploration of the meaning of Evil, of its congruence with the Goodness of God, is a theodicy.

Theodicy is a term coined by the German philosopher Wilhelm Leibniz, and denotes an apologetic response to the issue of how an omnipotent and benevolent God could permit Evil. Leibniz, for example, argued that God, in his Goodness, would create the best of all possible worlds. The best of all of possible worlds contains suffering, as a minimum of evil is required to contrast and therefore illumine the Good (of God).[3] As an elucidation of suffering in relation to a separate and distinct idea, the Good, theodicy functions within a logic of utility. It is thus that Kierkegaard's writings on suffering and Eternity have argumentative roots in Christian theodicy; and moreover that theodicy, and with that Kierkegaard's arguments, can be fundamentally understood as an attempt to conceptualise suffering as useful. By pursuing a project of theodicy, Kierkegaard confers meaning onto suffering through reference to that which follows suffering, and that which it brings about. In doing so, Kierkegaard interconnects the external and the suffering, isolated subject within an economy defined by utility.

> Yes, loving; that is why he would like you finally to will what he [God] for the sake of eternity wills for you: that you might resolve to will to suffer, that is, that you might resolve to will to love him, because you can love him only in suffering, or if you love as he wills to be loved you will come to suffer… if it is neglected, if you do not come to suffer, if you avoid it—it is eternally irreparable. (Kierkegaard 1998, p. 294)

Also within the same text Kierkegaard evoke suffering's other possibility—i.e. useless suffering, suffering no longer defined in terms of a logic of utility, as a state of affairs to be guarded against. Hence he writes 'Yet be careful, take care that time does not go by unused, perhaps in useless suffering; remember, one lives only once' (Kierkegaard 1998, p. 294). Kierkegaard presents his readership with a progressive exploration of existential stages. The first is the aesthetic, which gives way to the ethical, which gives way to the religious. It is within the religious sphere that an individual is able to foster the type of faith capable of shaping true selfhood. (And note that it is always self-hood in isolation.) Dependent on the success or failure of a subject's development of self through faith is his/her salvation or damnation before God. Indeed, according to Kierkegaard, such faith must be continually renewed. It is a consistent repetition of faith in the moment which brings forth eternal truth, as the moment is that point at which time and Eternity intersect.[4] Kierkegaard

---

but the definitive suffering: the loss of eternal life… The only begotten Son was given to humanity primarily to protect man against this definitive evil and against *definitive suffering*' (John Paul 1982, Part IV).

[3] Theodicy—[Greek] *theos*: God; and *dike*: Justice. See Leibniz (1952).

[4] 'The Moment' (*Øieblikket*—literally 'the glint of an eye') was Kierkegaard's final publication. Not only did Kierkegaard refer to the 'moment' as such an intersection of time and Eternity, but used the publication as a platform to undertake his own intervention in Church politics.

identified the moment as the moment of decision, the moment of transfiguring vision, the moment of contemporaneity with Christ. It was also the moment to let go of indirect communication and to speak directly. Given the intersection of time and Eternity within the moment, an actively faithful person has the chance to re-instate significantly their faith in the instant of suffering. The 'moment' yields the subject. Subjectivization occurs in the instant of suffering. In that way, suffering remains for Kierkegaard merely temporal; one suffers only momentarily, as in the face of the 'no time' of eternity, suffering can never transcend its 'one time', its temporality, which is but to be passed through.[5] Its temporality is in the same breath, however, an instance of a 'moment' to be seized, used in passing to relate with Eternity. It is evident that by linking suffering to a temporality which is defined by its relation to Eternity—eternal truth, eternal victory, 'no time', salvation, and the Good—Kierkegaard is positing suffering as meaningful only insofar as it can both illumine its counterpart (theodicy) and serve faith and eternal victory (teleology/utility).

The emphatic reference to 'victory' is indicative of what may be described as heroic terminology, employed in elucidations of suffering that take its overcoming as a focus. Nietzsche, for example, fundamentally responding to the 'senselessness' [*Sinnlosigkeit*] of suffering depicted by Schopenhauer, identifies both 'suppression/repression' [*Hemmung*] and 'resistance' [*Widerstand*] as constitutive components in an understanding of will to power.[6] Power cannot be understood without reference to 'suppression/repression' and 'resistance'. The result of their necessary pairing with power is suffering [*Leiden*]. Therefore, Nietzsche imbues suffering with both sense and necessity. In a gesture akin to Kierkegaard's active 'passing through' (by active persons), Nietzsche links the active 'overcoming' [*Überwinden*] of difficulty

[5] 'Temporality itself, the whole of it, is a moment; eternally understood, temporality is a moment, and a moment, eternally understood, is only once … Eternity is the very opposite. It is not the opposite of a single moment in temporality (this is meaningless); it is the opposite of the whole of temporality, and with all the powers of eternity it resists temporality's becoming more'. (Kierkegaard 1997, p. 98).

[6] Schopenhauer sees suffering as two-fold: the battle of all against all [*Kampf aller gegen alle*] is painful [*leidvoll*], and, given all individuals are but expressions/objectifications of the one substance, the Will [*der Wille*], such a battle is essentially self-destruction [*Selbstzerfleischung*]—see Schopenhauer, *Die Welt als Wille und Vorstellung* (see Schopenhauer 2009). The absurdity of such self-destruction stems from the contradiction between the motivating drive to preserve oneself, which is one of the central forces of the all-encompassing Will, and the resulting destruction of oneself. In fact, Schopenhauer argues that our task is to free ourselves from the chains of necessity, that is, to rid ourselves of the Will. This can take place on three levels: aesthetics, ethics, and religion (or soteriology), in order of efficacy/profundity. In this way, Schopenhauer is situated within a framework of Christian soteriology (suffering/grace), to which Nietzsche offers a response. (There is danger of *equating* Schopenhauer's push for asceticism as a form of soteriology with Christian soteriology. The point here is not to equate the two, rather to indicate a structural affinity.) Interestingly, Nietzsche seems to follow an ascetic ideal, in the Schopenhauerian spirit, in his *Unzeitgemäße Betrachtungen* (Nietzsche 1999, vol. 1): suffering is to be overcome through abstinence, withdrawal, leading eventually to redemption [*Erlösung*].

and resistance with suffering.[7] Critically, heroic rhetoric such as Nietzsche's reference to *Überwinden* and Kierkegaard's to 'victory on the day of suffering' is latent in the type of language used to refer to pain, illness, and suffering within some contexts of palliative care. One 'battles' with or 'fights' an affliction with 'courage' and 'bravery'. Such past affliction, as Levinas writes, 'is also thought to temper the individual's character' (Levinas 1998, p. 95).

Alongside the 'active persons', who pass through (overcome) suffering, able to relate themselves and their temporal sufferings to Eternity, Kierkegaard writes of 'real sufferers.' Suffering is real when it 'does not benefit others… but rather is a burden upon them.' The distinction drawn between active persons and sufferers corresponds to that between temporal suffering and 'useless suffering'. Given suffering is essentially a step on the way to Eternity, if one does not endure it as a step, then sufferings can pass by without being passed through. Such suffering is, at least can be expressed in language as, 'useless' and 'beyond the reach of comfort' (Kierkegaard 1948, pp. 153–154). Levinas writes that 'the bad and gratuitous meaningless of pain already shows beneath the reasonably forms espoused by the social (or otherwise) 'uses' of suffering'. That is perhaps 'real suffering', in Kierkegaard's sense. However, Kierkegaard's so-called real suffering is, firstly, incapable of being definitive, as 'as little as moth and rust can consume the treasure of eternity… just as little can all the suffering of temporality, no matter how long it might last, injure the soul in the remotest way' (Kierkegaard 1997, p. 102). Secondly, real suffering is subservient to and subsumed under the notion of suffering to be passed through, used. What is opened up therefore is the other economy. The one in which structures of guilt and a logic of utility will have ceded their place to the 'useless'.

Useless Suffering

One of the most significant critical responses to the articulation of suffering within a logic of utility, a location that determines the meaning of suffering, can be found in Emmanuel Levinas' paper 'Useless Suffering'. Prior to responding to and developing Levinas' position two preliminary points need to be identified in advance. What is important to note, in the first instance, is that what emerges is not simply another conception of suffering—as though the topos of suffering was a given and all that mattered were different accounts. Rather, his writings develop a different

[7] In this way, the anti-Christo-theological thinker Nietzsche is found to be espousing an understanding of suffering potentially subsumable under a logic of utility. It can be argued that Nietzsche does not see a *use* in suffering, especially in his arguments against the *legitimation* of suffering by Christo-Judaic theology in *Jenseits von Gut und Böse* (Nietzsche 1999, vol. 5) and *Zur Genealogie der Moral* (Nietzsche 1999, vol. 5). It is moreover difficult to claim that Nietzsche offers a response to 'why?' [*wozu?*]. However, Nietzsche certainly seems to position suffering in relation to resistance and overcoming, under the rubric of the will to power.

economy of suffering. 'Economy', as has been argued, is a concept that is central to this overall project. Suffering as a term has contrary designations insofar as it can be attributed different meanings. More significant however is the fact that differences on the level of meaning denote the presence of different modes of activity. Those modes position subjects. It is not simply therefore that there are different conceptions of suffering as though all that mattered was a debate on the level of meaning. The important point is that each conception of suffering, in its being lived out and thus in designating activity, brings with it different modes of subjectivization (and thus different conceptions of subjectivity)—as is clear from the discussion of Kierkegaard above. What they set in play are different practices. It is the link to activity and thus to institutional practices, a foundational and ineliminable link, which would allow a given philosophical account of suffering to give rise to one set of practices rather than another.

The second introductory point is that Levinas' work in relation to his writings on 'suffering', though this is true of his philosophical project in general, involves a form of radical transformation. What is transformed is the locus of the ethical. Rather than the isolated individual comprising that locus, the ethical is situated both within and structured by the effective presence of an already present relation. Levinas' writings on suffering invoke what he describes as the 'interhuman order' in order to describe that original setting. While it will be essential to pursue that setting in greater detail, it should be noted in advance that fundamental to Levinas' position is that as a setting—the setting of/for human being, being as acted out—it has a necessary form of originality. As such it can be understood as an 'order' that is already present within what can be described as the 'fabric of existence'. In a passage of telling importance towards the end of 'Useless Suffering' this original state of affairs is expressed in the following terms:

> The interhuman, properly speaking, lies in a non-indifference of one to another, in a responsibility of one for the other, but before the reciprocity of this responsibility, which will be inscribed in impersonal laws, come to be superimposed on the pure altruism of this responsibility inscribed in the ethical position of the I qua I. (Levinas 1998, p. 98)

If there is a way of giving great force to this position then it will emerge from the clear contrast to the setting that provides for a relation to death that is delimited by the individual. The latter emerges in Heidegger. It should be remembered that what is at work in both instances—Levinas and Heidegger—is a description of that which is proper to human being. What is important in Heidegger's attribution of centrality to 'being-towards-death' [*Sein zum Tode*] in *Being and Time* as that which defines the original propriety of Dasein, is not, in this instance, its link to a conception of authenticity—a conception in which death becomes one's own proper possibility. Rather, what is central is that death is a possibility that is inherently 'non-relational' (*unbezügliche*) (Heidegger wrote: 'death reveals itself as that possibility which is one's own most, which is non-relational, and which is not to be outstripped' (Heidegger 1978, p. 294)). While on one level what this means is that one cannot die in the place of the other, radical singularity and the impossibility of substitution is maintained on the level of the individuated Dasein (individuation and the non-relation is the setting of Dasein's authentic relation to death). While it remains the case for Levinas that substitution is an impossibility, that impossibility is set within relationality. There is a genuine possibility therefore of reading Levinas' concern with suffering, and in addition his voluminous writings on death, as a sustained engagement with the primordiality of 'relationality' and thus the inherently contradictory nature of the claim that death is delimited by its having been defined in terms of the 'non-relational'. While not expressed in Levinas' language, what has to emerge is the way the limited, if not contradictory nature of processes of individuation as defining human being are undone in Levinas' text 'Useless Suffering'.

The expression 'useless suffering' is intended, on the one hand, to interrupt an economy in which suffering is defined in terms of utility (one of the most emphatic forms of which is a theodicy). And, on the other hand, to insist that suffering means to have been 'overwhelmed'. Suffering comes from without. Suffering is to have been taken over. And yet having been 'overwhelmed' introduces not a pure form of subjection but a harrowing form of freedom: 'In suffering the free being ceases to be free, but while non-free is yet free' (Levinas 1969, p. 28). For Levinas the effect of the necessarily overwhelming nature of suffering and the sense of freedom to which it gives rise, is such that suffering is defined as a '*mal*' (evil). Moreover, present as 'evil', it undoes any continuity or congruity between life and being. Hence, suffering as 'evil' is both without meaning and 'absurd'. In drawing on the twofold possibility within the French term 'sens'—as both direction and meaning—suffering becomes meaningless and directionless, thus in general senseless (a positioning compounding its description as 'absurd'). Suffering, as a result, cannot be incorporated into any philosophical or theological project in which it is intended to lead somewhere. The latter would be that place—a placed possibility occurring after life—that would confer, albeit retrospectively, meaning and thus direction on suffering. Within such a setting suffering would have acquired meaning, though only after the event. Such a possibility is no longer operative from the moment in which suffering is refused a place within a logic of utility. In the place of utility there is a different economy.

It is at this precise point that the gulf between Kierkegaard and Levinas has its greatest acuity. Furthermore, it is the presence of 'pure suffering'—suffering in the other—that in having neither direction nor meaning opens up the necessity of the 'interhuman'. 'Useless suffering' becomes the affirmation of an already present form of relationality—a relationality that becomes manifest once the link between suffering and utility is exposed and undone. It is thus that what Levinas will describe as 'the useless suffering of the other' opens up a suffering within the self. The latter is a suffering for the 'unjustifiable suffering' of the other. Indeed, the force of this position becomes abundantly clear were the counter position to be allowed. The counter position is that suffering, once incorporated within a logic of utility, entails that the other's suffering had meaning in terms of what it allowed for the one who suffers, and as such there is no call on the other. Suffering would pertain to the one suffering. As a consequence, the suffering of the other would have a type of justification, and in so doing would have acquired both direction and meaning, and as a result any response to that suffering, in no longer having been opened up by an 'inescapable obligation', would as a result be both contingent in regards to presence (e.g. care as manifest) as well as arbitrary in regards to content.

Within the context of the text 'Useless Suffering' Levinas offers an emphatic critique of positions that try to attribute forms of meaning to the Holocaust and the other genocides that mark the twentieth century. This ever extends to well-intentioned projects such as Fackenheim's who sees in the Holocaust that which yields what Levinas, writing of Fackenheim, describes as 'a commandment of faithfulness'. While suffering has a particular configuration within modernity, it is the very impossibility of incorporating genocide within a logic of utility—of allowing the Holocaust a place within a logic of utility and thus of having a calculable economy—that opens up what can be described as an archaic setting within which the theological response is what Levinas describes as 'faith without theodicy', while the philosophical response (remembering that both responses are bound up with modes of activity and in which there is no clear divisions such that practice and thought would be held apart) starts from a suffering that is 'inspired by the suffering of the other'. What this opens up is the necessity to name that response as 'compassion'. While suffering will always be that which is meaningful in 'me', it remains the case it is 'useless in the other'. The full consequences of such a setting can be explored by looking at the force of the word 'compassion'.

Once rewritten as com-passion its two defining elements become clear. 'Com' designates a state of commonality. While 'passion'—coming from the Latin *patir*—involves the feeling of pity or suffering. (Passion, therefore, is mediated, *ab inito*, by the 'com'.) Thus compassion is to suffer together. On its own the identification of this founding mediation is not sufficient. What it opens up is the need to pursue how 'common' or 'together' are to be understood. As will emerge, in lieu of a relation defined by symmetry, within which the 'common' is the site of a pervasive sense of Sameness and a unity of self and other (equally a unity within both self and other), what suffering and thus com-passion gestures towards is what can be described as a relation defined in terms of the asymmetrical. To the extent that such a positioning is maintained then the asymmetrical reveals the way in which the 'interhuman' and by extension the 'com' of 'com-passion' is to be understood, namely as containing a sense of an original form of relationality. Passion, taken on its own, is inextricably bound up with suffering as incorporated within a logic of utility. Not only is such a setting integral to Christianity, it is also there in the attempts to incorporate those moments of suffering that mark the twentieth century within a conception of historical time where any event is determined by the necessity of progress (and thus progress' necessity). Passion is the site of the individuated subject who must attribute meaning to their suffering and only receive care because their suffering is taken to be meaningful. Care within such a context is no more than charity and as charity is inherently arbitrary. The only argument for its presence is the continual incorporation of suffering within a logic of utility. However, the force of recasting passion as com-passion is that once relationality involves a founding asymmetry then this will not just pertain to the relationship between self and other, it will inform equally the self's own self-relation.

Conclusion

Suffering in Kierkegaard provides for a subject's discovery of faith, self, and Eternity. By introducing a concept of absurd, useless suffering—that is, that which emerges at and brings about an impasse, incongruence, of life and being—Levinas interrupts the logic of utility underpinning such a discovery. Instead of subsuming suffering under a *telos* and the subject's control (in activity), suffering becomes the locus for radical passivity, a passivity that fissures self-mastery, opening up space for what was always already grounding human being—the interhuman order. This relationality is the nexus of human subjectivity, a subjectivity that can be realised through suffering together; com-passion.

As argued above commonality, along with a conception of suffering as inherently useless, in the Levinasian sense, allows an asymmetrical self-other relation to emerge, parrying and subverting any attempt to mould suffering into a logic of utility. The framework of 'care' that emerges out of asymmetry is one neither of charitable pity, nor of heroic battle, whereby the subject's autarky could, or should, be restored, through the instrumentalisation of woe. Rather, it will incorporate a recognition of the suffering Other, calling and demanding 'me' to respond to his/her unjustifiable suffering in my suffering, justifiable as com-passion.

Bibliography

Heidegger, Martin. 1978. *Being and Time*. Trans. J. Macquarrie and E. Robinson. Oxford: Blackwell.

John Paul II. 1984. *On the christian meaning of suffering*. Vatican: Liberia Editrice.

Kierkegaard, Søren. 1948. *Purity of Heart is to Will One Thing*. Trans. D. Steere. New York: Harper and Row.

Kierkegaard, Søren. 1997. The joy of it: That one suffers only once but is victorious eternally. In *Christian discourses: The crisis and a crisis in the life of an actress*. Trans. H. Hong and E. Hong. Princeton: Princeton University Press.

Kierkegaard, Søren. 1998. One lives only once. In *The moment and late writings*. Trans. H. Hong and E. Hong. Princeton: Princeton University Press.

Leibniz, G. W. von. 1952. *Theodicy: Essays on the goodness of god, the freedom of man and the origin of evil,* ed. A. Farrer. Trans. E.M. Huggard. New Haven: Yale University Press.

Levinas, Emmanuel. 1969. *Totality and Infinity: An Essay on Exteriority*. Trans. A. Lingis. Pittsburgh: Duquesne University Press.

Levinas, Emmanuel. 1998. Useless suffering. In *Entre nous: On thinking-of-the-other*. Trans. M. Smith and B. Harshav. New York: Columbia University Press.

Nietzsche, Friedrich. 1999. *Kritische studienausgabe,* 15 vols. Berlin: de Gruyter.

Schopenhauer, Arthur. 2009. *Die Welt als Wille und Vorstellung*. Munich: GRIN.

Chapter 5
The Other Thing About Suffering

Lucy Tatman

This is not about suffering, at least not directly, not suffering as such—that irreducible experience of pain and anguish. Rather, my concern is with 'the other thing' about suffering. This 'other thing' could be called the logic of suffering, if by this is meant the complex web of associations, connotations and implications wrapped so tightly around suffering *per se*. My problem is that each filament of this not quite arbitrary web seems by itself to be so insubstantial, so negligible, or so banal as to be not worth mentioning. *Our* problem is that when all these threads are knotted together in the western cultural imaginary—as I think they have been for over two thousand years—then we are all of us bound up in a most cruel logic, a logic which cannot but add insult to the injury that is suffering.

To begin with the deceptively banal: whether their suffering is a consequence of fate, chance, accident, deliberate attack, orchestrated misery, or the inescapable fact of human mortality, what sufferers have in common is that they are all the victims of something more powerful than they. They are weak in relation to its strength. But how do we 'know' that sufferers are weak? I suggest we 'know' it because they are in some obvious, which is to say interpretable, manner letting it 'get to them.' Swollen or dark shadowed eyes, hollow cheeks, clenched jaw, muscle tick, lethargy, passivity, or agitation, repetitive rocking or pacing, wild outbursts, uncontrollable (and ineffectual) rage, or howls, or tears, or or or. The symptoms are too numerous—each one evidence of the sufferer's inability to fix the problem, take control of the situation.[1] They are stuck: weak in relation to something stronger, more powerful than they.

According to the logic I am trying to make explicit, suffering seems to suffuse the sufferer, to affect the entirety of their being, to change them from someone who feels pain but conquers it, from someone who is victorious in their encounter with a

[1] My concern is with sufferers who are presenting as suffering, for the logic of suffering applies only to those assumed by others to be suffering. A colleague makes a similar argument with respect to assumptions which affect those deemed to be mentally ill—see Cox (2010).

L. Tatman (✉)
School of Philosophy, University of Tasmania, Hobart 7001, Tasmania, Australia
e-mail: Lucy.Tatman@utas.edu.au

J. Malpas, N. Lickiss (eds.), *Perspectives on Human Suffering*,
DOI 10.1007/978-94-007-2795-3_5, © Springer Science+Business Media B.V. 2012

potentially dangerous situation, into a defeated victim, an obviously damaged creature. The fact that they are suffering exposes their fragility, their frailty, their weakness. According to the inexorable logic of suffering, sufferers are, in a profound sense, an ontological sub-set of humanity. To put it bluntly, they are the ones who have succumbed, who have failed in their encounter with adversity. They are 'the other' in relation to 'us'; we are the resolute, the rock-solid, the implacable. We are strong, and they are weak. Further, the fact that they are weak exposes their inherent flaws, and not incidentally shores up our strength, our most excellent character, our innate superiority. 'They' are wusses; 'we' are real men. Ouch.

I am afraid this is the core element of 'the other thing' about suffering—that it feminizes all who suffer. This insight, its utter lack of nuance or subtlety, its sledgehammer-like quality, appalls me. As a gender theorist I feel as though I've been thrown back into an early second wave feminist cave, and I bristle at the thought. Why is this still here, why hasn't anyone warned me about this? And yet, there it is. I don't know how many indexes I've looked through, or how many times I've done web searches, or even resorted to pestering librarians—all to no avail. What I perceive to be an in your face association of suffering with weakness with the feminine has gone, if not entirely unmentioned, at least thoroughly unanalyzed.

Maybe this theoretical silence is related to the shocking corporeality of suffering. In Beauvoirian terms, those who suffer are mired in the immanence of their own flesh; they cannot transcend their embodied anguish. It does not matter if the cause of their pain had nothing to do with their own bodies, soon enough the anguish penetrates through their bones, their blood, their skin, their pores. It is as though the entire body of the sufferer becomes polluted with suffering. Again it is too obvious—they've succumbed to their feelings, their emotions.

Weakness, fragility, corporeality, pollution, emotion: the terms are stacking up, each one traditionally associated with the feminine, and all wrapped up in a shroud of silence. I wrote before that it is an old logic, but just how enduring are these associations? As fate would have it, I recently stumbled across the perfect quote, a summary of the 'élite free-status male values' that circulated in ancient Greek society. In Brent Shaw's words:

> Voice, activity, aggression, closure, penetration, and the ability to inflict pain and suffering were lauded as emblematic of freedom, courage, and good. Silence, passivity, submissiveness, openness, suffering—the shame of allowing oneself to be wounded, to be penetrated, and of simply enduring all that—were castigated as weak, womanish, slavish, and therefore morally bad. (Shaw 1996, p. 279)

I suspect he does not realize it, but Shaw's word choice reveals something of his cultural background. While in his context the meaning of 'womanish' is clear, and clearly negative, 'womanish' is, in African-American communities, a powerful word, a word used to describe girls who are acting with a degree of agency, purpose, wisdom and wit beyond their years (Walker 1983, p. xi). None of these are attributes associated with those who suffer, for their agency has been diminished, their wit dulled, their position in the world shifted away from the full-voiced human toward the mute, the child-like. Sufferers are not fully responsible for their actions. They must be looked after, often enough even their bodily needs attended to by someone more capable than they. To be caught up in suffering *is* to be somewhat ineffectual, less competent than one should be. Again the divisive logic cuts deep, separating with surgical precision the normative non-sufferer (effective, competent, masculine adult) from all those suffering others.

I said I was appalled by the other thing about suffering, by its relentlessly feminizing logic: that may have been an understatement. I am trying to understand that 'other thing' in order to discern a way out of its web, but so far everywhere I look there is yet another sticky thread. What I do not comprehend is, why? When a certain degree of suffering is in every life inevitable, why do we go to such great lengths to 'otherize' those who suffer? They are we, eventually. Or, if you are a Buddhist, they are we right now.

Aaaarrrrggggh. Frustrated, I've traded pen and paper for folding laundry, for tidying this little house. I would be muttering under my breath, but I cannot find the words. 'Harumph,' I say, and 'bleh.' A magnificently unjustified tirade directed against the editors of this volume takes shape. They are to blame for having ever so gently and thus irrefusably requested that I write about this blasted topic. It's complete nonsense, but I smile at the thought. The socks have been folded, the mugs and plates collected and stacked next to the sink. Glaring at a half-empty page, I begin to suspect that the distancing routine enacted by western non-sufferers is not inherently or essentially gendered, even if it is so thoroughly and historically feminizing. It's just, dare I write this, that suffering *is* icky. I understand the desire to avoid it, transcend it whenever possible. It really is nicer to fold socks than to think about suffering.

Accepting that it will touch our lives, that each of us will bear its scars, that if we are lucky we will one day escape from its clutches and thereby gain in status as a momentarily non-suffering subject, that if we are lucky we won't have to suffer again for a bit of a while—this all does seem to be a kind of acquiescence, a passive acceptance of precisely that which we have been taught to rail against. 'Do not go gentle,' etcetera. The deck is so stacked against anyone who might dare publicly to say, 'this is the way it is, all of us must suffer and so be it.'

Through my struggle to find a voice with which to speak the other thing about suffering, I have come to suspect that within western culture the discursive course of suffering simply followed the imaginary path of least resistance. Which is to say, there is great resistance to the appearance of suffering in public. The intensely private and personal character of suffering, its inextricability from the very body of the one suffering, seems to disqualify it as a matter for public discussion and debate. Sufferers are evicted from the world in common, and relegated to a private sphere which sometimes extends no farther than the surface of their own skin. Years ago Elaine Scarry made this point strictly in relation to bodies in pain, but I think it applies equally well to all who suffer (Scarry 1985). The public realm, that masculine dog-eat-dog world, provides no space for sufferers. For them room is made only in the private sphere. And there it is possible, I believe, to discern a language of suffering.

It is, however, a language spoken not so much with a voice but in a more material grammar, a physical syntax. I'm thinking of cups of tea, soft blankets tucked around hunched shoulders, pats on the hand or the head. I'm thinking of gooey casseroles brought to the door, or even of the cat who refuses to leave the lap of the sufferer for any reason whatsoever. Deep breaths, nods, head shakes. Pushing a bottle across the table toward the recently emptied glass. It is a language in the present tense, a language stripped of any memory or anticipation. Neither beginning nor ending can be told in this language; it's all about the middle, the suffering now. What was, what might be—these things cannot be discussed. Lacking the possibility of narrative arc, this language cannot be used to transmit heroic exploits—it can't even convey instructions for finding one's way out of a paper bag. It can, though, take the form of a paper bag handed over to relieve the hiccups which so often follow sobs. It is an immediate and attentive address, and one which requires no response. Dialogue is unlikely in this language, but monologue impossible.

Amazingly, the language of suffering is gender neutral; it's just that women are expected to be fluent in it, while manly mistakes are praised for the effort. I am reminded of a bad joke. 'What do you call a woman who suffers on behalf of others?' 'Mother.' 'What do you call a man who suffers on behalf of others?' 'God.' The logic wrapped around suffering is steeped in gendered expectations and value judgments. While the language of suffering is anything but 'a private language' in the strictly philosophical sense of the term, it is in fact a private language in the sense of belonging to the private side of the public/private divide, and this makes it feminine by association, expectation, and by practice. It is a language of immanence, of the material, of the corporeal. It is a language left unstudied as a language, for it doesn't count, it doesn't matter, even though, or perhaps because, it is made of matter.

Knowing when to offer whiskey and when to offer a slice of cheese on toast, this sort of knowledge—of epistemic excellence, I would suggest—has not been deemed to be excellent at all. Again the unsubtle, un-nuanced gendered irritation. Blokes are not impressed by that which they are not expected or required to know. I am, though. I am gobsmacked in the presence of those who can speak the language of suffering with ease, with fluency. What strikes me forcibly is (a) not many people I've met can speak this language without hesitation, and (b) I've discerned no actual gender bias one way or the other—not in the instances of suffering I've witnessed or experienced. Maybe my life has been truly odd, but if I take it as typical, then I must admit that in actuality (in contradistinction to the cultural imaginary) men seem just as likely as women to provide succour and solace in times of suffering. If this is true, though, if it can be generalized, then I am even more gobsmacked at the strength of the western cultural imaginary. In the face of an abundance of evidence suggesting otherwise (I'm thinking of you, John, and Gary and Jimbo and Steve and Ralph…), suffering remains resolutely feminine, private, pale and unspeakable.

By now it is clear, I hope, that the logic of suffering defies all logic. Irrational to an extreme—this is probably its greatest strength. It cannot be undone by any appeals to reason. That this magnificently masculine edifice, the otherizing logic of suffering, can only be described as a web (beloved feminist and feminine image[2]), that it is located so firmly in the realm of the irrational, the unreasonable—the irony

---

[2] See for example Keller (1986), the title of which is a reference to a line in a poem by Adrienne Rich. The poem is 'Integrity', and the line: 'Anger and tenderness: the spider's genius/to spin and

does not amuse me. A Buddhist might say I'm letting it get to me and I just need to renounce my attachment to the things of this world. I don't mean to pick on Buddhists, it's just, well, true. True in the same way that a particular sort of Christian might tell me to shut up and suffer in silence, because it's good for me. To the latter I would reply that I have yet to be convinced that suffering is in any way redemptive,[3] and to the former I might explain that I seem temperamentally inclined to love this world, and certain beings in it, very much indeed. The thought of renouncing my attachment to the things and critters of the world in order to reduce any associated suffering such attachment might bring, this seems to me, naively, like cutting off my nose to spite my face. There go all the joys and pleasures, too. So, no. I will not step away from the logic of suffering and say it doesn't matter, not when this logic is like the salt in suffering's wound.

What is less clear to me is what I can do. So I have untangled a few threads, exposed a pervasively feminizing (il)logic which seems to surround and suffuse suffering as such with the western cultural imaginary. So what? Or rather, so what now? A different grammar seems called for, a change of syntax. A language translated perhaps, laboriously, from uncontrolled shudder, to stutter, into slow-moving syllables. Soothing, calming, strong. Patient and implacable, light and weighty, all at once. It will need to be a language through which the inexorable force of reality may travel, a language stripped of all trivia. Thundering is out, and so is shrieking. It will be a language of the middle, but a middle occupied by many. Voiced by many, there is a chance it could become public, swell in time from a murmur into grounded and grounding reminder. All of us will suffer, and so be it.

Realistically, such a language does not have a hope in hell of coming into being. For this reason I am not entirely pessimistic. We live on earth, not in hell, and on earth the damnedest things happen with astonishing regularity. Nonetheless there is that pesky, thousands-of-years-long association between suffering and the feminine. There is also the fact that suffering does expose people's fragility and weakness. I'd like to think that on this point philosophers could make a contribution, an intervention which might also go some way toward dislodging that stubborn connection between suffering and the feminine. I'm thinking of ontology, or, for those who suffer from metaphysical allergies, of philosophical anthropology. To put it simply, it is in the nature of human beings to be fragile, weak, and, as individuals, ineffectual. It is in our nature to flail about, to be stunned into silence and, quite often, passively to bear whatever happens to be happening around us or to us. That ontological sub-set of humanity to which I alluded earlier—it is the whole shebang. If professional philosophers were to develop this message of ontological fragility or anthropological nakedness, then I think that within two or three hundred years, a blink of an eye, really, we will have made strong inroads against the insidiously feminizing logic of suffering. It might instead begin to be seen as a humanizing

weave in the same action/from her own body, anywhere–/even from a broken web', Rich (1981, p. 9).

[3] Christian feminist analyses and critiques of the theological glorification of suffering include Brown and Parker (1989) and Tatman (1996, pp. 220–221).

logic. If this be deemed neo-enlightenment thinking, so be it. I continue to be in favour of humanizing *Homo sapiens*. I think it is not until we are fully human that we realize 'the other thing' is always already our thing, too.

Bibliography

Brown, Joanne Carlson, and Rebecca, Parker. 1989. For God so loved the world? In *Christianity patriarchy, and abuse: A feminist critique,* ed. Joanne Carlson Brown and Carole R. Bohn. New York: The Pilgrim Press.

Cox, Peta. 2010. Passing as sane: Or how to get someone to sit next to you on the bus. Conference paper delivered at the Society for Disability Studies Annual Conference, Philadelphia, Pennsylvania, USA, June, 2010.

Keller, Catherine. 1986. *From a broken web: Separation, sexism, and self.* Boston: Beacon Press.

Rich, Adrienne. 1981. *A wild patience has taken me this far: Poems 1978–1981*. New York: WW Norton & Co.

Scarry, Elaine. 1985. *The body in pain: The making and unmaking of the world.* New York: Oxford University Press.

Shaw, Brent D. 1996. Body/power/identity: Passions of the martyrs. *Journal of Early Christian Studies* 4 (3, Fall): 269–312.

Tatman, Lucy. 1996. Suffering. In *An A to Z of feminist theology*, ed. Lisa Isherwood and Dorothea McEwan. Sheffield: Sheffield Academic Press.

Walker, Alice. 1983. *In search of our mothers' gardens*. San Diego: Harcourt Brace Jovanovich.

Chapter 6
'Giving the World a More Human Face'—Human Suffering in African Thought and Philosophy

Thaddeus Metz

> We believe that in the long run the special contribution to the world by Africa will be in this field of human relationship. The great powers of the world may have done wonders in giving the world an industrial and military look, but the great gift still has to come from Africa—giving the world a more human face
>
> *Steve Biko, I write what I like*

Introduction: A History of Suffering—First from Without, Then from Within

I am a healthy, middle-class, white, American male in his early 40s who earned his PhD from an Ivy League university and who has received a substantial amount of financial and other support for his education and career. Although my scholarly training was terrific by Western standards, it was parochial, having taught me virtually nothing of African worldviews and practices, where by 'African' I mean features salient among[1] the black peoples below the Sahara desert. My first visit to the African continent was to South Africa, by far the most wealthy country in the sub-Saharan region, but where half the population nonetheless lives on less than a dollar or so a day. I have lived in South Africa now for nearly a decade, have visited a few other countries on the African continent, and have devoted much of my recent research to critically exploring sub-Saharan moral and political philosophy.

[1] In speaking of 'salient' features, I mean those that are prominent in the sub-Saharan region in ways they tend not to be elsewhere on the globe. Hence, I am asserting neither that these features pertain to all sub-Saharan societies, nor that they are exclusive to them. Talk of things 'African' suggests to some people something that is unique to, and universal among, sub-Saharan peoples; but that simply is not how I employ the word here.

T. Metz (✉)
Department of Philosophy, University of Johannesburg, Johannesburg, South Africa
e-mail: tmetz@uj.ac.za

J. Malpas, N. Lickiss (eds.), *Perspectives on Human Suffering*,
DOI 10.1007/978-94-007-2795-3_6, © Springer Science+Business Media B.V. 2012

Although I believe I am qualified to speak about sub-Saharan, and particularly southern African, cultures to a global audience,[2] I realize that it might be a source of suffering to see me doing so here. Some Africans might be worried that I will misrepresent them, as European colonialists have so often done. Others might be pained, in fact, by an accurate representation of various sub-Saharan themes, disappointed that it is yet again a foreign white man doing the work, and miffed that an African was not invited to contribute. And still others might be offended that I do not always aim merely to *represent* African thought, but often draw on it selectively to reconstruct philosophical positions that I judge to be both particularly plausible and likely to be of interest to a global audience. Although not the most *deep* source of suffering that sub-Saharans have experienced in the past 100 years, these kinds of anxieties are probably the most *widespread* at the moment, affecting even those who are materially well off.

The need shared by many sub-Saharans to have something in which to take pride or to alleviate a sense of inferiority, trenchantly analyzed by Fanon (1967), is in large part the product of centuries of social, political and economic injustice. Psychological trauma is the natural consequence of wrongs that white people have systematically done to blacks below the Sahara, including: the kidnapping and enslavement of millions by Americans; the invasion of nearly all African territory by European colonialists who stole land, erected states and then ran them dictatorially; ethnic conflict heightened as a result of colonial powers using the tactic of 'divide and conquer'; the enforcement of apartheid by descendants of Dutch settlers; the neglect and often denigration of indigenous languages and cultures by Christian religious groups and Eurocentric educational institutions; the exploitation of natural resources and cheap labour by non-African governments and multinational companies; abuse by foreign firms using dodgy sales techniques, e.g., the Swiss firm Nestlé notoriously having marketed, in medical settings, baby formula to mothers who lacked access to clean water and the education to make it properly, resulting in widespread deaths of infants; the subjection of African participants to unethical procedures in clinical trials run by Big Pharma; the willingness of banks in the North to accept funds corruptly looted by post-independence African leaders; protectionist trade subsidies given to farmers by their American and European governments, making it difficult for sub-Saharan farmers to compete on the world market; and, most recently, being subjected to the worst effects of global warming, while being the least responsible for it. Such imperialism, exploitation and other injustice has, in turn, resulted in still more suffering, these days occasioned by more 'internal' factors, such as: the experience of widespread absolute poverty, with literally hundreds of millions living on no more than a US dollar a day; the shame that accompanies poverty in the face of white wealth; wars over natural resources perceived to be a ticket out of poverty, e.g., more than three million people killed in the Congo in the past decade, where systematic rape and mutilation were also used as a weapon;

[2] Having published widely on sub-Saharan ethics in international journals, having given dozens of talks on the topic to African audiences, and consequently having been appointed to an *ubuntu* advisory panel to South Africa's National Heritage Council.

genocide resulting from ethnic tensions, e.g., close to a million killed in Rwanda in about 30 days (where Belgian colonialism was part of the causal chain leading up to the slaughter); weak civil and political institutions and norms that enabled dictators and corrupt politicians to flourish after independence from colonial powers; poorly developed medical facilities and an ideological suspicion of Western medicine, resulting in the failure to prevent the spread of HIV/AIDS, which, for just one example, causes the death of close to 1,000 South Africans a day (Achmat 2006); the inability to fight tuberculosis, diarrhoea and malaria, which together are known to kill millions annually; a shockingly low incidence of per capita medical professionals; the widespread lack of infrastructure such as reliable electricity, clean water and easy access to books and journals, let alone the internet (estimates of paved roads in the Congo range from as little as 300 km to at most 2,500 km, for an area the size of Western Europe); patently base education, particularly in mathematics, statistics, logic, natural science, engineering and other abstract fields, including at the tertiary level; a lack of skilled professionals able to start small businesses or to run large governments efficiently; and the inability to make scientific discoveries or technological innovations of relevance to Africans, let alone to the globe.

All these sources of suffering have left many sub-Saharans feeling a desire to build something for their peoples, to contribute something to the world, to accomplish something worthy of great esteem, or, heck, just to have an African country do well at the Soccer World Cup.

To be sure, Africa cannot blame all its problems on the West, with age-old sexism and homophobia and present-day corruption being three faults that rest mostly on its shoulders, and which are, or should be, sources of shame. However, it is worth responding to an argument, sometimes voiced by whites I have encountered in Africa, that sub-Sahara, left to its own devices, would not have developed socially and economically as much as it has. Without the influence of colonialism, Africans would be suffering even more than they are, so the argument goes. Some suggest that people in Africa would not have become 'civilized' on their own because the geography of the continent hindered the development of agriculture and hence a specialized division of labour, or because indigenous cultural norms are inconsistent with a rationalized administration and economy, or because of racial, indeed racist, claims about the intelligence and industriousness of black people. However, such an empirical claim is simply irrelevant; even if it were true,[3] consider how much more prosperity and how much less conflict there would have been had Euro-Americans not violated their duties *not to harm*, and, furthermore, had they fulfilled their duties *to help*, say, by doing what was within their power to bring out what is best in others and to foster self-sufficiency on their part. That is the relevant benchmark by which to evaluate Africa's current standing, or so a characteristically African ethical perspective would entail, as I explain below.

The rest of this essay is less personal and more technical, its aims being to describe several sub-Saharan viewpoints on human suffering, to refine them as needed

[3] And of course many development theorists would argue that it is not, that under-development is a direct effect of Western imperialism. For a classic text, see Rodney (1972).

to make them philosophically attractive, at least to a global audience, and to argue that international theorists should take them seriously as plausible alternatives to influential Western accounts. I first focus on ways to describe suffering that are grounded in sub-Saharan worldviews, specifically, ideas that purport to account for its nature, causes and cures. Of particular interest is an under-appreciated account of the nature of human suffering that I submit is a genuine rival to a neurophysical view readily proffered by friends of Western science. Next, I take up and reconstruct normative judgements that are influential among Africans. I point out that, upon philosophical interpretation, they entail an ethical analysis of human suffering that is not only distinct from those entailed by standard Western moral philosophies, but also no less, and probably more, attractive than they. I conclude by suggesting that the reader has been given some reason for taking seriously the prophesy about what Africa will give the world made by Steve Biko, the influential Black Consciousness theorist murdered by the South African apartheid government.

Sub-Saharan Understandings of Suffering

Most traditional African societies have interpreted the world using what many Westerners would deem to be 'thickly metaphysical' categories.[4] For instance, a large majority of them believe in the continued existence of ancestors, people who were not merely forebears of a given people, but ones who both lived to a ripe old age and exhibited moral wisdom, i.e., were 'elders'. It is widely thought that elders whose bodies have died continue to live on and routinely interact with us, e.g., to the point of drinking beer at ceremonies, inhabiting certain animals or parts of land, and even becoming reborn in a baby. Hence, ancestors are often called the 'living-dead'.

To survive the death of one's body, or rather to be able to survive without a physical bearer, suggests the reality of something that Westerners would call 'spiritual'. It is not unusual for indigenous African cultures to posit the existence of something similar to what Westerners label a 'soul', a spiritual part of human nature created by God that is the essence of who we are. In addition to a spiritual part of our identity, many believe in immaterial forces that substantially affect the course of our lives. This includes the influence of the living-dead, who are deemed capable of determining such things as the weather and a person's state of health (typically via some human intermediary). It also includes the existence of extra-sensory powers such as witchcraft, the 'evil-eye' of jealous individuals and curses from bitter, spiteful people. And, for some (particularly southern and central) African peoples,[5] it further includes the existence of something often called 'life-force' ('*seriti*' in Sotho), an invisible energy that has its source in God and that permeates everything in the world,

[4] For overviews of metaphysical beliefs that are common below the Sahara, see Teffo and Roux (2003); Mkhize (2008).

[5] I again emphasize *not all* Africans; for one who denies that the notion of life-force is salient in his culture, see Kaphagawani (1998).

with rocks having a low degree of this power and human beings having the most of any creature in the physical universe. Hence, for the dominant strands of African thinking, the spiritual realm is not purely transcendent, but is rather immanent in a variety of ways in the material world.

This superficial background to salient African belief systems should be enough to help the reader grasp some common understandings of what suffering is, where it comes from and how to alleviate it. First, in terms of what constitutes suffering, it would cohere with the above to conceive of it as essentially being a loss of life-force.[6] On this view, to suffer consists of exhibiting less of the spiritual vital-energy that a human being is capable of exhibiting or that one would normally exhibit as such. Even if not all lack of life-force is suffering, given the metaphysical world-view prominent among a number of African peoples, it is fair to suggest that all suffering is a lack of life-force.

Such a supernatural interpretation of the nature of suffering would be familiar to many sub-Saharans, but it is worth thinking about whether this general perspective admits of a secular variant that could be found prima facie attractive by a wider populace. Consider, along this line, that when African theologians, cultural analysts and moral theorists describe a person as exhibiting a substantial degree of life-force, they often use what appear to be non-spiritual concepts, or at least physicalist words, such as: health, strength, growth, reproduction, generation, vibrancy, activity, self-motion, courage and confidence; and, correspondingly, they typically characterize a lack of life-force in terms of: disease, weakness, decay, barrenness, destruction, lethargy, passivity, submission, fear, insecurity and depression (Dzobo 1992; Kasenene 1994; Magesa 1997; Iroegbu 2005a, b, d; Mkhize 2008). Hence, one attractive conception of human suffering with an African pedigree is the idea that it is nothing but a *lack of liveliness* (relative to some conception of normality), a view that could admit of either a spiritual or purely physical understanding.

Such an *enervation theory* of the nature of human suffering should be compared with other accounts, say, a neurophysical view that it is nothing more than intense pain, a particular firing of A-delta and C fibers in the nerves. I lack the space to systematically evaluate the enervation theory against this and other competitors. Here I merely note a few argumentative strategies that should be pursued elsewhere. For one, I note that, on the face of it, one advantage of the enervation account is that it can naturally account for psychological suffering, which appears continuous with bodily suffering but not captured well by the neurophysical view. For another, though, one disadvantage of the enervation account is that it conceives of suffering as less of a positive, a state approaching zero on a uni-polar scale of well-being; one might reasonably object that suffering has an independently negative dimension, a state less than zero on a bi-polar scale of well-being and woe (with an intermediate, zero state that is neither of these). In other words, presumably a person being tortured and a person in a coma both substantially lack life-force, but only the former appears to be suffering.

---

[6] Or, in some cases, the misdirection of it, on which see Setiloane (1976, pp. 42–43).

I turn now to characteristic sub-Saharan views about where suffering comes from and how to avoid it. John Mbiti, a Kenyan theologian who was one of the first Africans to write sympathetically and systematically about the oral cultures of black Africa, says of human suffering that it is 'generally believed to be caused by the ill-will or ill-action of one person against another, normally through the agency of witchcraft and magic' (Mbiti 1990, p. 165; Setiloane 1976, pp. 44–45; Makinde 1988, p. 90; Magesa 1997, pp. 179–189; Manda 2008, pp. 125–139). For many traditional sub-Saharans, the natural world is, in Weberian terms, 'enchanted', a place where invisible agents can be responsible for, and immaterial forces can be tools for the occasion of, negative occurrences in life. So, for example, it is not infrequent for indigenous Africans to believe that one's suffering is a result of ancestors or other spirits being angry with one for having violated moral norms, or that it is a result of a wicked villager using sorcery against one. In a passage widely cited among African scholars, Mbiti remarks,

> Even if it is explained to a patient that he has malaria because a mosquito carrying malaria parasites has stung him he will still want to know why that mosquito stung him and not another person. The only answer which people find satisfactory to that question is that someone has 'caused' (or 'sent') the mosquito to sting a particular individual, by means of magical manipulation. Suffering, misfortune, disease and accident, all are 'caused' mystically, as far as African peoples are concerned. (Mbiti 1990, p. 165)

In short, it is common (not quite 'universal', as Mbiti's remarks suggest) to think of harm as produced by spiritual forces and ultimately caused by failures in relationship with another agent; either one has done wrong and is being punished for one's guilt by another's making one suffer, or another is doing one wrong in making one's innocent self suffer.

As far as the cure for illness and injury is concerned, many Africans visit shamans, with the World Health Organization estimating that up to 80% of a given population in Africa does so (World Health Organization 2002, p. 1). As Munyaradzi Felix Murove, editor of the first real anthology devoted to sub-Saharan ethics, sums up the nature of shamanic practice: 'African traditional doctors see human suffering as intrinsically linked to moral behaviour' (Murove 2009, p. 169); after all, if immorality is the cause of suffering, then it makes sense for the cure to involve some kind of response to immorality, often captured by the idea of repairing broken relationships through an intermediary trained in spiritual matters. For instance, if it was one's own wrongdoing that led to one's punitive suffering, then one is required to express contrition and seek forgiveness, say, by making a sacrifice to ancestors. And if it was another's wrongdoing that led to one's suffering, then one is permitted to act in self-defence by seeking protection from evil forces. Traditional healers are those deemed to be trained in facilitating these kinds of remedies. They use divination (e.g., the throwing of bones) to ascertain how and why a person is suffering, provide guidance about how to repair relationships with others and the ancestral world, and share charms and other magical properties to ward off harm from witchcraft or curses.

It might well be difficult for non-Africans, or at least Westerners, to find anything of use in this understanding of how suffering originates and of how it can be fought. However, it might help, here, to draw a distinction between a *relational* approach to medicine or the treatment of suffering, on the one hand, and a *spiritual* one, on the other. These are two logically distinct facets of a characteristically sub-Saharan interpretation of human suffering, and, even if many Africans would be disinclined to separate them, one could sensibly appeal to the former without the latter. Western medicine is becoming less strictly reductionist and mechanistic these days, acknowledging that certain mental attitudes and social conditions such as stress and isolation (or, conversely, equanimity and friendship) can substantially affect physical states of the body. So, Western medicine is recognizing a kernel of truth in the characteristically 'African' approach, acknowledging the relational or 'holistic' causes and cures of illness and even of proneness to accidents.

However, Western medicine will, and in all likelihood should, draw the line at appealing to any notion of a spiritual realm, which has not been verified and is, at this point, a matter of mere faith. Friends of African medicine often cite anecdotal evidence suggesting that cures have been effected by traditional healers (Setiloane 1976, pp. 60–63; Makinde 1988, p. 91; Manda 2008, pp. 125–126, 135–137), and they also point out that often a shaman accepts payment from patients only if they are satisfied with his work and deem themselves to have been cured (Setiloane 1976, pp. 59–60; Leonard 2009, pp. 178–187). This is very poor evidence for the thesis that anything ancestral or more broadly spiritual is doing the work of alleviating suffering. What it does support is the sensible call for scientific investigation into long-standing traditional healing methods, particularly those that involve the use of herbs. Until such studies have been conducted, though, it would be unreasonable—even potentially a matter of culpable homicide–for friends of African medicine to encourage people to take, say, an expensive potion for HIV/AIDS that a truck driver believes an ancestor communicated to him in a dream, as high-ranking health officials in South Africa did not long ago (Cullinan 2006).

Sub-Saharan Ethical Approaches Toward Suffering

The previous section addressed suffering descriptively, analyzing African-based understandings of what suffering is, how it is caused and how it may be alleviated. This section, in contrast, considers African-inspired accounts of how to approach suffering normatively. Sub-Saharan morality differs in many notable ways from typical contemporary Western views, and my aims in this section are to draw on some major strands of the former, to refine and unite them in the form of a philosophical principle, and then to apply this principle to the question of how to respond ethically to human suffering. I maintain that an African ethical philosophy that places basic value in communal relationships entails a very attractive, but under-appreciated, account of the way agents ought to deal with suffering. I also show how its prescriptions with regard to suffering stand in marked contrast to those of both Kantianism and utilitarianism, the two dominant moral theories in Euro-American philosophy.

Many sub-Saharan societies sum up morality with a phrase that is often (overly literally) translated into English as, 'A person is a person through other persons' or 'I am because we are'. To the unacquainted, such a maxim appears to say very little, and nothing at all normative, appearing at most to express the banality that people can exist only because they were looked after when they were young and helpless. While it is true that the maxim connotes the empirical (or, for many Africans, metaphysical) idea that we necessarily depend on one another for our lives, it also expresses a normative claim. Personhood or selfhood, in much African thinking about morality, is 'value-laden', meaning that it is a desirable state of affairs that not every human being attains.[7] One's ultimate goal should be to become a *real* person or a *true* self, or to obtain '*ubuntu*', the word for humanness widely used in southern Africa by Nguni speakers such as Zulus (Ramose 1999, pp. 49–53). How does one become a *mensch*? For a substantial part of African moral thought, it consists of exhibiting some kind of supportive engagement with community.

There are naturally differing conceptions of what community is and how it should be responded to, and I have sought in recent work to theoretically interpret what I contend are the most interesting and defensible ideas (Metz 2007, pp. 321–341; 2010, pp. 49–58). Specifically, I have argued that the best moral theory with an African pedigree prescribes honouring communal relationship, understood to be the combination of sharing a way of life, on the one hand, and caring for others' quality of life, on the other. To share a way of life is for people to identify with one another, centrally, for them to think of themselves as joint members of a group (as a 'we') and to participate in common projects. The opposite of sharing a way of life is division, thinking of oneself in opposition to others and seeking to undermine their goals and customs. To care for others' quality of life is for people to exhibit solidarity with each other, by helping one another and doing so out of sympathy with, and for the sake of, one another. The opposite of caring for others' quality of life is ill-will, trying to harm people and exhibiting *Schadenfreude*.

To honour, or prize, communal relationship does not mean promoting it as much as possible in the world. Of course, if communal relationship, *qua* the combination of identity and solidarity, has a basic moral worth, then it is something for a moral agent to foster, but she must do so in a respectful way or with integrity. That is going to involve, for two rough examples, refraining from sacrificing existing communal relationships of which the agent is a part for the sake of promoting others' relationships, as well as refraining from promoting community by using an anti-social means, viz., *via* division and ill-will.

In sum, then, according to this philosophical interpretation of sub-Saharan morality, one's basic aim should be to develop one's personhood, which one can do only by prizing communal relationships in which people share a way of life and care for one another's quality of life. Or as the Nigerian philosopher Pantaleon Iroegbu tersely puts it, '[T]he purpose of our life is community-service and community-belongingness' (Iroegbu 2005c, p. 442). Now, such sharing of life and caring for it, or belonging and service, is normally what people mean by 'friendship' or a broad

[7] For one clear analysis, see Menkiti (2004, pp. 324-331).

sense of 'love'. To love is just for people both to identify with each other (think of themselves as a 'we' and engage in common activities) and to exhibit solidarity with each other (be sympathetic and help the other for her sake). So, one way to understand a major element of African normative worldviews is to deem friendship or love to be the ground of morality, where wrong actions are roughly to be identified as those that are *unfriendly*.

This sketch of an African-inspired ethical philosophy should be enough to see how it entails dealing with human suffering in ways that differ from, and will for many readers be more attractive than, the most influential Western moral theories. Consider the principle of respect for autonomy first. According to this moral theory, articulated with care by Kant (1785), individuals have a dignity in virtue of their capacity for rational self-governance. We are the most important beings in the world, worth more than the mineral, animal and vegetable kingdoms, because we have a unique ability to deliberate or to make free decisions. For Kant and many Kantians, treating our capacity for voluntary decision-making with respect means acting in accordance with the way we have elected to exercise it. And that principle, in turn, is often interpreted to support a retributive approach to punishment, the view that it is right to punish just insofar as someone deserves it for having done wrong. Retributivism is the view that it is just to make another suffer in proportion to, and simply because of, his guilt, regardless of whether doing so promises to improve anyone's quality of life in the long run.

Retributivism is largely alien to an African ethic. Of course, sometimes African people will react to crime retributively, and some cultures believe that certain spirits are entitled to perform the function of imposing retributive penalties. However, the dominant themes in sub-Saharan discussions of how humans should respond to wrongdoing concern reconciliation (and, to a lesser extent, protection). That is, it can be appropriate to make an offender suffer, but usually on the condition that doing so is expected to rehabilitate him and to make others ready to accept him back into the fold. Where punishment is not necessary to foster communal relationships, or especially where it is likely to hinder them, then that is strong reason not to punish. Such a conception of criminal justice was widespread in small-scale, traditional societies, but many believe that it is apt for urban and modern environments, too. For just one example, an African-based injunction to respond to wrongdoing in a way likely to foster harmony was largely responsible for the establishment of South Africa's influential Truth and Reconciliation Commission, which granted amnesty for political crimes committed during the apartheid era in exchange for offenders' full disclosure of them (Tutu 1999; Louw 2006, pp. 161–172; Krog 2008, pp. 353–366).

The injunction to prize community or friendliness, which includes actual and potential relationships of solidarity, does more than merely rule out making another person suffer merely because he deserves it; it also entails that, generally speaking, people ought to try to reduce suffering they encounter, even if they are not responsible for having caused it. To esteem relationships in which people help one another and do so for each other's sake obviously means, in large part, avoiding making others suffer and trying to relieve their suffering. Hence, characteristic African morality includes substantial 'positive' duties to help others, even when one has not voluntarily assumed any obligation to do so by, say, having made a promise (Appiah 1998).

That said, it is *not* a salient part of African ethics to instruct a moral agent to minimize the amount of suffering in the world. The other major Western moral theory, a utilitarian approach, requires minimizing suffering and maximizing its opposite. From this perspective, a moral agent ought to act according to what an impartial cost-benefit analysis would dictate, performing whichever action would cause the least amount of unhappiness and the most amount of happiness, taking the interests of everyone into account. There are four respects in which typical sub-Saharan views about morality would probably forbid behaviour that is expected to reduce the amount of suffering in the world as much as possible.

First, and most interestingly, an Afro-communitarian morality often prescribes increasing the amount of suffering in the world for no long-term benefit, albeit not for retributive reasons. Part of exhibiting solidarity with another is being sympathetic toward her quality of life. That means feeling good when she flourishes, but also feeling bad when she founders. If, to realize their humanness, individuals ought to be persons who experience psychological pain upon awareness of the suffering of another, then morality does not require minimizing pain and other negative mental states. To be loving people sometimes means feeling more suffering, in themselves, than likely would have been felt in the absence of love; when one suffers, then so does the group—ideally!

A second respect in which the present African morality would not prescribe minimizing suffering is a product of the requirement to share a way of life. Suppose that suffering could be distributed so that either 18 units of it would be placed on a single person or 1 unit would be placed on each of 20 people, where the people are otherwise similar. Utilitarianism would require the former distribution, because there is less suffering overall (18 units instead of 20). However, so far as I am familiar with African ethics, it would clearly require the latter distribution, at least for the reason that people would be much more likely to experience a sense of togetherness thereby.

Thirdly, most interpretations of African morality assert that it can be justifiable to impose suffering in self- or other-defence, with some even summarizing the basis of sub-Saharan jurisprudence in these terms (Ramose 1999, p. 120). But distributing violence or other harm so as to redirect it away from the innocents, those who have been friendly, and toward the aggressors, those who have not, is often inconsistent with minimizing the overall amount of suffering. Suppose that four men are trying to kill an innocent woman merely because of her ethnicity, and imagine that an armed peacekeeper witnesses the attack. Imagine that they do not heed any pleas to stop attacking her, characterized as someone's daughter or mother, and that they also ignore a warning shot or two. If the only effective way to save the woman's life would be to shoot the four and hence make them suffer, the peacekeeper would be justified in doing so. But, then, four people would be suffering instead of one, as would happen if the peacekeeper stood by and did nothing.

Fourth, and finally, the respect-based nature of much of African ethics, or at least the philosophical rendition proposed here, often forbids performing actions that are likely to minimize suffering in the long run. To use some cases familiar to a philosophical audience, imagine that in order to get two suffering people to the hospital you must run over one healthy and innocent person. Or suppose that in order to save the lives of two people who need organ donations, you must kill one healthy and innocent person so as to harvest his kidneys and heart. Almost no one believes that it would be permissible to minimize human suffering by performing these actions. And an African morality would forbid them as failing to honour the value of communal relationship insofar as they, roughly, seek to promote friendliness with a very unfriendly means.

To sum up, from the perspective that one must obtain humanness or realize one's true self by respecting communal or friendly relationships, understood as the combination of identity and solidarity, the right approach to human suffering is neither that it should be minimized without regard to fault, as per the utilitarian, nor that it should be distributed in accordance with guilt, as per the typical Kantian. Instead, it recommends dealing with suffering in a loving way, very roughly, by being willing to take it upon oneself under certain conditions, by generally seeking to reduce suffering, and by usually not imposing suffering on others, unless doing so is necessary to direct it away from those who have been loving and toward those who have been unloving. Such an approach to suffering is under-theorized by contemporary philosophers, but is surely worth taking seriously in light of the many respects in which it accords well with moral common-sense.

Conclusion

In this chapter, I have sought to present a number of ideas about human suffering that are salient in sub-Saharan Africa, to reconstruct them in order to make them of interest particularly to an international audience, and to urge that audience to give them serious consideration as alternatives or correctives to some dominant Western approaches.

Two of the central explanatory and normative categories in African philosophy are vitality and community. I contended that the former is promising as a way to theorize the nature of human suffering, namely, as the loss of liveliness. And I argued, with regard to the latter, that deeming communal relationship to be the fundamental bearer of moral value shows great potential for understanding how we ethically ought to respond to human suffering. Biko predicted that what Africa would give to the world would be 'in this field of human relationship', a matter of 'giving the world a more human face'. As I have worked to explain, becoming more human is the fundamental theme of some major facets of sub-Saharan thought about ethics. More specifically, an attractive Afro-communitarian moral theory is the principle that everyone is required to develop her humanness by prizing communal relationships, ones in which people identify with each other and exhibit solidarity with one another. Such an approach instructs moral agents neither to make others suffer merely because they deserve it, on the one hand, nor to do whatever it takes to minimize suffering, on the other. Instead, it recommends responding to suffering out of love, which sometimes requires increasing the amount of suffering in the world, say, by taking it upon oneself (out of sympathy) instead of leaving it to others to bear on their own.

I do not know whether Biko's prophesy will come true, so that the world in fact receives from Africa the gift of a more human face. However, I strongly suspect that an ethic of becoming more human through community with others is indeed something that Africa is well positioned at least to offer the world, and I am certain that it is something in which Africans should take great pride.[8]

Bibliography

Achmat, Zackie. 2006. The tradition of Steve Bantu Biko and Rick Turner: The tradition of student mobilisation in the crisis of government and HIV/AIDS. http://www.tac.org.za/community/node/2187. Accessed Jan 2012.

Appiah, Anthony. 1998. Ethical systems, African. In *Routledge encyclopaedia of philosophy*, ed. Edward Craig. London: Routledge.

Cullinan, Kerry. 2006. Health officials promote untested uBhejane. *Health-E News*. http://www.health-e.org.za/news/article.php?uid=20031380. Accessed Jan 2012.

Dzobo, N. K. 1992. Values in a changing society: Man, ancestors, and god. In *Person and community; Ghanaian philosophical studies 1*, eds. Kwasi Wiredu and Kwame Gyekye. Washington D.C.: Council for Research in Values and Philosophy.

Fanon, Franz. 1967. *Black skin, white masks*. New York: Grove Press.

Iroegbu, Pantaleon. 2005a. Do all persons have a right to life? In *Kpim of morality ethics*, eds. Pantaleon Iroegbu and Anthony Echekwube. Ibadan: Heinemann.

Iroegbu, Pantaleon. 2005b. What is life: Body, mind and soul? In *Kpim of morality ethics*, eds. Pantaleon Iroegbu and Anthony Echekwube. Ibadan: Heinemann.

Iroegbu, Pantaleon. 2005c. Beginning, purpose and end of life. In *Kpim of morality ethics*, eds. Pantaleon Iroegbu and Anthony Echekwube. Ibadan: Heinemann.

Iroegbu, Pantaleon. 2005d. Right to life and the means to life: Human dignity. In *Kpim of morality ethics*, eds. Pantaleon Iroegbu and Anthony Echekwube. Ibadan: Heinemann.

Kant, Immanuel. 1785. *Groundwork of the Metaphysics of Morals*. Trans. A. Wood. New Haven: Yale University Press, 2002.

Kaphagawani, Didier N. 1998. African conceptions of personhood and intellectual identities. In *Philosophy from Africa*, ed. Coetzee and Roux. Cape Town: Oxford University Press.

Kasenene, Peter. 1994. Ethics in African theology. In *Doing ethics in context: South African perspectives*, eds. C. Villa-Vicencio and John de Gruchy. Cape Town: David Philip.

Krog, Antjie. 2008. 'This thing called reconciliation ...'. Forgiveness as part of an interconnectedness-towards-wholeness. *South African Journal of Philosophy* 27:353–366.

Leonard, Kenneth. 2009. African traditional healers: Are they as good at economics as they are at medicine? In *African ethics: An anthology of comparative and applied ethics*, ed. Munyaradzi Felix Murove. Pietermaritzburg: University of KwaZulu-Natal Press.

[8] For thoughtful written comments on an earlier draft, I express my gratitude to Mbongisi Dyantyi, Bernard Matolino and Pedro Tabensky. I am also thankful that Nicole Caunter and Motsamai Molefe took the time to read a draft and to express their support.

Louw, Dirk. 2006. The African concept of ubuntu and restorative justice. In *Handbook of restorative justice: A global perspective*, eds. Dennis Sullivan and Larry Tifft. New York: Routledge.
Magesa, Laurenti. 1997. *African religion: The moral traditions of abundant life*. Maryknoll: Orbis Books.
Makinde, M. Akin. 1988. *African philosophy, culture, and traditional medicine*. Athens: Ohio University Center for International Studies.
Manda, Lucinda Domoka. 2008. Africa's healing wisdom: Spiritual and ethical values of traditional African healthcare practices. In *Persons in community: African ethics in a global culture*, ed. Ronald Nicolson. Scottsville: University of KwaZulu-Natal Press.
Mbiti, John. 1990. *African religions and philosophy*. 2nd ed. Oxford: Heinemann.
Menkiti, Ifeanyi. 2004. On the normative conception of a person. In *A companion to African philosophy*, ed. Kwasi Wiredu. Malden: Blackwell.
Metz, Thaddeus. 2007. Toward an African moral theory. *The Journal of Political Philosophy* 15:321–341.
Metz, Thaddeus. 2010. African and Western moral theories in a bioethical context. *Developing World Bioethics* 10:49–58.
Mkhize, Nhlanhla. 2008. Ubuntu and harmony: An African approach to morality and ethics. In *Persons in community: African ethics in a global culture*, ed. Ronald Nicolson. Pietermaritzburg: University of KwaZulu-Natal Press.
Murove, Munyaradzi Felix. 2009. African bioethics: An exploratory discourse. In *African ethics: An anthology of comparative and applied ethics*, ed. Munyaradzi Felix Murove. Pietermaritzburg: University of KwaZulu-Natal Press.
Ramose, Mogobe. 1999. *African philosophy through ubuntu*. Harare: Mond Books.
Rodney, Walter. 1972. *How Europe underdeveloped Africa*. Dar es Salaam: Tanzania Publishing House.
Setiloane, Gabriel. 1976. *The image of God among the Sotho-Tswana*. Rotterdam: Balkema.
Teffo, Lesiba J., and A. P. J. Roux. 2003. Themes in African metaphysics. In *The African philosophy reader*. 2nd ed., eds. P. H. Coetzee and A. P. J. Roux. New York: Routledge.
Tutu, Desmond. 1999. *No future without forgiveness*. New York: Random House.
World Health Organization. 2002. *WHO traditional medicine strategy 2002–2005*. Geneva: World Health Organization. http://whqlibdoc.who.int/hq/2002/who_edm_trm_2002.1.pdf. Accessed Jan 2012.

Chapter 7
Suffering as Substantive and Subjective: Slavoj Žižek, Hannah Arendt and the Body's Pain

Michael Mack

> *You're craving depths that don't exist. This guy is the embodiment of nothing.*
>
> *Philip Roth, American Pastoral*

Parallax, Fetishism and the Disavowal of Suffering—Can We Do Justice to Suffering Without a Notion of Substance?

This chapter discusses the conception of substance as a ground on which we can do justice to the phenomenology of suffering. It analyzes how literature mediates between substance and subjectivity. A denial of substance comes close to a denial of truth. As Jeff Malpas has shown truth is a basis for a democratic form of government that attempts to alleviate or extenuate suffering (Malpas 2010). We live, however, in a world that does not acknowledge its constitution. What is certain about its constitution is its uncertainty. We seem to be suspended between subjectivity and substance, between the New Age form of a spurious spirituality and a pressing sense of suffering that has to do with issues of substance—be they physical or mental. As the father figure of Hanif Kureishi's novel *The Buddha of Suburbia* has put it:

> We live in an age of doubt and uncertainty. The old religions under which people have lived for ninety-nine point nine percent of human history have decayed or are irrelevant. Our problem is secularism. We have replaced our spiritual values and wisdom with materialism. And now everyone is wandering around asking how to live. Sometimes desperate people even turn to me. (Kureishi 1990, p. 76)

Here the aging father of the young protagonist offers a self-deflating diagnosis of the contemporary split between the spiritual and the material, between the subjective and the substantive, between the age old traditions of the religious and the secular loss of tradition. The acknowledgement that 'desperate people even turn to me' underlines the extent of how despairing our situation has become: the only

M. Mack (✉)
Department of English Studies, University of Durham, Durham, UK
e-mail: michael.mack@durham.ac.uk

J. Malpas, N. Lickiss (eds.), *Perspectives on Human Suffering*,
DOI 10.1007/978-94-007-2795-3_7, © Springer Science+Business Media B.V. 2012

alleviation of suffering seems to reside in a-would be Buddha or would-be Messiah of suburbia. The antagonism between the subjective and the substantive is here enmeshed in intergenerational dissonance. As Sander L Gilman has pointed, for Kureishi 'the religious conflict is a conflict of generations' (Gilman 2006, p. 142). Could the opposition between generations reflect the mutual exclusion of substance and subjectivity which is the subject matter of what the would-be Buddha of suburbia bemoans? Is the fictitious world of New Age spirituality not the mirror image of materialist overload? Instead of confronting the issues that shape much of our societal suffering and unease, our society escapes into various substitutes of substance (be it New Age or other forms of spurious intellectual gratification).

Ours seems to be an age that avoid a confrontation—at least on a consciously reflective level—with changes that are in the making or have already come to shape the way we live. Žižek has called fetishism the psychological mechanism involved in such refusal to engage with reality. In his application of psychoanalysis to political and cultural criticism, Žižek argues that we succumb to fetishism, when we know the rather pathetic consequences of our actions and yet perform them nevertheless.

Fetishism is the persistence of forms of behaviour that have become deprived of their validity and yet are still in force. The question of validity is bound up with that of a certain positioning. This will become apparent in a more detailed discussion of fetishism's cultural itinerary. The term fetish 'derives from the Portuguese *feitiço* and was applied first by fifteenth-century Portuguese traders to describe the cult objects of West Africa used in witchcraft' (Steiner 1995, p. 81). Seen from the vantage point of its history, the usage of the word goes with a certain perspective and the perspective in question can shift: what from a Christian point of view may strike you as superstitious may appear to a non-Christian as superstitious or fetishist in Christian practice (the wearing of crosses as talisman and so forth).

The term 'parallax' describes this shiftiness in perspective which characterizes the perception of what constitutes fetishism. Žižek has enmeshed his critical theory into a certain mobility of perspective which the term parallax denotes: "'Parallax,' according to its common definition, is the apparent displacement of an object (the shift of its position against a background), caused by a change in observational position that provides a new line of sight" (Žižek 2010, p. 244). In a discussion of Salman Rushdie's postmodernism, Wendy Steiner has shown how 'parallax' is a constitutive feature of a liberal (and postmodernist) coexistence of diverse and often contradictory traditions: 'Instead of a definitive, secure world, we have the parallax shifting of perspective' (Steiner 1995, p. 202). Criticizing the 'fetishism' of contemporary society, Žižek has recently taken issue with our contemporary 'parallax', bearing 'witness to how, in postmodernism, the parallax is openly admitted, displayed—and, in this way, neutralized: the antagonist tension between different standpoints is flattened out into an indifferent plurality of standpoints'(Žižek 2010, p. 253). Here Žižek does not attempt to do away with a multiplicity of perspectives but he rather wants to alert us to the loss of such plurality if it derives from a perspective of indifference.

The gap between different points of view can only be sustained through an engaged observer. An indifferent (as opposed to engaged) perspective flattens out the difference of antagonism that nourishes the life of diversity. In his most recent work Žižek implicitly corrects some aspects of his appraisal of philosophical parallax which deflates any substantive account of our existence and instead enthrones the subjectivity of perspective as sole motor of our existence in the shadow of Descartes's *cogito*, maintaining that 'the status of the Real is purely parallactic and, as such, nonsubstantial: it has no substantial density in itself, it is just a gap between two points of perspective, perceptible only in the shift from the one to the other' (Žižek 2006, p. 26). According to Žižek, it is such radical parallactic account of our humanity that empties the world of substance, which accounts for the plurality of our postmodern universe.

Previously, Žižek has made a strong case for the paradoxically consubstantiality of substance's disappearance and the multiplicity of our radical subjectivism, writing that 'the parallax Real is, rather, that which accounts for the very *multiplicity* of appearances of the same underlying Real—it is not the hard core which persists as the Same, but the hard bone of contention which pulverizes the sameness into a multitude of appearances' (Žižek 2006, p. 26). The hard bone of contention goes back to Hegel's famous equation of the spirit with the bone. According to Žižek 'Hegel converts the Fichtean I=I into the absolute contradiction Spirit=Bone, i.e. into the *point of absolute nonmirroring*, the identity of the subject *qua* void with the element in which we cannot recognize his mirror image, with inert leftover, the bone, the rock, the hindrance which prevents the absolute self-transparency of the pure performative: the subject is posited as correlative to an object which precisely cannot be conceived as the subject's objectivation' (Žižek 2001, p. 102). The absence of mimesis here coincides with the absence of any substance that could me mirrored. A radical contingency marks Žižek's nonsubstantive subject. It is a contingency born out of the void, which can be filled by so many contingent inert leftovers, by what Hegel calls the bone.

In his most recent work Žižek alerts his readers to the danger that the coexistence of so many contingent and contradictory leftovers that fill our subjectivity (having been emptied out of substance) may give rise to indifference and cynicism. When this happens then there is not so much a plurality of contingent worlds but rather a flattening out of difference where nothing matters any longer.

We may, however, ask how something can matter if matter (substance) does not exist in the first place. As we have seen via a brief glance at the history of its usage, the term fetishism adumbrates parallax: one object appears to be a fetish from a certain perspective, but is a holy relic seen from the insider's point of view. When Žižek criticizes contemporary society in terms of fetishism he presupposes some notion of substance that is either disavowed or extolled into a quasi-sacred realm. He argues that we know what is wrong with us, but nevertheless cannot believe in what is right. In this way we cling to the status quo and thus perpetuate what is harmful.

Fetishism precludes change in the face of obvious recognition to the contrary:

> The most basic coordinates of our awareness will have to change, insofar as today, we live in a state of collective fetishistic disavowal: we know very well that this will happen at some point, but nevertheless cannot bring ourselves to believe that it will. (Žižek2010, pp. x–xi)

This gap between knowledge and believe, which characterizes Žižek's usage of the term fetish, presupposes, however, a notion of substance (a matter of knowledge or a matter of belief).

The moot point is that Žižek has disavowed the validity of any substantive form. Žižek's work certainly partakes of a Heideggerian mode of thought that turns around the abyss of absence and the impossibility of full presence. This mode of thought has determined much postmodernist theory in literature, philosophy, architecture and jurisprudence. The logic of postmodernism is 'in keeping with a Heideggerian or existential analysis of modernity in which the awareness of departed meaning is all we can aspire to' (Steiner 1995, p. 202). In literary studies, Žižek's approach may well come closest to Paul de Man's rigorous demystification of literature as the absence of referential meaning. From his early wartime writings in the 1940s to his tenure as Sterling Professor at Yale, de Man and his adoring followers have insisted on the self-foiling of any form of enjoyment or meaning that literature may appear to evoke in its audience. As Wendy Steiner has put it, 'throughout his career de Man reiterated his early idea that literature is independent of life'(Steiner 1995, p. 195). Literature achieves this autonomy or independence from life, by dint of its referential void; signifying nothing. While we may be grateful to de Man for his rigorous insistence on the differentiation between life and art, he nevertheless succumbed to a literalism of sorts when he confused the empirical with the artistic: 'Far from mistaking art for reality, as he criticized modernism for doing, he—sometimes—mistook reality for art'(Steiner 1995, p. 205). In de Man's case this confusion of reality with art results in emptying life of substance and thereby of suffering. Reality turned into de Man's deconstructionist art, is nothing else but the void of the signifier; signs rather than bodies.

The polymath Žižek may appear to be far removed from the 'expert' literary critic de Man and yet both share a post-Heideggerian and postmodernist hostility toward substance or matter. In de Man's case the subject's referent foils the fulfilment of a substantive reference. In similar way Žižek insists on the void that is the real of our existence as substanceless subjects. How can we know and believe something within the abyss of the void? As we have seen Žižek's critique of our postmodern fetishism hinges upon knowledge and belief.

Here we reach the crux of Žižek's impasse: Žižek's is a postmodernist logic of the substanceless but in order to substantiate knowledge we cannot do without substance. In order to overcome this impasse, Žižek has recently resurrected the traditional Marxist notion of class struggle. The class struggle should give substance to something that is without substance. The proletariat comes to embody that which has no body, no substance: 'The first figure, corresponding to the enclosure of external nature, is unexpectedly perhaps, Marx's notion the proletariat, the exploited worker whose product is taken away from him, reducing him to a subjectivity without substance, to the void of pure subjective potentiality whose actualization in the labor process equals its de-realization' (Žižek 2010, p. 313). The de-realization of the labour process is part and parcel of what Marx critiques as capitalism's status quo. It is hardly an outline of better state of society. Idealizing this process comes close to what Benjamin criticized as the social democratic infatuation with the bourgeois work ethic of labour.

Žižek refers to the term proletariat in order to bring into relief his defence of social antagonism: we need proletarians in order to have a class struggle. Žižek's focus is political, Hegelian and Lacanian in its concern for the unacknowledged antagonisms and the spectre of social unrest and suffering that is not anticipatory but already present in the current condition and conditioning of the ecology and economy. The missing issue here is that about which the struggle could be about. There need be some form of matter about which we can argue or over whose possession we may struggle. The economy concerns the distribution of wealth and the class struggle is about such spreading of the goods of this world.

According to Žižek, the proletariat is 'subjectivity without substance', precisely because it has been dizenfranchized. Its loss of substantive power is what deprives the proletariat of substance. Deprivation does, however, presuppose something of which we could be deprived. Marx's point is precisely to remedy this state of affairs. So Žižek's recent discussion of fetishism and social antagonism reflects an unacknowledged missing link in his thought which revolves around substance and its lack. This is not to deny the importance of parallax for addressing suffering, aging and illness within our mobile global society. We should rather think the radical positioning of parallax together with what constitutes the increasingly mutating substance of our society. The substance in question here is not single but is itself split during transformations into ever new forms.

It is one of the central wager's of this chapter that we can only think together a new form of mobile as well as diverse substance with the creative freedom of Descartes's *cogito* via a novel understanding of art's social validity. Literature instantiates the paradoxical and hybrid state of residing in between the substantive and the non-substantive, the real and the non-real, the subjective and the objective: it 'is *of* reality and it is not' (Steiner 1995, p. 119). More importantly, literature's interstitial location outside and at the same time inside substance, prepares it not just for the narration of what is fictive but in doing so for a critique of the fictions that may have come to shape reality.

The interstices of literature question the all too simplistic and often misleading divide between the real and the constructed. When politicians admonish us to get real, they often promulgate their constructions of reality as the objective state of things. The reality projected by some politicians involves suffering and some form of sacrifice that is necessary 'to get real'. One example of financial sacrifice has been Gordon Brown's insistence that Britain's multibillion expenditure for Trident—a renewal of a highly costly nuclear weapon's programme—is necessary to meet the threat of terrorism. Any opposition to such dear military spending in the face of huge cost cuts in public finances (cuts in the range between twenty-five and forty percent in the education, health and home office budget) is met by the admonition to get real.

What is the real in question here? Žižek empties the real out of any substance and concomitantly inflates pure subjectivity as arbiter of what matters. His argument is accurate to a certain extent: up to a point the real is without substance and therefore radically dependent on the position of the observer. Humanity makes its world. It gives birth in various non-literal manifestations: in forms of buildings, artworks, technical innovations and so forth. Our constitution is indeed a constructivist one. Modern philosophy from Descartes and Kant onwards has alerted us to our constructivist nature.

Descartes's cogito as well as Kant's autonomy seem to do justice to our capacity for autonomous world creations. Postmodernism, however, has reflected upon both the history of modernity (from the catastrophes of constructing bio-political or total societies in the first part of the twentieth century) and Heidegger's existentialism. Dwelling on these reflections, it has given an account of how modernity's constructions can fail or even turn into their opposites: into sites of mass murder and limitless destruction (Derrida's work on autoimmunity is a case in point here).

Heidegger's existential analysis of our being towards death shows that creativity flourishes on the abyss of radical contingency, of meaninglessness, of the nothing without substance. His famous notion of a secularised or, in other words, god-less guilt describes "an owning up both to the radical contingency of one's thrownness and to the inescapability of an ever-threatening death, as well as to the practical necessity, in acting at all, of fleeing in some way from such nullity, of 'erring' in the ontological sense in order to be, in order to 'stretch one's existence along in time" (Pippin 2005, p. 71). The feast of our world making—as celebrated from a Kantian or Hegelian perspective—gives rise to fear and turns out to be so many escape routes from the inevitable lack of substance which is our being onto death.

We keep constructing our different versions of the world on the post-Heideggerian abyss of nothingness as manifested not in the world of our constructions but in the endpoint, or, ironically, in the aim viz. telos of our life which is death. As Robert Pippin has shown, Heidegger thinks within a Kantian framework of human autonomy while turning it upside down. He dwells on what Kant and Hegel would not bear to countenance: the failure of meaning and practical sense making. The issue here is not death but the lack of substantive meaning which death represents: 'The failure that Heidegger is trying to account for is not a failure to 'make sense' of death but an occasion on which the failure to make sense of, be able to sustain reflectively, sense making itself happens' (Pippin 2005, p. 75). Our autonomous construction of the world reveals itself as being premized on its failure. Temporality highlights the potentiality of such failure.

Now Žižek reads German Idealism through post-Heidggerian eyes. Our seemingly substantive constructions of different forms of world are essentially and existentially empty, without substance. The only thing remaining is the pure form of Descartes *cogito* or Kant's and Hegel's notion of autonomy. Yet how can Žižek refer to issues of knowledge and belief from the position of a substanceless subject? The fact that our attempts to create worlds are subject to failure does not necessarily invalidate such attempts. Some might fail and some might prevail. The eventual loss of substance in death, on an individual level, or on species level, 'in the end of times', does not impinge on our contemporary needs as embodied rather than substanceless subjects. There are clearly substantial issues and the contemporary cost cutting exercise concern matters that affect the lives and minds of millions (health, education and so forth). Žižek implicitly addresses these issue when he castigates our society for avoiding them, or disavowing their existence in fetishist behaviour.

We could read Žižek's critique of contemporary society's fetishism, as an unacknowledged acknowledgement of substance, of matters of knowledge and believe. We know that there is climate change underway and yet we refuse to believe it. Climate change is a question of substance, because it has huge impact on the material condition of our world (sea levels rising, severe storms and the massive increase in global temperature). Climate change is only one example for our fetishist disavowal of matters we know but refuse to believe. Literature might be what Žižek is looking for. The argument developed in this chapter maintains that literature is capable of changing the most basic coordinates of our awareness. With literature we enter an avenue where we come to believe what we know. This is due to its capacity to change the way we approach our world. It is capable of transforming our consciousness and in doing so our attitudes to the environment, human suffering and issues of demography and aging. In this way fiction might ironically have a much more realistic stringency and valence and than the get real admonitions of some politicians. Indeed literature's fictions may critique the way in which we believe in what we know not to be true.

Suffering, the Changing Demography, and Literature's Transformation of Consciousness

Mutatis mutundis, we have to move beyond 'a state of collective fetishistic disavowal' when we face human suffering as well as future demographic challenges. What is crucial here is that these challenges are part of the larger economic and socfial antagonisms that we consistently try to avoid. The truth here is apparent but we cannot face up to it. This reluctance to facing up to truth, however hurtful it may be, is intricately bound up with what I call a culture of flat mimesis. We attempt to copy the image of easy bliss, of simple fulfilment as presented in political slogans and advertizements, because we long for simplicity in a world that is increasingly complex and quick in its transformations. Biomedical advances drive much of the changes whose social repercussions we desperately try to disavow.

Biomedical advances have transformed and alleviated both aspects of suffering and the actual inception of aging: we are capable of working much longer than current coordinates of retirement would acknowledge. In addition huge changes in demography and new economic necessities are increasingly enhancing the working life of an apparently aging population. Due to biomedical advances our radically new form of aging has less and less to do with physical as well as mental suffering and a concomitant decline in cognitive capacities. Within in a knowledge-based economic system, however, the stable functioning of cognition in those who are deemed to be 'old' is a crucial factor. It should be a red flag alerting us to the dangers that go with denying those who physically appear to be old the capacity and the right to contribute to the welfare of society at large. The forces behind such demotion of the apparently 'old' are fictitious, because due to tremendous medical advances the facts of both suffering and aging are in the process of startling transformations that no longer warrant the application of out-dated standards and categorization. The persistent clinging to passé standards and categorization is the product of flat mimesis and ironically manifests an aging process irrespective of age: the copying of what we are familiar with but what no longer holds true debilitates young and old.

In this context we may wonder whether Žižek's notion of 'fetishism' may be better described by what I have called 'flat mimesis'. As we have seen the history of its usage, indicates that the word 'fetish' depends on the perspective of those who employ it in order to invalidate the religious and social practices of a culture other than their own. This emphasis on the position of the observer enmeshes the term fetishism within the conceptual field of the notion 'parallax' and, as has been discussed in the preceding section, parallax describes the change within the same object if perceived from different points of view. A fetishist approach clings to one perspective conferring on an ordinary thing sacred or supernatural status. Endowed with such status, the thing must not be seen in any other light. It has become incapable of change and undergoes a serious of copies that are aimed to provide a seemingly identical replication of the thing itself (crosses as talisman in a Christian context). The mimesis is a flat one, because the thing (the cross around the neck) has the fetishist capacity to be consubstantial with the supernatural power it arguably represents. This coincidence of the ordinary thing of representation with the sacred Thing represented characterizes the single minded and rather flat perspective which characterizes fetishism. The conviction that goes with such flat perspective hinges upon a certain disregard of substantial properties: the ordinary thing can only transmute into the sacred Thing of fetishism, if its rather sobering material qualities are disavowed and not taken in account. This is a perspective and a concomitant consciousness which the fetishist rejects at least apropos the object in question here. A change in perspective would work for a change in consciousness. This transformation of the way we perceive and think about certain issues of our world is precisely the intellectual domain of literature, the humanities and the arts.

It is crucial here to emphasize that such transformation of perception and cognition is not limited to a cerebral or subjective sphere. On the contrary it has a tremendous impact not just on subjectivity but also on embodied substance. The transformation of perception and cognition concerns both our subjectivity and our substance. We are clearly substantial—rather than 'substanceless'—subjects who relate to a given exterior or societal context in which we absorb as well as create the different texts and textures that shape our lives. Literature and the arts have a two pronged and radically divergent field of activity: one is ethereal or non-substantial—what the term fiction may denote in this context—and the other transmogrifies the way we relate to issues of substance in the embodied sphere of society.

Literature's independence from life paradoxically provides a new lease of life. It is operates in a free mental sphere beyond substance and yet impinges upon our embodied existence in a way that is capable of alleviating suffering. This alleviation is not immediate or direct one but rather does its work via a change of perception and consciousness. This change may seem ethereal and ephemeral but its subject matter is substantive. According to Elaine Scarry this state between non-material cognition and it materialization characterizes the sphere of human culture as whole:

> What gradually becomes visible (by inversion in its deconstructed form in torture and war and straightforwardly in its undeconstructed civilized form), is the process by which a made world of culture acquires the characteristics of 'reality', the process of perception that allows invented ideas, beliefs, and made objects to be accepted and entered into as though they had the same ontological status as the natural given world. Once the made world is in place, it will have acquired the legitimate forms of 'substantiation' that are familiar to us. That an invented thing is 'real' will be ascertainable by the immediately apprehensible material fact of itself: the city (not the invisible city asserted to exist on the other side of the next sand dune, but one within the sensory horizon) has a materialized existence that is confirmable by vision, touch, hearing, smell; its reality is accessible to all the senses; its existence is thus confirmed within the bodies of the observers themselves. (Scarry 1985, p. 125)

Literature certainly differs from the built environment as manifested in cities. Scarry's argument about the interaction between the non-substantial construct and its substantiating realization is nevertheless pertinent for a discussion of literature and its complex relationship with reality. Literature self-consciously sets itself apart from any pretension to be a substantial part of our material existence. If it is read in this way, the reading in question is literalist and as such affiliated with various forms of political and religious fundamentalism. Seen as literature, the Bible does not lay claim to be literally true. Only a literalist reading of the Bible would affirm that, say, the apocalypse, as outlined in the book of revelations is going to take place(or is going to take place in the way described therein). Literature is a form of make belief and as such it differentiates itself from forms of embodied truth.

Literature does, however, lay claim to truth in a non-literalist fashion. In this non-literalist way it impinges on our reality while being set apart from it. It is fictitious in the sense of being separate from the materialized and thus substantiated reality of culture as instantiated in the architecture and the skyline of our cities (as discussed by Scarry in the quote above). Being fictitious in the sense of separated from the reality we encounter on an everyday basis does not mean that literature tells lies about our world. On the contrary, its mental space has the capacity to change our ways of perception and cognition in a uniquely powerful manner precisely by dint of its separation from what we are used to see as presentations and representations of our world.

The creativity of literature thus differs from the reality making activity which is the focus of Scarry's writing in the above citation: it does not create a mental construct in order to translate it literally into a materializing and eventually materialized form; rather literature's truth keeps a distance from the literal and materialized world of human culture in order to change the way we coordinate and live our lives within this world. This is what I mean by its consciousness changing capacity: a mental space that is distinct from the materialized space of other arts and sciences and yet one that helps create a more fulfilling life within our embodied world due to the new perspectives it provides on how we can better coordinate our attitudes, beliefs and way of interaction in the ever changing material conditions of our society.

A substantial part of the changing conditions within contemporary culture and society are biomedical or are due to other scientific advances. In order to be able to keep up with the biomedical revolution we need change the way we engage with reality and in order to do so we need to attend to the transformational rather than merely representational work of literature. Literature turns out not so much *to produce fictions but to critique the fictional work of our perception of suffering, youth and aging*. Literature's achieves this critical stance not via mimetic techniques but through a transformation of our ways of thinking. It confounds oppositions and turns them complementary rather than mutually self-exclusive.

This work at the transformation of the ways we perceive us and our world is the so far un-acknowledged core of the critical expertize that has emerged in recent attempts to understand postcolonial literature. In his classic study *The Location of Culture* Homi K Bhabha has employed the term hybridity—as 'a strategy of ambivalence in the structure of identification that occurs precisely in the elliptical *in between*, where the shadow of the other falls upon the self' (Bhabha 1994, p. 60)—in order to describe the complementary rather than mutually exclusive relationship between the colonizer and the colonized, between East and West. What is hybrid is ambiguous, is difficult to pin down, in short, it is uncertain. Whereas the agenda of colonizers was to create clear cut distinctions between the 'civilized West' and the 'savage East', the actual colonial experience, as Bhabha shows, confounds such distinctions.

To be more precise literature outdoes the oppositional structure with which the social norms of the colonizers set out to colonize what they desire to be perceived as suffering and deficient: 'The colonial signifier—neither one or the other—is, however, an act of ambivalent signification literally splitting the difference between the binary oppositions or polarities through which we think cultural difference' (Bhabha 1994, p. 128). It has been rather underappreciated that Bhabha derives his notion of the ambivalent and the hybrid from Hannah Arendt's theory of action and inter-subjectivity, which, as I have shown elsewhere, is part of her philosophy of diversity.[1] Bhabha points out that Arendt's notion of action is premized on the acknowledgement of uncertainty and contingency as foundation of our shared—and thus social or political—human condition:

> Agency, as the return of the subject, as 'not Adam', has a more directly political history in Hannah Arendt's portrayal of the troubled narrative of social causality. According to Arendt the notorious uncertainty of all political matters arises from the fact that the disclosure of the *who*—the agent of individuation—is contiguous with the *what* of the intersubjective realm. This contiguous relation between *who* and *what* cannot be transcended but must be accepted as a form of indeterminism and doubling. The *who* of agency bears no mimetic immediacy or adequacy of representation. It can only be signified outside the sentence in that sporadic, ambivalent temporality that inhabits the notorious unreliability of ancient oracles who 'neither reveal nor hide in words but give manifest signs'. The unreliability of signs introduces perplexity in the social text. (Bhabha 1994, p. 189)

[1] For detailed discussion of this point see, Mack (2010b, pp. 13–26).

Bhabha ingeniously reads Arendt's notion of politics in terms of a splitting between *who* and *what*. This links up with the previous discussion of this chapter: the *who* is of course subjectivity and the *what* is the substance of the material world of our political-social interaction. Now this splitting is not actually separating two different entities. Instead the split raptures and fractures one substance: our substantial world experience is split between the non-substantiality of the subjective *who* and the substantiality of the *what*. As Bhabha points out these two realms are not disconnected but contiguous with each other and this very contiguity between ethereal subjectivity and the materialized body of the exterior world makes for the uncertainty and contingency of the human condition. We may be able to ascertain some of the *whats* that constitute our world. We are, however, unable to represent the *who*, the kernel of our substanceless subjectivity.

The contiguity of the *who* and the *what* shapes the paradoxical non-factual factuality of intersubjectivity. Our situation is more complex than what Žižek's notion of the 'substanceless subject' may insinuate: we are substantive subjects and at the same time we inhabit a sphere of endlessly subjective substances. The interaction between subjectivity and substance (and vice versa) constitutes the intersubjective realm of politics and accounts for its tendency to fall prey to various fictions which are taken be real with often deleterious if not lethal effects. This tendency of reality to be shaped by and sometime to be subsumed by fictions has a significant bearing on issues of substance such as suffering. Spinoza was the first philosopher who took seriously the role fictions play within our societal lives (Mack 2010a). His critique of both final goals and teleology is a critique of fictions: 'all final causes are nothing but human fictions' (Spinoza 1996, p. 27). Spinoza does not berate us for the constructions of fictions. Constructing fiction (of teleology and final causes and so forth) is part of our subjectivity and is an inalienable part of our humanity. He does, however, admonish us not to confuse fiction with reality, not to mistake subjectivity for substance. This is of course difficult to achieve in world where, as Bhabha's reading of Arendt has suggested, subjectivity is contiguous with substance.

Within a Heideggerian context of radical contingency, Spinoza's rationalist hope to separate substance from subjectivity seems to be doomed to failure. Spinoza's critique of the fictions of teleology gives, however, already some purchase on understanding contingency as substantial fact of our world. Arendt's writing and thought has been heavily informed not so much by Spinoza as by Heidegger's phenomenology. She keeps faith with Heidegger's attempt to do justice to substance as we encounter it not only in our embodied subjectivity but also in our sense of being placed within a particular context, within what Jeff Malpas has called *Heidegger's Topology*. Arendt calls that fictitious which distorts and potentially attempts to destroy, the unpredictability of our individual and highly idiosyncratic locations within the diverse and contingent cosmos of the human. She calls politics what sustains the plurality of our lives. Against this background, could it be that Arendt's notion of politics is akin to that of literature?

This may appear to be a rather odd, if not disingenuous idea. Does not Arendt insist on the importance of factual truth in political discussions? Her emphasis on actions and their materialization does not, however, call into question her literary and humanistic approach to political science and to the social sciences in general. It has been noted that narratives are of central importance to Arendt's work. Her post-Spinozan conception of the human condition has generated a shift away from grand philosophical schemes and systems to a concern with the particularity of literature. As Simon Swift has recently put it, 'the fact that the human condition is limited allows that condition to be the subject of story and narrative.'[2] Is literature nothing more than the subject and the subject matter of our limitations?

The recognition of epistemological limits may indeed make us wary of grand theories that presume to offer the key for the understanding of the universe and this wariness may let us appreciate the more limited sphere of literary narration. No wonder that post World War II thinkers from Arendt, via Paul Riccoeur to Alasdair McIntyre and Martha Nussbaum have turned their attention to the philosophical value within literature. Yet Arendt differs from these theorists in a crucial respect. Her approach to literature is not primarily a mimetic one. Neither does she read literary text, as Ricoeur does, in terms of 'a vast laboratory in which we experiment with estimations, evaluations, and judgments of approval and condemnation through which narrativity serves as a propaedutic to ethics' (Ricoeur 1992, p. 115). She does not question such an approach and would not necessarily dispute its validity. She abstains, however, from seeing literature exclusively as mimesis of reality. Her reading together of ethics, politics and literature goes much further: she implicitly reads purportedly non-literary, or, in other words, non-contingent or logical forms of political governance in terms of fictitious fabrication. Rather than upholding the common view of literature in terms of a representation of reality, she argues that reality is itself subjected to fictitious distortions of itself that result in forms of self-destruction. Within her writing and thought we may find an implicit conception of literature as a critique of fiction. We find this unacknowledged literary theory of Arendt only spelled out when we read, as I am suggesting here, her rather idiosyncratic notion of politics as another word for literature. Partaking of, while at the same being removed from a single-minded position within the *polis*, literature is best endowed to critique fictions of the non-contingent and the limitless that come to shape political life when it turns tyrannical or totalitarian.

It is appropriate to more adequately and clearly define what Simon Swift calls 'limited' as the contingent or inconsistent. In 'On the Nature of Totalitarianism: An Essay in Understanding' Arendt argues that 'ideologies are systems of explanation of life and world that claim to explain everything, past and future, without further concurrence with actual reality' (Arendt 1994, pp. 349–350). It is quite clear that she is far from conflating fact with fiction. Politics turns totalitarian, however, when it conflates the two and in doing so renders life a lie. The lie of totalitarian politics is a consistent one. It has eradicated contingency from the social realm. As has been argued above, the inconsistence of the public realm derives from the messy and pluralistic contiguity between substance and subjectivity. Totalitarianism reduces the plurality of subjectivity to one single point of view which claims to be the truth.

[2] Swift (2009, p. 28). For brilliant discussion of the role of narrative in the work of Arendt see Disch (1994) as well as Pirro (2001).

Through it monopoly of power totalitarian politics sets out to eliminate everything in substantial or real life that could question or contradict its monolithic view. Arendt explains this insidious form of politics that renders substance congruent with the fictitious as follows:

> The point here is that the ideological consistency reducing everything to one all-dominating factor is always in conflict with the inconsistency of the world, on the one hand, and the unpredictability of human actions, on the other. Terror is needed in order to make the world consistent and keep it that way; to dominate human beings to the point where they lose, with their spontaneity, the specific unpredictability of thought and action. (Arendt 1994, p. 350)

Via the infliction of tremendous suffering (i.e. terror), totalitarianism forces its fictitious world view upon the world. What it proclaims to be 'truth' is nothing but an opinion and yet, through terror the fictions of opinion are capable of shaping our embodied reality, if the terror in question is all-comprehensive viz. totalitarian within a given society. In this context Arendt draws attention to the darks aspects within the notion of the laboratory with which Ricoeur later on attempts to fathom the ethical value of literature. She reads Nazi concentration camps as 'laboratories in which human beings of the most varied kinds are reduced to an always constant collection of reactions and reflexes' (Arendt 1994, p. 304). Ricoeur's term 'ethical laboratory' differs from the context in which Arendt uses the word. It is, however, important, to emphasize how Arendt refrains from a scientific nomenclature (to which 'laboratory' belongs) in order to do justice to humanity's unpredictability and the world's contingency (here she writes and thinks from the perspective of Heidegger's phenomenology).

On this view literature's inconsistency and notorious refusal to be subsumed under logical or quasi-logical formulas that would predictably explain it—as outcomes of laboratory research are often exhibited in terms of predictable laws of behaviour or sequences of chemical reaction—are key elements of its realistic truthfulness. The truthfulness at issue is, however, not merely a mimetic one. Literature does not so much represent or copy our lives but provides a mental space in which we may come to realize how our subjectivity is contiguous with our substance and vice versa. In other words literature questions the coordinates of the consistent but untrue life to which we have to conform as professionals, as family members, as functionaries or managers and so forth. It not so much or not only represents the pressure to coincide with such de-individualized roles; instead it reveals how such conformity renders our lives into a lie. Lies inflict mental and potentially physical suffering. The rendition of life into a lie is premized on narrowing down and eliminating human diversity through the demand to behave in a predictable manner.

Thinking with Hannah Arendt we could say that suffering in its mental and its physical manifestations arises from the pressure to deny or abandon our unpredictability. A substantial part of this unpredictability is our creativity. Removing the term birth form its literalist, species-like connotation which prevailed during the Nazi reign of terror, Arendt implicitly developed a philosophy of birth, which defines the human as the non-definable and not to be programmed or predicted life that flourishes within a contingent world through its nascent capacity to begin anew. What is literature but infinite versions of new beginnings? Arendt quotes the theologian Augustine as godfather of her literary understanding of politics: '*Initium ergo ut esset, creatus est homo, ante quem nullus fuit*' ('That there might be a beginning, man was created before whom nobody was'). According to Augustine, who might rightly be called the father of all Western philosophy of history, 'man not only has the capacity of beginning, but is the beginning himself' (Arendt 1994, p. 322). We inhabit the space opened up by the splitting of subject and substance. A split assumes divergence and yet we unite what is divergent and in doing we embody the unpredictability of new beginnings.

Literature does justice to our unpredictable constitution, because, from a removed position, it reinforces the splitting and, at the same time, the unification of the subjective and the substantive. It also sheds light on the predicament that may go hand in hand with our unpredictability. The uneasy overlap between substance and subjectivity can make room for a conflation of the two. Then the subjective proclaims to be the only form of substance there is. This is the case in the totalitarian rendition of life as lie. Why, however, choose nations (the German nation under Hitler is the most striking example) to give credit to such lies? Arendt accounts for such deleterious choice on account of a desire to find easy answers to the contingency of our world. The allusion of consistency renders the world benign and beyond the reach of suffering. As Spinoza has shown, our sense of importance and self-esteem seeks succour in fictions of teleological consistency. In middle of the twentieth century, Arendt argues that totalitarian rulers momentarily turn reality in to such a fiction: 'Before the seize power and establish a world according to their doctrines, totalitarian movements conjure up a lying world of consistency which is more adequate to the needs of the human mind than reality itself; in which, through sheer imagination, uprooted masses can feel at home and are spared the never-ending shocks which real life and real experiences deal to human beings and their expectations' (Arendt 2004, p. 464). Here a fictitious kind of subjectivity does violence to substance: it attempts to eliminate the inconsistency of the world into which it is place in order to count as true the fiction of a non-contingent and predictable universe. Such easy comfort comes home to roost, precisely because we are not substanceless subjects. The proof of this is not least to be found in suffering. As Malpas has put it, 'Totalitarianism attempts to deny the limits truth imposes, but it must inevitably fail in this attempt, simply because of the way in which no matter what strength is exerted, that strength is inevitably constrained by the world' (Malpas 2010, p. 139). Totalitarian regimes can only enforce their fiction of a consistent reality at the cost of substance itself. People purchase 'the most rigid, fantastically fictitious consistency of an ideology' while paying 'for it with countless sacrifices' (Malpas 2010). Suffering is the price of a fictitious reality. Literature as a critique of societal fictions helps alleviate such suffering. Here, in their endeavour to alleviate, if not to avoid, suffering, philosophical and literary ethics truly meet and encompass each other.

Bibliography

Arendt. 1994. *Essays in understanding 1930–1954: Formation, exile, and totalitarianism* (ed. with an introduction by Jerome Kohn). New York: Schocken.
Arendt. 2004. *The origins of totalitarianism* (with a new introduction by Samantha Power). New York: Schocken.
Beer, Gillian. 1999. *Open fields: Science in culural encounter*. Oxford: Oxford University Press.
Beer, Gillian. 2009. *Darwin's plot: Evolutionary narrative in Darwin, Eliot and nineteenth-century fiction*. Cambridge: Cambridge University Press.
Benjamin, Walter. 1996. Metaphysics of youth, vol. 1. In *Collected writings,* eds. Marcus Bullock and Michael W. Jennings. Cambridge: Belknap.
Bhabha, Homi. 1994. *The location of culture,* 60. London: Routledge.
Bowie, Andrew. 1997. *From romanticism to critical theory: The philosophy of German literary theory.* London: Routledge.
Disch, Lisa Jane. 1994. *Hannah Arendt and the limits of philosophy.* Ithaca: Cornell University Press.
Gilman, Sander. 2006. *Multiculturalism and the Jews*. London: Routledge.
Kureishi, Hanif. 1990. *The Buddha of Suburbia*. London: Faber and Faber.
Mack, Michael. 2001. *Anthropology as memory: Elias Canetti and Franz Baermann Steiner's responses to the Shoah*. Tübingen: Niemeyer.
Mack, Michael. 2003. *German idealism and the Jew: The inner anti-semitism of philosophy and German Jewish responses*. Chicago: University of Chicago Press.
Mack, Michael. 2009. Modernity as an unfinished project: Benjamin and political romanticism. In *Walter Benjamin and the architecture of modernity*, eds. Andrew Benjamin and Charles Rice. Melbourne: re.press.
Mack, Michael. 2010a. *Spinoza and the specters of modernity: The hidden enlightenment of diversity from Spinoza to Freud*. New York: Continuum.
Mack, Michael. 2010b. Hannah Arendt's philosophy of plurality: Thinking and understanding and *Eichmann in Jerusalem.* In *Power, judgment and political evil,* eds. Andrew Schaap, Danielle Celermajer and Vrasidas Karalis. Burlington: Ashgate.
Malpas, Jeff. 2010. Truth, politics and democracy: Arendt, Orwell and Camus in Andrew Schaap. In *Power, judgment and political evil: In conversation with Hannah Arendt*, eds. Danielle Celermajer and Vrasidas Karalis. Burlington: Ashgate.
Man, Paul de. 1979. *Allegories of reading: Figural langauge in Rousseau, Nietzsche, Rilke, and Proust*. London: Yale University Press.
Pippin, R. 2005. *The persistence of subjectivity: On the Kantian aftermath*. Cambridge: Cambridge University Press.
Pirro, Robert C. 2001. *Hannah Arendt and the politics of tragedy.* DeKalb: Northern Illinois University Press.
Ricoeur. 1992. *Onseself as Another*. Trans. K. Blamey. Chicago: University of Chicago Press.
Spinoza. 1996. *Ethics,* ed. E. Curley, with an introduction by Stuart Hampshire. Trans. E. Curley. London: Penguin.
Steiner, Wendy. 1995. *The scandal of pleasure: Art in an age of fundamentalism*. Chicago: University of Chicago Press.
Swift, Simon. 2009. *Hannah Arendt.* London: Routledge.
Žižek, Slavoj. 2001. *Enjoy your symptom! Jacques Lacan in Hollywood and out*. 2nd ed. with a new preface by the author. London: Routledge.
Žižek, Slavoj. 2006. *The paralax view*. Cambridge: The Massachusetts Institute of Technology Press.
Žižek, Slavoj. 2010. *Living in the end times.* London: Verso.

Chapter 8
Suffering and Forgiveness: An Heroic Journey

Andrew Brennan and Norva Y. S. Lo

There is an important sense in which all suffering stands in relation to the possibility of forgiveness. This is obviously true of suffering that occurs as a result of the actions of others, but one might also say that that even suffering that arises as a result of natural events may call for something at least analogous to forgiveness—those who are incapable of this may find themselves simply angry at an apparently uncaring world. Forgiveness is thus a key concept for any attempt to engage with suffering in a way that attends to the larger context in which it is embedded, and our engagement with suffering here will be one that moves by means of an engagement with the concept of forgiveness.

Arendt and the Unforgivable

Many contemporary treatments of forgiveness take their point of departure from the works of Hannah Arendt, Jacques Derrida and Vladimir Jankélévitch. Accordingly, we start by giving an initial assessment of their accounts, focusing on what is most problematic about them. In our journey into this territory, it is perhaps Hanna Arendt's work that provides the clearest orientation, since she captures in her writing what are at once the most traditional and also the most puzzling of the features of a concept which Derrida described as 'obscure in its limits, fragile in its foundations' (Derrida 2001, p. 30).

Arendt notes that forgiveness and punishment share the same *function*, namely one of freeing both victims and those who perpetrate wrongs from the consequences of past acts. In the absence of these devices, we should be prey to cycles of vengeance, ones which—in her words—'enclose both doer and sufferer in the relent-

A. Brennan (✉)
Department of Philosophy, LaTrobe University, Bundoora 3086, Victoria, Australia
e-mail: A.Brennan@latrobe.edu.au

N. Y. S. Lo
Department of Philosophy, LaTrobe University, Bundoora 3086, Victoria, Australia
e-mail: N.Lo@latrobe.edu.au

J. Malpas, N. Lickiss (eds.), *Perspectives on Human Suffering*,
DOI 10.1007/978-94-007-2795-3_8, © Springer Science+Business Media B.V. 2012

less automatism of the action process, which by itself need never come to an end' (Arendt 1958a, p. 241). In place of endless vendettas, struggles for revenge and other dysfunctional processes, forgiveness, like punishment, offers—in her view—at least the possibility of a fresh start, of beginning again with a clean slate. She writes:

> Without being forgiven, released from the consequences of what we have done, our capacity to act would, as it were, be confined to one single deed from which we could never recover; we would remain the victims of its consequences forever, not unlike the sorcerer's apprentice who lacked the magic formula to break the spell. (Arendt 1958a, p. 237)

In what looks like a mistake of logic, Arendt infers from the similarity of their functions that punishment and forgiveness share the same limit. As she puts it: 'It is therefore quite significant, a structural element in the realm of human affairs, that men are unable to forgive what they cannot punish and that they are unable to punish what has turned out to be unforgivable' (Arendt 1958a, p. 237). In particular, offenses of 'radical evil' are both unpunishable and unforgivable. According to Arendt, such offences have been revealed through the actions of totalitarian regimes, which

> [I]n their effort to prove that everything is possible, … have discovered without knowing it that there are crimes which men can neither punish nor forgive. When the impossible was made possible it became the unpunishable, unforgivable absolute evil which could no longer be understood and explained by the evil motives of self-interest, greed, covetousness, resentment, lust for power, and cowardice; and which therefore anger could not revenge, love could not endure, friendship could not forgive. (Arendt 1958b, p. 459)

While punishment is founded on the idea of justice, and associated ideas of restoring the balance and paying one's debt to society or the victims, it is hard to see how forgiveness could be associated any of these. Think of the accountant's notion of punishment, according to which punishment for a misdeed is a kind of balancing of the books, whereby the debt incurred by doing something wrong is countered by paying an appropriate penalty. In terms of this idea, punishment can be assessed for its capacity to fit the crime. It is not an uncommon thought that some crimes—in particular, those that involve radical evil—appear to lie beyond the scope of appropriate or proportionate punishment. For such crimes, as is often said, no punishment would be enough to redress the wrong—to balance the books.

Arendt's idea of forgiveness having the same limit as punishment can seem puzzling, given that the two concepts have radically distinct logic. Unlike punishment, forgiveness is not motivated by the demand of justice or any part of the apparatus of justice. Derrida recognized this clearly when, following Jankélévitch, he put forward the idea that forgiveness—in at least one of its senses—is something exceptional, with the character of a gift. 'One could never, in the ordinary sense of the words,' Derrida wrote, 'found a politics or law on forgiveness' (Derrida 2001, p. 39). Forgiveness, according to him, can be transcendent, something that 'exceeds the juridico-political' system (Derrida 2001, p. 47). This idea of the gift of forgiveness is, in Derrida's view, one aspect of an inconsistent pair of ideas lodged in what he calls the 'Abrahamic' religious tradition: 'Sometimes, forgiveness (given by God, or inspired by divine prescription) must be a gracious gift, without exchange and without condition; sometimes it requires, as its minimal condition, the repentance and transformation of the sinner' (Derrida 2001, p. 59).

Perhaps a better way to make sense of Arendt's statement that we cannot forgive what we cannot punish is to consider her description of radical evil which, according to her, shares some of the same dehumanizing structure as totalitarianism. According to her account of totalitarianism, 'radical evil has emerged in connection with a system in which all men have become equally superfluous' (Arendt 1958b, p. 459), that is where humans are no longer treated as intrinsically valuable centres of beliefs and values, and of worth for their own sake. The instrumentalism of totalitarian regimes extends to those who apparently are in power, and work the system, as well as to those who are oppressed—all alike are dehumanized. This notion of radical evil is essentially Kantian, involving a breach of the categorical imperative, which demands that we never treat a human being (an end in itself) as a mere means to other ends. By saying that he was merely following orders in his administration of the death camps and therefore it was not his crime, the Nazi bureaucrat Adolf Eichmann was not just denying the humanity of the Jewish victims, but also his own humanity by treating himself as a mere instrument in the Nazi machinery.

In a chilling anticipation of what we might call the *bureaucratic totalitarianism* of the present age, Arendt warned:

> Totalitarian solutions may well survive the fall of totalitarian regimes in the form of strong temptations which will come up whenever it seems impossible to alleviate political, social, or economic misery in a manner worthy of man. (Arendt 1958b)

Radical evil of this sort does not need to be on a large scale. In Australia, the state of Western Australia has long had a sorry record of high levels of incarceration of Aboriginal people combined with high levels of Aboriginal deaths in custody. In a recent shocking case, an Aboriginal elder by the name of Ward, was picked up in a remote settlement and charged with being drunk in charge of a vehicle. The trainee magistrate before whom he was brought, ordered Mr Ward be transferred to a prison 360 km away, and this instruction was carried out on the following day. Mr Ward was confined in a small, unventilated steel cell, or pod, mounted on the rear of a Mazda truck. Although the pod was meant to be air-conditioned, apparently no check was made on the system's operation by the two staff charged with driving him to the prison. The external temperature on the day of the transfer was in excess of 40°C and Mr Ward was given only one 600 ml bottle of water for the journey. No stop was made during the transit, which took 3 h and 45 min, and at the end of the journey Mr Ward was found to be in a very bad way, suffering from serious burns, and died of heatstroke shortly after being transferred to hospital. The air-conditioning in the pod had not been working, and temperatures in the pod itself were estimated—after a re-enactment of the journey—to have involved air temperatures of around 50°C and surface temperatures, on the seat and floors of the pod, of up to 56° (Hope 2009, pp. 34–37). The pod itself was an object of horror to the coroner, who wrote in his report: 'It is difficult to imagine a more uncomfortable environment for travelling over even short distances. In my view, the use of this pod for long distance travel was inhumane' (Hope 2009, p. 17).

More horrors emerged in the course of the inquest. The two staff, who failed to check the air-conditioning, who did not stop to check on Mr Ward's condition at any point during the journey, and who gave somewhat unsatisfactory answers to the coroner's questions were found not to have breached any of the procedures laid down by their training or in the codes of practice laid down by their employer. Although they had treated Mr Ward without due care, there was no legal basis for charging them with any offence. Nor was there apparently any occupational health or safety regulation they had breached when they put their duty to their company's procedures above their concern for the prisoner. One of them, a former paramedic, described her reaction when, near the end of the journey, she had looked into the pod and seen Mr Ward in a state of collapse: 'my first reaction in normal circumstances would have been to rip that door off its sockets and gone in there and dragged him out and done gave him mouth to mouth, but that is against our procedures' (Hope 2009, p. 76). Like Eichmann, this officer followed procedures. But while Eichmann was executed, she was not even charged with any offence at all.

Some commentators on the West Australian case commented that if there was a category of 'bureaucratic murder' then that was the charge that should have been laid in this case. The idea that someone who has not breached any company rule or standard operating procedure has done nothing wrong is precisely what Arendt would have seen as a source of radical evil. Those who see their lives as committed to following procedures, are—like Eichmann—presenting themselves as mere instruments for a larger-than-individual cause. In trying to justify their neglect of Mr Ward in this way, the two officers not only denied Mr Ward's humanity and his fundamental human rights, but also denied their own humanity. While the cost of escaping responsibility in this way may be very high, in moral terms, it is quite low in our current socio-political world. After all, the officials in question were not even disciplined by their company, nor was that company subject to prosecution.

How, then, do we go about deciding on who is responsible for Mr Ward's death? Arendt's writings inspire the thought that bureaucracy is worse than tyranny, not just because bureaucracy dehumanizes, but also because of the diffusion of responsibility it entails. Rule by no-one, she points out, is not absence of rules, but rather a rule by system, not by person. The result of this is that bureaucracy leads to a corrosion of responsibility. In recent years, the term 'accountability' has been brought into company and organizational parlance, a term that has replaced the notion of responsibility with a much weaker and more fluid notion. Everyone is accountable under rules and procedures, but no-one is any longer responsible. In a situation where no-one is supposed to act as a human being responsible for their own actions any more, then no one can act wrongly, and no one need be responsible for anything. Collective responsibility easily transforms into no responsibility at all, where failures are blamed on the system and not on the individual.

If no one is responsible any more, there is no target on which blame can be laid, and there is no one who can be or should be punished. Now think of the implications of this for our study of forgiveness. Even in the face of appalling suffering, the language of pardoning and forgiving no longer makes any sense. If no one can be blamed, *a fortiori* no one can be forgiven. Arendt's claim that we cannot forgive what we cannot punish now makes perfect sense. Our interpretation of her views on radical evil in the context of totalitarian bureaucracy—and the consequent dehumanizing of both victim and perpetrator—means that in these cases we cannot punish and we cannot forgive. The perpetrators of evil are no longer moral agents who are ends in themselves, but are no more than instruments, some mere mechanical things not capable of personal responsibility.

As we have seen earlier, despite the fact that punishment and forgiveness appear to exemplify two different kinds of logic—one of justice, the other of the gift—Arendt thinks that punishment and forgiveness share the same positive function of liberating both victim and perpetrator from the consequences of past acts, and opening a wider range of future possibilities for both. Following her ideas through, we may ask under what circumstances we should adopt one strategy instead of the other—when is it right to demand punishment, when is it right to make a gift of forgiveness? These are urgent and important practical questions, yet Arendt leaves them unaddressed. Any adequate theory of forgiveness, we say, must actually address this question, and have at least something to say about when, where and under what conditions forgiveness is preferable to punishment and vice versa. This will be a task to which we return later in the paper.

A vital feature of forgiveness according to Arendt is that it opens up some new possibilities for the future, and also puts paid to the capacity of the past to haunt us and trap us in patterns of behaviour determined by former deeds and misdeeds. She also talks about the complementary functions of forgiving and promising. One of them is backward-looking, serving to 'undo' the past, while the other is forward-looking, serving to 'secure' the future. She writes:

> The remedy for unpredictability, for the chaotic uncertainty of the future, is contained in the faculty to make and keep promises. The two faculties belong together in so far as one of them, forgiving, serves to undo the deeds of the past, whose 'sins' hang like Damocles' sword over every new generation; and the other, binding oneself through promises, serves to set up in the ocean of uncertainty, which the future is by definition, islands of security without which not even continuity, let alone durability of any kind, would be possible in the relationships between men. (Arendt 1958a, p. 237)

Oddly enough, Arendt apparently overlooks the fact that forgiving itself is a tacit promise. Forgiving, when carried out sincerely and with commitment, provides some islands of certainty in the unpredictability of the future, since to forgive someone is to promise to forgo vengeance, grudges and ill will, and hence to provide some security in respect of our future behaviour.

Like all other acts of avoidance and refraining from doing, forgiveness is an ongoing and uncertain pursuit, always open to the risk of being ruined by one single slip even when someone has a previously perfect record of restraint. It would be incoherent to say that today I genuinely have forgiven you but tomorrow my grudge against you will come back and I will take revenge on you. Since, then, forgiveness with an expiry date is no forgiveness at all, but—given the fragility and vulnerability to which all promises are prone—there is no absolute certainty that people will keep their promises, we are seldom in a good position to judge that people have forgiven until the nails are in their coffins. Aristotle's conception of human flourishing (*eudaimonia*) is the conception of a state that is always subject to loss: to have a flourishing life is itself partly a matter of luck, of avoiding the vulnerabilities and tragedies to which human lives are inevitably exposed. Likewise, there are multiple possibilities of risk associated with forgiveness, and these apply both on the side offering to forgive and on the part of those receiving it. Even when the perpetrator of an evil has died, apparently been forgiven by his contemporaries, history may subsequently reverse the decision. There can be no expiry date on the risks of loss of forgiveness.

Suppose in certain circumstances, we do decide to offer forgiveness instead of inflicting punishment. In such cases, how do we effectively achieve forgiveness—especially when the wrong involved and the injury people suffer are both grave? Although Arendt also neglects this question, we can derive from her brief remarks some hints of what can motivate forgiveness.

She contrasts the political and public situation of forgiveness with the private, other-worldly condition of lovers: we love others for *who* they are, not for *what* they are, she claims. This distinction between *who* and *what* enables us to forgive the person (the *who*) for *what* he or she has done. In the public realm of political matters, she thinks that a correlate for love can be found—a correlate that also distinguishes the *who* from the *what*—and that this is respect for other people. 'Respect,' she tells us, 'because it concerns only the person, is quite sufficient to prompt forgiving of what a person did, for the sake of the person' (Arendt 1958b, p. 243).

The appeal to respect is tantalizingly brief, and raises a number of problems. Three of these are worth noting here. First, what do we say about cases where respect for a person is lost as a result of the wrong that has been done? This is not an unusual case. If respect is the basis of forgiveness, it seems that there can be no possibility of forgiving someone for whom we have lost respect. Can this be right? It may be that Arendt is able to defend her position from a Kantian perspective. Suppose, according to this viewpoint, that all rational agents are entitled to a degree of respect, no matter what they do. Now what do we say about apparently rational human beings who commit atrocities? Is it that the sleep of reason brings forth monsters (to cite the inscription on one of Goya's etchings)? Or is it that through the very horrors they inflict, the perpetrators put themselves beyond the pale of humanity? The Kantian interpretation makes sense of the way Arendt seems to throw up her hands in despair when confronted with radical evil. Of radically evil deeds she states:

> … all we know is that we can neither punish nor forgive such offenses and that they therefore transcend the realm of human affairs and the potentialities of human power, both of which they radically destroy wherever they make their appearance through the very atrocities they commit. (Arendt 1958b, p. 241)

The problem is that if evil-doers of a sufficiently radical kind do expel themselves from the community of rational agents through the very acts they undertake, then the Kantian position that demands respect for all rational beings is impotent to safeguard them from any actions we take against them. It would not be intrinsically wrong to torture a mass killer, according to this point of view. Recall that when confronted with the question of our duties towards animals, Kant himself appealed to the special dignity of humans, distinguishing them as 'altogether different in rank and dignity from things, such as irrational animals, with which one may deal and dispose at one's discretion'. In regard to animals, we have to consider the instrumental damage cruelty may cause since, as Kant remarks in the *Lectures on Ethics*, 'he who is cruel to animals becomes hard also in his dealings with men'. We do nothing wrong to the dog by torturing it, so the argument goes. Rather we run the risk of hardening our hearts to other rational beings by treating a non-rational being—the dog—in such a way. Torturing animals, then, is not intrinsically wicked, but instrumentally wrong to the extent that it desensitizes us to human suffering. The same would apply to mass-murderers if they no longer belong to the community of rational beings.

If this is Arendt's position, then it seems quite implausible. Horrified as we are in the face of genocide, mass murder, the use of rape as a weapon of war and other such monstrosities, it is doubtful if the appropriate reaction is to strip the perpetrators of their humanity and their moral standing. In terms of a theoretical strategy, Arendt seems to have taken far too extreme a line, one that is liable to render her overall approach unsatisfactory. Incidentally, this problem emerges in much more recent writings too, as in remarks like this: 'The agent whose self-governance is profoundly and persistently vicious may merit our loathing to such a degree that we experience doubts about his standing as a participant in the moral order' (Jacob 2003, p. 243).

A further problem, independent of this first one, is that the appeal to Kantian respect for persons supports taking the route of punishment no less than that of forgiveness. For the Kantian, it is rational agents and they alone who deserve respect. Likewise, it is only rational agents who can be seen as culpable when they do wrong and should take responsibility for what they do. The rational agent of Kant's philosophy deserves appropriate punishment as part of what it is to merit respect: punishment involves respect for the victim of wrong-doing and also respect for the perpetrator, who should receive his or her 'just deserts'. This is because punishment is one significant way by means of which an agent can take responsibility for what he or she has done. The punished agent, having paid the debt, can then resume life in the moral community, the books having been balanced and harmony restored. But then how can an appeal to respect give a special motivation for forgiveness rather than punishment? As we have already pointed out, a satisfactory theory of forgiveness has to give at least some account of the motivation for granting it: so far, Arendt's account fails to do this.

Finally, there is the case of irrationality. In a very broad sense of *rationality*, common in western philosophy since the time of Socrates, the person who is rational attempts not only to make valid inferences, but also tries to ensure that his or her beliefs track the truth. In this broad sense, a classic case of irrational behaviour is action from ignorance, since it is irrational for agents not to be fully informed about a situation before they act in it. As a result, people who are victims of ignorance often do not undertake courses of action that fully rational agents would undertake. A sympathetic, or benevolent, observer might none the less forgive such people their mistakes, aware of their limitations and sympathizing with their plight. To say this is to suggest that sympathy may motivate forgiveness. When Jesus asked for forgiveness on behalf of those who condemned him to death, he said 'forgive them for they know not what they do'. Here is a case of benevolence, possibly intermingled with sympathy. But it is certainly not a case of Kantian respect for the rational agent. While there are various emotional and moral outlooks and stands that can motivate forgiveness, respect for rational agents does not seem a plausible candidate, and certainly fails to be explanatory in a wide range of cases.

Romantic and Magical Forgiveness

Arendt is unapologetic in advocating a thesis of the unforgivable, arguing in effect that forgiveness of radical evils is beyond all human capacities. Her account of forgiveness is tied closely to religious ideas, and this may be why some large issues can only be left to God's judgment. By contrast Derrida argues that forgiveness, worthy of the name, is precisely the forgiving of the unforgivable. As he writes: 'there is the unforgivable. Is this not, in truth, the only thing to forgive? The only thing that calls for forgiveness? If one is only prepared to forgive what appears forgivable, what the church calls 'venial sin', then the very idea of forgiveness would disappear' (Derrida 2001, p. 32).

Strongly influenced by the earlier treatment of the subject by Vladimir Jankélévitch, Derrida—in our view—also repeats some of Jankélévitch's mistakes. As often noted, Jankélévitch seems to have held two different views. According to his first view, forgiveness, like love, is something that can occur in a instant, that can change the world, and which lies outside the normal chain of events and habits in which humans are usually cocooned. Forgiveness, like love, has a miraculous quality (Jankélévitch 1967, p. 208), and involves risk—risk that is worth taking in view of the potentially world-changing nature of forgiveness. Moreover, forgiveness proper—as opposed to reconciliation, forgetting or other ways in which resentment can fade and the sense of injury decline—is freely given, a gift, something excluded from economic transactions of exchange and balancing. Like love—in at least some of its manifestations—forgiveness is a kind of mad act, returning good for evil rather than following the path of justice:

> When a crime can neither be justified, nor explained, nor even understood, when, with everything that could be explained having been explained… when the atrocity has neither mitigating circumstances, nor excuses of any sort… then there is no longer anything else to do but to forgive. (Jankélévitch 1967, p. 206)

It is precisely this view that Jankélévitch appeared to abandon a few years later in an essay on the holocaust entitled 'Should We Pardon Them?' as if he realized how extraordinarily implausible his earlier view had been. While he had been prepared to claim that forgiveness: 'forgives in one fell swoop and in a single, invisible *élan*, and it pardons undividedly; in a single, radical, and incomprehensible movement, forgiveness effaces all, sweeps away all, and forgets all. In one blink of an eye, forgiveness makes a tabula rasa of the past, and this miracle is as simple for it as saying hello and good evening' (Jankélévitch 1967, p. 153), his later view is that 'pardoning died in the death camps' (Jankélévitch 1971, p. 567).

Like Jankélévitch, Derrida wants to face up to the remarkable nature of forgiveness, but unlike his predecessor, Derrida also wants to find space for the idea that forgiveness did not die in the camps. Instead, he claims that there is an ideal—perhaps unattainable—at which we can aim. For him, genuine forgiveness—forgiveness in the face of radical evil, of what is completely unforgivable—must be in some way conceivable, even if impossible. Such pardoning is unconditional, *non-instrumental*, *non-calculative*, and therefore *spontaneous* not planned. Moreover, it can be given in the absence of any request for forgiveness, and in the absence of any evidence of remorse on the part of the wrong-doers:

> From the inexpiable or the irreparable, Jankélévitch concludes the unforgivable. And one does not forgive, according to him, the unforgivable. This connection does not seem to me to follow. For the reason I gave (what would be a forgiveness that forgave only the forgivable?) and because this logic continues to imply that forgiveness remains the correlate to a judgement and the counterpart to a possible punishment… (Derrida 2001, p. 36)

In common with both Arendt and Jankélévitch, Derrida sees forgiveness as something that lies outside of everyday transactions; unlike them, he sees forgiveness as independent of any request, not a response to repentance, hence not a way of balancing the books.

How could such pardoning happen? This is an important question. However unusual, exceptional or ideal, we need to know how the kind of forgiveness that Derrida has in mind can happen. More modestly, even if the idea is unattainable, are there at least some steps we can take that would enter us onto a path like the path of forgiveness? Disappointingly, Derrida openly admits that he has no idea of how to answer this question, and that he can provide no explanation for such extraordinary acts of forgiveness. For him, genuine forgiveness is as mysterious as it is mad:

> …if I say, as I think, that forgiveness is mad, and that it must remain a madness of the impossible, this is certainly not to exclude or disqualify it. It is even, perhaps, the only thing that arrives, that surprises, like a revolution, the ordinary course of history, politics, and law. (Derrida 2001, p. 39)

While Derrida does not compare forgiveness to love, it is tempting to read some of his remarks on forgiveness as mimicking a somewhat callow account of love. The phenomenology or psychology of what Derrida describes seems rather similar to having a crush, or *falling in love* as sometimes described in pulp literature. Think of the following ways in which a somewhat clichéd account of romantic love would parallel what Derrida has written. First, forgiveness, like romantic love, is supposed to come with *unconditional* commitments. Just as the one who is madly in love often makes unconditional promises of affection, care and sacrifice, the one who genuinely forgives makes unconditional promises of forgoing all vengeance (both in action and attitude), wiping the slate clean and making a fresh start. That is why Derrida argues that forgiveness is a gift, not an exchange based on calculation.

Furthermore, 'madness' is an extremely appropriate term for describing romantic love for highlighting its mystery and unexplained (if not inexplicable) origin and motivation. The combination of madness with self-sacrifice is the depiction of something that, in its extraordinary unconditionality, has a precious, angelic, and other-worldly feel. This may in part explain the attraction of Derrida's comments to a wide range of readers, secular and religious, young and old. When such a depiction is combined with a treatment that relishes contradiction and inconsistency, the result is a heady brew. It is easy to be thrilled by the claim that 'pure and unconditional forgiveness, in order to have its own meaning, must have no "meaning", no finality, even no intelligibility. It is a madness of the impossible…' (Derrida 2001, p. 45).

However exciting the fantasy, reality obtrudes in the end. Although romantic love and crushes have their excitements, they also have a tendency to fade away quickly. While falling in love is spontaneous, supposedly unconditional, beautiful, angelic, and mysterious, when lovers fall out of love things can quickly turn very ugly. If forgiveness is like this kind of love, then it is likely to be short-lived, especially if it is without any independent support. Strangers in the night may indeed be lovers at first sight, but if their love is to survive more than a few nights or days, then they will need to find some common interests, shared values and joint purposes that will help them build a more stable and enduring relationship. In international diplomacy, for example, there is no shortage of sudden infatuations, diplomatic surprises, peace conferences that promise much followed by a further breakdown in relationships and the resumption of hostilities. Even if we suppose that Derrida has captured some of the phenomenology of forgiveness—at least in some cases—he has failed to provide any prescription for how to establish the relationship, how to remake the previously broken world, and how to maintain the forgiving stance. We cannot assume that the gift of forgiveness will go on giving day after day, any more than we can assume that the lovers of a whirlwind romance will simply live happily ever after.

A Hero's Journey

We asked earlier when to forgive and when to punish. On Arendt's view both forgiveness and punishment are alternatives and can apparently achieve the same ends—namely freeing both the perpetrators and the victims from the consequences of past acts. This claim raises a doubt: why should we ever opt for forgiveness if punishment can achieve the same desired results? Before tackling this question, we need to lay aside a number of cases where there is no choice to be made between punishment and forgiveness, and where Arendt's analysis would just be inappropriate. One of these is where no question of punishment would properly arise. In many close relationships, forgiveness is an important element in restoring trust and relationships, even when questions of punishment would not arise at all. When families suffer rifts, brothers feel wronged by sisters, children are scolded for wrongs they did not commit—in these and a thousand other cases, forgiveness does not present as an alternative to punishment but rather serves as an independent means of opening the way to reconciliation and restoration of closeness. A second case that fails to fit Arendt's remarks concerns timing. While punishment seems to be appropriate at any time after a legal wrong has been committed, forgiveness often requires time. After a deep hurt, it can be difficult for the victim to forgive, and forgiveness can seldom be offered swiftly. By contrast, just punishment can be swift and sure. Finally, there are cases where no legal wrong is committed, or where the wrongdoer is no longer accessible through the legal system (because he or she is dead, or in another country). In such cases, there is no alternative to forgiveness in the form of punishment, yet forgiveness can play an important part in the healing journey undertaken by those who have suffered a wrong.

Arendt's analysis does seem to apply to a number of social and political situations where there is a choice between punishing and forgiving. In many of these, it is often much easier for a victim of crime to want the perpetrators to be punished than to forgive them. So what is the point of opting for forgiveness? Are there any principles that will indicate when one strategy makes more sense than another? We suggest that it can be useful to look at a case where, after much suffering and in the face of demand for punishment, the argument for forgiveness has been put forward with some success. This has happened, for example, in Timor-Leste, where the first president, and former guerilla leader Xanana Gusmao argued for the unpopular choice of forgiveness rather than punishment.

Portuguese Timor was a colony, unilaterally abandoned to its fate in 1975 when Portugal decided to dissolve its colonial empire. Under Portuguese rule, the colony had been known for production of sandalwood, but had received little investment. Within a few days of the announcement of its independence, it was taken over in a brutal fashion by Indonesia, and—despite popular resistance to Indonesian rule—little attention was paid to the situation there until 1991 when Indonesian forces shot dead more than 250 people taking part in a procession in the capital Dili. After the Dili massacre, increasing international pressure forced the Indonesian government to permit a referendum on independence in 1999, a referendum that was opposed by pro-Indonesian militia forces, apparently armed and supported by the Indonesian military. It is estimated that when the referendum revealed overwhelming support for independence, the resulting rampage by the militias led to the destruction of 70% of the territory's infrastructure, and caused the deaths of hundreds of people (BBC 2010). The mayhem was only stopped when an international peace-keeping force under the auspices of the United Nations was sent to end the violence. In a truth commission report jointly commissioned by the Timorese and Indonesian governments and handed down in 2008, it was claimed that crimes against humanity committed by the armed militias in 1999 had included murder, torture and sexual violence, and that the Indonesian army had continued to arm and support the militias engaged in these acts in full knowledge of what was happening.

During the last six years of Indonesian occupation, Xanana Gusmão had been either in prison or under house arrest, but he emerged as the only serious contender for the presidency. Although many people wanted punishment for those in the militias who had committed atrocities during the struggle for independence, and during the mayhem after the 1999 referendum, Gusmão insisted that East Timor must not take what he called 'the path of justice'. In contrast to Arendt who saw both forgiveness and punishment as ways of bringing closure to the past, Gusmão says in his commentary to the film *A Hero's Journey* that 'to take the path of justice, there is no beginning and no end. And we all stay stuck in the past.' The context of this remark is a meditation on the fact that there was not a one-sided history of atrocity in Timor:

> You must understand that during our recent history atrocities were committed on all sides. It was not only Indonesian soldiers that killed Timorese. Timorese killed Timorese too. Some Timorese collaborated with Indonesia to fight those who wanted self-determination. This was all part of our struggle, all part of our history. When people call for justice, they must understand that there are no clear lines. Where do you begin? In 1974? In 1999?

What Gusmão is suggesting here, we propose, is that the use of punishment—the path of justice—was not politically viable, for two reasons. First, since atrocities were committed from both sides, any policy of punishment where justice is the goal would have to impose punishment on many people on each of the sides. The result would be the alienation of people who have very different political alignments. Moreover, punishment, like vengeance, is unlimited. Wherever a line is drawn, where we say that people fitting a certain set of criteria will be punished, that line can be challenged—and the challenge itself would likely be couched in terms of fairness. Hence Gusmão's query—'Where do you begin?' The unanswerability of this question implies endless debates about justice and fairness, justice in this case being prey to the very problem that Arendt identified for vengeance: '… far from putting an end to the consequences of the first misdeed, everybody remains bound to the process, permitting the chain reaction contained in every action to take its unhindered course (Arendt 1958a, pp. 240–241).'

The destabilizing effect of arguments about justice and fairness would not only be political, but would also impact on the economy of a country rendered one of the poorest in the region. For punishment to be carried out according to justice and proper standards, there would be massive financial strains put on a nearly bankrupt economy, and establishing cases, setting up trials and hearings, allowing for appeals and so on would use up many human resources that could be more effectively deployed in reconstructing the nation and its infrastructure. In crude terms, Gusmão's argument could be stated in terms of costs and benefits: on any political and economic calculation, it would be more beneficial overall for the people who committed atrocities to be forgiven so that everyone can work together to rebuild the nation. Locking such people up, or excluding them from the rebuilding process, would be a cost that the new nation could not afford. From the point of view of such a calculation, forgiveness can be seen as materially necessary for the rebuilding of the country.

There is a larger scope for forgiveness too. In the film, Gusmão is shown hugging one of his former prison guards, an Indonesian, while he explains how much he hated Indonesia and everything to do with the oppressor country. Yet, in almost the same breath, he points out that Timor-Leste needs to forgive Indonesia, for Indonesia is too important a neighbour to hold as an enemy. Forgiveness of Indonesia is in the interests of Timor-Leste, he states, for it is the first step toward reconciliation. Here again, Gusmão seems to be urging that forgiveness is an alternative to punishment—after all, given the evidence of the Indonesian military's complicity in crimes against humanity, it would be legitimate to call for punishment and reparations. Here is how he puts it:

> Forgiveness and reconciliation: they are complementary processes. To reconcile with other people, you first must forgive. If you don't forgive, any shake hand that you can do, any embrace that you hate to do but you do because many people are looking at you will not mean anything. You must be strong enough to forgive first. Then you make the step forward to shake hand, or to embrace somebody. But forgiveness is the first thing, the first challenge you face. You forgive or not. If not, no reconciliation can happen.

This interesting comment suggests that forgiveness and reconciliation are complementary processes. The forward-looking character of forgiveness prepares the way for, and can possibly motivate, reconciliation. On the other hand, punishment by itself could do very little toward reconciliation, especially because it is essentially a backward looking process. In saying this, we may seem to have departed a long way from Arendt's analysis. However, it should be recalled that forgiveness is just as forward-looking as promising, as we have already argued. Certainly, in the political sphere, forgiveness consists in a promise to forgo revenge, or to behave in the future in a way that can re-establish good relations. If reconciliation is the longer term goal, then there are very good reasons for offering forgiveness rather than seeking punishment.

This brief examination of Gusmão's views on forgiveness, brings a flavour of *realpolitik* to our discussion. It also draws attention to the discrepancy between the situation in Timor-Leste and the situation in Europe at the end of the Second World War, a situation which provided the setting and background for Arendt's work. In that case, the allied forces were not so materially devastated as to be lacking the means to establish procedures for tracking down, arresting, prosecuting and punishing those who had committed acts of radical evil. The new state of Israel was likewise well-equipped to make an investment in tracing and prosecuting those who designed, operated and supported the machinery of genocide, including Adolf Eichmann, the administrator with a skewed conscience, so brilliantly depicted in Arendt's account of his trial (Arendt 1963). Forgiveness of Eichmann and the Nazis—let alone reconciliation with them—was not a necessary option, required for establishing and building the state of Israeli.

If these suggestions are correct, then there is more to forgiveness than is dreamed of in the romantic pronouncements of Derrida and Jankélévitch. In some situations, the offering of forgiveness is—and has to be—materially driven. In such cases, it is a carefully considered and rational political decision rather than a spontaneous feeling of unconditional commitment of the kind found in romantic love and spiritual conversion. We previously pointed out that forgiveness has a certain fragility, the same frailty that is associated with all promising. Forgiveness in the Timor case as we have described it is an instrument, a means to a larger than individual end. It is precisely because the strategy has solid material justifications and benefits, that it is likely to last longer than otherwise, like a marriage founded on more than romantic impulses. Derrida's proposal that the unconditional, uncalculated and unthinking version of forgiveness is the only genuine form is by contrast like someone insisting that a crush is the only genuine form of love.

How to Forgive

After why and when, we come to the question of how to forgive. Again, there are many different cases to consider, and for the present we look only at the most dramatic of these—serious trauma. For example, how does a victim of horrific crime effectively achieve long lasting forgiveness? As in the previous section, we use the example of Timor-Leste, as a *prima facie* plausible example of how to go about coping with trauma and forgiving it.

For Gusmão, trauma is something that we cannot avoid carrying, but something we should resist feeding. What does this mean? In the film he introduces the story of a girl, Flavia de Jesus, who was disfigured by being slashed in the face with a machete while her mother was murdered in front of her eyes. Of this terrible individual tragedy he says:

> I wanted to understand the problem of trauma. What is trauma? If trauma is something we have to feed every day, we have to carry every day,… like her [*indicating Flavia*]—she has a signal that will accompany her for all of her life. Or trauma is something that will reveal our weakness, our psychological weakness, to accept that the past is the past. Many people complain and accuse myself or the state of forgetting the suffering of the past, forgetting the sentiments of the victims. I always say that during a liberation struggle, we cannot use the term 'victims'. They are all heroes.

These remarks require some comment, and we propose the following, in an experimental mode. To carry traumas is to remember them while to feed them is to refresh the emotions associated with them. The suggestion we draw from Gusmão's words is that only when people stop feeding their traumas can they be ready to forgive and reconcile. If this is right, then an important point about time order emerges. It is not that people forgive, and then change their emotional orientation, but things are instead the other way round. Distancing oneself from the emotions association with traumas can prepare the way for forgiveness, and then forgiveness prepares the way for reconciliation. Here is an important point about forgiveness and time.

The past is of course important according to Gusmão. That is why the events that caused trauma must not be forgotten. But the future is even more important. By not feeding the negative emotions associated with trauma, people can become more ready to move forward and rebuild their lives. Gusmão emphasizes that people need to dream how to live in a better future of independence. We can supplement this point with the cost-benefit analysis given in the previous section. If we use too many resources in feeding the past, then we have less left for building a better future. Unlike investing in the future, investment in the past gives no returns.

Gusmão's language of 'hero' and 'victim' is meant, in our view, to encourage a certain view of past and future. The victimological stand is one in which people feed their trauma, seeing themselves as passive rather than active, trapped in situations not of their own making rather than working for change. To help people change their stance, they need a model, such as Flavia, who is courageous in the face of loss and disfigurement. Flavia is young, someone for whom the future has meaning, and with less investment in the past than an older person. Immediately after the commentary above, Flavia talks to the camera:

> [*Flavia*] My nose has a scar but I am not ashamed because this is the result of a war. [*Gusmão*] What I say is that children like her are more courageous to leave the ghost of the suffering than adults. I have many cases, a mother or a father, they will cry all the time. They just will express the sadness. The past was, of course, something important. But now the future is in each one's hands.

The suggestion here is that focus on the future is an imperative, and that children and young people, with their high investment in the future, will be more willing to forgive than their older peers. Moreover, the goods of the future are larger than individual goods. As Gusmão says: 'now the two countries can sit together to look at the future of our people, the future of our children'—and then affirms his key message—'We put the past to the past. We are looking for the future'. In country with potentially rich oil and gas reserves, such a dream is at least persuasive.

In this context, we can start to see why Gusmão puts emphasis on the notion of the *hero*. Notice that heroes volunteer for their roles, while victims do not. Heroes are moved by altruistic motives, while victims may be onlookers who were hoping not to get involved. Heroes expect injuries. Victims flee from them. Put in more detail, we can flesh out the hero-victim dialectic like this. Heroes see injuries as a cost they pay for the cause they stand for. By contrast, victims see injuries as uninvited misfortunes. Flavia, like other heroes, is not ashamed, but even proud of, the injuries received in fighting for the cause. Heroes are outward and forward looking. Victims are inward and backward looking. Victims seek compensation for injuries but heroes are less inclined to do so. Victims get sympathy and help, but in the end they can become objects of irritation and contempt. Heroes get respect and trust and are much less likely ever to become objects of derision. Against this set of oppositions, it is hardly surprising that heroes are more likely than victims to forgive those who done them personal injuries—especially if such a move would achieve some important altruistic goal.

Gusmão's invocation of the hero is a clever political and rhetorical strategy, and—given the continuing uncertainty about the prospects for reconciliation in Timor-Leste—it is unclear if it will be a successful one. The idea of a hero working for the people, and of a heroic people's army also working for the people (hence not stealing from them, not exploiting them and not operating in a corrupt way) is hardly novel. Cynical observers would be able to point to similarities between these strategies as adopted by Gusmão and those adopted by other successful charismatic leaders such as Mao Tse Tung. It is wise, then, to adopt a cautious stance towards the material we have cited in this and the previous section: as already emphasized, it provides some suggestions for thinking about forgiveness in ways that go beyond the frame of Arendt's and Derrida's thought.

With such a *caveat* in mind, we still think it worth pursuing the idea of heroic forgiveness. As already seen, we live in a bureaucratic world where it can be difficult to identify who to blame, and who is responsible, when evils occur. There are cases where forgiveness is impossible because no-one is there to be forgiven, and instead evils are attributed to a system or set of procedures. There will therefore be no easy way in which those who are victims of systematic abuse of evil, where no individual has done evil to them, can move from the victimological to the heroic stance. Moreover, few have the moral authority to ask others to give up victimhood and adopt instead the stand of the hero. In particular, bureaucrats have no such authority.

If these experimental suggestions are right, then forgiveness must remain inspirational. It cannot be replaced by a machine-like bureaucratic process run by officials whose motive for working is largely just to make a living out of it. But *pace* Derrida, inspiration is not the opposite of rationality or calculation. The fact that forgiveness is to be inspired rather than administered does not mean that it is not also a result of rational and political calculation. By taking the example of Gusmão, we have tried to show how forgiveness as a stage on the path to reconciliation can be both inspirational and calculative.

'Forgiveness to me means peace of mind,' Gusmão says towards the end of the film. 'If we can forgive, we liberate ourselves from all bad sentiments, from revenge, from self-flagellation. If we forgive we stop a part of our life. We say no—now we are entering a new phase of my life. If not, I live everyday a sense that I am the worst victim in the world. God! Why me? Why it happened to me and not to other people?… Forgiveness is the way to live in peace. Peace not with other people, firstly, with him- or herself.' The 'why me' echoes the incomprehensibility that Arendt expressed in the face of radical evil. When evils befall us, whether wrongs inflicted by others, or natural catastrophes, we often resort to the plea that we do not understand, that it is inexplicable. The statement, 'I don't understand,' is in these circumstances not so much a statement about the world as an expression of the degree of trauma felt. Arendt herself perhaps give expression in her own writings to just such a feeling of trauma, and this is something that anyone commenting on her work is bound to respect. Derrida's response to her trauma is to commend us to do the impossible, to forgive the unforgivable. As he put it, 'forgiveness is thus mad. It must plunge, but lucidly, into the night of the unintelligible' (Derrida 2001, p. 49). What we have tried to show, however, is that even a curative and healing notion of forgiveness need not be unconditional and uncalculated. When you forgive, you may not get any benefit from the perpetrator, from the one you forgive, but you gain nonetheless. So, even if it is not a form of exchange with the people you forgive, there is a way in which forgiveness is nonetheless a form of exchange: you forgive in exchange for your own peace of mind.

Bibliography

Arendt, Hannah. 1963. *Eichmann in Jerusalem. A report on the banality of evil.* New York: Penguin Books.

Arendt, Hannah. 1958a. *The human condition,* 2nd edn. Chicago: University of Chicago Press.

Arendt, Hannah. 1958b. *The origins of totalitarianism,* 2nd edn. Cleveland: World Publishing.

BBC. 2010. East timor country profile. http://news.bbc.co.uk/2/hi/asiapacific/country_profiles/1508119.stm. Accessed 16 March 2010.

Derrida, Jacques. 2001. *On Cosmopolitanism and Forgiveness*. Trans. M. Dooley and M. Hughes. London: Routledge.

Hope, A. N. 2009. *Record of an investigation into death reference 9/09*. Western Australia: Government of Western Australia Coroner's Court.

Jacobs, Jonathan. 2003. *Some tensions between autonomy and self-governance*. In *Autonomy*, eds. Ellen Frankel Paul, Fred D. Miller Jr. and Jeffrey Paul. Cambridge: Cambridge University Press.

Jankélévitch, Vladimir. 1971. *Should We Pardon Them*. Trans. A. Hobart. *Critical Inquiry* 22 (1996): 552–72.

Jankélévitch, Vladimir. 1967. *Forgiveness*. Trans. A. Kelley, 2006. Chicago: University of Chicago Press.

Part II
Humanities Approaches

Chapter 9
The Suffering of Job: He is Every Person and No-One

Peta Jones Pellach

There was a man in the land of Uz and his name was Job ...
The Book of Job

In the Jewish canon, the Book of Job seems oddly out of place. It has no liturgical role, it tells no epic story of Jewish history, it is not prophecy or poetry, nor does it fit neatly into the genre of Wisdom literature[1]. Ostensibly, it tells the story of one man. Job is depicted as exceedingly righteous, beset by calamity and tragedy, yet he does not falter in his allegiance to God. There are only hints in the story as to any historical or geographical setting that we can recognise and Job has no genealogy. For those reasons, the Malbim (Pfeffer 2003)[2] (19th Century) saw the Book as a parable, just as many of Rabbis of the Talmud (5th–6th Century) had done earlier.[3] The importance of the story is not that it tells the tale of one man; it lies in lessons that this story teaches about the place of suffering in human experience. The 'answer' it offers is that God is responsible for suffering. The current chief Rabbi of the British Commonwealth, Rabbi Jonathan Sacks, describes Job as 'the most dissident book ever to be included in the canon of sacred scriptures (Sacks 2005, p. 27).'

In Post-Holocaust Judaism, there has been a renewed interest in the problem of evil and suffering. The idea of an omnipotent God Whose 'mercy endures forever'[4] is inconceivable for many Jews in light of their recent historical experience. Traditional and dominant explanations for evil and suffering in the world—that suffering

[1] The name applied to some pieces of Jewish writing from the late Second Temple period. The genre is characterized by praise of *God*, often in *poetic form*, and by sayings of *wisdom* intended to teach about God and about *virtue*. While sections of Job match the genre, the Book as a whole has a narrative structure that makes it exceptional.

[2] Acronym, Meïr Leibush ben Jehiel Michel Weiser, 19th Century Rabbi and commentator, whose views can be found in Pfeffer (2003).

[3] Talmud *Bava Bathra,* p. 14b.

[4] Psalm 100:6.

P. J. Pellach (✉)
Director of Educational Activities for the Elijah Interfaith Institute, Jerusalem, Israel
e-mail: peta@elijah-interfaith.org

J. Malpas, N. Lickiss (eds.), *Perspectives on Human Suffering,*
DOI 10.1007/978-94-007-2795-3_9, © Springer Science+Business Media B.V. 2012

is punishment for sin, that suffering is 'instructive', that suffering is character-building, that suffering brings rewards either in this world or in the 'world-to-come', that we have a responsibility to find meaning in suffering—all rely on the belief that the infliction of suffering is consistent with divine mercy. When Fackenheim called victims of the Shoah the 'Job of the gas chambers' (Fackenheim 1982, p. 196) he was hearkening to an alternative theology. Although it is found in the Hebrew Bible, its complexity and the challenge is poses to the warnings of the Prophets meant that, Job's message was not the ascendant one. Today, it is viewed with renewed interest.

For contemporary readers, the historical veracity of Job is unimportant; his torment is timeless. As Wiesel (1994) points out, every person who has experienced loss and suffering, in every generation, every person who asks 'Why?' or 'Why me?' What makes him stand out and what justifies his place in the Biblical canon is his steadfast faith, which earns him a response, though not an explanation, from God.

The Theological Question

The question explored in the Book of Job, the suffering of the righteous, is part of the larger question of whether a clear moral order exists in the world. The book stands in contrast to the clarity of a divinely-ordained moral order, governing the world from the time of creation, which rewards virtue and punishes evil. (See, for example, Deuteronomy 28, Hoseah 14, Amos 5 et al. Also in the Mishna[5], in Kiddushin 1:10 et al.). Job is righteous yet he suffers. God is all-powerful yet he allows the righteous to suffer. Indeed, he initiates their suffering. Conventional understandings of God as 'good' and 'just' are challenged and perhaps undermined by the story of Job.

Recognising the reality of suffering of the righteous, the Talmud posits in its tractate *Kiddushin*[6] that rewards for righteousness may not be received in this world but in 'the world to come'. Consequently, suffering in this world does not undermine the system of reward and punishment. In another tractate, *Berakhot*[7], there is further discussion. Suffering may come to educate a person or to elevate one. The concept of 'chastenings of love' (*yissurim shel ahavah*) is introduced, implying that the virtuous may suffer as a sign of divine favour. The Rabbis allude to Job and argue over his virtue. They do not, however, seek to interpret the Book as providing a definitive answer to the meaning of suffering, nor do they consider it a rebuttal of various conceptions of divine justice.

[5] Mishna is the earlier of the two parallel texts that comprise the Talmud. Redacted by the end of the 2nd Century, it is a record of the oral tradition and debates extant during the period of the Second Temple (destroyed 70CE).

[6] Kiddushin 39b—Kiddushim is the section of the Talmud concerned with marriages.

[7] Berakhot 7a, 5a *et al*—Berakhot is the section of the Talmud dealing with obligatory blessings.

It may be that the Book does not intend to solve the mystery of human suffering at all. Talmudic and Midrashic[8] writers were more interested in the character of Job, some seeing him as exemplary of how one ought to behave in times of great suffering and others criticizing him. Oliver Leaman points out that whereas philosophical approaches seek to elicit the underlying argument posited in the text of Job, the Rabbinic commentators did not feel constrained by the particulars of the text they were studying (Leaman 1995). They were interested in the experience of suffering and in the experience of theophany, more powerful than suffering and an 'argument' against it. Subsequently, Jewish philosophers have attempted to reconcile a philosophical and a theological reading of the text itself.

The Narrative

The modern orthodox rabbi and bible scholar Moshe Greenberg describes the Book of Job as dealing with the way in which "one man suddenly awakened to the anarchy rampant in the world, yet his attachment to God outlived the ruin of his tidy system (Greenberg 1995, p. 327)." Greenberg believes that Job's suffering comes in order to educate him, adopting one of the Talmudic explanations for the existence of suffering. He says, "The terrible paradox is that no righteous man can measure his love of God unless he suffers a fate befitting the wicked..." (Greenberg 1995, p. 328) Greenberg is drawing on a key narrative of Judaism's national mythology, the story of Abraham. According to the Bible, the founding father of the Jewish people, Abraham, was tested terribly to measure his love of God, including a final test in which he was asked to sacrifice his child. Known as the 'Binding of Isaac', this story is read on the Jewish New Year, as Jews enter a ten day period of penitence. Job's story, according to Greenberg and others, is an extension of Abraham's.

As Job's narrative opens, a veiled character, the 'Adversary', Satan, appears in the heavenly court. Job's anguish is initiated when God says to Satan 'Did you pay any attention to My servant Job? There is no one like him on earth, a sound and honest man who fears God and shuns evil' (1:8). The expression, 'fears God', is a direct allusion to Abraham at the end of the *akeidah* (Binding of Isaac). So is the setting in the land of 'Uz' (one of the relatives of Abraham, who is somewhat cryptically mentioned after the story of the *akeidah.*) The language suggests that Job starts out at the level of righteousness that Abraham achieves only after the Binding; his unfaltering loyalty is testament to that.

Apparently Satan had not noticed Job, until God drew his attention to him. Immediately, Satan expresses doubts about Job's faith, telling God that Job's devotion is only due to his blessings. If Job's fortunes were to be reversed, Satan slyly suggests, his faith would not stand up to the trial.

[8] *Midrash* refers to the tradition of Rabbinic commentary and speculation on the Biblical text. Classical midrashim (plural) were composed from the 3rd–12th Century.

Satan is only doing what Satan must do. In Jewish tradition, he is one of God's angels, responsible for a particular task and only that task. Satan is created in order to stir up trouble, to cause doubt and to wreak havoc. God permits him to test Job, and he does so most cruelly.

Satan is told not to touch Job himself. This limitation did not include Job's children, despite his having taken responsibility for their moral and religious upbringing, making burnt offerings for each of them in case 'my sons have sinned and in their heart blasphemed' (1:5). In this sense, also, the testing of Job is compared to the testing of Abraham at the *akeidah*, but this time the offering is accepted. We note that it is Job, not Abraham, who merits the statement 'no one [is] like him on earth.' (1:8)

When Satan expresses his certainty that Job will curse God, the Hebrew word for 'curse [*k'llal*]' is not used, but rather the euphemism 'bless [*barukh*]' (1:11). (The meaning of 'curse' is clear from the context). Once Job's suffering is set in motion and he is beset by disaster, Satan's predictions are proven false. There is no cursing. The irony is heightened when Job thwarts Satan's predictions and says, 'The Lord has given and the Lord has taken away, Blessed be the name of God' (1:21). Sadly, this is not the end of the challenge.

In Chap. 3 there is a second interchange between God and the Adversary. The Adversary has been 'roaming all over the earth' but God has continued to take interest in both Job's affliction and his righteousness. It is at this point that God hands Job's immediate fate over to Satan: the One Who notices but does not interfere cedes power to the one who has been roaming the earth, not at all interested in the individual except as he may prove a point in the otherwise hypothetical discussion about human fidelity. This seems to be a key to understanding the remainder of the Book. God notices the pain and the joy of the individual but allows other forces to intervene in his life.

Although we, the readers, understand something of the farce in heaven that is the cause of Job's suffering, Job himself knows nothing. The fate of Job, until late in the narrative, represents the concept of '*Hester Panim*', which means that God 'hides His face' and is not readily perceptible to us in our everyday lives.[9] Thus, inexplicable suffering endures, the righteous seem to be punished and the wicked appear to prosper.

Job's friends, the other characters in the extended dialogue that follows Job's affliction, are ordinary people. They have ordinary understandings of God and providence. For these naïve acquaintances of Job, who provide the voice of the human yearning for an uncomplicated moral order, the narrative is simple—the favoured one is no longer favoured. Once Satan inflicts personal suffering on Job, they admonish him to repent for his sins, insisting that his tragedies must be divine punish-

[9] The concept is first found in Devarim (Deuteronomy) 31:17 and is expounded upon by commentators including Nachmanides (Ramban), whose explanation is most widely accepted. According to Ramban, God hid His face in response to human sin but is waiting for the opportunity to reconnect with human history, when there is full repentance. God's apparent absence from the world is not the total reality—nor does God remove Himself from one individual or another but is imperceptible to everyone. Although Rashi and others see the hiding as punishment, many see it as a test for humanity.

ment for wrongs he committed. Why else, they declare, could he be suffering this way? "Think now, what innocent man ever perished?" (4:7) they ask him. "Where have the upright been destroyed?" (4:8)

These words come from Eliphaz, who is described by Rashi as one who, raised in the house of Isaac, acquired great levels of wisdom. According to his argument, God is always fair. Misfortune comes about when humans choose an evil path and God responds accordingly. Eliphaz views man as a creature who possesses absolute freewill. He begins his argument tentatively but eventually employs sarcasm and even vitriol in his accusations that Job's suffering must be the direct result of his greed. He articulates the conviction that suffering is always the result of sin.

Job knows he has done no wrong and refuses to repent. He pleads with God to explain why this evil has befallen him.

Bildad and Zophar enter the fray, also convinced that God is both just and merciful, and accuse Job of not reflecting sufficiently on his own shortcomings. They use phrases reflected in Wisdom Literature suggesting that it is simple-mindedness or ignorance that make a man deny his sin. Job responds that he accepts the central contention that God is all-powerful but denies that divine power is used only for the type of justice that his friends assert.

Job's 'friends' and the community make him a scapegoat. They need Job to be guilty, therefore they declare him so. Their concept of religion, reconciling a just God with the existence of evil, has a built-in need for a scapegoat. 'Those who plough iniquity … By the breath of God they perish' (4:7–9).

When Job does not agree, they effectively excommunicate him. Job expresses his anguish, blaming God for his loss. 'He has alienated my brothers from me, my relatives take care to avoid me, my intimate friends have gone away and the guests in my house have forgotten me. My maid servants regard me as a stranger… my servant does not answer me. My breath is unbearable to my wife and my stench to my brothers. Even the children look down on me … all my dearest friends recoil from me' (19:11–18).

Job has been a model of pious behavior (31:1–39). He was wealthy and influential, possibly the most influential man in the community, and apparently much loved: 'If I smiled at them, it was too good to be true, they watched my face for the least sign of favor, As their chief, I told them which course to take, like a king living among his troops and I led them wherever I chose' (29:24–25).

The animosity shown by his friends when his fortunes change is striking. From Eliphaz: '… writhe in pain all their days … [you] sent away widows empty-handed and crushed the arms of orphans' (15:21, 22:9); from Bildad: you will be 'driven from the light into the darkness, … without … a single survivor' (18:18, 19); from from Zophar: he 'used to suck vipers' venom … [and] destroyed the huts of the poor plundering houses … his avarice never satisfied' (20:16, 19–20).

There is a striking dissonance between Job's virtues noted by God and those accusations voiced by his friends. In his refusal to admit guilt, Job has 'rebelled' against what he formerly considered and what the community, led by his friends, still considers to be the natural order of things. In their eyes Job has become the enemy of God and the enemy of the people. The friends become the zealous defenders of God as they understand Him.

Job finds comfort in the wisdom of Elihu ben Barachel, a younger companion who waits to hear the contributions of his elders before offering an opinion. Job's answer to his own suffering is that he is the victim of fate, until Elihu finally convinces him otherwise. 'Fate' might imply an absence of a moral order, making any search for understanding futile. Although Elihu is not mentioned outside the Chapter in which he speaks, through him, Job is encouraged to continue his quest to comprehend his own situation. Elihu's words resonate with Job but they do not bring closure to the argument.

At the end of the narrative, after a lengthy period of Job searching for reasons for his suffering, God speaks from the whirlwind but He does not answer Job's questions. Nevertheless, Job is quieted. On an intellectual level, the enigmatic quality of the divine response provides most readers with a less than satisfactory answer. For Job, it is enough. Maimonides (1963, pp. 22–23) sees Job's transformation as attributable to his defective knowledge of God being superseded by greater knowledge—a knowledge that it is almost impossible for the reader to experience because it is the result of a revelatory process.

The divine voice replies to Job, speaking 'out of the whirlwind,' challenging the premise of the whole discussion: 'Where were you when I laid the Earth's foundations?' 'Speak if you have understanding'. 'Do you know who fixed the Earth's dimensions, or Who measured it with a line?' 'Onto what were its bases sunk?' 'Who set its cornerstone when the morning stars sang together and all the heavenly beings shouted for joy?' (38:4–7) In order for Job to 'understand', the Almighty responds with an admonition that takes him back to the time of creation, before humans existed.

God has confirmed Job's view that his suffering was not a result of any sin he had committed. For Job, this is a relief. He has reconciled himself to the existence of suffering and accepted the adage from Ecclesiastes 'For in much wisdom is much grief: and he that increases knowledge increases sorrow.'[10] For those who seek a clear relationship between 'good' and 'prosperity' and 'evil' and 'suffering', this is a blow.

For the next four chapters, the story has God repeating in great detail the same basic theme: humans cannot know how the universe operates, or why it came to be one way rather than another. God's justice manifests in ways that humans cannot understand.

Job as the Man We Know

As possibly the only imaginary hero of Biblical personalities, Job is at the same time the most universal of all of them in his experience of a life radically removed from the type of 'justice' for which humans yearn. Job's comfortable situation in the opening verses of the Book is familiar to many of us in our Uz (Oz)—healthy

[10] Ecclesiastes 1:18.

children, happy family life, he is a successful businessman, wealthy, hospitable. He is humble and pious. His expressions of faith, as they are described, are not very sophisticated. He does what is right and expects his life to follow a pattern of peace and prosperity.

Elie Wiesel (1994, p. 211) calls Job 'Our Contemporary'. He is the father who has inexplicably lost his job and has no means of supporting his family. He is the mother who has just been told her child has terminal cancer. He is the Holocaust survivor who still wakes up screaming in the middle of the night. He is the central character in the latest Coen Brothers film, 'A Serious Man'. He is an imperfect man but one whose flaws do not warrant extraordinary suffering; when he is afflicted, he seeks answers; no one is able to satisfy his yearning to understand.

Each of us who has known loss or suffering can identify with this man. When we listen to those who have suffered, we hear in them the anguish of Job. 'Job: a moment of obsession, a gleam of anguish, a cry contained but not stifled trying to pierce our consciousness, a mirror a thousand times shattered reflecting the image of a solitude bursting with madness'.

The Book of Job is not the story of a tragic figure of old. The Book of Job resonates with contemporary men and women who try to make sense out of the unfair circumstances of their lives even as they struggle to hold onto their beliefs. Most of all, the Book of Job is about a dilemma with which every thinking person struggles.

The Dilemma of Job

This dilemma is the apparent contradiction between the basic assumptions that God is just and rewards the good and punishes the wicked, that God is all-powerful and that nothing happens in the world without His willing it, and the fact that we see the suffering of the innocent.[11]

God determines that Job will be able to withstand the test of suffering and come to terms with the dilemma. This is the case. Job remains confident of his own virtue and equally confident that divine wisdom must prevail, despite the suffering it brings him. The concept of suffering being a test for the righteous is discussed in the Middle Ages by Saadiah Gaon in his *Book of Beliefs and Opinions*. (9th Century) 'It is not, however, His wont to act in this fashion with him who cannot bear these trials, since there would be no benefit therein. For the whole purpose of the suffering of the upright is that the rest of God's creatures might know that He has not chosen the former for nothing. This is known to thee from the case of Job and his suffering (Gaon 1967, p. 213).'

Job, for Saadiah Gaon (9th Century), becomes the exemplar of a righteous person suffering as a test of his faith in and love of God. Through it Job elevates himself; he serves as a role model to others of one who suffers greatly, yet maintains his

[11] The Rabbis of the Talmud described the paradox in term of 'tzaddik ve' ra lo', literally, "the righteous one and it's bad for him." (Talmud Brachot, pp. 4–7).

fidelity; and he is ultimately rewarded by God. He knows that his suffering is not punishment and his quest is for an alternative explanation. Ultimately, he accepts that divine justice is beyond human comprehension. His steadfastness of faith in himself is contrasted to all around him.

Some Talmudic thinking wants to assert the view of the friends of Job. It suggests that a person who suffers may have committed some secret sin that even the sufferer might not know about. Alternatively, a person might be rewarded or punished for good deeds or sins of their parents. If that is not satisfactory, Rabbinic discourse posits the idea that God rewards goodness and punishes sin not in this world, but in the afterlife. Therefore, suffering in this life facilitates full reward in the afterlife. This leads to the idea that suffering is given to those whom God especially loves, as a test or opportunity to show faith, an idea not incompatible with the experiences of Abraham or of Job.

One *Midrash* explains Abraham's test in these terms:

> If you go to the marketplace you will see the potter hitting his clay pots with a stick to show how strong and solid they are. But the wise potter hits only the strongest pots, never the flawed ones. So too, God sends such tests and afflictions only to people He knows are capable of handling them, so that they and others can learn the extent of their spiritual strength. (Genesis Rabbah 32:3)

Modern thinkers, such as Mordecai Kaplan and Harold Kushner, resolve the paradox by having us rethink our image of God. For them, God is not a conscious Being controlling the events of the world but a spiritual presence or force that comforts and strengthens humans in hard times, and enables people to grow and evolve. Kaplan rejects the idea that God is All-Knowing, preferring to think of God as 'The Power that Makes for Salvation (Mordecai 1958).' Kushner (1982), on the other hand, says that God is not All-Powerful; God does not act to do good things for one person and bad for another, but instead suffers with the suffering, acting in empathy rather than history.

The end of the Book of Job offers another alternative and for some it is comforting. When God responds out of the whirlwind, Job experiences a theophany, comparable only to those of Abraham (Gen. 15), Moses (Ex. 19:16), and Elijah (I Kings 19:11–12). Job requests that God respond (31:35). God does not answer Job, but rather appears and challenges Job himself. 'Who are you obscuring my intention with your ignorance' (38:2). Job's 'ignorance' can only be understood as his insistence on retributive justice and on a moral order.

God does not respond to Job's quest for answers, and Job does not respond to God. Job's first words of response (40:4) have many layers of meaning: 'What can I reply?' Then Job states that 'I spoke once, and I will not answer, twice, and I will add nothing' (40:5). This is a non-response to God's non-response. It appears that this is not sufficient contrition for God, so God retorts by more clearly challenging Job.

> Do you really want to reverse My judgment, put Me in the wrong and yourself in the right? Has your arm the strength of God's? … I will be the first to pay you homage, if your right hand is strong enough to save you (40:8–9, 14).

The Unfathomable Nature of God

God reprimands Job saying that man, who does not understand the mysteries of nature, cannot hope to understand the Creator. Job accepts his ignorance: 'therefore I have uttered that which I did not understand, things beyond me that I knew not' (42:3). Job is changed by the theophany: 'Before, I knew you only with the hearing of my ears, but now I have seen You with my own eyes' (42:5). Job both hears and sees God. 'I withdraw what I have said, and recant [or: repent] as I am but dust and ashes' (42:6).2 Job repents that he mistakenly thought the world ran on the basis of a discernible moral order. He has heard and seen that it does not. His experiences enlighten us to a new way of understanding the role of God in human suffering.

God has no retort to Job's specific questions because no answers exist. He does not mention retribution, which is a theme of the dialogues and of Job's questioning. God insists on asking questions rather than answering Job's questions. Thus God tells Job that in fact he understands nothing. Neither Job nor any human can understand the moral order of the world.

God, then. rejects not just the logic, wisdom and orthodoxy of Eliphaz, Bildad and Zophar but, simultaneously, of all the Prophets of Israel who assume that the suffering of the Israelites is incurred by their being sinners. The essence of their messages is that repentance will avert national disaster, and it is thrown into doubt by the revelation to Job.

The Suffering Inherent in Creation

Greenberg (1987, p. 327)[12] points out that the account of creation in Job differs from the those in Genesis and in Psalms. In these more familiar accounts, human are the pinnacle of creation and give purpose to it; in Job, humans are incidental. The Malbim (see above, fn. 2) noted the flaws in the arguments proposed by Job's acquaintances: although human activity plays a significant part in determining the course of history, there are forces greater than human endeavour. Job's actions do not determine Job's fate. There is only one answer to Job's suffering: that suffering is inherent in the divine creation. God created everything; He is responsible for suffering, too, and He does not recoil from that responsibility.

In the beginning of creation there was '*tohu vavohu*'[13], utter disorder, and the act of creation was an act of applying Divine order. God created the world by the power of His word—'*Abra K'dabra*'[14], 'He created as He spoke'. The Divine utterance had the effect of creation. The word itself was sufficient for five-and-a-half days;

[12] Sacks (2005, p. 191) reiterates that the significance of the account of Creation in Job is that it is not anthropocentric.

[13] Translated as 'unformed and void' (Genesis 1:2), but perhaps best understood as 'chaos'.

[14] Aramaic/Hebrew: bara—created; k'dabra—as spoken.

but not so with humans. Before God created humans, He consulted, *Midrash* says, with the angels, and said 'Let Us make man in Our image'[15]. Humans were created differently and 'in the image of God'[16]. And when He saw His creation it was 'very good'[17].

Yet the description of the creation at the end of the first chapter of Genesis[18] is premature as a summary of the condition of the world. Humans are not completely finished, not yet quite 'in God's image'. God warns them (Adam, the first human,) not to eat of the fruit of the tree of knowledge of good and evil and the snake is able to taunt that eating the fruit would make humans 'like angels, knowing good from evil'.[19] Like angels, in OUR image, knowing good from evil—the intention inherent in the creation of humans from the beginning.

When the world was created, it contained the potential for both good and evil. Humans, in the image of God, were intended to know good from evil, to experience the full expanse of creation, and their eating from the tree in the centre of the garden was their destiny. Humans could not remain in the Garden of Eden if they were to fulfill their role as divine representatives on earth. They needed to know what was beyond. With such knowledge comes suffering. It is part of the human condition.

For the first ten generations, humans had no reason to suspect that suffering was anything other than punishment. Adam and Eve suffered as a result of their disobedience. Cain was sent into exile because of his sin. Noah watched his entire generation drown because they had become so evil. It was not until Abraham, that there was any suggestion that suffering could be part of the divine plan, quite apart from divine retribution.

Abraham's tests, particularly his final test, the *akeidah*, were not punishments. One Jewish understanding is that the purpose of the tests was to help Abraham learn precisely the lesson that is inherent in the Book of Job: although God has promised blessings as a reward for obedience, the reasons for obedience cannot and must not be the rewards. Humans cannot demand the rewards or blessings they believe they have earned from God—not in this life and not even in the world to come. Although Abraham was not, ultimately, required to sacrifice his son, the possibility that God might demand such suffering is firmly posited. The creation, which is God's ultimate act of providence, includes evil and suffering. It is a narrow understanding of what constitutes 'very good' that denies the possibility of the suffering of the innocent.

Disinterested Piety

Job's suffering is God's doing. In the Epilogue, Job's previous material possessions are restored to him in double measure. Robert Gordis noted that theft requires a double repayment (Ex. 22:3, 6) as if God is admitting the theft of Job's property

[15] Genesis (Genesis) 1:26.

[16] Genesis 1:27.

[17] Genesis 1:31.

[18] Genesis.

[19] Genesis 3:5.

(Gordis 1978, p. 576). Job has another seven sons and three daughters, his children allegorically resurrected.

Can the death of his seven sons and three daughters be forgotten or forgiven? Can seven more sons and three more daughters ever replace his original children? Can a dead child, let alone ten dead children, ever be replaced? Elie Wiesel says he "was offended by [Job's] surrender.... He should have said to God: very well, I forgive you... but what about my dead children, do they forgive you (Safire 1992, p. 35)?" Can Job die old and full of days (42:17), that is, be fulfilled, after having buried ten children? The reader wishes to cry out, as Levi Yitzchak of Berditchev once suggested as a prayer on The Day of Atonement: 'So on this holy night, our sacred Yom Kippur, if You forgive us, we will forgive You!' (Rabbi Reiss).[20] As Sacks says, 'On trial in the Book of Job is not Job but God (Sacks 2005, p. 192).'

Sacks summarises Job as follows: 'The Book of Job is the space God makes for the human voice to be taken to its very limits and beyond—sacred scripture giving human protest its hour on the stage and conferring on it a lonely but unshakeable dignity. Job is a sustained cry of pain at the inequity of misfortune (Sacks 2005, p. 189).'

The message that some learn from the Book of Job is that God is God; neither a just God nor an unjust God (Tsevat 1981). Humans must simply accept that and expect nothing. Maimonides (13th Century), acknowledged as the greatest and certainly the most influential Jewish philosopher of all times, posited this in his foundational work, *Guide to the Perplexed,* and this is what Tsevat has defined as "disinterested piety (Tsevat 1981)." God states that humanity must love God for the sake of heaven and for love of God. Satan states that humanity loves God for fear of the consequences. God insists that true piety is 'disinterested'.

Job never learns the cause of his suffering, (the challenge by Satan,) but after seeing God and speaking to Him, he accepts God's management of the world. Job is disinterestedly pious. At the end of the Book, he concludes that to see God and to know that you cannot know God are sufficient rewards in themselves.

This interpretation is consistent with the philosophy of modern Israeli philosopher, Yeshayahu Leibowitz, who focuses on man's function in the world as being simply that of love of and service to God. Leibowitz maintains that Job is being tested by God—and his trial is the continuation of that of Abraham's in the a*keidah.* Job, after his encounter with God: [He]... understands that he must decide whether to commit himself to faith in God and to His service in the world as it is, to believe in Him and serve Him not for his (Job's) benefit, but because of His divinity (Goldman 1992, p. 52).

[20] Known as the Berdichever Rebbe, Rabbi and Hasidic leader (1740–1810), quoted in (Rabbi Reiss).

God's Justice is Beyond Our Justice

The message of Job is not dissimilar from the Talmudic story recounting the fate of Rabbi Akiva, who, we are told, understood his personal suffering as an opportunity for serving the Almighty.

Rav Judah said in the name of Rav: When Moses ascended on high he found the Holy One of Blessing, engaged in affixing coronets to the letters. Said Moses, "Lord of the Universe, Who stays your hand?" He answered, "There will arise a man, at the end of many generations, Akiba B. Joseph by name, who will expound upon each letter of Torah heaps and heaps of laws." "Lord of the Universe," said Moses; "permit me to see him." He replied, "Turn around." Moses went and sat down behind eight rows [and listened to the discourses upon the law]. Not being able to follow their arguments he was ill at ease, but when they came to a certain subject and the disciples said to the master "Whence do you know it?" and the latter replied "It is a law given to Moses at Sinai" and he was comforted. Thereupon he returned to the Holy One of Blessing, and said, "Lord of the Universe, you have such a man and you give the Torah by me!" He replied, "Be silent, for such is my decree." Then said Moses, "Lord of the Universe, you have shown me his Torah, show me his reward." "Turn around," said He; and Moses turned around and saw them weighing out his flesh at the market-stalls. "Lord of the Universe," cried Moses, "such Torah, and such a reward!" He replied, "Be silent, for such is my decree." [21]

Moses is told to be silent. He cannot hope to understand the Divine decree. He needs to recognize that justice, as we know it, is not part of that decree. Job, too, is forced into silence. When Job declares that he withdraws and recants, he recognizes first that God has responded to him, and secondly that God's essence is more than justice. He is the Sovereign of the world. For God, justice and power are congruent, even if not for man. Job searched for justice and found God's truth and knowledge, just as Abraham having known of God's justice, found in obedience to Him God's truth and knowledge.

We Are Still Responsible

As Martin Buber said of Job: "He believes now in justice in spite of believing in God and he believes in God in spite of believing in justice (Buber 1949, p. 192)." Perhaps as Elie Wiesel commented on Job "we know that it is given to man to transform divine injustice into human justice and compassion (Safire 1992, p. 29)." Thus God has put the onus back where it belongs—on Man. The idea that we cannot understand suffering does not relieve us from the obligation to prevent it if we are able. The paradox of Divine Justice is in God's realm. The problem of human injustice and suffering is in ours.

---

[21] Talmud *Menachot* 29a–b.

Bibliography

Bowker, J. 1970. *Problems of suffering in religions of the world.* Cambridge: Cambridge Univ. Press.

Buber, Martin. 1949. *The prophetic faith.* New York: Macmillan.

Fackenheim, Emil. 1982. *To mend the world.* New York: Schocken Books.

Frankl, Viktor. 1997. *Man's search for meaning*, rev. edn. New York: Washington Square Press.

Gaon, Saadia (Sa'id'Ibn Yusuf). 1967. *Book of beliefs and opinions*, Part 5, Chap. 3. Trans. S. Rosenblatt. New Haven: Yale Univ. Press.

Goldman, Eliezer, ed. 1992. *Judaism, human values, and the Jewish state.* Cambridge: Harvard Univ. Press.

Gordis, Robert. 1978. *The Book of Job.* New York: Jewish Theological Seminary.

Greenberg, Moshe. 1987. Job. In *The literary guide to the Bible*, eds. R. Alter and F. Kermode. Cambridge: Harvard Univ. Press.

Greenberg, Moshe. 1995. *Studies in the Bible and Jewish thought.* Philadelphia: Jewish Publication Society.

Pfeffer, Jeremy I. 2003. *Malbim' Job: The Book of Job, newly translated and interpreted according to the commentary of Rabbi Meir Lebush Malbim.* Jersey City: KTAV Publishing House.

Josephus. 2003. *The Jewish War.* Trans. G. Williamson. Harmondsworth: Penguin.

Kaplan, Mordecai. 1958. *Judaism without supernaturalism.* New York: Reconstructionist Press.

Kraemer, David. 1994. *Responses to suffering in classical rabbinic literature.* New York: Oxford Univ. Press.

Kushner, Harold. 1982. *When bad things happen to good people.* London: Pan Books.

Leaman, Oliver. 1995. *Evil and suffering in Jewish philosophy.* Cambridge: Cambridge Univ. Press.

Levi, Primo. 2006. *If this is a man and the truce.* London: Abacus.

Levinas, Emmanuel. 1989. *The Levinas reader*, ed. Sean Hand. Oxford: Blackwell.

Maimonides, Moses. 1963. *The guide of the perplexed*, vol. 3. Trans. S. Pines. Chicago: Univ. of Chicago Press.

Neusner, Jacob. 1999. *The theology of the oral torah: Revealing the justice of God.* Montreal: McGill-Queen's Univ. Press.

Reiss, Rabbi Moshe. *The fall and rise of job, the dissenter.* www.moshereiss.org/articles/14_job.htm. Accessed Jan 2012.

Rosenberg, Shalom. 1989. *Good and evil in Jewish thought.* Tel Aviv: MOD Books.

Sacks, Rabbi Jonathan. 1982. *'Explaining suffering' in issues in Jewish thought*, 2nd series. London: United Synagogue.

Sacks, Rabbi Jonathan. 2005. *To heal a fractured world.* New York: Schocken Books.

Safire, William. 1992. *The First dissident: The Book of Job in today's politics.* New York: Random House.

Spinoza, Baruch. 1996. *Ethics*, ed. E. Curley. Trans. E. Curley. London: Penguin.

Tsevat, M. 1981. *The meaning of the Book of Job and other biblical studies: Essays on the literature and religion of the Hebrew Bible.* New York: Ktav.

Wiesel, Elie. 1994. *Messengers of God.* New York: Random House.

Wiesel, Elie. 1996. *Night.* London: Penguin.

Zornberg, A. G. 1995. *The beginning of desire: Reflections on genesis.* New York: Double Day.

Chapter 10
The Meaning and the Experience of Suffering: A Historian's Perspective

Nicholas Tarling

You will expect an historian to think and speak in terms of time, and of what Adrian Moulyn calls 'objective' time, time that is measured by clocks and calendars, rather than 'subjective' time, time that is less mathematically measured by an individual's memory and recalled experience (Moulyn 1982, p. 15).

In the course of time—both kinds, but particularly the former—the historian will point out, with the aid of the lexicographer, that the meanings of words change: they 'slip, slide, perish,' as Eliot put it, but are also revised or reappropriated. The verb 'suffer' has two main meanings. One relates to the undergoing of generally painful experience. 'A brave man suffers in silence.' 'He had suffered from delirium tremens.' The other relates to allowing or tolerating. 'I was not suffered to stir far from the house, lest I should run away.' 'Suffer the little children to come unto Me.' The second meaning has largely perished. Perhaps it retains a foothold in an adjectival opposite, 'insufferable', though even that useful word has been displaced, like 'wrong,' by the pussy-footing 'inappropriate.'

Yet the two meanings may have had a connexion, and that may introduce a discussion, not of the meaning of the word 'suffering', but of the 'meaning', if any, of the experience. The connexion surely implies that the experience was something to be borne, to be endured, put up with. 'Suffering' as a noun was indeed defined as patient endurance, long-suffering, and as an adjective it suggested 'inured to suffering,' 'submissive.'

Perhaps these shifts point to changes over time in the conception of the experience, in the ways it is given 'meaning'. That raises fundamental questions to which all our disciplines offer but a partial answer, and history, perhaps, not one of the larger. They relate to the mysteries of the human condition itself. 'Suffering' relates to a whole range of experiences and it is both general and individual. What some experience as a major form of suffering, others find quite minor. Some cope better than others with what are among its major sources: the dread of death, the fear of loneliness.

N. Tarling (✉)
New Zealand Asia Institute, University of Auckland, Auckland, New Zealand
e-mail: n.tarling@auckland.ac.nz

J. Malpas, N. Lickiss (eds.), *Perspectives on Human Suffering*,
DOI 10.1007/978-94-007-2795-3_10,

In the past religions offered meanings now less readily acceptable. They also offered the prospect of redemption. For the Buddhists suffering was a fundamental constituent of being, a punishment for sins committed in a previous incarnation. To supersede the suffering that arose from desire, one must leave desire behind, leave the world behind. For the people of Israel, suffering was the punishment of sins committed by individuals and by the whole community. A messiah would bring redemption. In Christianity suffering comes from sin. But God loves the world and gives his Son as a promise of redemption to those who are penitent and love Him.

These ideas remained and remain potent. They were, of course, challenged, by both the Enlightenment and by Romanticism. What alternatives did they offer? For the Romantic artist, the answer might be an 'heroic' approach. Through a work of your own creation, you would both use and displace suffering, investing in a hedge against annihilation.

It was not necessarily, however, entirely a matter of finding alternatives. In the grip of his own suffering—torn between spiritual aspiration and fleshly pleasure—Wagner focused his creative work on the theme of 'redemption'. In *Parsifal* the Redeemer himself is redeemed, since his sacrifice is shown not to be in vain. 'The intended outcome of Christ's voluntary deed of suffering is fulfilled through imitation.' Parsifal is the redeemer of the Redeemer. He imitates Christ and 'completes Christ's deed of salvation through this imitation' (Kienzle 2005, pp. 128–129).

Wagner's sufferings were not material. Though at times in poverty or in flight, he was seldom at a loss for support or patronage, however outrageous his behaviour. When the outlook was bleak, he called, rightly perhaps, for champagne. Yet for many Romantics material suffering was essential for the production of 'great' art.

Certainly that was the background for the 'Bohemia' of the Paris of Louis Philippe, so brilliantly depicted by Henri Murger, and later, by a process just short of sentimentalisation, made into the most popular of operas by Puccini. It was inhabited by men like the Desbrosses brothers, one nicknamed 'The Christ', one 'The Gothic'. They spent 'half the day not eating and the other half of dying of cold.... As for a fire, all they have is their pipes—very often without tobacco' (Richardson 1982, p. 36). It was also inhabited by 'amateurs.' 'To enter that paradise they leave their home, or the study which would have brought about a sure result, turning their backs abruptly on an honourable career for the quest of adventures and a life of uncertain chances. But since the most robust can hardly cling to a mode of life which would send Hercules into a consumption, they throw up the game before long, scamper back in hot haste to the paternal roast, marry their little cousin, set up as notaries in some town of thirty thousand inhabitants, and of an evening by the fireside they have the satisfaction of telling "what they went through in their artist days", with all the pride of a traveller's tale of his tiger hunt' (Murger 1908, pp. xxvi–xxviii).

The legend of the artist in his garret had been born. If it did not exist, suffering had to be invented if 'art' were to be created. 'If you are really to develop to your full stature,' W.H. Auden told Benjamin Britten in 1942, 'you will have, I think, to suffer, and make others suffer in ways which are totally strange to you at present' (Tippins 2006, p. 248).

The notion that there is a connexion has endured, and there may be a truth in it. Shostakovich, Richard Taruskin has suggested, 'was perhaps the most pestered composer who ever lived.' The Soviet regime feared the 'uncontainable' in his music, tried to contain it 'whether by denunciation or adulation, coercion or cajolery, censorship or co-option,' though never by 'neglect or indifference' (Taruskin 2005, p. 372). How did that affect it? Did the suffering the regime caused the composer indeed improve his music? 'Millions of people, the flower of the nation,' lived under the regime, 'vacillating,' as Levon Hakobian puts it, 'between fairly understandable and conscious conformism and an awareness of being constantly faced with something alien, objectionable, and sinister.' That 'engendered an extraordinarily rich psychological background for every kind of reflection on the ultimate and most profound metaphysical questions' (Hakobian 2005, p. 226).

What is certain is that audiences responded to his works, which, by demonstrably sharing their ambivalence, in a measure redeemed their suffering. 'For many of us,' a Russian emigré said, 'listening to a new piece by Shostakovich was a sacred experience' (Mitchinson 2005, p. 318). 'He could not disregard the inner deception of our existence,' Victor Bobrovsky wrote, 'the pain he experienced for us all, for our spiritual impurity, for the daily desecration of the truth, this was what summoned his muse to life' (Kovnatskaya 2005, p. 250).

If artists can achieve that, can others? Perhaps artists are fortunate inasmuch as their creativity may be shared, its power redoubled. Is suffering creative for others? Or, at least, can it be made so? Most of us are aware that some suffering is often a condition of achievement: we agonisingly practise, we train, we are nervous before we go on stage, give a lecture, make a speech; and many would argue that what we do is better as a result—our performance has an edge, an excitement. Less obvious, perhaps, is the possibility that such achievement, though attained with some suffering, holds at bay, if it does not defeat, the deeper suffering brought by the fear of loneliness and, deeper yet, the dread of death.

Such arguments are offered by Moulyn, and are surely to be placed in the context of a yet more recent historical trend. On the one hand, advances in biotechnology suggest a yet more mechanistic and deterministic approach to the mysteries of the human condition. On the other hand, advances in medical science, in particular in the invention and use of drugs, make it possible to eliminate some of the sources of suffering and to reduce the pain of other sorts. We live longer. But some live only part of a life, dumbed by drugs, demented in old age. In the late twentieth century, as Joanna Bourke puts it, '[n]ot only was the soul absent from deathbed considerations, the body itself was hooked to a machine that took precedence over the free will of the dying person.... The medicalisation of death finally stripped the Beyond of both heaven and hell, leaving dying people with little to ward off their fears of annihilation' (Bourke 2005, pp. 320–321). Is it death that is to be dreaded or an unintelligent existence? Has suffering been unnecessarily prolonged? Who is to say?

I take it that there is, as a result, a number of arguments in the medical and caring professions which others can conduct better than historians, or at least this historian. But I cannot help wondering whether Moulyn's answer is more than a partial one. '[E]ven if all suffering had some beneficial office, it would still be impossible to defend the amount of suffering that exists,' writes John Laird. 'Cancer may give an occasion for fortitude and for a certain melancholy dignity, but, in its case, anodynes are better than dignity and most of the suffering is sheer waste' (John Laird in Fisher et al. 2002).

In extreme circumstances—such as the death camps—some have been able to resort to creativity, both prompted by and assuaging their suffering, and Moulyn writes of 'sagas of creative people who do not give in and do not give up.' He advocates 'the heroic life-style' (Moulyn 1982, p. 195, 289). But while he is at pains to suggest that the concept does not apply only to Socrates or Beethoven, we cannot help wondering whether we can hope to live up to it, and whether, even if we have kept loneliness at bay by albeit painful creativity, we shall be able to cope with the dread of death, the end of subjective time, and, perhaps, the end, so far we are concerned, of objective time as well.

Yet another recent change, at least in part a connected one, may be signalled by the historian. We have increased our capacity to recall; we have also increased our recourse to 'memory.' It is, of course, nothing new to honour ancestors, to remember the dead, to set up memorials, to find that place evokes past. Maybe, however, we now go further, substituting human memory for God's enumeration.

Visiting the family home, the great early twentieth-century Polish composer Karol Szymanowski heard it 'whisper, quietly telling the tale of days long ago.' He listened: did he not hear his father's voice? 'That evening, I realised that people do not completely die; the sweet shades of their words and smiles become for ever one with everything which surrounded them in life—one has only to know how to summon the dead and to hear what they have to say' (Wightman 1999, p. 53).

> [T]he vanishing of people we love, forever, is not an easy thing to continue to live with. But we can give their lives and their dying meaning by letting go—letting go because of what the person has meant to us, and because we love that person for the memory of what he or she continues to mean for us. That is the hope we can give to the suffering of those we love. This is a way of redeeming suffering.' (Fisher et al. 2002, p. 73)

Robert Fisher is writing of those we know and love and of the risk that we prolong their suffering though hope is lost. Yet what of those we have never known and might have found it impossible to love? Perhaps that is the point of memorials, of 'sites' of memory, even though they may be constructed in a spirit of vainglory.

The historian before you is not a music historian, whether that is obvious or not, but a political one, in particular an historian of imperialism and international relations. Though it may be his dearest wish, the historian, as J.A. Froude recognized, cannot hope to enter the mind of others. The motivation even of the heroes remains obscure. What can the historian hope to say about the sufferings of those who fought in wars or suffered tortures? Only a little, and rather generalised. To some extent, it may be that the fear of loneliness overcame the dread of death. Men risked death together.

They also created other worlds of meaning. The enforced submission of Cambodia to reunited Nguyen Vietnam, along with increased corvée and Vietnamese colonization, prompted rebellion in the eastern provinces in 1820–1821, led by a monk called Kai. He

> washed the heads of his soldiers, reciting sutra to give them strength, and shaking drops of water on to them to keep the Vietnamese from dispersing them in battle. If the Vietnamese fired guns, the power of the Khmer would keep the bullets from going far or coming close to them. When Kai's blessings were over, his soldiers lost their apathy, and went out to battle the Vietnamese. (1869 poem, Chandler 1975, pp. 16–24)

That may seem incomprehensible, until we recall the men who went away to war in 1914.

In the Philippines—which had not known Buddhism, nor, for the most part, Islam—such popular attitudes took on Christian features. As Rafael Ileto has shown, the dramatised epic of Christ's resurrection helped to shape a view of the world that fused elements of the remote past and of the introduced religion. A Kristo was a man of power, lowly and humble, but superior to the priests of the establishment. To die for his cause was to see Heaven. Maybe here we see a popular version of the 'creativity' of which Moulyn writes. Certainly we can see an elite version in the Spanish Philippines. There elements of the elite identified the suffering of the people and identified with the people. The same happened in Europe. Dimitri Karakozov wondered

> why my beloved simple Russian people has to suffer so much!… why next to the eternal simple peasant and the labourer in his factory and workshop are there people who do nothing—idle nobles, a horde of officials and other wealthy people, all living in shining houses?… The man really responsible is the Tsar. (Venturi 1960, pp. 345–346)

He would kill the Tsar, Alexander II, and die for the people. He tried in vain. Years later another was to succeed, and kill others as well. For Mazzini, the nation had displaced God: it was [again] beautiful to die pro patria mori. For Ben Anderson, it is too impoverished an idea to justify such sacrifice. Why have so many died for 'such limited imaginings' (Anderson 1991, p. 7)?

Attempting to create a unified nation, Indonesian leaders pictured a community of suffering under the Dutch, shared for 300 years, though in fact Dutch rule had not extended so far for so long.

For others Christianity provided a metaphor, a powerful one, though clearly not the only possible one. It was, of course, strongest of all in the Philippines, Christianised from the late sixteenth century onwards. The great nationalist polymath, Jose Rizal came, it seems, to construct his life as a sacrifice, giving it meaning by seeking or accepting martyrdom.

'Alas, Jose!' a townmate wrote to him in 1889. 'All the people here ask about you and pin their hope on you. Even the poorest people of the mountains are asking about your return. It seems that they consider you the second Jesus who will liberate them from misery (Ileto 1979, p. 313)!' He returned to the Philippines, was arrested, and, when the Katipunan revolt broke out in 1896, was executed.

> Land of my idolatry, my misery of miseries,
> Beloved Philippines, hear this last farewell.
> I give you now my all, my parents, all I have loved.
> I go to where there are no slaves, no hangmen, no oppressors,
> Where faith does not slay, where he who reigns is God. (Coates 1968, p. 323)

Nationalism, the nation state, and the relations among nation-states continue to construct our lives. They construct deaths, too, including the death of those in the past, who were or may be retroactively made members of a nation. The Second World War produced great suffering. After the first war, the discourse was of guilt; after the second of apology, and subsequent globalisation has expanded it. The suffering caused by disease and dementia remains a mystery, no easier to explain or accept than it was. For the suffering inflicted by human beings on other human beings, apology is possible. Even in the case of individuals, however, its redemptive character may be undermined by inadequacy or by suspicion of insincerity. Apologising for the actions of a people, or the majority of a people, or a government that may have acted for it, must surely be still more questionable, particularly if those who suffered are dead, and those who are apologising, or on whose behalf apology is being tendered, were not themselves involved. Sincerity may not be obliterated. But it is hard to avoid the conclusion that such apologies may have additional, if not alternative, purposes. Apology—sometimes accompanied by monetary payment—may be designed to shape consensus within the nation-state, for whom the past is often a source of legitimation. It may be designed to improve relations with another nation-state.

The first President Bush apologized in 1990 for the incarceration of Japanese Americans at the outset of the Pacific war. In 2002 the Clark government in New Zealand apologized for the discriminatory poll tax levied on early Chinese settlers in New Zealand. The main focus of the discourse has, however, been on German and Japanese actions in the 1930s and 1940s, and more particularly on the Japanese. Meeting the President of Korea in 1990 Prime Minister Kaifu Toshiki apologized in respect of the 'unbearable grief and suffering' caused by 'the actions of our country,' and Miyazawa Kiichi repeated the words in 1992 (Yamazaki 2006, p. 42, 60). But, for Japan, as Yamazaki puts it, 'the apology has become a ritual of remorse that… has yet to reach its potential in providing reconciliation with the past, with its neighbors and with the international community' (Yamazaki 2006, p. 139).

Perhaps academics should not be too hard on such politicians, for there is a risk, too, in their activities, even though they focus on explanation rather than expiation. 'Academics observe, analyze, and try to explain human behavior. In so doing… we exploit the experience, and even perhaps, the suffering of others.' In our attempts to explain, as Yamazaki says, 'we distance ourselves and the reader from truly recognizing the suffering and wrongdoing of our subjects. In explaining, we somehow explain away' (Yamazaki 2006, p. viii). There is another risk, however, one that, say, James Warren does not avoid in his fascinating alternative histories of Singapore, his account of the rickshaw coolies, for example: the work comes to seem sentimental, the author preachy (Warren 1986). Perhaps there is no better way, at least for the historian, than trying to tell it as it was, and evoking memory, stimulating reflection, rather than calling for apology.

Bibliography

Anderson, Benedict. 1991. *Imagined communities*. London: Verso.
Bourke, Joanna. 2005. *Fear*. London: Virago.
Chandler, David. 1975. An anti-Vietnamese rebellion in nineteenth century Cambodia. *Journal of Southeast Asian Studies* 6: 16–24, 21.
Coates, Austin. 1968. *Rizal, Philippine nationalist and martyr*. Hong Kong: Oxford Univ. Press.
Fisher, Robert, N., Daniel T. Primozic, Peter, A. Day, and Joel, A. Thompson, eds. 2002. *Suffering, death and identity*. Amsterdam: Rodopi.
Hakobian, Levon. 2005. A perspective on Soviet musical culture during the lifetime of Shostakovitch. In *A Shostakovitch casebook*, ed. Brown, Malcom Hamrick. Bloomington: Indiana Univ. Press.
Ileto, Reynaldo. 1979. *Pasyon and revolution*. Quezon City: Ateneo de Manila Univ. Press.
Kienzle, Ulrike. 2005. Parsifal and religion: A Christian music drama? In *A companion to Wagner's Parsifal*, eds. W. Kinderman and Katherine R. Syer. Rochester: Camden House.
Kovnatskaya, Ludmila. 2005. Dialogues about Shostakovitch. In *A Shostakovitch casebook*, ed. Brown, Malcom Hamrick. Bloomington: Indiana Univ. Press.
Mitchinson, Paul. 2005. The Shostakovitch variations. In *A Shostakovitch casebook*, ed. Brown, Malcom Hamrick. Bloomington: Indiana Univ. Press.
Moulyn, Adrian C. 1982. *The meaning of suffering*. Westport: Greenwood.
Murger, Henry. 1908. Preface to *Scènes de la vie de bohème*. Paris: Lévy Frères. English edition: Murger, Henry. 1908. *The Latin Quarter*. Trans. E. Marriage and J. Selwyn. London: Greening.
Richardson, Joanna. 1982. Henry Murger and La vie de bohème. In *English National Opera Guide*, no. 14. London: Calder; New York: Riverrun.
Taruskin, Richard. 2005. When serious music mattered. In *A Shostakovitch casebook*, ed. Brown, Malcom Hamrick. Bloomington: Indiana Univ. Press.
Tippins, Sherill. 2006. *February house*. London: Pocket Books.
Venturi, Franco. 1960. *Roots of revolution*. London: Weidenfeld and Nicolson.
Warren, James. 1986. *Rickshaw coolie: A people's history of Singapore*. Singapore: Oxford Univ. Press.
Wightman, Alistair. 1999. *Karol Szymanowski*. Aldershot: Ashgate.
Yamazaki, Jane W. 2006. *Japanese apologies for World War II: A rhetorical study*. London: Routledge.

Chapter 11
Jewish Responses to Suffering

Paul Turner

Introduction

In terms of a religious framework, the dilemma of suffering presents two challenges—how can the Divine permit the existence of suffering, and as members of a religious group, how can we maintain our faith when we experience it? We seek meaning and structure to our lives; nothing threatens our sense of order and being more than the experience of suffering. It is a phenomenon that all religions have had to deal with, and Judaism is no exception.

For over 2,500 years, the Jewish people have lived through events which have challenged their very existence. From the conquest of Israel and Jerusalem by the Babylonians in 586 BCE to the persecutions of the Crusader period, mass expulsions, blood libels and pogroms culminating in the European Holocaust—nothing has challenged Jewish theology more than anti-Semitism. Suffering and evil is difficult enough to comprehend at a personal level; but at a national level, state-sponsored persecution has raised additional challenges. As Elie Wiesel, a Holocaust survivor, writes:

> Some talked of God, of His mysterious ways, of the sins of the Jewish people and of their future deliverance. But I had ceased to pray. How I sympathised with Job! I did not deny God's existence, but I doubted His Absolute justice… Why should I bless His name? The Eternal, Lord of the Universe, the all-powerful and terrible was silent. What had I to thank Him for? (Wiesel 1996)

The religious leadership of the Jews—the rabbis—were therefore left with little option but to provide a response. This paper does not suggest *solutions* to the challenge of theodicy, rather an insight into the range of responses that are found within the early rabbinical tradition.

P. Turner (✉)
Sydney Medical School, University of Sydney, Sydney 2006, NSW, Australia
e-mail: paulyt@doctors.org.uk

J. Malpas, N. Lickiss (eds.), *Perspectives on Human Suffering*,
DOI 10.1007/978-94-007-2795-3_11, © Springer Science+Business Media B.V. 2012

Rabbinical Literature

The earliest rabbinical writings originate from the *Tannaitic* period, a time which encompasses the Roman invasion of Israel leading to the destruction of the second Jewish Temple in the year 70 CE. Politics had not succeeded in preventing this tragedy, and subsequent rebellions by the Israelites (including the events at Masada and the Bar Kochba revolt around 135 CE) resulted in the decimation of the community (many historical records reporting over 500,000 deaths) (Josephus 2003). With the failure of political and military leadership, the rabbis took charge. In the second century CE, Rabbi Judah the Prince (also known simply as 'Rabbi'), the patriarch of the Jewish community in Israel, feared that the oral tradition of Jewish law, composed by the rabbis who had preceded him and which complemented the bible texts, would soon be forgotten in the turmoil of the day. He took the historical decision to canonize the core of the tradition to ensure its preservation, and the resulting work was known as the *Mishnah*, meaning 'repetition' or 'teaching'. Rabbi Judah arranged the material into subject area, the vast majority being legal in nature (termed *halakhah*).

A few hundred years after the compilation of the *Mishnah*, the leaders of the remaining community in Jerusalem and the larger, exiled community in Babylon had the same fears as Rabbi Judah. They decided to commit many of their discussions about the *Mishnah* to writing. The resulting works are known either by the Hebrew name *Talmud* or the Aramaic *Gemara* (both meaning 'learning'). The Babylonian *Talmud* was compiled around 600 CE, the Palestinian version (also known as the *Yerushalmi* or Jerusalem *Talmud*) around 200 years earlier. Both are written as a commentary to the *Mishnah*, although they frequently digress onto other issues. The *Talmud* is a record of the rabbinical discussions on legal matters ('*halakhah*') but there are also a significant number of factual or fictional stories ('*aggadah*') and explanations of biblical passages. The *Talmud* continues to be the essential Jewish source text for scholars today, second only to the five books of Moses (Pentateuch or *Torah*).

There are also a number of other rabbinical texts which constitute the *Midrashic* literature. *Midrash*, meaning 'seeking' or 'investigation', is a work that expounds biblical texts. There are two primary categories: *halakhic* and *aggadic*. Unsurprisingly, there are a number of similarities between *Midrashic* works and the *Talmud*, and the same stories will often appear in both. Many *Midrashic* sources are thought to predate *Talmudic* works and provide an insight into rabbinical thought after the Roman invasion.

Early Rabbinical Responses to Suffering

In the Jewish Bible, suffering is typically 'disciplinary' in nature, a consequence of disobeying the word of God. The biblical debate on theodicy is therefore limited, with the notable exception of the book of Job (a subject which is beyond the remit of this essay). While there are instances of suffering as a transitory or illusional phenomenon—for example, in the books of Habakuk and Psalms—for the most part suffering is viewed as a punishment.

The rabbis of the *Mishnaic* period were faced with the challenge of having to provide spiritual leadership in a time when the surviving community was broken and traumatized. Perhaps surprisingly, the *Mishnah* is silent on these events. Indeed, large sections of the *Mishnah* are devoted to the rules of temple life with barely a mention of the fact that with the destruction of the Temple, those rules no longer applied. Jacob Neusner, a 20th century scholar, suggests that for the rabbis to speak about these circumstances would have required the people to confront the pain of recent events. Instead, they focus on a time when the Temple would be rebuilt, thus maintaining a belief in a happier future (Neusner 1999). There is but a single reference to the destruction of the Temple in *Taanit* 4, a text which briefly discusses the mourning rituals to commemorate the destruction. Otherwise, in general, the *Mishnah* perpetuates the biblical concept of suffering: 'For three sins women die in childbirth: because they are not cautious in [their observance of the rules of] family purity, in *challah*[1] and in the lighting of the [Sabbath] candles'.[2]

It is in the later writings that the perspective becomes a little more interesting: 'Rabbi Yannai said: It is not in our hands to explain either the tranquillity of the wicked or the suffering of the righteousness.'[3] There is, therefore, a transition from disciplinary suffering to a theological system where mankind is limited in its understanding of divine events. Indeed, we are told elsewhere that 'You do not know the reward of the commandments'[4] and therefore cannot even begin to comprehend the divine system of reward and punishment.

A further device is introduced in these later texts, that of a belief in the world-to-come. One might suggest that given the turmoil of the times, it was no longer possible to believe in a system where justice could be seen to apply in this physical world, and so the world-to-come offered a theological answer to the paradigm of reward and punishment:

> God causes the righteous to suffer in this world, in order that they will inherit the World to Come… In contrast, He makes the wicked prosper in this world, in order to destroy them and place them at the lowest level… (Babylonian Talmud, Kiddushin 40b)

This theme is taken up by the Jerusalem *Talmud*, though the text continues to discuss the destruction of the Temple in terms of divine retribution, explaining that the Israelites 'loved money and hated one another without cause' and 'worshipped idols and engaged in prohibited sexual relations and shed blood'.[5] In contrast, perhaps due to the remoteness of Babylon from events in the holy land,

---

[1] This is the act of taking a portion of unbaked dough during baking as an offering to God.

[2] *Mishnah,* Shabbat 2:6.

[3] *Mishnah,* Ethics of the Fathers 4:19.

[4] *Mishnah,* Ethics of the Fathers 2:1.

[5] Jerusalem Talmud Yoma 1:1 (38c).

alternative approaches are seen to evolve in the Babylonian writings. There are, of course, many references to biblical interpretations of suffering, but the Babylonian rabbis were not afraid to diverge from the traditional position. For example, in commenting on the story of Cain and Abel, the *Talmud* states:

> This may be compared to a man who struck his son a strong blow, and then put a plaster on his wound, saying to him: 'My son! As long as this plaster is on your wound, you can eat and drink at will, and bathe in hot and cold water, without fear. But if you remove it, it will break into sores.' Thus the Eternal spoke to Israel: 'My children! I created the Evil Desire, but I [also] created the Torah as its antidote; if you occupy yourselves with Torah, you will not be delivered into his hand... But if you do not occupy yourselves with Torah, you shall be delivered into his hand.' (Babylonian Talmud, Kiddushin 30b)

This can be seen as a traditional approach, but one has to ask why the father strikes his son in the first place? The issue is dealt with in another *Midrashic* work:

> As soon as the Eternal said to him, 'Where is your brother Abel?' Cain replied 'I do not know: am I my brother's keeper?'[6] You are the keeper of all creatures; notwithstanding this, you seek him at my hand? To what may this be compared? To a thief who stole something by night, and escaped. In the morning, the guard caught him and asked him: Why did you steal the object? To which the thief replied: I stole but I did not neglect my job. You, however, your job is to keep watch—why did you neglect your job? Now you talk to me like that? So too, Cain said: I killed him because You created in me the evil inclination. You are the keeper of all, yet You allowed me to kill him? It was You who killed him, for if You had accepted my sacrifice, I would not have been jealous of him. (*Midrash Tanhuma,* Genesis 1:9)

In case the point has been missed, Rabbi Shimon b. Yohai, one of the leaders of the early rabbinic tradition, relates in reference to the episode:

> This is a difficult thing to say, and it is impossible to say it clearly. Once two athletes were wrestling before the king. If the king wants, they can be separated; but he did not want them separated. One overcame the other and killed him. The loser cried out as he died: 'Who will get justice for me from the king?' (*Midrash Rabbah,* Genesis Rabbah 22:9)

The interpretation would appear to be this—that it is God who is ultimately responsible for the murder of Abel, an accusation that appears to indict God as the creator of evil and suffering. Christian theodicy is often portrayed in the following terms: 'Either God cannot abolish evil, or He will not. If He cannot, then He is not all-powerful. If He will not, then He is not all-good.'[7] There is an assumption that God is good, a view shared by the rabbis: 'Nothing that is evil descends from above.'[8] The rabbis therefore had to confront the challenge of how suffering can exist in the world, if one is to reject the concept of God creating evil. But one should note the assumption that suffering is necessarily an evil. As we shall see, the rabbis did not always view it as such.

---

[6] Genesis 4:9.

[7] This probably originates from the writings of Augustine—see (Augustine.2008), Book 7, Chap. 5.

[8] *Midrash Rabbah,* Genesis 51:3.

Theodicy—One Dilemma? or Two?

The existence of evil and suffering in the context of a 'good' God was not the only dilemma facing the rabbis. A further challenge was that of divine dualism or Gnosticism—a belief in two deities, a 'good God' who created the world, and another power (referred to as the Demiurge in Greek writings) who seeks to destroy it. In monotheistic thought, the latter might be represented by Satan or the Devil. Gnosticism is thought to have its origins in Greek philosophy from 3rd century BCE. There is no doubt that Platonic thought influenced the rabbinical writings of the period, and the Talmud makes frequent derogatory reference to them. Indeed, the threat to the monotheism was so great that an early Palestinian Sage, Elisha b. Avuyah, is described as becoming a heretic in trying to reconcile the challenge of theodicy:

> How was it that Elisha acted in this manner? They related that once he was sitting and studying by the sea of Galilee when he saw a man who climbed to the top of a date tree and took the dam with the young [so transgressing the commandment of Deuteronomy 22:6] and descended safely. At the conclusion of the Sabbath, he saw another man climb the tree and take the young, but let the dam go; when he descended a snake bit him and he died. He said: It is written: 'You shall let the dam go, but the young you may take for yourself, in order that it may be well with you and your days will be prolonged'.[9] Where is the goodness, and where the length of days for this man? (*Midrash Rabbah,* Ruth 77–78)

Elisha b. Avuyah is asking the time-old question—why do the wicked prosper, and the righteous suffer? The *Talmud* relates the same incident, answering: '[the verse] means on the day that is wholly good; and in order that your days may be long, on the day that is wholly long'[10]—namely, that the reward will come in the next life. But whether the *Talmud* accepts this answer, it clearly sympathises with the injustice of the situation. It is in a third text (*Chaggiga* 15a) that Elisha b. Avuya is accused of the heretical belief in two divine beings (and even here, there is textual evidence to suggest that this reference was a later addition).

The rabbis therefore had two challenges: To explain both the existence of suffering and to clarify how it could originate from the Divine, something tradition readily acknowledges: 'I am the Eternal, there is none else; beside me there is no god. I form light and create darkness, I make peace and create evil—I, the Eternal, do all these things.'[11] Jonathan Sacks suggests that the threat from dualism was so great the rabbis, incredibly, introduced this verse into the daily liturgy, (Sacks 1982) but only after amending the wording to read: 'Blessed are You, Lord, King of the Universe, who forms light and creates darkness, who makes peace and creates *everything*.' We can only guess as to the reason for this, though one can postulate that the recital of a daily blessing attributing evil to the Divine might prove controversial. Nonetheless, there is no doubt as to the rabbis' own beliefs. Commenting on the creation story in Genesis, the *Midrash* states: 'God saw all that He had made,

---

[9] Deuteronomy 22:7.

[10] Babylonian Talmud, Kiddushin 39b.

[11] Isaiah 45:5,7.

and behold it was *very* good.'[12]—this [use of emphasis] refers to the evil inclination, to sufferings, to *Gehinnom*, to punishments, to the angel of death.[13] The *Talmud* does not elaborate further on this concept, and it is the rabbinical philosophers of the middle ages who provide further explanation. Maimonides, a prominent 13th century philosopher, provides a useful summary in his *Guide of the Perplexed*:

> It will be known with certainty that it may in no way be said of God that He produces evil in an essential act; I mean that He has a primary intention to produce evil. This cannot be correct. Rather, all His acts are an absolute good; for only he produces being and all being is good. On the other hand, all the evils are privations… (Maimonides 1963, III 10, 17b)

Maimonides describes three domains of suffering: those due to the limitations inherent in the physical nature of man; those that are self-inflicted; and those inflicted by others upon man. All three are, in his opinion, a consequence of an absence—in the case of the latter two, an absence of reason which permits irrational thoughts and actions to result:

> Just as the blind man, since he cannot see, and also since there is no one to show him the way, hurts himself and inflicts wounds on others, so are there sects among men: each of them, in the measure of its foolishness, inflicts great evils on itself and on others. (Maimonides 1963, III 11)

In his essay Good and Evil in Jewish Thought, Shalom Rosenberg provides a suitable commentary:

> Let us assume that someone has entered a lighted room and turned the light off. Someone else now enters and asks, colloquially, 'Who has made darkness by turning off the light?' … Evil in comparison with good is like darkness in comparison with light. It is not the contrast between one being and another being, but between a being and its absence. It is something which is missing; and although you can say, apparently, that someone 'made darkness', it is only language which is deceiving you, or by means of which you deceive yourself. Thus we should realise that we do not really 'make' darkness, since darkness is nothing but a privation. In the same manner, God, who is the source of all and of the whole of reality, is also the source of evil. The prophet says that God 'forms the light and creates darkness, makes peace and creates evil' meaning, in fact, that God made light, and this is the creation of something positive. But in the nature of things, together with the formation of light, the possibility of darkness also arises. With the creation of good, there appears also to the possibility of its privation, of evil… (Rosenberg 1989)

Maimonides does not explain in explicit terms why God created a system to function in this way, though he hints at it in his discussion of divine providence. In allowing man to exist, God has necessarily created an imperfect world which man can improve. This imperfection allows for the possibility of suffering. Maimonides believes that those who attract divine providence do not experience suffering, though he also provides a limitation that 'providence watches over thoughts and not the bearer of those thoughts' (Maimonides 1963, III 51, 127a). Unfortunately, a consequence of his approach is that the experience of evil/suffering becomes so distant from the Divine that perhaps the Divine is irrelevant in the theological response to

[12] Genesis 1:31.

[13] *Midrash Rabbah,* Genesis 9:7–11.

suffering. This is a common problem in texts on theodicy, and we shall therefore return to the rabbinical writings to further analyse responses to this challenge. In the Talmud, the question is not 'Why is there evil', but rather, why does evil seem to affect the wrong people? The issue involves the unfair distribution of suffering, rather than its existence.

Suffering in the Babylonian Talmud

In contrast to the Jerusalem *Talmud*, the Babylonian writings frequently include texts which question the biblical premise that the righteous do not suffer. One example is the treatment of Job in the book of *Bava Batra*. A number of accusations are levelled at Job, that he somehow deserved the suffering inflicted upon him. However, the context in which the *Talmud* brings the example of Job is a legal text dealing with the appropriate behaviour of the righteous in matters of property. Job is thus cited as an example of a righteous man, despite the accusations made. The text clearly considers Job to be righteous, and that this status was not diminished through his protests against his experience of suffering.

Elsewhere, the *Talmud* describes a number of Sages all of whom reject suffering as a consequence of sin, as well as denying any reward that suffering may bring. This is the concept of 'sufferings of love'—that God brings suffering upon the righteous in order for them to earn a reward:

> Rava (some say Rabbi Chisda) says: If a person sees suffering coming upon him, he should examine his ways, as it says: 'Let us search and examine our ways, and return back to God'.[14] If he searched but did not find [anything wrong]—let him attribute it to [wasting an opportunity to study] Jewish law… If he attributed it thus but still did not find [this to be the cause]—then it is clear these are 'afflictions of love', as it says: 'God reproves those He loves.'[15] Rava recalled Rabbi Sachora said in the name of Rabbi Huna: Anyone whom God has affection for, He afflicts with suffering, as it says: 'And the one whom the Eternal desires, He crushes with illness.' (Isaiah 50:3)

Taken out of context (as this passage often is), one might think that the rabbis are supportive of the notion of 'suffering of love'. Indeed, the passage reminds us of the opinion of Rabbi Shimon b. Yohai, that the Jewish bible, land of Israel and the world-to-come were all given by means of suffering (Babylonian Talmud, Brachot 5a). But the subsequent text makes a number of objections. The first is a requirement for 'sufferings of love' to be accepted willingly; non-acceptance equates to the suffering not being a 'suffering of love'. The text has already rejected the possibility of a sin or inattention to a religious duty being a causative factor, and so the cause of the resulting suffering cannot be explained. The passage continues:

> Rabbi Chiya b. Abba became ill. Rabbi Yochanan went in to him. He said to him: Is suffering dear to you?

---

[14] Ecclesiastes 3:40.

[15] Proverbs 30:3.

> He said to him: Neither it nor its reward.
> He said to him: Give me your hand.
> He gave him his hand and raised (healed) him.
> Rabbi Yochanan became ill. Rabbi Chanina went in to him. He said to him: Is suffering dear to you?
> He said to him: Neither it nor its reward.
> He said to him: Give me your hand.
> He gave him his hand and raised him. (Babylonian Talmud, Brachot 5a)

The text continues to relate a third example, only this time providing additional elaboration. The characters involved are major *Talmudic* figures: Rabbi Eleazar was famous for being childless, while Rabbi Yochanan was a father many times over, but had also experienced the trauma of his tenth son dying in childhood. Elsewhere, he is described as offering 'comfort' to others by showing them a bone, or more likely, a tooth from this tenth son. The passage from *Brachot* 5a quotes an opinion that 'anyone who engages in Torah or deeds of loving kindness, or buries his children, all his sins are forgiven.' However, Rabbi Yochanan objects to this opinion, and the Talmud does not question his view. Thereafter, the text continues:

> Rabbi Eleazar became ill. Rabbi Yochanan went in to him. He saw that he was lying in a dark room. He uncovered his arm and a light fell [over the room] and he saw Rabbi Eleazar was crying. He said to him: why are you crying?
> If it is because of Torah that you have not [studied] sufficiently, we have taught 'it makes no difference whether one does much or little, provided that he directs his heart to heaven.'[16]
> And if it is because of food, not every man may merit two tables [i.e. wealth].
> And if it is because of children, this is the bone of my tenth son [i.e. the pain of burying your own child is more than the pain of being childless].
> [Rabbi Eleazar] said to him: I am crying on account of this beauty that will rot in the earth.
> [Rabbi Yochanan] said to him: For this you should surely cry. And the two of them cried together.
> He said to him: Is suffering dear to you?
> He said to him: Neither it nor its reward.
> He said to him: Give me your hand. He gave him his hand and raised him. (Babylonian Talmud, Brachot 5a)

Despite multiple explanations for the experience of suffering, none are accepted. The suffering, if divine in origin, is relieved by a visiting sage without recourse to prayer to God, and any premise that the suffering might be beneficial is clearly rejected by the sages concerned. This is by no means the only example of such an objection. Perhaps the most astounding case is a discussion of the opinion of Rabbi Ammi, who states: 'There is no death without sin, and no suffering without transgression' (Babylonian Talmud, Shabbat 55a–b).

Rabbi Ammi supports his assertion with a number of biblical quotes, but despite this, the redactor of the *Talmud* cites two anonymous objections to his statement:

> They (the other rabbis) object [quoting a source]: The Ministering Angels said before God: 'Master of the Universe! For what reason have you punished the first person with death?' He said to them: 'I commanded him only one simple commandment, yet he transgressed it!' They said to Him: 'But didn't Moses and Aaron, who observed the whole Torah, die?' (Babylonian Talmud, Shabbat 55a–b)

---

[16] *Mishnah,* Menachot 13:11.

The first objection is that Moses and Aaron died despite obeying the entire Jewish law. The text answers with an opinion from Rabbi Shimon b. Elazar, who states that they died because they failed to obey God's command during the biblical wanderings of the Israelites in the desert, a view which would be familiar to every student of the Bible. The rabbis therefore bring their second objection: 'Four died because the urging of the snake [i.e. the sin of Adam], and who are they? Benjamin the son of Jacob, Amram the father of Moses, and Jesse the father of David, and Calev the son of David' (Babylonian Talmud, Shabbat 55a–b).

The rabbis concede that Moses and Aaron sinned. But what about these other four figures—what sin did they commit? The lack of response indicates that indeed they are blameless. But in order for this view to refute Rabbi Ammi's, the source must be reputable. The text then performs a *Talmudic* sleight of hand, attributing the source to be Rabbi Shimon b. Elazar, the only other figure mentioned in this passage, who coincidentally is senior enough to 'trump' Rabbi Ammi, and therefore: 'We learn from this [that] there is death without sin, and there is suffering without transgression, and the refutation of Rabbi Ammi is a [definite] refutation' (Babylonian Talmud, Shabbat 55a–b).

Although the *Talmud* has only 'disproved' part of Rabbi Ammi's assertion (that death can occur without sin), the text concludes that the entire assertion (i.e. suffering without transgression) must likewise be false. The redactors seem to be pushing the boundaries of *Talmudic* process in order to force the conclusion that suffering is *not* to be understood as punishment for sin.

Perhaps the most unique text on our theme appears in the book of *Chagiga*, where the *Talmud* relates:

> When Rabbi Joseph came to the following text, he cried: 'There are those who find their ends without judgment.'[17] He said: But is there [anyone] who passes [away] before his time? Yes, as [in] the [case] of Rabbi Bibi b. Abbaye, who found himself in the presence of the Angel of Death. [The Angel of Death] said to his messenger: Go bring me Miriam the hairdresser. He went [and] brought him Miriam the kindergarten teacher. [The Angel of Death] said to him: I said to you Miriam the hairdresser. He said to him: If so, I will return her. [The Angel of Death] said to him: Since you have brought her, let her be added to the number. But how were you able [to take] her? [He answered:] She was holding a shovel in her hand and raking the oven. She took it and [accidentally] placed it on her knee and burnt [herself]; her luck went bad [so] I brought her.
> [Having witnessed this exchange] Rabbi Bibi b. Abbaye said to him: Have you permission to do this? [The Angel of Death] said to him: Is it not written 'There are those who find their ends without judgement?' He said: But is it not written, 'One generation goes, another comes?'[18] [The Angel of Death] said: [This verse merely requires] that I accompany them until the generation is completed, and then I give them to Duma [the angel in charge of the dead]. (Psalms 115:17)

> [Rabbi Bibi] said to him: In any case, what did you do with her [missing] years? He answered: If there is a student of sages who forgives [others], I will add them to him instead. (Babylonian Talmud, Chagiga 4b)

---

[17] Proverbs 13:23.

[18] Ecclesiastes 1:4.

David Kraemer finds this passage unique—the only text in the entire *Talmud* where one angel sends another to do his bidding, and so the story is totally bereft of any mention to the Divine (Kraemer 1994, p. 202). The idea of mistaken identity accounting for suffering is not unique to this passage. Elsewhere, Job suggests that he has been mistaken for another, but the *Talmud* explicitly rejects that notion—God does not make these types of errors.[19] In contrast, in this example, the heavenly bureaucracy seems to do exactly that. The commentaries on this passage seem more interested in 'balancing the books' than the issue of 'bad luck' causing the taking of a life before its time. The inference is thus—this premature death, at least, has nothing to do with God.

Conclusion

In this brief review, I have sought to demonstrate that early rabbinical Judaism did not concur with the biblical view of suffering, instead providing a number of alternative responses. The examples suggest that it is better to be angry with God than to deny God. By being free to converse with the Divine and remonstrate against the injustice of suffering, the tradition allows us to maintain a relationship with God at a time when we might need it most. To quote Clifford Geertz:

> As a religious problem, the problem of suffering is, paradoxically, not how to avoid suffering but how to suffer, how to make of physical pain, personal loss, worldly defeat, or the helpless contemplation of others' agony something bearable, supportable—something as we say, sufferable. (Geertz 1973, p. 70)

Bibliography

Augustine. 2008. *Confessions*. Trans. G. Wills. Harmondsworth: Penguin.
Geertz, Clifford. 1973. *Religion as a cultural system*. New York: Basic Books.
Josephus. 2003. *The Jewish war*. Trans. G. Williamson. Harmondsworth: Penguin.
Kraemer, David. 1994. *Responses to suffering in classical rabbinic literature*. New York: Oxford University Press.
Maimonides, Moses. 1963. *The Guide of the Perplexed*. Trans. S. Pines. Chicago: University of Chicago Press.
Neusner, Jacob. 1999. *The theology of the oral torah: Revealing the justice of god*. Montreal: McGill-Queen's University Press.
Rosenberg, Shalom. 1989. *Good and evil in Jewish thought*. Tel Aviv: MOD Books.
Sacks, Rabbi Jonathan. 1982. Explaining suffering. In *Issues in Jewish thought*, 2nd series. London: United Synagogue.
Wiesel, Elie. 1996. *Night*. London: Penguin.

[19] Babylonian Talmud, Bava Batra 16b.

Chapter 12
Suffering and Ancient Therapy: Plato to Cicero

Dougal Blyth

Greco-Roman Conceptions of Suffering

The Roman politician, orator and amateur philosopher Cicero provides, in the *Tusculan Disputations,* the following indicative list of forms of suffering, easily recognisable as such to a modern reader: poverty, lack of recognition, exile, national disaster, slavery, disability, blindness, and so on;[1] for each kind of calamity, he asserts, following the Greeks, philosophy can provide the appropriate consolatory advice in a book. To us today, used to the intervention of international aid organisations, governments with highly resourced social policies, economic policies, private and public health and education systems, disability commisioners, and the roving eye of the media, Cicero's answer to human misery might at first glance seem a little underwhelming.

Yet we too attribute a certain efficacy to the counselling of those who have been traumatised, at least in the richer nations. When we think of suffering today we normally distinguish, I suppose, between objective and subjective factors in human misery. While the subjective, or psychological, factors are often treated with drugs for various purposes and with varying degrees of success, nevertheless counselling and psychotherapy are also prominent forms of therapy used today.[2]

When we compare the modern distinction between objective and subjective aspects or kinds of suffering with the ancient world, we find a partly similar but partly

[1] Cicero (1945), *Tusculans* 3.81; see also 5.15–5.16, 5.29. For the benefit of non-specialists classical texts are cited in modern English translations wherever possible, but individual passages are referred to by book (or page in a standard edition of the text), section and/or lines, as normally printed in the margin of modern translations.

[2] Gill (1985) shows that there was no precise equivalent of modern psychotherapy in antiquity; similarly Lampe (2010), after comparing the various portrayals of Socrates with Lacanian analysis, concludes 'Socrates' erotic relationships with young men, we must affirm, are *not* psychoanalytic relationships', (p. 213, original emphasis; see pp. 189, 212–213 with ns. 89–90).

D. Blyth (✉)
Department of Classics, University of Auckland, Auckland, New Zealand
e-mail: dj.blyth@auckland.ac.nz

J. Malpas, N. Lickiss (eds.), *Perspectives on Human Suffering,*
DOI 10.1007/978-94-007-2795-3_12,

different conception shared by many ancient philosophers, in particular Plato, Aristotle and their schools and successors. A common feature of their ethical theories is to distinguish goods of the soul, of the body and external goods; correspondingly there are evils, causes of suffering, of each of these three kinds: respectively, for example, poverty, ill-health and viciousness. It is noteworthy here that psychic suffering is identified primarily in terms of immorality. Contemporary doctors were aware of medical diseases that affected what we would call the mind,[3] but this is always of secondary concern to the philosophical schools, who seem to have had most influence on ancient views generally, at least to judge from Greek and Roman literature.

Common Philosophical Assumptions

Five further initial assumptions need to be noticed here, shared by the Platonic, Aristotelian and the later Stoic schools, those that are of most relevance to Cicero's conception of therapy.[4] Firstly they all argue that, compared with bodily and external goods and evils, what is good and bad for the soul has a much greater influence upon (or, in the case of the Stoics, is the only factor affecting) human well-being. Secondly, the concept of a soul (*psychê*, Greek; *animus*, classical Latin), although explained in various metaphysical terms in the schools, is essentially a functional and not a religious one: the soul is whatever it is that is responsible for physical life, perception, self-movement and thinking.

Thirdly they all approach human beings as parts of the natural order (although how this is explained in practice is one key area of disagreement among the schools), and by reference to nature they derive normative conclusions about our proper goals and how to pursue them. Fourthly, since they think of what we call morality in terms of this orientation to philosophically discoverable objective norms, the primary subject of their moral evaluation is our intellectual capacity to understand, reason and decide. Finally, since they all conceive of morality in terms of the virtues, or functional states of excellence, of the soul, i.e., what is primarily good for

[3] Cicero, *Tusculans* 4.30 (in Graver 2002): 'There is also another sort of 'health' of mind which can be found also in the non-wise person, when some mental disturbance is removed by medication and the care of doctors'. This idea is almost certainly taken from the Stoic Chrysippus (see further below). See also Pigeaud (1981, esp. pp. 46, 70–138, 537), discussing 'phrenitis', 'mania', 'hydrophobia' and 'melancholia'; and Gill (1985), pp. 316–319 with further references, and see also Plato (2000b), *Timaeus* 86b–87a.

[4] In this essay I will not discuss Epicureanism, for which see, e.g., Nussbaum (1994), Chaps. 4–7. Cicero rejects Epicureanism entirely, although making use of some of its ideas instrumentally in the *Tusculan Disputations*, on which see below. The other important philosophical movement between the age of Aristotle and the revival of Platonism after Cicero's time is the sceptical turn Plato's Academy took in the Hellenistic period which informed Cicero's own outlook, on which see below. A later form of scepticism (Pyrrhonism) developed thereafter but is beyond the scope of this study.

it, they conceive of human thriving, or happiness, as constituted solely or at least primarily by this moral-intellectual condition. Hence they argue that the primary, or sole, constitutive cause of human suffering is individual moral-intellectual failure.

It is easy to see, then, that the prescribed cure for suffering, according to these schools, is philosophical wisdom, the central moral-intellectual virtue. This is evident in the comparison of philosophy with medicine found first in a fragment of the atomist philosopher Democritus, 'medicine heals the body's diseases; but wisdom the soul's sufferings (*pathê*)'.[5] Thereafter this comparison is repeatedly invoked by Socrates in Plato's dialogues, and inspires and structures the Stoic philosopher Chrysippus' account of psychic *pathê* (see Tieleman 2003, pp. 142–57), of which Cicero in the *Tusculans* makes much use (see below).

Poetic Alleviation of Suffering

The idea and practice of healing with words was not unique to philosophy in ancient Greece. Given Plato's radical criticism of the moral educational influence of poetry in the *Republic* (Plato 2000a, 376e–403c and 595a–608b), it is important to see that these two prominent features of Greek culture share this conception of themselves. The difference between them is in their mode of operation, and the way poetry and philosophy each invite us to conceive of suffering. Socrates criticises a version of Homer's *Iliad*, which in our text runs:

> There are two urns that stand on the door-sill of Zeus. They are unlike
> for the gifts they bestow: an urn of evils, an urn of blessings.
> If Zeus who delights in thunder mingles these and bestows them
> on man, he shifts, and moves now in evil, again in good fortune.
> But when Zeus bestows from the urn of sorrows, he makes a failure
> of man, and the evil hunger drives him over the shining
> earth, and he wanders respected neither of gods nor mortals. (Homer 1962, *Illiad*, pp. 24.527–24.533)[6]

The implications here are that all humans suffer, only some more than others, and moreover the king of the gods is responsible, to which Socrates objects on theological grounds, and also because it discourages us from seeking elsewhere for the causes of our own suffering and perhaps alleviating them (Plato 2000a, 379c).

The alternative, poetic, perspective nevertheless claims its own power to assuage suffering. Hesiod most explicitly claims the power of poetry to charm it away:

> So if someone is stricken with grief of a recent bereavement
> and is torturing his heart with mourning, then if some singer
> serving the Muses sings of past glory and the heroes of old and
> tells of the blessed immortals who have their homes on Olympos,

[5] Democritus B31 in Diels and Kranz (1966–1967), my translation.

[6] See also Plato 2000a, 379d. See Murray 1997, pp. 143–144 for discussion of Plato's divergence from our text of Homer.

> swiftly the grief-stricken one is forgetful and remembers
> none of his sorrow; quickly the gifts of the Muses divert him. (Hesiod 1983, *Theogony* pp. 98–103)[7]

One significant method of consolation is clearly revealed in Homer by Telemachos' response when his mother Penelope asks the bard Phemios not to tell the story of the Greeks who returned from sacking Troy, since she misses her own husband Odysseus:

> So let your heart and let your spirit be hardened to listen.
> Odysseus is not the only one who lost his homecoming
> day at Troy. There were many others who perished, besides him. (Homer 1967, *Odyssey* 1.353–1.355)

Conceiving of suffering as universal leads to sympathy for others sharing our common condition and lessens our own misery.[8] Later Greek lyric poetry contains many shorter pieces originally composed with a particular occasional consolatory function, which have been preserved and valued precisely because of the universalising appeal central to the effect. Other common themes include the unpredictability of fortune for all, and the impermanence of the human condition.[9] Subsequently such arguments are absorbed into the philosophical consolatory literature, beginning with the lost work *On Grief* by Crantor from Plato's school, the Academy.[10]

Plato's Rejection of Poetry

Plato's own rejection of this method of alleviating suffering by means of sympathetic identification with human limitations thus requires further explanation. Much scholarship exists on his explanation of, and attitude to poetry and the arts (see, e.g. Murray 1997, with further references); but for present purposes it may be sufficient to point to Plato's frequent rejection in the dialogues of such human limitations themselves. This includes two tendencies, one that inspired Stoicism, for Socrates to assert or argue that the just man, or the true philosopher, does not in fact come

[7] See also Homer 1967, *Odyssey*, pp. 1.337–1.339, 8.62–8.95, 11.333–11.334, 12.39–12.44, 13.1–13.2, 17.514–17.521; Pindar 1997, *Pythian*, pp. 1.6–1.12.

[8] Homer (1962), *Iliad* Bk 24, esp. 507–524 dramatizes this effect clearly, when Achilleus, having heard Priam tell of the loss of his sons, and being reminded of his own father, is finally freed of his anger at the death of Patroclus and rehumanized; they weep together, and their passion for lamentation is sated.

[9] See e.g. Archilochus, *Elegy* 13, and Simonides, 520–524 and 531, in West (1994). See Nussbaum (1986), esp. p. 52 (Nussbaum makes particular reference to tragedy, and also notes the extension to the prose rhetoric of Gorgias and Isocrates of the conception of a cure through words). I have not yet seen all of Baltussen (2012b).

[10] See Graver (2002) Appendix A, 'Crantor and the Consolatory Tradition', pp. 187–194.

to any harm,[11] and a second one, although recognising the suffering inevitable in human embodiment, to assert and argue that the true self is the soul alone, which is only circumstantially and impermanently connected with the body.[12] This latter view seems to be adopted from the earlier Pythagorean tradition, whichtaught that the true self is a god that has been trapped in a body, suffers reincarnation, and by practicing philosophy can become free again.[13] Scholars have long noted the similarities here with Orphic religious doctrines (Kirk et al. 1983, pp. 220–222).

In Plato's treatment of such ideas, in the context of accounts of reincarnation (*metempsychosis*), one clear theme is that there is a variety of diverse lifestyles possible (Plato 2000a, *Republic* 10.617d–10.620d; *Phaedrus* 248c–249c, in Plato 1997). These are conceived in terms of distinct social roles with their attendant rewards and costs, and are each attractive or not depending on individual moral-intellectual character. Consequently the extent of someone's suffering depends on the soul's choice of lifestyle on rebirth and so ultimately its moral character. Plato essentially here treats life as a competition amongst these lifestyles for overall happiness. Each has its costs, and in that sense all embodied humanity suffers, but the suffering in the case of the philosopher, at least, is dismissed in the same way an athlete dismisses the discomforts required in training to excel in competition. It is the need to belittle and dismiss one's own suffering in order to excel in virtue, then, that motivates the complete rejection of the poetic means of alleviating suffering by sympathetic identification, what Homer calls 'charming' or 'enthralment' (*thelxis*; see earlier references).

Tragedy and Aristotle

Surviving works of Athenian tragedy provide us with the most intense, nuanced and evocativeportrayals of human suffering of any genre of Greek poetry (see recently Hall 2010 and her chapter in this volume), and thus are the particular focus of Plato's attack in *Republic* Bk 10 for their ability to stimulate grief in the audience. It seems from the evidence of Aristophanes' comedy *Thesmophorizusae*, which contains systematic parody of several of Euripides' tragedies, that the word *pathos* (pl. *pathê*) had by that time (411 BC) become a technical term for a scene in which a character laments at length.[14] I will return to this term shortly.

---

[11] See *Apology* 41cd, *Gorgias* 477d, in Plato (1997), and note the *Republic* as a whole sets out to show that the just man is happy in any conceivable circumstance; see also Cicero (1945), *Tusculans* 5.34–5.36.

[12] See *Phaedo* 69c–d, 70c–d, 76d–77d, 79b–d, 80d–81e, *Phaedrus* 245c–257a, in Plato (1997) and Plato (2000a), *Republic* 611b–612a.

[13] See, e.g. Kirk et al. 1983, pp. 219–220, and also pp. 314–317 on Empedocles.

[14] Aristophanes (1994), *Thesmo* 1058; see Liddell et al. (1940), *s. v. pathos* V. "Rhet., *emotional style or treatment*".

Aristotle's *Poetics* is commonly regarded as responding to Plato with a defence of tragedy that provides the first theoretical account of the therapeutic value of art. Aristotle defines tragedy as an imitation (*mimêsis*: as did Plato), but of action (*praxis*), not suffering (*pathos*), nor of character, as Plato does. Nevertheless he describes in detail the ways that it will produce pleasure for the audience by eliciting pity and fear in them (Aristotle 1968, Chap. 13, 1453a36). This corresponds with the older poetic conception discussed above, even where at one place Aristotle describes the effect as a *catharsis* (purification) of these particular emotions (Aristotle 1968, *Poetics*, Chap. 6, 1449b28).

Notwithstanding the extensive scholarly interest in the precise interpretation of Aristotle's claims,[15] what seems most noteworthy here is the way a more or less purely theoretical approach to art (as opposed to Plato's engagement in a cultural polemic) brings about a reconciliation between the philosophical and poetic modes of therapy for human suffering. This extends also to the art of rhetoric, which Plato aligns with tragedy, and castigates equally (at least in the *Gorgias*; although cf. the *Phaedrus*), but on which Aristotle wrote a textbook (his *Rhetoric*). The evidence of Crantor's book *On Grief* (and what we can learn of this tradition from Cicero's *Tusculans*) shows that the art of persuasion could be used to apply the kinds of reasoning and consolatory effects earlier typical of poetry, for circumstantial relief, alongside the more strictly philosophical claim that only wisdom is truly effective as a cure for human suffering.

Aristotle's influential contribution to moral philosophy has particular importance in relation to the question of suffering, as it was developed later in the tradition as reported by Cicero.[16] His moral theory fits closely the set of common philosophical assumptions discussed above, and further involves treating the moral virtues as each a mean between two extremes (thus, e.g., courage is between overboldness and cowardice), where the extremes are characterised by what Aristotle calls *pathê*.[17] These are clearly such things as desire or anger in the case of overboldness, and fear in the case of cowardice. Such *pathê* are normally interpreted as emotions by scholars, but I shall return to this point. The idea that the virtuous person experiences just the right degree of *pathos* in relation to circumstances as reason judges was developed subsequently in his school into the claim that virtue involves moderate *pathos* (*metriopatheia*).[18] This is a reaction to the view of the Stoic school that the virtuous person extinguishes all *pathos* in the soul, to be discussed below. In brief, the two schools take the term *pathos* in different senses, Aristotle's Peripatetic school to mean 'external influence' on our souls, the Stoics to mean 'suffering'.

A second point of conflict with the Stoics arises because Aristotle and his followers hold to the distinction among psychic, bodily and external goods (and cor-

[15] See, with further bibliography, e.g., Andersen and Haarberg (2001), or Rorty (1992).

[16] For a brief summary of both these aspects, adapted to the present topic, see Gill (1997, pp. 6–7).

[17] For virtue as a mean, see Aristotle, *Nicomachean Ethics* 2.2, 1104a12–1104a27, and for the *pathê* 2.3, 1104b14, in Aristotle (1984); Aristotle thinks of these as pleasures and pains (see *Nicomachean Ethics*, 2.3), i.e. ways we can be motivationally affected by things.

[18] In addition to Gill (1997), *Thesmo* see Dillon (1983).

respondingly evils), whereas the Stoics argue that only virtue and things associated with it are good, only viciousness and associated things evil, and everything else is a matter of indifference. Aristotle in the *Nicomachean Ethics* resists the implication threatened by his recognition of lesser goods and evils, that a virtuous man's happiness is subject to fortune, by distinguishing between happiness or thriving (*eudaimonia*, dependent on virtue alone) and *makaria* (blessedness, the product of additional goods),[19] but (according to Cicero) Theophrastus, his successor as head of the Peripatetic school,conceded the point, and it was up to later Peripatetics such as Critolaus to come to Aristotle's defence, restating the view that virtue makes much more difference to our wellbeing than any amount of other goods. By contrast, claiming to follow Socrates, the Stoics assert that the wise man is as happy as Zeus under all circumstances whatsoever.[20]

Pathos and Emotion

Both Aristotle and the Stoics thus define the role of reason in securing happiness by reference to *pathos*. This Greek noun is formed from the verb *paschô* (aor. *epathon*), cognate with *patior* (Latin), and they share the root meaning 'to have something done to one' and, when used without modification, 'to suffer'.[21] *Paschô* thus functions from Homer onwards, in the sense 'to be acted upon', as the opposite (and as if grammatically the passive form) of verbs of doing or acting upon. A *pathos* is thus the event or result of being acted upon, or absolutely, a suffering or misfortune.[22] Thus to experience a *pathos* is to be passive in relation to something. In particular, an individual's distinctively human reactions to significant events or objects can be called *pathê* to which he is subject. These are the psychic *pathê* (such as grief, anger or love), as opposed to physical ones.[23] But if we call these 'reactions', we must be aware that the Greek word implies that the human subject is primarily passive, not active, in relation to what stimulates a *pathos*, and is not, in Aristotle's terms, the moving cause of the reaction.

Amélie Oksenburg Rorty has studied in detail the metaphysical implications of Aristotle's psychological use of the term *pathos* (Rorty 1984). She shows that he preserves the normal range of its meanings (being affected, suffering), but that in

[19] *Nicomachean Ethics,* 1.8, 1099a31–10, 1101a22, in Aristotle (1984).

[20] For the Stoic view see conveniently the sources collected in Long and Sedley (1987), Chaps. 60–61; on the conflict see Cicero (1945), 5.21–5.36, 75–87, and Bk 5 *passim.*

[21] Liddell et al. (1940), *s. v. paschô* I.

[22] Liddell et al. (1940), *s. v. pathos* I.

[23] On the basis of the argument I present here, the meaning given in Liddell et al. (1940), *s. v. pathos* II.1 of the soul, *emotion, passion* (see Liddell et al. (1940) *s. v. paschô* I.2 and *pathêma* II), which cites exclusively philosophers and Dio Cassius (2nd–3rd c. AD), ought to be corrected to a literal sense, something more neutral like 'affect or influence upon the *psychê*' or 'psychic reaction'. See further below.

accordance with his normal practice, his uses have to be interpreted in relation to phenomena given under particular descriptions. Aristotle does recognise that we can develop dispositions to react in certain ways, so that these reactions become our own characteristic behaviour, subject to our agency, and we are ourselves responsible for them. Nevertheless in calling such reactions *pathê* he still thinks of them as in each instance causally dependent upon their stimulus.

This is quite contrary to the idea of an emotion (as such), as an essentially subjectively constituted experience, which may or may not be expressed, as a revelation of one's inner life. Thus we should not conceptualise Aristotle's account of *pathê* in the *Rhetoric*, where he discusses a series of them individually at 2.1–11 (and cf. 1.10–11), nor in his moral theory, in terms of emotion as such. Rather he conceives of psychic *pathê* literally as the ways we are affected by, and react to, external influences. Although the subject matter covers that range of reactions which we today interpret in terms of the concept of emotion, there is a significant formal difference involved, which is everything when it comes to the interpretation of modes of thought.

Notwithstanding this, in the scholarship both on Aristotle's *Rhetoric* and on the Stoic account of the *pathê* the term is regularly translated as 'emotion'. There is sometimes some initial acknowledgement that this is not the literal meaning of the word, but then the use of the English 'emotion' is substituted.[24] This is partly driven by the urge to show that ancient philosophy can contribute to the contemporary growth of philosophical interest in the emotions as such.[25] It is also partly due to the radical claim made by the Stoics that such *pathê* are indeed generated by the subject (see Auerbach 1965, p. 67). But there is particular reason to be careful here.

As David Konstan has shown in some detail, local cultural norms have a large part to play in what particular 'emotions' (scarequotes mine) are recognised in a given society, and more importantly, what range of experience or activity they are individually thought to encompass in any given case.[26] Konstan further argues that what we today conceive of in general as an emotion (as such)does not have the same characteristic structure as what was recognised by the classical Greeks (of which he is nevertheless prepared to use the word 'emotion').[27] I would rather say here that at a more precise level, it is misleading to think of what Aristotle and the Stoics are concerned with as 'emotion' (as such) at all, since that is not to think of this range of phenomena in the way that they did.

[24] Thus, e.g., Rist (1969, p. 26); Nussbaum (1994, p. 319 n. 4, see also pp. 366–367); Annas (1992, pp. 103–104 (with n. 1)); Sihvola and Engberg-Pedersen (1998, p. viii); Knuuttila and Engberg-Pedersen (1998, p. 1); see Cooper and Procopé (1995, p. 9 n. 8 and p. 4 (note also their use of 'emotion' to translate the Latin *adfectus*, e.g. *On Anger* 2.3.1)). By contrast Inwood (1985, pp. 127, 130, 144–145, 162); Frede (1986, esp. p. 96) and Tieleman (2003, pp. 15–16), are unusual exceptions.

[25] See, e.g. Graver 2007; Sorabji 2000; Sihvola and Engberg-Pedersen 1998; Fortenbaugh 2000.

[26] Konstan (2006, Chap. 1 '*Pathos* and Passion', pp. 3–40).

[27] Konstan (2006, pp. 28–29). I should note that Konstan continues by suggesting that in the Hellenistic period (of the Stoics) a conception of emotion more like our own (static, internal) one arose. But see further my discussion of what differentiates the Stoic conception from Aristotle.

Notice in passing that the word 'emotion' according to the OED only attained its modern sense in the nineteenth century.[28] The first scientific studies of emotion (in the modern sense) date from this period (Darwin 1872; James 1884; see Konstan 2006, pp. 10–11), suggesting it was only then beginning to be recognised as a unitary category (non-physical feeling), as opposed to the earlier distinction between 'sentiment' and 'passion'.[29] The latter term reflects the sense hitherto recognised in English for the word 'emotion', of a disturbed or agitated feeling, itself seemingly an extension of the earliest attested sense of 'emotion' in English as 'public disturbance'.[30] The word is derived *via* French from the use of *emoveo* first in Virgil's *Aeneid* in the sense 'shake' or 'shatter'.[31] Its evolution in English has thus abandoned its etymological origins, which imply something public, not private, intense and destructive, not placid, and externally caused. Paradoxically, these lost implications, as we have seen, are all appropriate to the Greek word *pathos*.

---

[28] *Oxford English Dictionary s. v. emotion* 4.b—here I discount the first citation (1808), since, although this is presumably non-metaphorical (contrast 4.a '*fig.* Any agitation … of mind,' etc.), it clearly implies significant mental agitation (viz, as a cause of sea-sickness); remaining citations for the sense b. '*Psychology.* A mental "feeling" or "affection" (e.g. of pleasure or pain, desire or aversion, surprise, hope or fear,' etc., date only from the 1840s, although see below for a slightly earlier use.

[29] *Oxford English Dictionary s. v. passion* II. 'Sensesrelating to emotional or mental states' (all of these, 6.a–9.c, are defined with use of the adjectives 'strong', 'overpowering', or 'intense',or the noun 'outburst', except 8.b 'Sexual desire or impulses' and 8. c'An object of sexual love'); see *Oxford English Dictionary s. v. sentiment* 7.a–9.b, and note esp. 7.a 'A mental feeling, an emotion' (1652–1872), and 9.a 'Refined and tender emotion', etc. (1768–1888): note that no senses here represent 'emotion' in the generic modern sense since they all specify that sentiment is either or both (1) intellectual and/or (2) refined, with the single exception of 7.b '*Phrenol.* In *pl.* used as the name for the class of "faculties" … which are concerned with emotion'. Note here esp. the citation from Combe's *Syst. Phrenol.* (2nd ed. 1825), p. 153 'Genus II Sentiments. This genus of faculties corresponds to the "emotions" of the metaphysicians…. Dr. Spurzheim has named these faculties Sentiments, because they produce a propensity to act, joined with an emotion or feeling of a certain kind.' This is the only citation of its kind, but perhaps does seem to anticipate the modern conception of emotion, by extending the latter term beyond the earlier sense, perhaps unwittingly in reference to earlier metaphysical usage, and by a similar extension from the opposite direction of the term 'sentiment', assimilating them to a new genus.

[30] *Oxford English Dictionary, s. v. emotion* 4.a. ('mental agitation') discussed above, and 3. '*transf.* A political or social agitation; a tumult, popular disturbance. *Obs.*' (first 1579); see 1. ('local movement', 1603 and 1695) and 2. ('physical agitation' of blood, air, horses, earthquake, etc, from 1692).

[31] Virgil (1952), 2.610. The senses of *émotion* in French parallel and anticipate early uses in English: (1) 'agitation caused by a sensation', (2) 'intense affective reaction to a stimulus', and (3) prior to the French Revolution, 'popular revolt': see *Dictionnaire Larousse de la langue francaise* (Paris: Larouse [www.larousse.com]), *s. v. émotion*. More precisely, *Dictionnaire du Moyen Français* (2010), *s. v.*, lists four medieval senses, (1) 'causing of a movement', i.e. 'instigation' (1429), (2) 'riot' or 'uprising' (1429–1502), (3) 'externally stimulated movement' or 'agitation' (c. 1494) and (4) 'disorder' or 'moral disturbance' (1456–1471). The formation **emotio, -nis* does not occur in classical or late ancient Latin, nor is there an entry in Niemeyer (1976).

The Stoic Theory of the *Pathê*

Accordingly I advocate interpreting the Stoic doctrine of the extermination of the *pathê* as one of escaping from all suffering, as such, not one of ridding ourselves of emotion. One problem this solves is the disagreement amongst scholars as to whether the Stoics mean us to remove all emotions or only excessive ones. The Stoics distinguish between *pathê*, which everyone else experiences, and *eupatheiai* (commonly understood as good feelings), which are unique to the Stoic sage. On the explanation of Michael Frede,[32] since our emotions are qualitatively different from the sage's, all our emotions are to be eradicated. But according to Tad Brennan the Stoics are not concerned with emotions such as 'laughter and tears and whatever may underlie them', but only those identifiable as 'vicious motivations'.[33] Yet if both these views are translated into an understanding of *pathê* as suffering-involving reactions and *eupatheiai* as good responses to appearances, they will be seen to be consistent.

On the Stoic theory, children and animals live by reacting directly to appearances ('impressions'; Greek *phantasiai*), whereas from the age of fourteen people are capable of first judging whether to accept a given appearance, either that of fact or value.[34] This represents the emergence of our capacity to reason, unique in the animal kingdom, as a result of which the human soul as a whole is of a quite different kind, renamed by the Stoics the 'leader' (Greek *hêgemonikon*; Latin *principale*) of our life. What this implies is that because, in virtue of our 'leader', we can decide to accept ('assent to') an appearance or not, we are responsible for our own lives.

When we assent to an appearance that proposes a response, the decision to assent automatically involves the generation of an impulse which sets us in motion. If the decision is truly rational, in the case of a wise person, what motivates it is a particular kind of reliable appearance (called *katalêptikê*: 'cognitive') that he or she recognises as such, concerning what really is good or bad (virtue or vice). Incidentally this may involve a choice among indifferent bodily or external circumstances or objects, in which the sage follows nature and chooses what is accordingly appropriate but without thinking that any such circumstances or objects themselves are independently good or bad.

---

[32] Frede (1986, p. 94); see similarly Cooper (1998, p. 78).

[33] Brennan (1998, pp. 33–34); see Rist (1969, pp. 26–27). Annas (1992, pp. 114–115) is indicative of the confusion here, claiming that for the Stoics (1) emotions are not good, (2) we should not be affectless, and (3) appealing to the Stoic concept that the sage experiences *eupatheiai*, but not explaining how these can be affects without being emotions, on her view.

[34] The main sources for the Stoic theory of *pathê* are Galen (1978–1984), *Deplacitis, Hippocratis et Platonis* (hereafter *PHP*) Bks 4–5; Diogenes Laertius (1925), 7 (esp. 7.110–7.117); Cicero (1945), *Tusculans* Bks 3–4 (esp. 4.11–4.33), Plutarch (1939), *On Moral Virtue*, esp. 3.441c–d, 7.446f–447c, 9.449a–10.450d, 12.451b; Pseudo-Andronicus (1977), 1–5; and Stobaeus (1884), *Eclogae*, 2.90 (for a more recent text and translation see Arius Didymus (1999). See conveniently the extracts in Long and Sedley (1987), Chap. 65. Among shorter modern discussions I have found most helpful Rist (1969), Chap. 2; Inwood (1985), Chap. 5, Frede (1986); Brennan (1998), along with other essays Sihvola and Engberg-Pedersen (1998); and Sorabji (1997, pp. 197–209). Longer studies include Tieleman (2003), Chaps. 3–4, Graver (2007); Sorabji (2000) and Nussbaum (1994), Chaps. 9–11.

Essentially what the wise person does in all cases is to act to preserve the good of his orher rationality, by not succumbing to the impression that anything inconsistent is actually good orbad, and so being impelled towards or away from that in defiance of reason. By contrast all ordinaryhumans regularly assent to the appearance that something else is good or bad, and so on this basiswe experience impulses to embrace or reject, pursue or avoid their objects. In such cases the assentis still an action of the rational 'leader' within us, but one that rejects the valueof rationality as an end in itself, and in this sense is irrational. The Stoic explanation of this is that the appearances are seductive ('persuasive'), and furthermore, that we are influenced by one another in society to believe wrongly that bodily and external things are good or bad, and not really indifferent (Galen 1978–1984, *PHP* 5.5.19 (p. 320. 16–320.19); Diogenes Laertius 1925, 7.89; Cicero 1945, *Tusculans* 3.2–3.4).

This leads us to the explanation of *pathos* in Stoicism.Zeno the founder is reported to have called it an 'excessive impulse' (*hormê pleonazousa*) and alternatively 'an irrational and unnatural movement of the soul' (irrational as rejecting the intrinsic goals of reason, and unnatural because by nature only virtue and what is associated with it are goods).[35] A *pathos* is at root a judgment, according to Chrysippus, the third head of the school, and, as examples show, it is the judgment that something non-virtuous is good, or something non-vicious bad (Diogenes Laertius 1925, 7.111; Cicero 1945, *Tusculans* 4.15). There are four basic kinds of judgment, and these constitute four general kinds of *pathê*. These are those related to apparent present goods (pleasure: *hêdonê*), present evils (pain or grief: *lupê*), future goods (desire) and evils (fear), each subdivided into myriad particular kinds (e.g. Cicero 1945, *Tusculans* 3.24–3.25, 4.11–4.22). By pleasure they do not mean physical pleasure but 'an irrational elation over what seems to be worth choosing',[36] and correspondingly the Greek term *lupê* refers to mental grief, not physical pain (*ponos*).

What is entirely paradoxical, as with much of Stoicism, is the doctrine that *pathos*, suffering—normally in the sense of something inflicted upon us, is, according to Chrysippus, something we do to ourselves. This follows immediately from the assertion that *pathê* are judgments. As much of the discussion in the sources makes clear (particularly in Galen), the key difference between this and the Academic and Peripatetic schools' doctrines is that the latter both allow that, besides reason, the soul includes irrational parts, responsible for our vulnerability to *pathos*. Chrysippus has to explain the irrationality of *pathos* without appeal to other irrational parts that are independent sources of impulse, since on his doctrine the whole human soul is always dependent upon its rational 'leader'.[37]

[35] For the definitions see, e.g., Diogenes Laertius (1925), 7.110; Cicero (1945), 4.11; Galen (1978–1984), 4.2.8 (pp. 240.11–240.16).

[36] Diogenes Laertius, in Inwood and Gerson (1997), 7.114. On the ambiguity see further Annas (1992, p. 112).

[37] The only other parts the early Stoics recognise are the sense organs, voice and reproductive-capacity (e.g. Diogenes Laertius 1925, 7.110; see Long and Sedley 1987, Chap. 53), which are merely biological functions.

As an aid to his explanation Chrysippus says that an excessive impulse is analogous to a man running, who, unlike a man walking, cannot immediately stop his legs.[38] We are precipitated into action in a way that cannot be recalled by an immediate change of mind. Thus under the grip of *pathos* our rational 'leader' has lost control of itself temporarily.[39] Whereas other schools explained unself-controlled action as involving conflict between different parts of the soul (for instance appetites and reason), according to Zeno it is a 'fluttering' (*ptoia*) of the 'leader' (Galen 1978–1984, 4.5.6 (p. 260.17)), in which inconsistent motivations alternate rapidly in succession, so that we come to think they are simultaneous.

What is actually happening then is that we have contemporaneous dispositions to inconsistent value judgments, or beliefs, which in the case of a certain appearance will alternate in proposing opposed decisions. Reason is reduced to irrationality and is at war with itself, contrary to its own intrinsic goal of rational consistency.[40] In this circumstance where an appearance of value contrary to virtue is assented to,impulse has been enacted, and reason is abandoned. In the case of future-oriented *pathê*, the impulse leads to action, as the contractions and expansions of the soul (in Stoic physiology a light physical fluid), precipitate bodily behaviour automatically, whereas present-oriented *pathê* are completed in the psychophysical contraction that constitutes grief or the expansion of irrational elation.[41] We must think here of the over-excitement of children at birthday parties that drives adults crazy and, as we say, always ends in tears. According to the Stoics, all the pleasures of the non-wise are no better than this, and are intrinsically disturbing, and forms of suffering.

According to Chrysippus' medical analogy our individual pathology and the effects of habit generate dispositions in people to various characteristic kinds of *pathê* (love of this, hatred of that, for instance avarice and irrascibility), and these dispositions are mental diseases.[42] He then distinguishes as a separate category those that are so severe as to destroy the whole soul. These chronic dispositions are all features of viciousness, the opposite of a virtuous disposition, so the severe kind of mental disease seems to be that which completely destroys our rationality. In relation to

---

[38] Galen 1978–1984, *PHP* 4.2.8 (pp. 240.15–240.16), 4.2.14–4.2.18 (pp. 240.33–242.11) and 4.6.35 (pp. 276.34–278.2).

[39] Plutarch (1939), *On Moral Virtue* 3.441c–d, and Galen (1978–1984), *PHP* 4.6 (pp. 270.10–280.17) which contains quotations and reports interspersed with criticism; see for discussion Tieleman (2003, pp. 170–190), who divides it into two topics, the rejection of rationality, and resultant madness and mental blindness.

[40] See Inwood (1985, pp. 163–165), whose explanation here suggests that since consistency of judgments, for the Stoics, is virtue, (i.e., the only good), the only consistent set of judgments will be those that accord with this principle, so that any *pathos*-generating judgment (which assumes that there is some other good) will be inconsistent with other beliefs of the sufferer.

[41] Galen (1978–1984), *PHP* 4.3.2 (pp. 248.1–248.3), Cicero (1945), *Tusculans* 4.15. For the medical background to the conception of physical psychic movements of expansion and contraction in the fluid called *pneuma* ('breath') see Tieleman (2003, p. 156 n. 67), Annas (1992), Chap. 1, Pigeaud (1981), Chap. 1, and see Aristotle (1978).

[42] Galen (1978–1984), *PHP* 5.2.22–5.2.27, 31–33, 47 and 49, with interspersed criticism by Galen (pp. 298.27–304.21);Cicero (1945), *Tusculans* 4.23–4.32; Diogenes Laertius (1925), 7.115; Stobaeus (1884), *Eclogae* 2.902 (pp. 93.6–93.10).

this, individual *pathê*, as discrete events, are the symptoms of mental disease (at least if regularly repeated) as well as its reinforcing causes.

It seems clear that this pathology is not reducible to an account of the emotions as such. Itis essentially a pathology of the malfunction of reason, our 'leader'. What the Stoics are claiming is that all our suffering in life is produced by our own judgments, and takes the form of the experience of being irrationally out of control. In order to make out this claim, they have to demonstrate that other things apart from virtue are not at all goods or evils, or else some of our assenting to such appearances would be in fact rational. (They argue that everything of this kind, what other schools call bodily and external goods and evils, depend entirely on circumstances as to whether they benefit us or harm us, and so are intrinsically indifferent.[43])

Now since the Stoics conceive of *pathê* as impulses originating in ourselves, the use of the term has lost its primary implication that a *pathos* is a passive reaction. (It is in a sense a reaction, but merely to an appearance, not something external, and the generative cause is now conceived to be a dispositional belief, activated as a judgement about the appearance.[44]) Thus the operative element in the semantic range of the word is now just, and distinctively, 'suffering', as is clear by the contrast with the three *eupatheiai*, which are thus the good ways in which the sage is moved in judgment: joy, caution, and wishing (see, e.g. Diogenes Laertius 1925, 7.116; Cicero 1945, *Tusculans* 4.12–4.13). For the Stoics, *pathos* denotes *self-harm*, as such.

Although we might be tempted to re-characterise the two terms *pathos* and *eupatheia* as both forms of *self-affecting*, there is in Stoicism still no conception of a neutral category 'emotion'. Firstly, the concept of impulse itself does not imply the idea of emotion in Stoicism, since it is conceived as an objective matter of our rational 'leader' acting upon itself so as to produce in itself physical movement (contraction and expansion), not as a distinctively subjective dimension of experience (cf. Tieleman 2003, p. 157; Engberg-Pedersen 1990, pp. 172–175).

Secondly, beyond the ideas of judgment and impulse as such there is no other common ground between acting rationally and losing control of oneself. The sage's *eupatheiai* are determined negatively, as the complete absence of the irrational excess of externally-directed impulse that constitutes self-harm. Joy, caution and wishing, by contrast, are internally-directed impulses to virtue and away from vice (cf. Brennan 1998, pp. 34–36, pp. 54–57). Thus so long as the distinction between virtue and vice is regarded as both natural and fundamental to human well-being, an affective component of judgment or impulse in general cannot be separated off as a common category. In the case of the virtuous and the vicious these have only

[43] Diogenes Laertius (1925, pp. 7.101–7.103) (in Long and Sedley 1987, Chap. 58 A, at 5–6), with Long and Sedley (1987, pp. 357–358).

[44] There are also 'preliminary reactions' (Greek: *propatheiai*) to the mere appearance as such, even in the wise person, but these are not sufficient to produce real *pathos*: see, e.g., Cicero (1945), *Tusculans* 3.81, Seneca, *De ira*, in Cooper and Procopé (1995), 2.1–2.4; further refs. Graver (2002, pp. 125–126), and also Sorabji (2000), Index, p. 481 *s. v.* 'First Movements' and Annas (1992, p. 110 n. 17).

a formal similarity, while in the latter case judgment and impulse produce a radical deformation of the subject, in terms both of orientation and internal condition.[45]

Cicero's Relationship to Chrysippus

Cicero frequently discusses his translation of Greek philosophical terms into Latin, and scholars have occasionally reacted critically to his statement:

> A literal translation for *pathê* would be 'sicknesses' [*morbi*], but that would run counter to normal Latin usage. For pity, envy, elation, gladness, and so forth are all called by the Greeks 'sicknesses', as being movements of the mind not obedient to reason. But I think I was right to refer to these same movements of the mind when aroused as 'disturbances' [*perturbationes*], since 'sicknesses' would sound peculiar. (Cicero, *Tusculans* 3.7, translation adapted from Graver 2002; cf. Cicero 2001, *On moral ends* 3.35)

The term *pathos* is used in relation to illness, among other things, although there are also other Greek terms with this meaning (*nosos*, *astheneia*).[46] It seems likely that the Stoic Chrysippus used the term *pathos* for both bodily and psychic suffering, since he treats them as parallel cases. Accordingly Cicero's first claim here is not as exceptional as some have made it out to be, although since it assumes Chrysippus' doctrine it is not theory-neutral. He is not trying to match the lexical range of the Greek word in Latin, but to find a term that expresses its relevant sense, as his second sentence shows.[47] Thus his preferred Latin term *perturbatio* (meaning 'disturbance', rather than Graver's 'emotion'), is not theory-neutral either, since it picks

[45] We might imagine a limited modification to the theory whereby there were, contrary to Stoic doctrine, in addition to virtue and vice also bodily and external goods and evils; in that case some pursuit of such other goods might be rational, and not all externally-directed impulses would be directly self-harming. Nevertheless this would still not produce the category of emotion, as the meaning of *pathos*. In that case, given the vicissitudes of fortune, *pathos* as suffering would be divided into two distinct primary species, self-harm, in the case of irrational judgements, and, in the case of external evils, externally inflicted suffering, a traditional sense of the term. In a third sense, the fortuitous influence of external goods would also be a pleasant *pathos*, but the *eupatheiai* of the wise would still not be *pathê* in any sense.

[46] For reaction see e.g. Erskine (1997, p. 45 with n. 22), and Inwood (1985, pp. 127–128). On the medical sense of *pathos*, contra Erskine here, see Plato (2000b), *Timaeus* 86b, Hippocrates (1923), *Airs, Waters, Places,* 22 (admitted by Inwood, p. 128 n. 3), and Vegetti (1995), cited by Tieleman (2003, p. 16 n. 30).

[47] The phrase *e verbo*, which Graver translates as 'literal', implies only that Cicero considers a word here that corresponds with all uses of *pathos* in the given philosophical context, not quite generally. Inwood (1985, pp. 128, 144), criticises Cicero for confusing disease, as the underlying state (of body or soul), in Chrysippus' theory (Galen 1978–1984, *PHP* 5.2–5.4), with the symptom, or outbreak; we might rather say that Cicero has here assimilated disease to its effects, and in any case Inwood notes (1985, p. 144 n. 69) that for both Aristotle and the Stoics bad actions and bad psychic states are related as the chicken and the egg, and (1985, pp. 163 and 168) that the diseased mental state is identified in Stoicism as an opinion (*doxa*: Stobaeus, *Eclogae* 2.93; Diogenes Laertius (1925), 7.115), which is equally true of the *pathos*: see above. See also Pigeaud (1981), pp. 289–290.

out just what characterises psychic suffering under the Stoic account of the *pathê* as judgments made in rebellion to reason.[48]

As Cicero's discussion of terminology here shows, his approach to Stoic doctrine in the *Tusculans* is quasi-medical, and therapeutic (see Cicero 1945, *Tusculans* 3.1, 3.5–6), in contrast, for instance to his theoretical treatment in *On Moral Ends*, Books 3–4. This distinction can be paralleled for Chrysippus. The key text for which we have evidence in which the Stoic theory of *pathos* was worked out was Chrysippus' lost *On pathê*.[49] This originally consisted of three theoretical books (i.e. ancient scrolls), to whichwas added a fourth book he wrote separately, called the Therapeutic, or Ethical, book.[50] Tieleman's recent study of the evidence concludes that the contents of this book included (1) a statement and justification of the medical analogy for psychic *pathê* and their treatment, (2) definitions of *pathos*, (3) an account of how in individual *pathê* the subject deliberately rejects reason, (4) an account of how they are consequently irrational states of mind, and (5) advice on two kinds of therapeutic intervention: preventative, and responsive.[51]

What this seems to show is that although Chrysippus provided some extended discussion of distinct forms of therapy for two different stages of each of various kinds of *pathê*, this book did not itself constitute a therapeutic work.[52] Cicero states 'when Chrysippus and the Stoics discuss mental disturbances [*animi perturbationes*], they concern themselves primarily with classifications and definitions, and the part of their discourse devoted to healing the mind, and preventing it from being agitated [*turbulentos esse*] is very small'.[53] For a depiction of practical philosophical therapy for human suffering we must turn to Cicero's own *Tusculans*.[54]

Cicero in the *Tusculans* admittedly does discuss some therapeutic principles he derives from Chrysippus, in addition to the use he makes of Stoic psychological

---

[48] See Rist (1969, p. 26), and Graver (2002, p. 80). Auerbach (1965, p. 67) calls *perturbatio* 'perjorative', by comparison with the Greek *pathos*.

[49] For the fragments and reconstruction see esp. Tieleman (2003).

[50] For the name, see Tieleman (2003, p. 140 with n. 1).

[51] Tieleman (2003, p. 326) summarises the topics with evidential references; for discussion see Chap. 4.

[52] Moreover (contra Nussbaum (1994) and Sorabji (2000)) nor does Chrysippus propose a theory-neutral form of therapy, according to Tieleman (2003, pp. 142–143 and 166–170), with further references. Inwood (1985, p. 144 n. 73 (see pp. 152–153)) rightly calls this, rather, 'first-aid'; see further below.

[53] Cicero, *Tusculans* 4.9 (translation adapted from Graver 2002); see Cicero (2001), *On moral ends* 4.6.

[54] Pigeaud (1981, pp. 245–246) emphasises Cicero's influence on later western ideas about the passions, madness and vices,extending to Philippe Pinel, 'the father of modern psychiatry'; Pigeaud (see, e.g., pp. 287–289, 298) argues that Cicero achieved this by reducing Chrysippus' analogy between body and soul to a metaphor, rejecting Stoic materialism and medical theory, which enabled him to treat the soul independently. This overlooks the fact that Cicero himself offers aquasi-stoic material theory of the soul in *Tusculans* 1.39–1.49 (and see the 'Dream of Scipio' from *Respublica* 6 in Cicero 1998), probably derived from Antiochus, and that his non-materialist psychological terminology derives from, and is motivated by, his rhetorical therapeutic approach (see further below).

and ethical theory. He follows Chrysippus' distinction between two judgments upon which *pathos* depends, the judgment that something present or expected is good or bad, and the judgment that the *pathos*, as a response, is appropriate. (Presumably the former judgment, insofar as it can be addressed by persuasion, must be the disposition to believe, rather than the occurrent belief, since once the latter occurs the *pathos* as an impulse, is practically automatic, except as follows).

Cicero further follows Chrysippus in arguing that it is normally more effective at first topersuade the sufferer that his response is inappropriate, rather than that his value judgment is incorrect (Cicero 1945, 3.76, see 4.59–4.60). This initial form of therapy focuses only on allaying the *pathos* as a symptom, and does not require any particular philosophical commitments of the patient; but it is merely preparatory to the full philosophical cure which can only begin once the sufferer has been sufficiently relieved of immediate symptoms that it is possible to question the value judgment itself.[55]

Accordingly, Cicero correctly understands the Stoic observation that an episode of *pathos* only lasts so long as the motivating belief is fresh (Greek *prosphatos*; Latin *recens*: Cicero 1945, *Tusculans* 3.54–3.55, 3.75; see also 3.52, 4.64). *Tusculans* 3.75 reports that according to the Stoic founder Zeno this is not just a matter of temporal immediacy, but of the belief's vitality;[56] Inwood seems right to interpret this vitality as intended to explain the final point of the previous chapter, that a belief that *pathos* is an appropriate response is linked to a false value judgment.[57] Note that *recens* has also the sense 'vigorous', while *prosphatos* is primarily applied to what is newly killed, from which the vigour of life has not quite departed; thus freshness, or vigour, in a false value judgment consists in its continuing power to suggest that we ought to be experiencing *pathos*, something that can be independently soothed rhetorically by re-contextualising and diminishing the importance of the circumstance.

Form and Content of the *Tusculan Disputations*

The *Tusculans* itself consists of five books, each with a preface addressed to Cicero's friend Brutus followed by a dramatised report of a purported conversation between a teacher and a student.[58] These are held on five consecutive days and each

[55] See Inwood (1985, pp. 144 n. 73, 152). Thus (with reference to Tieleman's distinction) the philosophical cure is only preventative with respect to subsequent occasions of *pathos*.

[56] Pigeaud (1981, pp. 276–287), contrasts the later Stoic Posidonius' view (according to Galen) that Chrysippus understood freshness exclusively in terms of time.

[57] Inwood (1985, pp. 147–148,151–152), citing Stobaeus, *Eclogae* 2.90 and Pseudo-Andronicus, in von Arnim (1964, p. 3.391).

[58] Although not original, to these have become attached the speaker identifications 'M' and 'A', perhaps representing *magister* (teacher), or Marcus (i.e. M. Tullius Cicero), and *adulescens* (youth), *auditor* (listener, i.e. student) or *alius* (another); see Dougan and Henry (1905–1934, vol. 1, p. 13).

takes the form Cicero calls a *schola*, i.e. a class or lesson taught by a philosopher, in which the student initially states a claim, and the teacher refutes it at length.[59] The five claims refuted are that death is an evil, that pain is the greatest evil, thatthe wise man is subject to distress or grief (*aegritudo*), that the wise man cannot be free of all psychic disturbance, and that virtue is not sufficient for a happy life (*beate vivendum*).[60]

Cicero (as the teacher) does not adopt a Stoic stance until Bk 3, and this requires-some comment. Firstly, his own philosophical allegiance is to the sceptical Academy, although he wastrained in all forms of Hellenistic philosophy (see, e.g., Powell 1995, pp. 17–20 with further references). On the basis of the doctrine of plausibility (*to pithanon*) propounded by the sceptic Carneades which he follows, Cicero claims in several places that he can consistently adopt the views of whichever school he finds most plausible on a given topic.[61] Secondly, Cicero had just recently lost his daughter, which caused him profound grief.In response to this he had researched the tradition of Greek consolatory literature and written his own consolation for himself, now lost (Cicero 1945, *Tusculans* 1.83, 3.76, 4.63; 1.65–1.66, 1.76; cf. Baltussen 2012a). This is what seems to have led him first to the view that the only sufficient response to grief is to extinguish it entirely in accordance with Stoic doctrine (Bk 3),[62] then on to the more general Stoic positions of Bks 4–5.

The *Tusculans* are written, notwithstanding the scholastic setting, in a highly rhetoricised style, reflected in the structure of each book. Each tends, with individual variations, towards a pattern whereby the student's thesis is very quickly disposed of, more or less dialectically, at which he announces himself compelled to agree, but not yet fully convinced (Cicero 1945, *Tusculans* 1.16, 2.14–2.15; cf. 3.22, 4.33, 5.37). Thereafter the style and organisation becomes much more oratorical, sometimes divided into sub-philosophical and philosophical argumentation.[63] In Bk 1 there is even an explicitly signalled rhetorical epilogue.[64] Cicero comments, as elsewhere, on the awkwardness of Stoic syllogisms[65] and the more congenial Peripatetic rhetorical treatment: of such topics.

Cicero imagines himself, while at his villa in Tusculum with some young guests, as following the practice of his Academic teacher of 88–7 BC, Philo of Larissa, each day teaching rhetoric in the morning and philosophy in the afternoon, the lat-

[59] Cicero (1945, *Tusculans* 1.7–1.8). On the term *schola* see Douglas (1995).

[60] These are stated respectively at *Tusculans* 1.9, 2.14, 3.7, 4.8 and 5.12. For an analytical outline of the contents of each book see MacKendrick (1989, pp. 149–163).

[61] Cicero (2006), *Academica* 2.66; Cicero (1991), *Onduties* 2.7–2.8; see Cicero (1945), 2.5. According to Cicero (1945), *Tusculans* 5.33 this sceptical liberty extends to changing his mind day by day.

[62] On the relation between Cicero's own experience and the *Tusculans* see especially Erskine (1997) and White (1995), pp. 223–224, who downplays the link.

[63] E.g. Cicero (1945), *Tusculans* 1.26–1.38 vis-à-vis. 1.39–81; and 1.89–1. 111 vis-à-vis. 1. 82–88.

[64] Cicero (1945), *Tusculans* 1.112–1.119; see the recapitulations at 2.65–2.67, 4.82–4.84.

[65] Cicero (1945), *Tusculans* 2.29, 3.22; cf. Cicero (1997), *The nature of gods* 2.20; and Cicero (2001), *On moral ends* 4.5–4.7; see also Schofield (1983), Cicero (1945), *Tusculans* 4.9; see also Graver (2002), p. 133.

ter constituting the dialogue (Cicero 1945, *Tusculans* 2.9; cf. 1.7–1.8, 5.121). Elsewhere Cicero reports that Philo had adopted the teaching of technical, professional, rhetoric (of the kind in which Cicero was himself independently an expert practitioner), not merely the philosophical treatment previously taught in the Academy.[66] It seems to be from Philo that Cicero has learned the idea that technical rhetoric-should be used as a part of philosophy (what Cicero 1945, *Tusculans* 1.7 calls 'the culmination of philosophy': *perfecta philosophia*), in the form of practicaltherapy for human suffering.[67] Charles Brittain asserts of Philo what we may apply equally to Cicero here, 'he thought the rhetorical practice of *theseis* on these issues could be used to refine and make *effective* the ethical beliefs of his "patients" (Brittain 2001, p. 289).' This explains the division of each of Cicero's books into a first, theoretical and dialectical, section, followed by a more oratorical treatment, and the dramatic, quasi-practical presentation.

Cicero's treatment includes both direct demonstration of the therapeutic process upon the student's beliefs and state of mind, and also more theoretical rhetorical reflection on tactics for alleviation of suffering by means of persuasion (see above). This also reduces the presentation of philosophical doctrine to an *ad hoc* status; for instance in Bk 1 the rhetorical strategy (after the preliminary dialectical exchange) is to argue at length that, if there is an afterlife, death is not to be feared (recycling Platonic arguments and adopting a reformulation of Platonic eschatology in Stoic terms, probably due to Antiochus: Cicero 1945, *Tusculans* 1.18–1.81), and then that otherwise, if death is the end, it is not to be feared (applying Epicurean and popular arguments: Cicero 1945, *Tusculans* 1. 82–1.111).

In Bk 2 Cicero does not adopt the Stoic view that pain is not evil, but rather the Peripatetic position that it is an evil, but less so than viciousness (Cicero 1945, *Tusculans* 2.29–2.30). This position is adopted rhetorically: it is a more believable starting point, and will produce the same result. Cicero presumably both here and in Bk 1 follows Antiochus of Ascalon, an Academic who had abandoned scepticism for an assimilation of Stoic, Peripatetic and Platonist doctrines. What is most interesting with regard to practical therapy in Bk 2 is the extended argument for the human ability to develop endurance of pain, derived from the quasi-empirical evidence of human behaviour in various contexts under various motivations (Cicero 1945, *Tusculans* 2.46–2.57), along with the argument that the motivation of virtue will be more effective than others (Cicero 1945, *Tusculans* 2.58–2.65, esp. 63–65).

Of philosophical significance is the non-Stoic doctrine that the soul has two parts, the rational and irrational (also stated in Bk 1, attributing the *pathê* only to the irrational part),[68] which suits the explanation of how the ability to overcome

---

[66] For discussion see Brittain (2001), pp. 296–297 and 328–342, concluding that Philo's aim was to open up philosophical ethics and politics to non-philosophers.

[67] Brittain (2001) and Schofield (2002) discuss the independent confirmation of this given by the report of Philo's approach in Stobaeus, *Eclogues* 2.39.20–2.41.25.

[68] Respectively Cicero (1945), 2.47 and 1.80. See Vander Waerdt (1985), who shows this comes from a doxographic tradition assimilating Platonic psychology to the Peripatetic view (see esp. p. 376 and n. 13, and pp. 382–383); see also Inwood (1985, p. 141 n. 55).

pain can be developed with the aim of virtue. What is more surprising is the repetition of this psychological division in Bk 4, where Pythagoras and Plato are given as authorities, immediately before, and supposedly in concert with, the adoption of Zeno's Stoic account of *pathos*.[69] There are several possible sources for Cicero's adoption of this doctrine (the recent Stoic Posidonius, or one of Cicero's teachers Philo and Antiochus),[70] but it is certainly inconsistent with Zeno and Chrysippus' 'monistic' psychology, according to which *pathê* are produced by malfunction of the rational 'leader' in us alone.

According to Galen Posidonius wrote a work *On pathê* attacking Chrysippus and arguing for a separate irrational part of the soul as source of the *pathê* (Galen 1978–1984, *PHP* Bks 4–5). There is some doubt how far Galen can be trusted, but it seems clear that Posidonius did at least claim that *pathê* must be anticipated by irrational 'pathetic' movements (whether or not originating from a separate irrational soul part, and even if these must then be confirmed by the rational 'leader').[71] Paul Vander Wardt, assuming bipartition in Posidonius, argues that he is very likely to be Cicero's source for a bipartite soul in the *Tusculans*.[72] If so, it is possible that, contrary to Galen's claims, Posidonius did not set out explicitly to attack Chrysippus, and Cicero did not notice any inconsistency when he turned to use Chrysippus as a source in Bks 3–4. However if this is the case it is surprising that Posidonius is not mentioned in the *Tusculans*, apart from a story about him which came down in the Latin tradition.[73]

But another explanation is possible. I have already remarked the common structure of the individual books of the *Tusculans*, with a dialectical refutation of the thesis followed by oratory, including in Bk 1 sub-philosophical argument, and in all cases much illustration with poetic passages, and historical exempla, and in particular the distinction made between intellectual acceptance and thorough conviction (Cicero 1945, *Tusculans* 1.16, 2.14–2.15). This all suggests the rhetorical theory applied here is based on a working model of the soul to be persuaded as composed of two factors, a rational and a sub-rational part. In that case the distinction will have

[69] Cicero (1945), *Tusculans* 4.10. Inwood (1985, p. 141) calls Cicero's adoption of psychic dualism in connection with Stoic doctrine 'breathtaking', and Annas (1992, p. 118), 'an edifying muddle', but Pigeaud (1981, pp. 248–249, 252, 274, 287–289, 297–298) treats it as a consequence of what he regards as Cicero's deliberate and (apparently) coherent rejection of Chrysippus' reduction of psychic phenomena to their material basis in strict parallelism with other bodily pathology; this view does not seem to have gained any further support.

[70] Since Cicero (1945), *Tusculans* 1.42 and 1.79 himself tells us that the Stoic Panaetius asserted the soul was made of a single material element, and not immortal, he cannot be the source, contrary to the apparent suggestion of Inwood (1985, p. 131 n. 19).

[71] Esp. Galen (1978–1984), *PHP* 5.5.21 (pp. 320.23–320.28). See the articles by Gill, Cooper and Sorabji in Sihvola and Engberg-Pedersen (1998).

[72] Vander Waerdt (1985, esp. pp. 383–389); similarly Inwood (1985), p. 141 n. 55 (and see p. 142 with n. 62).

[73] Cicero (1945), *Tusculans* 2.61. Moreover as Pigeaud (1981, pp. 276–279 (see p. 272)), has shown, Cicero does not follow Posidonius' mistaken interpretation of the 'freshness' of a judgment as only a matter of time.

arrived in the *Tusculans* as an element of Cicero's own working rhetorical theory, perhaps derived *via* Philo, and ultimately from the Peripatetic rhetorical practices of which Cicero approves (1945, *Tusculans* 4.9), as adopted into the late Academy.

Nevertheless, by contrast with the case in psychology, Cicero does reject Peripatetic ethicshere, in particular the doctrine of *metriopatheia* (i.e., that *pathos* should be moderated, not excluded from the soul: Cicero 1945, *Tusculans* 4.34–4.57). Here a series of individual Peripatetic justifications of (what we would call) emotions, as useful to moral life, are first presented then individually rejected. As mentioned, on this point Stoics and Peripatetics were talking at cross-purposes: for the former *pathos* means 'self-harm', but for the latter 'external psychic influence'.

Conclusion: Therapeutic Method in the *Tusculans*

Bk 5, on the sufficiency of virtue for happiness, states the extreme Stoic position on the complete philosophical therapy for human suffering, and is not a matter of practical day-to-day treatment for particular instances. For the latter, the use Cicero makes of Stoic doctrine in Bks 3–4 is significant. He addresses the range of particular sources of misery indicated by the list with which I began. Our concern with these is in every case to be treated as an instance of self-harming, mental disturbance produced by our own beliefs. The discussions of the fear of death and pain from Bks 1–2 are reconceptualised in Bk 4 as Stoic therapy for fear, *pathos* in relation to future evil (Cicero 1945, *Tusculans* 4.64). Bk 3 has covered grief (at all present evil), and Bk 4 extends this to the two other primary *pathê*, overexcitement, and desire. For therapeutic material here see the advice to apply shame to the former (Cicero 1945, *Tusculans* 4.66–4.68), and to belittle amorous love,[74] while the discussion of anger (regarded in antiquity as another form of desire, viz, for revenge) argues that anger is madness, useless and unnatural, with advice on intervention:separating those quarrelling and making time for people to cool down.[75]

In all cases our suffering can be alleviated by persuasion, according to Cicero, ultimately that the object of the agitation is not in fact good or bad, or immediately, at least, that it is not practically or morally appropriate to respond to it as such. In some circumstances the therapist should argue for the former, philosophical, point, in others for the latter; sometimes he or she might argue the point in general, at others in relation to the particular circumstances (such as that someone does not in fact have a duty to mourn); Cicero also evaluates the use of truisms from the poetic tradition such as that others too have suffered, and recommends positive examples of endurance as more effective (Cicero 1945, *Tusculans* 3.75–3.79, 4.58–4.60). Moreover timing is crucially important, since fresh grief is inconsolable, but this will continue until attention abates (Cicero 1945, *Tusculans* 3.74–3.75).

[74] Cicero (1945), *Tusculans* 4.68–4.76; see Lucretius (1997), 4.1058–4.1191 for a similar Epicurean attack on love.

[75] Cicero (1945), *Tusculans* 4.76–4.81; see Seneca,'On Anger' in Cooper and Procopé (1995).

What Cicero's *Tusculan Disputations* demonstrate is that Greco-Roman antiquity claimed to possess, in the combination of philosophical theory and rhetorical expertise, a methodology for addressing the whole range of human suffering with a cure through words. This operated in two co-ordinated ways, at the general level of conversion and training in a philosophical school (a life-changing experience when philosophy was conceived as a way of life), and at the particular level of individuated therapy for particular problems, as persuasion applied by the trained orator to another (or even himself) in private. It is clear that at least in some schools, philosophy as a discipline was conceived doctrinally in detail as psychic therapy co-ordinated with medicine as bodily therapy (this applies to our evidence of Philo's Academic programme as much as to the Stoics). Moreover Cicero's commitment to this conception is supported by his reports of the private experience of healing his own grief at the death of his daughter by these means.[76]

Bibliography

Andersen, Olivind, and Jon Haarberg, eds. 2001. *Making sense of Aristotle: Essays in poetics*. London: Duckworth.
Annas, Julia. 1992. *Hellenistic philosophy of mind*. Berkeley: University of California Press.
Aristophanes. 1994. *Thesmophoriazousai*, ed. A. Sommerstein. Trans. A. Sommerstein. Warminster: Aris & Phillips.
Aristotle. 1968. *Aristotle: Poetics* (ed. D.W. Lucas). Oxford: Clarendon Press.
Aristotle. 1978. *De motu animalium*, ed. M. Nussbaum. Trans. M. Nussbaum. Princeton: Princeton University Press.
Aristotle. 1984. *The complete works of Aristotle: The revised Oxford translation* (ed. Jonathan Barnes), 2 vols. Princeton: Princeton University Press.
Arius Didymus. 1999. *Arius Didymus: Epitome of Stoic Ethics*, ed. A.J. Pomeroyand. Trans. A.J. Pomeroy. Atlanta: Society of Biblical Literature.
Auerbach, Erich. 1965. *Literary Language and Its Public in Late Latin Antiquity and the Middle Ages*. Trans. R. Manheim. Princeton: University Press.
Baltussen, Han. 2012a. Cicero's self-consolation: The social and intellectual dimensions of grief in the late Roman republic. Chap. 3. Balthussen (2012b).
Baltussen, Han. ed. 2012b. *Greek and Roman Consolations. Eight Studies of a Tradition and its Afterlife*. Swansea: Classical Press of Wales.
Brennan, Tad. 1998. The old Stoic theory of the emotions. In *Emotions in Hellenistic philosophy*, eds. Juha Sihvola and Troels Engberg-Pedersen. Dortrecht, Netherlands: Kluwer
Brittain, Charles. 2001. *Philo of Larissa: The last of the academic sceptics*. Oxford: University Press.
Cicero, M.T. 1945. *Tusculan disputations*. rev. ed. Trans. J.E. King, Loeb Classical Library. London: Heinemann.

[76] Cicero (1945), *Tusculans* 1.83; see 4.63. There is disagreement whether Cicero reports at the latter place that he ignored the inconsolability of fresh grief in unnaturally curing himself by writing the *consolatio* for his daughter's death, contrary to Chrysippus' advice on this point, or, *vice versa*, that he ignored Chrysippus' advice not to grieve, and indulged himself to the full, and so produced a measure of the power of consolation when that succeeded. For the former view see, apparently Dougan and Henry (1905–34), vol. 2, p. 177 and Graver (2002, p. 62); for the latter King (1945, p. 401) and MacKendrick (1989, p. 159).

Cicero, M.T. 1991. *On Duties*, eds. M.T. Griffith, E.M. Atkins. Trans. M.T. Griffith and E.M. Atkins. Cambridge: Cambridge University Press.
Cicero, M.T. 1997. *The Nature of the Gods*. Trans. P.G. Walsh. Oxford: Oxford University Press.
Cicero, 1998. *The Republic and The laws*. Trans. N. Rudd. Oxford: Oxford University Press.
Cicero, M.T. 2001. *On moral ends*, ed. Julia Annas. Trans. R. Woolf. Cambridge: Cambridge University Press.
Cicero, M.T. 2006. *On Academic Scepticism*. Trans. C. Brittain. Indianapolis: Hackett.
Cooper, John M. 1998. Posidonius on Emotions. In *Emotionsin Hellenistic philosophy*, eds. Juha Sihvola and Troels Engberg-Pedersen. Dortrecht, Netherlands: Kluwer.
Cooper, John M., and J.F. Procopé. eds. 1995. *Seneca: Moral and political essays*. Cambridge: Cambridge University Press.
Darwin, Charles. 1872. *Expression of the emotions in man and animals*. London: Murray.
Dictionnaire du Moyen Français. 2010. ATILF: CNRS-Nancy Université. www.atilf.fr/dmf. Accessed 26 Oct 2010.
Dictionnaire Larousse de la langue francaise. 2010. Paris: Larouse. www.larousse.com. Accessed 26 Oct 2010.
Diels, Hermann, and Walther, Kranz. eds. 1966–1967. *Die Fragmente der Vorsokratiker*. 6th ed. 3 vols. Dublin: Weidmann.
Dillon, John. 1983. Metriopatheia and apatheia: Some reflections on a controversy in later Greek ethics. In *Essays in ancient Greek philosophy*, vol. 2, eds. John P. Anton and Anthony Preus. Albany: SUNY Press.
Diogenes Laertius. 1925. *Lives of eminent philosophers*, vol. 2, ed. R.D. Hicks, Loeb Classical Library. Trans. R.D. Hicks. London: Heinemann.
Dougan, T.W., and R.M. Henry. 1905–1934. *M. Tulli Ciceronis Tusculanorum disputationum libri quinque*, 2 vols. Cambridge: Cambridge University Press.
Douglas, A.E. 1995. Form and content in the Tusculan disputations. In *Cicero the philosopher*, ed. J.G.F. Powell. Oxford: Clarendon Press.
Engberg-Pedersen, Troels. 1990. *The Stoic theory of oikeiosis*. Aarhus: University Press.
Erskine, Andrew. 1997. Cicero and the expression of grief. In *The passions in Roman thought and literature*, eds. Susanna Morton Braund and Christopher Gill. Cambridge: Cambridge University Press.
Fortenbaugh, William. 2000. *Aristotle on emotion*. 2nd ed. London: Duckworth.
Frede, Michael. 1986. The Stoic doctrine of the affections of the soul. In *The norms of nature: Studies in Hellenistic ethics*, eds. Malcolm Schofield and Gisela Striker. Cambridge: University Press.
Galen. 1978–1984. *On the doctrines of Hippocrates and Plato*. 3 vols., ed. P.d. Lacy. Trans. P.d. Lacy. Berlin: Akademie.
Gill, Christopher. 1997. Introduction II: The emotions in Greco-Roman philosophy. In *The passions in Roman thought and literature*, eds. Susanna Morton Braund and Christopher Gill. Cambridge: Cambridge University Press.
Gill, Christopher. 1985. Ancient psychotherapy. *Journal of the History of Ideas* 46: 307–325.
Graver, Margaret. trans. and comm. 2002. *Cicero on the emotions: Tusculan disputations 3 and 4*. Chicago: University of Chicago Press.
Graver, Margaret. 2007. *Stoicism and emotion*. Chicago: University Press.
Hall, Edith. 2010. *Greek tragedy: Suffering under the sun*. Oxford: University Press.
Hesiod. 1983. *Theogony*. In *The poems of Hesiod*. Trans. R.M. Frazer. Norman: University of Oklahoma Press.
Hippocrates. 1923. *Hippocrates*, vol. 1, ed. W.H.S. Jones, Loeb Classical Library. Trans. W.H.S. Jones. Cambridge: Harvard University Press.
Homer. 1962. *The Iliad*. Trans. R. Lattimore. Chicago: University of Chicago Press.
Homer. 1967. *The Odyssey*. Trans. R. Lattimore. New York: Harper and Row.
Inwood, Brad. 1985. *Ethics and human action in early Stoicism*. Oxford: Clarendon Press.
Inwood, Brad, and L.P. Gerson. eds. and trans. 1997. *Hellenistic philosophy: Introductory readings*. 2nd ed. Indianapolis: Hackett.

James, William. 1884. What is an emotion? *Mind* 9: 188–205.

Kirk, G. S., J.E. Raven and M. Schofield. 1983. *The presocratic philosophers*. 2nd ed. Cambridge: University Press.

Knuuttila, Simo, and Troels, Engberg-Pedersen. 1998. How the philosophical analysis of emotions was introduced. In *The emotions in Hellenistic philosophy*, eds. Juha Sihvola and Troels Engberg-Pedersen. Dordrecht, Netherlands: Kluwer.

Konstan, David. 2006. *The emotions of the ancient Greeks:Studies in Aristotle and Greek literature*. Toronto: Toronto University Press.

Lampe, Kurt. 2010. "Socratic Therapy" from Aeschines of Sphettus to Lacan. *Classical Antiquity* 29: 181–221.

Liddell, H.F., R. Scott and H.S. Jones. 1940. *A Greek English lexicon*. 9th ed. Oxford: Clarendon Press.

Long, A.A., and D.N. Sedley. eds. 1987. *The Hellenistic philosophers*, vol. 1. Cambridge: Cambridge University Press.

Lucretius. 1997. *On the Nature of the Universe*. Trans. R. Melville. Oxford: Oxford University Press.

MacKendrick, Paul. 1989. *The philosophical books of Cicero*. New York: St Martin's Press.

Murray, Penelope. 1997. *Plato on poetry*.Cambridge: Cambridge University Press.

Niemeyer, J.F. 1976. *Mediae latinitatis lexicon minus*. Leiden: Brill.

Nussbaum, Martha. 1986. Therapeutic arguments: Epicurus and Aristotle. In *The norms of nature: Studies in Hellenistic ethics*, eds. Malcolm Schofield and Gisela Striker. Cambridge: Cambridge University Press.

Nussbaum, Martha. 1994. *The therapy of desire: Theory and practice in Hellenistic ethics*. Princeton: Princeton University Press.

Oxford English dictionary. 1989. (eds. J Simpson and E Weiner, 2nd ed). Oxford: Clarendon Press.

Pigeaud, Jackie. 1981. *La maladie de l'âme: étude sur la relation de lâme et du corps dans la tradition médico-philosophique antique*. Paris: Belles Lettres.

Pindar. 1997. *Pindar: Olympian odes. Pythian odes*, ed. W.H. Race, Loeb Classical Library. Trans. W.H. Race. Cambridge: Harvard University Press.

Plato. 1997. *Complete works*, ed. John M. Cooper. Indianapolis: Hackett.

Plato. 2000a. *The Republic*, ed. G.R.F. Ferrari. Trans. T. Griffith. Cambridge: Cambridge University Press.

Plato. 2000b. *Plato: Timaeus*. Trans. D. Zeyl. Cambridge: Hackett.

Plutarch. 1939. *Moralia*, vol. VI, ed. W.C. Helmbold, Loeb Classical Library. Trans. W.C. Helmbold. Cambridge: Harvard University Press.

Powell, J.G.F. 1995. Introduction: Cicero's philosophical works and their background. In *Cicero the philosopher*, ed. J.G.F. Powell. Oxford: Oxford University Press.

Pseudo-Andronicus. 1977. *Peri pathôn*, ed. A. Glibert-Thirry. Leiden: Brill.

Rist, J.M. 1969. *Stoic philosophy*. Cambridge: University Press.

Rorty, Amélie Oksenberg. 1984. Aristotle on the metaphysical status of *pathê*. *Review of Metaphysics* 37: 521–546.

Rorty, Amélie Oksenberg. 1992. *Essays on Aristotle's poetics*. Princeton: University Press.

Schofield, Malcolm. 1983. The syllogisms of Zeno of Citium. *Phronesis* 28: 31–58.

Schofield, Malcolm. 2002. Academic therapy: Philo of Larissa and Cicero's project in the Tusculans. In *Philosophy and power in the Graeco-Roman world*, eds. Gillian Clark and Tessa Rajak. Oxford: University Press.

Sihvola, Juha, and Troels Engberg-Pedersen. eds. 1998. *The emotions in Hellenistic philosophy*. Dortrecht, Netherlands: Kluwer.

Sorabji, Richard. 1997. Is Stoic philosophy helpful as psychotherapy? In *Aristotle and after (BICS Supplement 68)*, ed. Richard Sorabji. London: Institute of Classical Studies.

Sorabji, Richard. 2000. *Emotion and peace of mind: From Stoic agitation to Christian temptation*. Oxford: Oxford University Press.

Stobaeus. 1884. *Ioannis Stobaei Anthologii libri duo priores*, vol. 2, ed. C. Wachsmuth. Berlin: Weidmann.

Tieleman, Teun. 2003. *Chrysippus' on affections: Reconstruction and interpretation*. Leiden: Brill.
Vander Waerdt, Paul. 1985. Peripatetic Soul-Division, Posidonius, and Middle Platonic Moral Psychology. *Greek, Roman and Byzantine Studies* 24: 373–394.
Vegetti, M. 1995. Tra passioni e malattia. *Pathos* nel pensiero medico antico. *Elenchos* 16: 217–230.
Virgil. 1952. *The Aeneid*. Trans. C.D. Lewis. Oxford: Oxford University Press.
von Arnim, Hans. ed. 1964. *Stoicorum veterum fragmenta*. 4 vols. Stuttgart: Teubner.
West, M.L. trans. 1994. *Greek lyric poetry*. Oxford: Oxford Univerity Press.
White, Stephen. 1995. Cicero and the therapists. In *Cicero the philosopher*, ed. J.G.F. Powell. Oxford: Oxford University Press.

Chapter 13
Ancient Greek Responses to Suffering: Thinking with Philoctetes

Edith Hall

> I heard a thumping sound,
> the sort always made by a man worn away by pain.
> It came from over there.
> What a harsh, harsh noise it makes—it hurts my years—
> the unmistakable sound of someone
> staggering along as if he's being tortured.
> The howl of a man in agony is instantly recognisable,
> even from a distance. His groans are all too audible.
>
> *Sophocles, Philoctetes*

These are the words with which the chorus of twelve Greek soldiers respond to the disturbing sounds they can hear from offstage shortly before Philoctetes, the hero of Sophocles' tragedy which bears his name, staggers into view. The play was first performed in the spring of 409 BCE, at a time when Athens, the city where it was produced, had been at war more at less continuously for more than two decades, and had sustained terrible casualties.[1] Few members of Sophocles' audience would not have suffered either a war injury or a close personal bereavement within the last few years. And in this drama, the now elderly playwright (he was at least seventy) made his citizen audience watch a soldier suffering horrifically and for extended sequences in front of their eyes.

Over the last hundred years before the premiere of *Philoctetes*, an unprecedented intellectual revolution had been taking place in all the ancient Greek-speaking communities, which were spreading from western Asia, the Black Sea and the Aegean islands to North Africa, Greece and Sicily. The revolution was manifested in the emergence of several new branches of enquiry and corresponding genres of writing. The first treatises on the nature of the gods, on the physical world, on history, on rhetoric, and on comparative anthropology all stemmed from this period. But so did

[1] For excellent studies of the historical evidence for the way that pity and sympathy functioned as social forces in classical Athens, see Sternberg (2005, 2006).

E. Hall (✉)
Department of Classics, King's College London, London, UK
e-mail: edith.hall4@btinternet.com

J. Malpas, N. Lickiss (eds.), *Perspectives on Human Suffering*,
DOI 10.1007/978-94-007-2795-3_13, © Springer Science+Business Media B.V. 2012

the first discourses on political philosophy (by Socrates as recorded by Plato and Xenophon, and by Socrates' coevals Protagoras and Antiphon), the first handbooks of practical medicine (by Hippocrates, or if not by him personally, by the doctors of the fifth century associated with the medical school named for him which already centred on the island of Cos), and the first surviving Greek tragedies (by Aeschylus, and Euripides as well as Sophocles). These last three genres share one crucial feature in common: they all confront, very directly, the problem of suffering in human life.

The Greek moral philosophers asked how communities can be run so as to maximize the happiness of individuals within them (Amato 1990, pp. 30–34). The doctors asked why their patients experienced pain, and through empirical observation and study of precedent created regimes of increasingly scientific treatment with which to ameliorate it. The tragedians brought back long-dead mythical heroes to suffer both physically and psychologically, at great length and with great intensity, in front of audiences in the Athenian theatre of Dionysus. It is surely no coincidence that these three distinct responses to suffering developed almost precisely at the same time. Nor is it accidental, given the religious, social and cultural values shared by the ancient Greeks, that all three media are unanimous that suffering is regrettable, largely random, has nothing whatsoever to recommend it, and needs to be cured or prevented altogether. Ancient Greeks did not believe that suffering ennobled the sufferer. They did not believe that suffering was distributed providentially: they were well aware that good people often suffered, and bad people had been known to die at advanced ages without apparently suffering much at all. As Philoctetes says in reference to the cynical and pitiless Odysseus, 'While the gods have apportioned me no enjoyment whatsoever, you are alive and gratified. I endure so much pain and suffering, as well as being mocked by you and the Atridae' (i.e. Agamemnon and Menelaus, the Greek commanders at Troy) (Sophocles 1994, lines 1020–1024)[2].

The ancient Greeks also knew that they were all, as individuals, very likely to suffer extreme and life-threatening physical pain, whether on the battlefield as men or in childbirth as women, at some point in their lives, and the psychological pain of bereavement was ubiquitous in close-knit communities where premature death happened every day. Moreover, a large proportion of the inhabitants of most ancient Greek communities were not free, but of slave status, and slaves were legally vulnerable to all kinds of physical and mental abuse at the hands of their owners. It is hardly surprising that the ancient Greek vocabulary of suffering, while not differentiating between physical and psychological pain (see below) is nevertheless so extensive and nuanced; (Rey 1993, pp. 10–40) indeed, Rem Edwards (1984) has suggested that thinking about the classical taxonomy of suffering could help us create new modes of language more adequate to the apprehension and representation of pain and distress in our own society.

There is a large range of words traditionally translated into English as 'suffer' or 'suffering'—certainly more than are available in English, as a glance into any Ancient Greek-English dictionary will demonstrate. The very sound of even some of the most frequently used substantives, most of which occur in *Philoctetes*, gives

[2] All references are to line numbers in the Greek text, which can be found with a parallel English translation in Sophocles (1994), lines 202–208.

an idea of the aural effect of the laments in Greek tragedy—*ponos*, *pēma*, *pathos*, *pathēma*, *pēmonē*, *penthos*, *kaka*, *lupē*, *odunē*, *algēdōn*, *algēma*, *algos*, *achos*, *ania*, *athlos*, *mochthos*, *oizus*, *dusphora*, *talaipōria*. Moreover, as in the English word 'suffering', almost all of these words can mean both physical and mental pain: indeed, the Greeks of Sophocles' day would have had great difficulty in making a hard-and-fast distinction between the two. We shall see shortly that one writer categorized together as the (to us) rather distinct forms of suffering constituted by extreme poverty, acute illness, physical handicap and bereavement. The ancient perception of the psychosomatic indivisibility of suffering was partly a result of the beliefs that emotion had physiological effects on the internal organs, and that thinking took place somewhere in the area of the midriff or spleen (Hall 2010a). It was also partly because a key word in the ancient Greek vocabulary of suffering was *kaka*, a term as all-embracing as the French *mal* in French studies of suffering since Durkheim (Pickering and Rosati 2008). *Kaka* can mean 'evil', but it can also refer to illness, disease, pain, harm, suffering, misfortune, and even cowardice in the face of these afflictions.

It would be quite impossible to cover the attitude to suffering in classical Greek moral philosophy, tragedy and medicine in a single essay. This is why I have chosen to represent classical Mediterranean thought on suffering by a detailed examination of just one Greek tragedy, Sophocles' *Philoctetes*, in which both moral philosophy and medicine also feature. Philoctetes, who has longstanding infection of some kind from a snake-bite received ten years ago, screams in physical pain for two extensive portions of this drama. He did not do anything immoral to deserve the injury, and nor did anyone else: the play is not about the problem of evil, unlike, for example Euripides' *Trojan Women*, which does conduct a metaphysical enquiry into the possible cosmic as well as terrestrial causes of suffering (Hall 2007). Philoctetes is not ennobled by his suffering and learns nothing from it. Suffering in this play has no inherent metaphysical or ethical status, although it does raise the rather practical as well as ethical question of how other human beings can and should respond to the sufferer. There is a remarkable degree of what we would call 'realism' in the depiction of the suffering. Philoctetes is not cured of his pain even by the end of the play; his symptoms are not only enacted but (albeit briefly) described. The younger Greek man Neoptolemus, when he finds the cave in which Philoctetes lives, sees 'some rags drying out in the sun, full of the acute infection' (Sophocles 1994, lines 38–39). Neoptolemus also observes, after Philoctetes' first major paroxysm, that 'his head sinks backward. Yes, a sweat has broken out over his whole body, and a dark, haemorrhaging vein has burst from his heel' (Sophocles 1994, line 825). Just one palliative is mentioned:Philoctetes says that he has collected the leaves of a particular plant which help to 'put the wound to sleep and calm it down' (Sophocles 1994, lines 649–650). Moreover, a complete cure is predicted in the future (see below). The play would certainly have interested doctors in the ancient audience. But it is far more important that the play examines in close detail how an individual's acute suffering deforms his everyday life and his relationships with his or her community. It also shows how very differently individuals respond to the suffering of others. It even asks the proto-Utilitarian question of whether the suffering of a single individual should be allowed to outweigh the interests of the whole community. The crisis which the suffering individual causes, by creating a social rift between people who react to it in different ways, is actually irresolvable except by divine intervention. At the end of all this intellectual questioning, however, what the spectator remembers is Philoctetes' screams. It is almost impossible to imagine a modern dramatist or film-maker presenting his audience with a comparable portrayal of unremitting agony; I know of no other artwork which explores so intensely the problem which incurable suffering presents to the community to which the sufferer belongs.

David Morris has advised us to address ourselves to recovering the wisdom of Greek tragedy. He argues (correctly, in my view) that this genre of literature identifies pain and suffering as an inevitable aspect of human life, however wasteful and senseless these phenomena may be experienced as being. I certainly agree with Harold Schweizer when he argues that the 'rhythm and syntax of speaking orders and articulates the movement of suffering towards another. In speaking we acknowledge, and indeed claim, the social space in which mourning and empathy can take place. Greek theater fulfilled this function of an empathic space' (Schweizer 2000). But where I depart radically from Morris's view is when he argues that the Greeks emphasized the 'social meaningfulness' of suffering, and the human potential to 'rise to moments of awesome fortitude, grandeur, and almost inconceivable endurance' (Morris 1991, p. 262; Wilkinson 2005, p. 29). This was, to be sure, arguably one aspect of the way in which the Roman Stoic Seneca interpreted the Greek tragedians more than five centuries later. Admiration for heroic endurance has also certainly been an important strand in thinking about heroes in tragedies composed since the Renaissance, inflected by Christian models of asceticism (although I concur with Terry Eagleton that the idea that tragedy somehow ennobles the sufferer has been vastly—and often with distasteful insensitivity towards 'real-life' sufferers—exaggerated) (Eagleton 2002).[3] But in my view no classical Greek tragedy (which means in effect a play composed by an Athenian in the fifth century BCE) remotely construes suffering as having any immanent value or inherent 'social meaning' whatsoever. A few contemporary comments do admittedly show that the point of representing suffering in the theatre was discussed, at least in the fourth century. One comic writer proposed that spectators take comfort from the fact that in tragedy, the heroes experienced even worse suffering than they did themselves: Telephus' poverty comforted those who were poor; sick ones were comforted by the fits Alcmaeon suffered; those with eye problems by the sons of Phineus, who were blinded; and the bereaved were consoled by Niobe, who had lost far more children than they had (Hall 2006, pp. 16–17). Aristotle proposed that we can learn about suffering in a paradoxically *pleasurable* way through experiencing it vicariously in theatrical mimesis (Aristotle 1968; Hall 2006, pp. 126–127). But no classical Greek thinker, as far as I know, ever recorded the view that suffering was itself in any sense whatsoever advantageous, constructive, or 'socially meaningful'. In tragedy, by staging suffering in concentrated form, the dramatists confronted head-on 'the irreducible dilemma or the uncircumventable paradox that human cultures must give meaning to suffering, yet they cannot' (Amato 1990, p. xxiv). That is why, I believe,

[3] On ancient asceticism see Perkins (1995).

we do have something to learn from classical Greek tragedy's fearless confrontation with the sheer randomness, pointlessness, and absolute misery of undeserved suffering.

Philoctetes was a skilled warrior and archer who had joined the Greek expedition against Troy. But he had suffered a wound that made his presence intolerable to his comrades. All we are told is that he had, apparently by complete accident and unwittingly, intruded into the shrine of Chryse, the nymph who lived on an island named after her, and been bitten by the poisonous snake who guarded it (Sophocles 1994, lines 1327–1328). The snakebite on his foot remained an open wound and festered atrociously. The Greek leaders, the Atridae, ordered their lieutenant Odysseus to take Philoctetes away from their camp at Troy, and abandon him on the uninhabited island of Lemnos, a boat ride away in the north-eastern Aegean Sea. Ten years have passed, and now the Greeks desperately need to recover Philoctetes, since an oracle has told them that without him and his special bow (which Philoctetes inherited from his friend Heracles) they can't win the war at all.

The cynical, now middle-aged Odysseus arrives at the island with the young Neoptolemus. His purpose is to trick Philoctetes into returning to Troy with them (he is, they correctly predict, unlikely to cooperate voluntarily with the community which abandoned him). On this desert island there are no cities, institutions, lawgivers, judges, priests, prophets, or other authority figures to provide any moral framework for the action. Distinctions between right and wrong have to be made up as they go along. There is therefore absolutely nothing in this simple scenario to distract the audience from the problem of Philoctetes' suffering. Unusually amongst Greek tragedies, there is neither a death nor even any reported combat. Uniquely amongst Greek tragedies, there are no females at all. Also uniquely among Greek tragedies, no character is related by blood to any other. Yet inter-subjective relationships are central, since Odysseus and Philoctetes are rivals for the fatherless Neoptolemus' filial attachment. By removing the biological and kinship elements, therefore, the social and moral ramifications of the way in which individuals respond to Philoctetes' suffering are engineered by Sophocles so as to appear in the clearest possible light, uncomplicated by questions of familial obligation or affective ties.

Indeed, Sophocles has gone out of his way to turn his theatre into something akin to a laboratory, where Philoctetes, as sufferer, is to be inspected by both his internal audience and the external one in the ancient Athenian performance space on the south side of the Acropolis in the sanctuary of Dionysus. The responses to Philoctetes' suffering are different, and fluctuate even within the psyche of each involved party, but certain images and metaphors recur, above all the notion that Philoctetes' state of suffering somehow aligns him with wild animals rather than with human beings (Avery 1965, pp. 284–285). It is partly that his bodily debility has made it impossible for him, alone as he is on Lemnos, to practise the arts and crafts of civilization—farming, weaving, the manufacture of tools—which the Greek pre-Socratic philosophers, especially Protagoras (as recorded in Plato's dialogue *Protagoras*), had argued divided humans from the animal world (Hall 2006, pp. 178–181). His pain also makes him lose the ability to express himself adequately or precisely in the Greek language. Philoctetes' cries, as Odysseus says in the opening speech, are 'wild'. When we meet Philoctetes, movingly, his first response is great pleasure at hearing the Greek language spoken by others after so long in solitary confinement on the island (Sophocles 1994, line 234), but it soon becomes apparent that this animal-like linguistic and social isolation is a metonymy for his psychological situation. In his private world of pain, when the spasms strike, language can scarcely reach him at all.

By far the most important feature of the play is its portrayal, in Philoctetes, of a man suffering terribly. His part requires the actor to communicate a series of subjective responses to pain, both aurally and visually, through gesture, posture and movement. The play explores several possible behaviours in the sufferer himself. He repeatedly expresses degrees of death wish, asking his own personified Life why he has not been allowed to slip down to Hades, (Sophocles 1994, lines 1348–1349) or describing his existence as equivalent to being dead (Sophocles 1994, line 1216). During his first convulsive fit of agony, he begs Neoptolemus to cast him into the fires of the volcano on the island, and let him burn to death (Sophocles 1994, lines 800–801); the volcanic fires also function as an analogy for the pain which surges within Philoctetes' flesh. In his convulsive spasms, he screams for a weapon to cut himself up with—'a sword, or an axe, or any weapon—just get me one!' He wants 'to mangle this flesh, to hew limb from limb with my own hand; all I can think of is death' (Sophocles 1994, lines 1207–1209). Besides his suicidal and self-destructive impulses, he is also extremely angry about his helplessness when he actually passes out from pain, and when his bow (which in his maimed state is all that keeps him alive, by enabling him to eat), has been removed (Sophocles 1994, line 1281).

Philoctetes has also become obsessed by the question of who is responsible for his suffering, on an incorrect and paranoid impulse blaming the Atridae (who did abandon him but did not actually cause his injury). This is an incorrect reaction to a wholly correct perception on his part–that his problem is quite as much social as physiological. He desperately needs to have his suffering *acknowledged*. The worst aspect of his mental suffering is his fear that absolutely nobody except Odysseus and the sons of Atreus is even aware of what he his going through (Sophocles 1994, lines 254–260). What he finds even harder to bear than the pain itself is that the Atridae saw it as a justification for making him forfeit all social standing. They forcibly removed all his normal rights as a fellow Greek prince in the army—to recognition, respect, freedom to express himself and his opinions, to self-determination and autonomy, to move around physically, and to the protection of his group. This is a form of social erasure—what Orlando Patterson, in the context of transatlantic slavery, called 'social death' (Patterson 1982; Patterson 1999)—which does all too often accompany physical suffering in modern as well as ancient societies. Philoctetes is so outraged at his 'social death' that he even rejects the offer of being cured at Troy by the sons of Asclepius (Sophocles 1994, line 1332).[4] As Neoptolemus complains towards the end of the play, this now makes him responsible for his own continued suffering, which makes it more difficult 'to excuse or pity' him: 'You have become wild, and can't tolerate advice; even if someone counsels you with good

[4] Machaon, the archetypal surgeon, and his brother, who represented medicine and pharmacology.

will towards you, you hate him, and treat him like an enemy' (Sophocles 1994, lines 1317–1324). Yet unlike the other characters, Neoptolemus does, unconditionally, support Philoctetes' right to make the decision himself and can also, unlike the chorusmen, tolerate being verbally abused by a man in pain.

Everyone internal to the play finds Philoctetes' pain difficult to be near and especially difficult to hear: although there is some discussion of the obnoxious smell his foot gives off (Sophocles 1994, lines 876, 891), and the rank blood which oozes from it, what people really can't tolerate is the terrible noise he makes when the pain as at its worst. But Sophocles also portrays four discreet subjectivities—Odysseus, Neoptolemus, the chorus of Greek soldiers and finally the spirit of Philoctetes' dead friend Heracles–responding to their exposure to his suffering. Through these different reactions Sophocles asks his audience to think about where their own responses fall on the spectrum, from total lack of sympathy (Odysseus), to conditional support (the chorus), unconditional but rather passive support (Neoptolemus) to proactive intervention which Philoctetes can accept because the individual who offers it has been a fellow-sufferer himself (Heracles).

For the first two hundred and twenty lines—a good fifteen or twenty minutes of action—Philoctetes is not to be seen. The play begins when the Greek party arrives and Odysseus immediately identifies the location to Neoptolemus as a headland in Lemnos. It was here, ten years ago, that he exposed Philoctetes, 'with his foot oozing from the disease that devoured it', because 'we weren't even able to conduct libations or sacrifices at our ease, so wild were the obscenities to which he subjected the whole encampment, with his shouting and groans' (Sophocles 1994, lines 7–11). This is how the suffering subject, Philoctetes, is verbally introduced. The lexical terms that describe his wound suggest the dripping of a viscous pus or other matter and a malady that actually eats away at his flesh. But the most telling words here is actually the one which I have translated 'at our ease', *hekēlois*, an adjective often used to describe the gods' carefree enjoyment of their banquets. The sufferer, implies Odysseus callously, was acting distastefully when he spoilt the non-sufferers' civilized pleasure. The sufferer made terrible noises (the word I have translated 'wild' is usually applied to undomesticated animals), which penetrated his comrades' consciousness and compromised their peace of mind.

Odysseus' response to Philoctetes as a sufferer has always been comprehensive repudiation. Now, years later, Odysseus remains completely unmoved, and as unconcerned by Philoctetes' desires or needs as he always was. He is simply determined to force Philoctetes to Troy, however unwilling he may be. Odysseus' reaction to Philoctetes never changes in the course of the drama. He expresses no pity, offers no apology, and does not even acknowledge Philoctetes' plight. He regards Philoctetes' suffering as a ground for forcing him to forfeit all his rights as a human being of equal status, and to a role in determining what should happen to him. Repudiation of this kind is of course is one possible human reaction to suffering—to put it as far out of sight, hearing and mind as feasible, deny all responsibility for the protection, care or survival of the sufferer, and effectively to exploit their helplessness by removing from them fundamental rights as a person to self-determination and autonomy.

Yet Odysseus knows that suffering can elicit other reactions in other individuals. When he is trying to keep Neoptolemus focused on tricking Philoctetes, he is aware of the transformative power of pity on a more sensitive person: 'Don't look at him, since you have a gracious nature, and may wreck our chances' (Sophocles 1994, lines 1068–1069). And indeed Neoptolemus does turn out to be an instinctively empathetic character. He is so shaken by direct contact with Philoctetes' suffering that he eventually decides to agree to take him back to Greece himself. His support for Philoctetes, which does not exist at the start of the play, is something he *learns* through witnessing the older man's suffering: he describes the emotional experience he himself undergoes as 'a startling pity' which 'fell hard upon' him from the start (Sophocles 1994, lines 965–966). What happens to Neoptolemus is a change of perspective. His encounter with the suffering of Philoctetes makes him 'change his opinion' (*metagnōnai*, (Sophocles 1994, line 1270)—an ethically neutral term which editors under the influence of Christianity used to translate, misleadingly, 'repent' (Jebb 1898, p. 197). The support which pity creates in him becomes unconditional. At the critical moment towards the end of the action, he does stand by his promise to take Philoctetes on his own ship back to mainland Greece even if though it means wrecking his own relationship with the sons of Atreus and his 'career prospects' at Troy. Neoptolemus is the only one of the Greek party who takes Philoctetesseriously as a social being with intact 'human rights', entitled to expect complete candour in his interlocutors and to have his opinion about his own future consulted and respected regardless of how irrational it may seem.

The play is structured around a long, terrible paroxysm of agony which strikes Philoctetessometime after the arrival of the Greeks. This paroxysm creates the psychological shift in Neoptolemus which in turn, somewhat later, results in his 'conversion' to Philoctetes' cause. And in this paroxysm, Philoctetes himself utters cries that in ancient Greek poetry indicate wordless vocalizations of pain or despair. In order to suggest the powerful effect of this scene, which extends for over a hundred lines, here is approximately the first quarter:

Neoptolemus	Why have you gone quiet for no reason? What has suddenly paralysed you like this?
Philoctetes	*a! a! a! a!*
Neoptolemus	What is it?
Philoctetes	Nothing serious. Carry on, son.
Neoptolemus	Are you in pain from the usual affliction?
Philoctetes	Not at all. I think it's passing... *i-ō, gods!*
Neoptolemus	Why are you groaning and calling on the gods?
Philoctetes	…the ones who can come and help, soothe the pain... *a! a! a! a!*
Neoptolemus	What's happened to you now? Tell me….. Don't try to keep it quiet… Something's obviously wrong.
Philoctetes	I'm done for, child. I can't hide the problem from you. attatai! It pierces straight through me, it pierces straight through me. I can't stand it. I'm done for, child. It's devouring me, child. *papai! apappapai, papappapappapappapai!* For the gods sake, if you have a sword with you, child, strike my ankle, cut my foot off there! Now! Don't worry about killing me! Do it!

Neoptolemus	But what is the sudden change that makes you scream so very loudly?
Philoctetes	You know...
Neoptolemus	What?!
Philoctetes	You do know, child.
Neoptolemus	What is the matter? I *don't* know!
Philoctetes	You must know. *Pappapappapai…*
Neoptolemus	The burden of disease you are carrying is dreadful.
Philoctetes	Yes, dreadful. Beyond words. But pity me.
Neoptolemus	So what should I do?
Philoctetes	Just don't leave me because you're frightened. She comes only intermittently, when she has had enough of wandering.

There are several significant features of this interchange. First, Philoctetes' striking personification and externalization of the pain as a female who visits him intermittently between bouts of wandering (the word for disease, *nosos*, is indeed feminine in gender, but rarely personified so forcefully). Secondly, the painful part of his body feels somehow objectively *separable*, and he wants it removed, however violently. Thirdly, his attempt to suppress the pain and explicitly deny that he is in pain, until it becomes uncontrollable. Fourthly, it forces him to repeat himself, as if he can't find alternative words to express the sameness and repetition of the waves of pain assaulting him. Fifthly, the metaphors are not unlike those used to describe pain today—the pain *piercesright through* him and *devours* him.[5] Sixthly, though it is difficult co convey the full effect in translation, Philoctetes' verse form actually dissolves during this episode. The usual verse of Greek tragic dialogue is the iambic trimeter, which has an effect not very different from the blank verse of Shakespearean tragedy. But here Philoctetes has 'extra-metrical' utterances, such as '*a! a! a! a!*'and '*apappapai'*, which break up the rhythmical flow of his speech. And lastly, his pain, as he says, is 'beyond words'. That is why Sophocles wrote those strange non-verbal noises for him, the sounds emitted by bodies in pain—by animals as well as humans–almost regardless of language or culture. Philoctetes has great difficulty explaining to Neoptolemus what the matter is, and Neoptolemus has equal difficulty in understanding the nature and extent of the problem; as affected witness he also feels helpless and at a loss what action to take. The communication between the sufferer and the witness, despite the witness's best intentions and efforts, is thoroughly deficient. In the hands of expert actors, the effect of this scene is still devastating. As Iain Wilkinson puts it, citing Arthur Frank's insight that the most significant part of suffering concerns what we cannot say about the pains of our adversity, 'part of the negativity of suffering appears to consist in its capacity to oppose and destroy the "meaning of language" (Wilkinson 2005, p. 17; Frank 2001).'

Neoptolemus goes on to ask if Philoctetes would like him to touch him anywhere. As another spasm of pain arises (the metaphors here are 'it crawls on me, it comes over me' (Sophocles 1994, lines 787–788)), Philoctetes can't stand the thought of any physical contact, but he remains adamant that he does not want to be left alone. Eventually he passes out, but insists that Neoptolemus stay with

[5] For a brilliant comparative study of the metaphors for pain in ancient Greek and contemporary English, see Budelmann (2010).

him until he regains consciousness. It is intensely important to him that his suffering takes place in the sympathetic, although non-intrusive, listening presence of another human being. Indeed, his greatest anxiety, expressed over and over again, is that he is going to end up alone again, 'with no human companion' (Sophocles 1994, line 1105). One of the most moving moments in the play is when he regains consciousness after this first major bout of pain, and finds that Neoptolemus and his men, although helpless to alleviate it, have stayed with him throughout:

> Oh light, returning to me after sleep.
> Oh, you have kept watch over me, my friends—
> something I never dared even hope for!
> I would never have expected you to put
> up with my pain so sympathetically,
> and to stay beside me and assist me!
> Certainly the sons of Atreus, those fine generals,
> were not prepared to tolerate this with equanimity! (Sophocles 1994, lines 867–876)

Neoptolemus does not immediately change his mind about tricking Philoctetes, and does at first go along with Odysseus' scheme by removing the bow while the sick man is asleep. But when he returns to the stage, after mentally digesting the appallingly traumatic scene he has witnessed, he has completely changed his mind.

The reaction of Neoptolemus' men, the chorus of twelve lower-status Greeks soldiers, is carefully and subtly distinguished from his. At first they are the chief mouthpiece for pity, shocked by the situation in which Philoctetes has been trying to survive, and moved by the terrible sounds of pain he emits. In a central song they linger on the horrors that he must have suffered over the years:

> He did nobody any wrong, and was fair to people who treated him fairly,
> but was left to perish so undeservedly…
> Left alone, unable to walk,
> with nobody anwhere in the land to be his neighbour while he suffered, nobody from whom he could get a response
> when he cried in pain at his devouring, bloody wound;
> nobody to soothe, with gentle herbs that grew in the earth,
> the scalding blood which seeped from the ulcers of his envenomed foot, whenever the torment attacked him.
> He was forced to creep this way and that,
> tottering like a child without a kindly nurse,
> going anywhere he might find any relief,
> whenever the anguish sank its teeth into him. (Sophocles 1994, lines 684–705)

Moreover, the soldiers volunteer to stay behind and look after Philoctetes while Neoptolemus and Odysseus make arrangements at the ship for leaving Lemnos with the bow, and try to persuade him to leave with them. But their support, however sorry they feel for him, turns out (unlike that of Neoptolemus) to be conditional. They are increasingly frustrated by his refusal to serve his own medical interests, since he refuses to leave the island on the ground that his social 'personhood' has not been recognized by the Atridae and Odysseus. The interchanges between Philoctetes and the chorus reveal both how the sufferer's psychological state can alienate him from his community, and that the community can show crass psychological insensitivity in terms of the humiliation which may accompany the offer of help to the sufferer.

The exchange becomes increasingly bitter, and the chorus are on the point of going back to the ship in the face of Philoctetes' continuing hostility, but then, once again, a paroxysm of agony overwhelms Philoctetes, and he screams at them not to leave:

> *Ai-ai, ai-ai!*
> *O God! O God!* This has finished me!
> My foot, my foot! What am I going to do with you
> for the rest of my life?!
> Friends, you must come back... (Sophocles 1994, lines 1186–1190)

Sophocles is trying to find ways to convey the sensory world inhabited by the suffering subject through the juxtaposition of the use of the second person to address both 'god' (i.e. the unseen metaphysical power that runs the universe) and his foot (the all too physical reality of the source of his pain). For Philoctetes, malign god and agonizing foot are as real presences as the Greek soldiers on his island, which explains why it is difficult for him to deal politely or rationally with them. He knows he has been harsh with these visitors:

> There is no reason to be angry when a man,
> who is beset with a storm of agony,
> says crazy things. (Sophocles 1994, lines 1193–1195)

But the chorus, while still horrified at what he is suffering, are indeed finally alienated and at the play's climax are about to abandon him themselves. If he won't be helped on the terms offered by the community, the community wants to put as much space between themselves and the defiant, noisy, noisome compatriot as they possibly can.

At this climax, Neoptolemus, with considerable reluctance, stands by his promise to look after Philoctetes, recognizing his status as a social entity as well as his needs as a physical sufferer. The chorus and Odysseus are equally determined that he must be brought to Troy—the chorus believe that he should be forced, even without consent, to undergo medical treatment with Asclepius' sons, and Odysseus cares solely about what Philoctetes and the bow can do for the community. Only divine intervention can resolve this impasse, but Sophocles' choice of figure to introduce in the theatrical machine is of profound importance. It is the demigod and hero Heracles, son of Zeus and a mortal mother, whose terrestrial life is over but who has now joined the immortals. He resolves Philoctetes' problem—that a medical cure can only come at the unacceptable price to his pride of forfeiting all social autonomy and dignity—by making the return to Troy and the cure by Asclepius' son Machaon (see Fig. 1) a command from the gods. But it is the reason why Philoctetes trusts and obeys Heracles that needs to be emphasized. Heracles was a friend—not a blood relative—and bound to him by precious reciprocal ties of mutual loyalty, respect, and promises of protection and aid should the need arise. But even more importantly, Heracles had suffered a degree—although not a duration—of physical agony equivalent to Philoctetes' own, as the demigod reminds him (Sophocles

Fig. 1 Etruscan scarab from the fourth century BCE engraved with Machaon, seated and bearded, healing Philoctetes, who leans on a staff. (Image reproduced courtesy of the British Museum)

1994, lines 1418–1419). Heracles' death was caused by putting on a garment infused with terrible corrosive poison, which gradually devoured his skin, flesh and bones. Indeed, Heracles' own writhing agony is portrayed in another tragedy by Sophocles, his *Women of Trachis*.[6]

Philoctetes knew how badly Heracles had suffered because he had been there. Moreover, he had done Heracles the ultimate kindness of putting him out of his misery: he had agreed to build him a pyre and set light to it on Mount Oeta, a deed he recalls proudly to Neoptolemus as having been 'the act of a benefactor' (Sophocles 1994, line 670). Philoctetes, in the world of modern medicine, might have faced trial in agreeing to assist Heracles, who was dying a slow and agonizing death, to a swifter demise. But in Sophocles' ethical universe this act of assistance in euthanasia was conceived as doing the sufferer a substantial favour.

Philoctetes is the ultimate example of the Greek tragic hero because his suffering is constant, 'in-your-face', and yet is never given any acceptable justification. As the play ends he is still suffering, but feeling strengthened sufficiently by his deceased fellow sufferer's intervention to be persuaded to return to Troy. He is given a promise, with divine authority, not only of a cure but of social rehabilitation as the hero who will (with Neoptolemus' help) win the war. But the problem of the cruelty shown to Philoctetes formerly, when he was put out of sight, out of hearing, and as far as possible out of mind, is never resolved. What the play does, despite all the attempts of the Greek leaders at Troy to erase him, is make Philoctetes' anguish just about as visible and audible as possible within the limits of theatre, and expose

[6] For a recent study of the ethics of *Women of Trachis*, see Hall (2009). For an outstanding analysis of the importance to cultural history of the representation of physical pain in both *Philoctetes* and *Women of Trachis*, see Budelmann (2007).

Fig. 2 The gay rights activist Ron Vawter (*right*), shortly before his death, as Philoctetes at the Kaaitheater, Brussels (1994). (Image reproduced courtesy of the Archive of Performances of Greek & Roman Drama)

and explore the subtle (as well as not so subtle) differences in human reactions to it. Surely ancient Greek tragedy' combination of directness about suffering, as well as its complexity in dissecting the impact of suffering on human relationships, has been a main reason for its renewed popularity over the last few decades in the theatres of the modern world.

It is precisely since the mid-1990s that there has been a call for closer attention to the *experience* of suffering, an awakening to the 'need for the social sciences to inquire more substantially into the existential components of the phenomenon of suffering' (Cohen 2001, p. 3). It was at that time that the great actor Ron Vawter, who was suffering from AIDS, chose to perform in an important Brussels production of plays about Philoctetes shortly before his death in 1994 (Fig. 2).[7] Much more recently, Bryan Doerries has directed readings of his translation of the play as a part of the training of medical students at Cornell's Weill Medical College.[8] It must of course be true that Sophocles, like everyone else who has ever ventured 'to fashion symbolic forms of culture to reveal the character of suffering', was of course liable to the charge that his theatre is 'woefully inadequate' to the task of accounting 'for the multidimensionality of this experience' (Wilkinson 2005, p. 17). Yet it remains

[7] See Hall (2004, pp. 11–12), with Fig. 2. The production was entitled *Philoktetes Variations*, directed by Jan Ritsema, and performed at the Kaaitheater. Vawter's naked body, covered with purple Kaposi rash, 'spoke a more forceful language than his and his fellow actors' words', according to Laermans (1994, p. 68).

[8] See http://www.philoctetesproject.org/pdf/Philoctetes_Project.pdf

a constructive way to approach the phenomenon and problem of suffering in human life to ask ourselves this question: do we want to react to Philoctetes like Odysseus, or the Greek sailors, or Neoptolemus, or with the understanding that nobody who has not suffered equivalently, such as Heracles, has any grasp whatsoever of what is really at stake?

Bibliography

Amato, Joseph D. 1990. *Victims and values: A history and theory of suffering*. New York: Greenwood Press.

Aristotle. 1968. *Poetics,* ed. D.W. Lucas. Oxford: Clarendon Press.

Avery, Harry C. 1965. Heracles, Philoctetes, Neoptolemus. *Hermes* 93:279–297.

Budelmann, Felix. 2010. The reception of Sophocles' representation of physical pain. *American Journal of Philology* 128 (4): 443–467.

Cohen, Stanley. 2001. *States of denial: Knowing about atrocities and suffering*. Cambridge: Polity.

Eagleton, Terry. 2002. *Sweet violence: An essay on the tragic*. Oxford: Blackwell.

Edwards, Rem. 1984. Pain and the ethics of pain management. *Social Science and Medicine* 18 (6): 515–523.

Frank, A. W. 2001. Can we research suffering? *Qualitative Health Research* 11 (3): 353–362.

Hall, Edith. 2004. Introduction: Why Greek tragedy since the late 1960s? In *Dionysus since 69: Greek tragedy at the dawn of the third millennium,* eds. E. Hall, F. Macintosh and A. Wrigley. Oxford: Oxford University Press.

Hall, Edith. 2006. *The theatrical cast of Athens: Interactions between ancient Greek drama and society*. Oxford: Oxford University Press.

Hall, Edith. 2007. Trojan suffering, tragic gods, and transhistorical metaphysics. In *Tragedy in transition,* eds. Sara Annes Brown and Catherine Silverstone. Oxford: Blackwell.

Hall, Edith. 2009. Deianira deliberates: precipitate decision-taking and Trachiniae. In *Sophocles and the Greek tragic tradition: Studies for patricia easterling,* eds. S. Goldhill and E. Hall. Cambridge: Cambridge University Press.

Hall, Edith. 2010a. Bringing together nature and culture: On the uses and limits of cognitive science for the study of performance reception. In *Theorising performance reception: Greek drama, cultural history, and critical practice,* eds. Edith Hall and Stephe Harrop. London: Duckworth.

Hall, Edith. 2010b. *Greek tragedy: Suffering under the Sun*. Oxford: University Press.

Jebb, R. C. 1898. *Sophocles: Philoctetes*, 2nd edn. Cambridge: Cambridge University Press.

Laermans, Rudi. 1994. Halfway to the Grave. *Theater* 25:67–70.

Morris, D. 1991. *The Culture of pain*. Berkeley: California University Press.

Patterson, Orlando. 1982. *Slavery and social death: A comparative study*. Cambridge: Harvard University Press.

Patterson, Orlando. 1999. *Rituals in blood: Consequences of slavery in two American centuries*. New York: Basic Civitas Books.

Perkins, J. 1995. *The suffering self: Pain and narrative representation in the early Christian era*. London: Routledge.

Pickering, W. S. F., and Massimo Rosati. 2008. Introduction. In *Suffering and evil: The Durkheimian legacy,* eds. W. S. F. Pickering and Massimo Rosati. New York: Durkheim Books.

Rey, R. 1993. *The history of pain*. Cambridge: Harvard University Press.

Schweizer, Harold. 2000. Against suffering: A meditation on literature. *Literature and medicine* 19:229–240.

Sophocles. 1994. *Philoctetes*, vol. 2. Loeb Classical Library. Trans. H. Lloyd-Jones. Cambridge: Harvard University Press.
Sternberg, Rachel Hall. 2005. *Pity and power in ancient Athens*. Cambridge: Cambridge University Press.
Sternberg, Rachel Hall. 2006. *Tragedy offstage: Suffering and sympathy in ancient Athens*. Austin: University of Texas Press.
Wilkinson, Iain. 2005. *Suffering: A sociological introduction*. Cambridge: Polity Press.

Chapter 14
Historicizing Suffering

Wayne Hudson

According to the standard account suffering is a universal human experience described as a negative basic feeling or emotion that involves a subjective character of unpleasantness, aversion, harm, or threat of harm to body or mind (Spelman 1997; Cassell 1991). A distinction is then drawn between *physical suffering*, which can often be ameliorated by medical, political, and economic measures, *mental suffering*, which can continue to resist treatment, and *ontological suffering*, including death, where the suffering turns on the lack of positive meaning and the ultimacy of the experience rather than the amount of pain as such. The standard account then goes on to note different treatments of suffering in the world's religions (Bowker 1970) and philosophies, and the different ways in which individuals may respond to suffering: becoming defeated and embittered; by using suffering as a spur to achievement; by making a positive out of suffering as a path to transcendence; or by providing help and support. The standard account is *framed in generic terms*, and can at times occlude both the historicity of suffering and its social constitution. At the very least it may be possible to raise such considerations without giving support to the excesses of postmodernism and the various forms of relativism associated with it.

The approach to suffering I argue for here accepts that generic accounts of suffering should be developed and that major human performances such as hatred and friendship have recurrent and largely commensurable elements. I urge only: 1. that we need to be more sensitive to the fact that suffering has changed historically, assuming that we can gain some knowledge of this from the records that survive and taking into account the lack of records from most of those who suffered; and 2. that we need to pay more attention to the social construction of suffering in particular contexts, whereby social construction applies both to the experience of the one who suffers and to the interpretations others place on their suffering, although in some cases these obviously interact. My view does not imply an extreme form of social

W. Hudson (✉)
School of Philosophy, University of Tasmania, Hobart 7001, Tasmania, Australia
e-mail: Clement.Hudson@utas.edu.au

Centre for Public and Contextual Theology, Charles Sturt University, Canberra, Australia
e-mail: Wahudson@csu.edu.au

J. Malpas, N. Lickiss (eds.), *Perspectives on Human Suffering*,
DOI 10.1007/978-94-007-2795-3_14, © Springer Science+Business Media B.V. 2012

constructivism of the type associated with discourse idealism. Nor do I deny that a certain species-wide intelligibility applies to the overwhelming majority of known cases. In many ways the view I put is neither surprising nor unexpected. However, I will suggest that the degree to which it is the case has not been generally grasped, and also that the implications of my view for the alleviation of suffering have not yet been fully taken into account. What follows prepares the reader for these substantive claims.

An extensive literature already alerts us to the possibility that suffering is *socially constructed, interactive* and *hermeneutical*, and arises with our need to impose meaning on our lives. Suffering is not found everywhere in the same universal and unmediated form. It is different in different geographies.[1] Studies of the Chinese peasantry, for example, reveal a concept of the 'sufferer' (*shoukuren*), with the implication that those who cultivate the land experience both 'bodily suffering' (*shenti de ku*) and 'spiritual suffering' (*xinling de ku*), where neither term implies exactly the type of ego-based reflexivity associated with suffering in the modern West.[2] There is also evidence that understandings of suffering have changed in clinical medical contexts in the West.[3] Further, there are reasons to argue that suffering has *a narrative character*, and is *intra-social* and *dialogic*, at least in societies which have developed more than very limited forms of reflexivity (Bakhtin 1981). But this, in turn, means that for certain purposes suffering may need to be understood contextually, that is, with regard to social and cultural situations which differ over space and time. Thus the Mongols, for example, were well aware that their military tactics terrorized populations of areas they were seeking to occupy. Indeed, this was the reason they adopted the tactics they did. On the other hand, the way they constructed the suffering of their victims is less immediately accessible to us, and there is little evidence that they were concerned about the suffering of the peoples they conquered, except in so far as it impacted on their own military objectives.

To give a very different example, it seems likely that torture, which has been carefully studied (Scarry 1985), has different narrative content in different cultures in which it occurs, with the implication that this narrative content may impact on the actions of the torturers and also in part on the responses of those tortured. Some American Indian societies, for example, took great pleasure in torturing captives to death and regarded such practices as central to their honour code. They were not inclined to feel pity for those they tortured and there were cases when the tortured also understood their experience in terms of honour rituals.

---

[1] The literature on suffering often reveals a pronounced localism, of the kind which applies to one's personal pain. For example, an emphasis on morally outrageous suffering colours the literature on suffering in the American civil war. See (Gilpin 2008).

[2] The evidence supports the social construction of suffering. Granted that there are problems about interpreting the suffering of millions of peasants who left few records of their reflections on their experience, we do have some evidence about how Chinese peasants interpreted their suffering in recent times and also evidence about how they were re-socialised to interpret it in Marxist ideological terms by the Chinese Communist party. See (Guo 1993, p. 4; Liu 2002, p. xii).

[3] See (Rey 1995) which gives detailed evidence of historically variable conceptions of pain and responses to it in the Western tradition.

To say this is not to imply that suffering cannot be transculturally explicated in generic terms. Clearly it is possible to explicate suffering by reference to phenomenological descriptions of grimacing, tears and weeping and so forth. Nonetheless, it is important not to fail to attend to the sociocultural construction of such suffering even at the level of facial display (Mauss 1973). Further, it is crucial not to assume that experiences of suffering and their cultural interpretations have remained static over time. On the contrary, refined studies suggest that even rather simple features of interpreted human experience vary historically. Thus there are endemic problems about attempts to separate subjective and objective conceptions of suffering in sources from ancient Greece and the ancient Middle East, partly because the subject-object distinction known to Western philosophy may be local and in some respects historically emergent. It is generally conceded, for example, not to be present in Homer, and there is now argument that it may not be found in the form we expect in St. Paul.[4] Finally, it is crucial not to ignore the cosmological contexts in which suffering occurs, that is, what suffering means for those who suffer and for those who impose suffering, given their cosmologies, which, of course, often differ. Thus in the case of the Aztecs their attitudes to the sufferings of the human beings they slaughtered were inseparable from the fact that they believed that human sacrifice was necessary to prevent the destruction of the universe.

If we accept that interpretations of suffering are in part socially constructed, then it is possible to problematize in some respects contemporary Western attempts to understand suffering as intrinsically ‘bad’. The modern Western social judgement that suffering is bad can sometimes be anachronistic, and also insensitive to the plurality of human meaning systems over time, even though all human communities associate extreme pain with negativity at some level. This is clear enough from the records which survive from ancient cultures. In Hinduism, for example, there is no notion that suffering is bad or cosmologically illegitimate, even though suffering is deemed to have negative features. In Hinduism the ever-changing outer world is called the *wheel of samsara*. To live on that plane of existence is to encounter suffering after suffering. According to the Upanishads:

> This vast universe is a wheel, the wheel of Brahman. Upon it are all creatures that are subject to birth, death, and rebirth. Round and round it turns, and never stops. As long as the individual self thinks it is separate from the Lord, it revolves upon the wheel in bondage to the laws of birth, death, and rebirth. (Svetasvatara Upanishad 1. 6–8)

The problem of suffering is real, but individual suffering may be compensated for in the next life, while the unchanging reality is beyond all suffering.

For Buddhism as well suffering is a pervasive cosmological circumstance rather than a contingent personal misfortune. Deprivation pervades life, and the problem therefore is to learn how not to be reborn. As the Buddha explains:

> The Noble Truth of deprivation (*dukkha*) is this: birth is deprivation; aging is deprivation; sickness is deprivation; death is deprivation; sorrow and lamentation, pain, grief, and

[4] For a partial anticipation on this view see the very thorough, albeit iconoclastic, study by (Campbell 2009).

> despair are deprivation; association with the unpleasant is deprivation; dissociation from the pleasant is deprivation; not to get what one wants is deprivation—in brief, the five aggregates of attachment are deprivation. (Samyutta Nikaya, 56)

Sanskrit discussions of 'deprivation' are related to cosmological premises which ensure that all deprivation and sorrow are deserved, even though Western theorists, including some Buddhist philosophers, sometimes play down this dependency.

The ancient Semites also constructed suffering in complex ways which differ quite considerably from attitudes we now take for granted. Thus the *Book of Job* explores the limitations of any approach which posits a happy theodicy and draws out the ethical complexities of a God who sends suffering to the just. Likewise, the notion of suffering as redemptive appears in many Hebrew stories and songs. Isaiah, for example, declared: 'By his suffering shall my servant justify many, taking their faults on himself'. On the other hand, the Hebrews expressed no concern for the men, women and children they killed at Yahweh's command, although they were prepared to criticise Yahweh when underserved suffering occurred.[5] They also insisted that it was a sin against Yahweh not to hear the cries of the poor i.e. they constructed the problem of suffering in theistic or, to be more precise, henotheistic terms, and not only with reference to social immanence.

In the early Christian world view suffering was also socially constructed in historically specific and emergent ways. It was not seen as necessarily undesirable, meaningless or without value.[6] On the contrary, salvation depended upon the suffering of Christ in his paschal mystery (Moltmann 1974; John 1984). Moreover, according to St. Paul 'suffering produces endurance, and endurance produces character'.[7] In later Latin Christianity there was a widespread view that it was original sin which led to punishment and so suffering, with the implication that such suffering might be a proper consequence of earlier evil actions. Christians were also conspicuous in their concern for others who suffered (the sick, widows, orphans) and in some contexts recognised that they were obligated to alleviate suffering,[8] a comportment which could be sometimes seen as new and remarkable in the Roman world. Later medieval phantasmagoria produced a God who tormented the wicked with suffering in hell, but the medieval Christian enthusiasm for suffering cannot be understood in modern psychological terms, and even Aquinas seems to have regarded the sufferings of the wicked as a matter of celebration. Subsequent Christian asceticism ascribed even more positive value to suffering, to the extent of institutionalising the use of whips and cilices for religious men and women.[9] Indeed, religious persons regularly reported looking forward to sharing in the sufferings of Christ.

---

[5] *Psalm* 44, 23–6.

[6] On one Jewish view Jesus' career is connected to the emergence of a catastrophic Messianism for which the suffering, humiliation and death of the Messiah were part of the redemptive process—see (Knohl 2008).

[7] *Romans* 5:3.

[8] *Matthew* 5:1–12 and *Luke* 6:20–26.

[9] Opus Dei has attracted negative publicity for its contemporary advocacy of such practices, but they were much more widespread in religious orders in the past. Islam also has the notion of

Nor does the secularism of the modern West, which strips suffering of most of its theological and cosmological connotations, provide access to an unmediated form of suffering. In the West totalitarian regimes have been conspicuous for their political appropriation of suffering as something supremely glorious in the context of war. Indeed, the idea of suffering for a righteous cause probably became stronger in Nazi Germany and in the USSR than it had been in previous regimes. When ameliorist approaches to suffering emerged in the nineteenth and twentieth centuries in medical and economic contexts, this ameliorism involved much greater concern for the sufferings of some peoples than others. Indeed, it is extraordinary how slow European colonial powers were to express concern about the suffering of slaves if those slaves were coloured. Once again there is nothing in my argument that downgrades the importance of ameliorist efforts to end suffering. But the modern utopia of the amelioration of suffering also needs to be understood as a social construction of suffering rather than as a belated recognition of suffering's real nature. And much the same applies to the vast psychological literature in European languages which accepts modern suffering as somehow beneficial: as 'part of the journey' or as the outcome of 'a conflicted self'.[10]

To go beyond unnuanced generic accounts of suffering we need to be careful not to assume that we know what suffering is in specific instances, as if the nature of suffering manifested without a history of cultural attitudes and theoretical ideas to colour it. To grasp this point it is only necessary to consider some well-known approaches to suffering in the history of Western philosophy, which is only one of the world's major philosophical traditions. In Western philosophy accounts of suffering are found in Plato, Aristotle, Epicurus, the Stoics, Bentham, Mill, Schopenhauer, Nietzsche, Scheler, Arendt and Levinas, to give only key cases. Thus Plato attacked Homer and the Greek tragedians for educating Athenians in wrong conceptions of the role of grief in individual and collective life. He also had access to a refined distinction between grief connected with the spirited part of the soul (*thumoeides*) and grief connected with the appetitive part of the soul (*epithymetikon*), which was later lost, and so was able to make subtle differentiations (Spelman 1997, Chap. 1). Aristotle, on the other hand, denied that slaves could be associated with suffering on the grounds that they did not have the social status needed to acquire such experiences. Slavery was natural and necessary, and Aristotle did not show concern for or interest in slaves as subjects of experience (Spelman 1997, Chap. 2). More generally, Greek approaches to what might now be dubbed 'suffering' in context hinged more on the exact theory of the soul and the polis they assumed than many of the standard accounts tend to suggest. In the same way, later German ruminations on suffering relate to particular terms and to the type of universe assumed by different philosophers. Hence when Schopenhauer emphasized that human suffering

---

suffering for a righteous cause, and the idea of suffering as an instrument for realizing the greater purposes of God (*Qur'an* 5:35) and the Sh'iah put a related emphasis on physical suffering and accept whipping as a religiously meaningful act.

[10] For a different view exploring the problem of social theodicy, see (Wilkinson and Morgan 2001).

was intensified by thinking of absent and future things, he assumed that suffering had no effect on ultimate meaning and destiny (Schopenhauer 1970, p. 40), just as when Nietzsche denounced the Western devaluation of suffering as a form of decadence and insisted that suffering had an essential role to play in developing the *Übermensch*, he relied on a specific conception of how struggle formed part of the workings of the universe.

Likewise, when French existentialists such as Jean-Paul Sartre and Albert Camus argued that there was no meaningful way to comprehend the suffering of life and that all human beings could do was to create their own meaning in an absurd universe, they depended crucially on assumptions about the cosmos they presumed to be in. In Germany Max Scheler attempted to revise the traditional accounts of suffering from Plato to Schopenhauer by arguing that suffering was not essentially passive and could be a source of growth, (Scheler 1963, p. 46) while Hannah Arendt argued that the suffering of others cannot become public without becoming dangerously distorted, relying upon a specific conception of the public (Arendt 1998, pp. 240 ff; Chouliaraki 2006, Chap. 9). Both, however, for the most part understood suffering in generic and not in historical and sociocultural terms. Later still, the philosopher and Talmudic scholar Emmanuel Levinas explored the phenomenology of suffering, while insisting that the torment of suffering is most acute in the realisation that it is for nothing, an analysis which again takes a specific conception of human life in our universe for granted (Edelglass 2006; Levinas 1969). In the long history of philosophical discussion of suffering in the West the relationship between the generic nature of suffering and its contextual realisations has never been satisfactorily resolved. And what is true for philosophy is also true for other domains as well (Metz 1980; Matthiesen 1986). Thus theological approaches to suffering are also often weakened by over-generic approaches to suffering. The German political theologian Johann Baptist Metz, for example, argues that attempts to offer a theological solution to the history of human suffering display a 'non-identity' which cannot be overcome by any alleged salvation history—but significantly without the multiple contextualisations which would test his claims (Matthiesen 1986, p. 49).

Generic approaches to suffering without adequate contextualisation at the level of social ontology also limit many treatments of suffering in the human sciences. In the social sciences, suffering has now been addressed in fields such as medical anthropology, ethnography, mass media analysis and holocaust studies. Certainly suffering needs to be studied more closely by the discipline of sociology, as Iain Wilkinson argues.[11] The best contemporary sociological work on suffering seeks to understand and explain the relationship between individual suffering and changing social structures. However, the new sociology of suffering is only weakly historical. The sociological exploration of suffering as inherently social derives from Durkheim's classic theory of suicide as a social fact. More recently, in *The Weight of the World: Social Suffering in Contemporary Society*, (Bourdieu 1999) the French sociologist Pierre Bourdieu has examined the diverse everyday sufferings of ordi-

[11] Wilkinson (2005) reviews in detail the contributions of Marx, Durkheim Weber and Arendt. Wilkinson explores ways in which people make suffering productive for thought and action and to cases in which suffering is associated with innovation and social change.

nary people in contemporary society. In bringing to light the social character of individual suffering, Bourdieu and his colleagues assert that the individual is simultaneously social and that what appears to be the most individualised is at the same time the most de-individualised (Bourdieu 1999). Difficulties in individual circumstance may be seen as subjective anxieties and conflicts, yet what they actually reveal are the structural contradictions embedded in the stratifications of the social world. Bourdieu also noted that religious change impacted upon the character of suffering by depriving it of the *raison d'être* it had in theistic cosmology, and well as removing the promise of supernatural assistance and ultimate justification (Bourdieu and Wacquant 1992, p. 278; Bourdieu 1997). But, once again, while contemporary ethnographic approaches seek to provide explanations of the explanations social actors offer, they still tend to do so in terms of a trans-societal mythology of 'social classes' and with reference to 'the larger processes of social history' rather than with reference to contextually specific formations of human suffering in the context of specific narratives and horizons of meaning and purpose.[12]

The term 'social suffering' is also used by the medical anthropologist Arthur Kleinman, but again without detailed contextual determinacy. Kleinman writes that 'Social suffering…brings into a single space an assemblage of human problems that have their origins and consequences in the devastating injuries that social force can inflict on human experience. It reveals too the interpersonal grounds of suffering: in other words, that suffering is a social experience' (Kleinman et al. 1970, p. ix). Critical community psychologists also now seek to show that individual concerns, anxieties and suffering, especially associated with mental illness, unemployment and suicide, are 'social suffering'. Once again, however, generic accounts of suffering are sometimes allied with context sensitive accounts of the social causes of suffering without the contextualisation of the suffering itself which would seem to be required.

Given the background of these considerations, and many others which could be cited, I now urge that our understanding of suffering be *historicised* to bring current discussion of suffering up to the level of contemporary histories of sexuality and the emotions. Tracing the history of suffering is an immense task, especially since most of the literature is still Eurocentric. Philology is only a partial guide because real social contexts determine how words are used in specific situations. Thus it is clear that *dukkha* in Sanskrit cannot be translated as suffering because it encompasses both mental and physical perspectives. It does not imply that the experience is undeserved and it means more than sorrow (Larson 1984). Related problems afflict *passio* in Latin, while *ku* in Chinese emphasises the bitterness of the experience, not reflexivity. Equally, different strata in different societies responded to suffering differently, and pity has only been extended historically to certain groups in particular situations. Thus in most human societies there is only limited evidence of pity from higher social classes for the disabled, for prisoners, or for those injured in war until very recent times. In China, for example, it is said that no army picked up and cared for wounded soldiers until the Peoples Liberation Army did so. Once, however, it is

[12] Bourdieu, to be fair, has a considerable sense of this, but does not entirely overcome the structural functional influences on his thought.

accepted that there is *a social history of suffering* (how it is constructed, interpreted and responded to), then more contextual approaches are pertinent. Here post-Foucauldian perspectives which draw attention to radical and specific discontinuities in cultural history have some purchase, provided we avoid the relativism that implies that everything about X is constructed and the cultural and linguistic idealism which asserts that human experiences are incommensurably different in different societies and languages.[13] Instead, it is useful to explore *ensembles of suffering* under particular types of socio-political and ethical regimes. Diverse ensembles of suffering impose meanings on the lives of the individual. They also tend to have formative historical and cultural effects over time within any particular history and culture. It is also useful to note that suffering often has *spectatorship features*, and can be related to its reception by historically changing media, including popular culture (Chouliaraki 2006). How others see and interpret our suffering sometimes modifies its character. This is so both for traditional societies, in which witch doctors and shamans were crucial mediators, and for contemporary technoscientific social spaces in which the suffering of peoples far away feature prominently.

Granted that suffering cannot be entirely an a-historical condition, let alone the putative 'human condition' beloved of pundits, some current conceptions of suffering may need to be called into question, or at least tested against culturally more challenging instances. Thus the current view that suffering has no meaning must be confined to conceptions of reality for which this is the case, just as the modern view that suffering should be avoided at all costs is more socio-culturally specific than its advocates realise.

If, however, historical and social contexts are taken more seriously in the area of suffering than they have been to date, then this may have implications for the ways in which we respond to suffering in the present, and also for how suffering is constructed in the future. Grasping the interactive, meaning dependent nature of human performances has policy implications. Specifically, it may be possible to generate more culturally and contextually relevant responses, including responses in the form of relevant moral meanings. If so, then it may be possible not only to affirm the role of critical memory or *anamnesis* as a response to the sufferings of the dead, as Walter Benjamin famously did, but to generate culturally specific ways of rendering suffering meaningful in contemporary people's lives, and so modify at a sociocultural level what suffering is for the people concerned. Such a stance in no way minimises the need for effective practical help, for example, in the form of medical treatment. It does, however, learn from historical examples that suffering is not entirely independent of the schemes through which we construct it because we are, in a profound sense, the results of the meaning systems on which and through which we operate. This, in turn, requires a major shift in our own comportments towards human life and its problems, a shift in comportment which will hopefully become increasingly common as our century progresses. My argument can be restated as a plea for caution. But it also contains the elements of a programme to respond to suffering in cultures in which reflexivity and communication through media play an immensely enhanced and increasingly constitutive role.

[13] For Foucault's impact on the history of sexuality, see (Halperin 2004).

Bibliography

Arendt, Hannah. 1998. *The human condition*, 2nd edn. Chicago: Univ. of Chicago Press.
Bakhtin, M. M. 1981. *The dialogic imagination: Four essays*, ed. M. Holquist. Trans. C. Emerson and M. Holquist. Austin: Univ. of Texas Press.
Bourdieu, Pierre. 1997. *Pascalian meditations*. Stanford: Stanford Univ. Press.
Bourdieu, Pierre. 1999. *The weight of the world: Social suffering in contemporary society*. Cambridge: Polity Press.
Bourdieu, Pierre and Loïc Wacquant. 1992. *An invitation to reflexive sociology*. Chicago: Chicago Univ. Press.
Bowker, J. 1970. *Problems of suffering in religions of the world*. Cambridge: Cambridge Univ. Press.
Campbell, D. A. 2009. *The deliverance of God an apocalyptical reading of justification in Paul*. Grand Rapids: Eerdmans.
Cassell, E. J. 1991. *The nature of suffering and the goals of medicine*, 1st ed. New York: Oxford Univ. Press.
Chouliaraki, L. 2006. *The spectatorship of suffering*. London: Sage.
Edelglass, W. 2006. Levinas on suffering and compassion. *Sophia* 45:43–59.
Gilpin, D. G. 2008. *This republic of suffering: Death and the American civil war*. New York: Knopf.
Guo Yuhua. 1993. Suffering, Civilisation and Oral History. http://inter.ishlyon.cnrs.fr/iDocuments/Texte_Communication/Guo Yuhua Suffering Civilization Oral Historypdf.
Halperin, D. M. 2004. *How to do the history of homosexuality*. Chicago: Univ. of Chicago Press.
John, Paul II. 1984. *On the Christian meaning of human suffering*. Vatican: Liberia Editrice.
Kleinman, Arthur, V. Das, and M. Lock, eds. 1970. *Social suffering*. Berkeley: Univ. of California Press.
Knohl, I. 2008. *The messiah before Jesus: The suffering servant in the dead Sea scrolls*. Berkeley: Univ. of California Press.
Larson, G. J. 1984. The relation between 'Action' and 'Suffering' in Asian philosophy. In *Philosophy East and West* 4:352–3.
Levinas, Emmanuel. 1969. *Totality and Infinity: An Essay on Exteriority*. Trans. A. Lingis. Pittsburgh: Duquesne Univ. Press.
Liu, Xin. 2002. *The otherness of self: A genealogy of the self in contemporary China*. Ann Arbor: Univ. of Michigan Press.
Matthiesen, M. M. 1986. Theological anthropology in Metz and Elie Wiesel. *Religion and Literature* 18:47–63.
Mauss, Marcel. 1973. Techniques of the body. *Economy and Society* 2:70–88.
Metz, J. B. 1980. *Faith in history and society: Toward a practical fundamental theology*. New York: Crossroad.
Moltmann, J. 1974. *The crucified God*. New York: Harper and Row.
Rey, R. 1995. *The history of pain*. Cambridge: Harvard Univ. Press.
Scarry, Elaine. 1985. *The body in pain: The making and unmaking of the world*. New York: Oxford Univ. Press.
Scheler, Max. 1963. Schriften zur Soziologie and Weltanschauungslehre. In *Gesammelte Werke*, vol 6. Munich: Francke Verlag.
Schopenhauer, Arthur. 1970. *Essays and aphorisms*. Harmondsworth: Penguin.
Spelman, E. V. 1995. *Fruits of sorrow framing our attention to suffering*. Boston: Beacon Press.
Wilkinson, Iain and David Morgan. 2001. The problem of suffering and the sociological task of theodicy. *European Journal of Social Theory* 4:199–214.
Wilkinson, Iain. 2005. *Suffering: A sociological introduction*. Cambridge: Polity Press.

Chapter 15
The Politics of Suffering: Aboriginal Health in Contemporary Australia

Peter Sutton

Health is one of the most highly politicised domains of Indigenous affairs in Australia.[1] Acting out of altruism, ardent goodwill, or political ambition, sometimes perhaps all three, activists and progressives have made improvements in this field. Some have also created a web of self-censorship and other-censorship that has become counterproductive. In this partly historical exploration, I examine the way in which politics has connected, or in many cases failed to connect, with the need to address the real problems of Aboriginal health in contemporary Australia. These problems entail a level of suffering that threatens not only individuals, but entire communities.

The standard progressive line on the causes of the gap between Indigenous and non-Indigenous health is that these are pretty much entirely the historical outcomes of past dispossession, ill treatment and racial discrimination. But there is a deep-seated problem with this partial picture. These same catastrophic events have been endured by others, and in more recent times, and on a far larger and more diabolical scale, in the European Holocaust of the 1940s, yet without anything like the same health outcomes for the survivors and the following generations of their descendants.

So a wounded history of domination and discrimination, while a significant historical factor, is not enough, on its own, to explain the Indigenous/non-Indigenous health gap in Australia. Fourth World health profiles, even where very similar historical processes were at work over the same period, also vary considerably among themselves and do not reveal a single uniform reaction to colonisation. Aboriginal Australians, Maori, Aztecs, ancient Britons and Ainu (Japan) have experienced

This chapter draws on material included in Chap. 5 of Peter Sutton (2009), *The Politics of Suffering: Indigenous Australia and the End of the Liberal Consensus* (Melbourne: Melbourne University Press).

[1] The most sophisticated academic analysis of the recent history of the subject is Kowal (2008).

P. Sutton (✉)
School of Earth & Environmental Sciences, University of Adelaide, Adelaide 5005, South Australia, Australia
e-mail: Peter.Sutton@samuseum.sa.gov.au

J. Malpas, N. Lickiss (eds.), *Perspectives on Human Suffering*,
DOI 10.1007/978-94-007-2795-3_15, © Springer Science+Business Media B.V. 2012

widely differing outcomes from conquest and colonisation. One key factor causing these differences is the pre-existing differences between the cultures people bring to their disasters. Differences between colonisers form the other main factor.

Every human community that is relatively homogeneous culturally has what might be called an identifiable health culture that can be systematically described. Accounts of this kind form one of the elementary tasks of medical anthropologists. In the Australian Aboriginal case, the communities have a range of health cultures, which are now clearly an amalgam of old, classical traditions and other, newer patterns of health-related practices that have grown up since conquest. Where old elements in a health culture come into collision with new environmental or other factors, the clash can be deleterious. People whose sanitation and hygiene practices derive significantly from the period when their ancestors were semi-nomadic, usually naked and living mostly in the open, but who themselves now live in fixed dwellings and use clothing, sheets and blankets, face dangerous biological conditions that were not a problem, or not so great a problem, for their forebears. Combined with large household sizes, these and similar elements in the health culture of many communities help underpin high levels of a range of different diseases, some of them life-threatening.

Health cultures are largely reproduced by being acquired by each generation in infancy, childhood and youth. If there is a problem with the capacity of such a culture to cope with modern conditions then it is at this early life stage that shifts critically need to occur, although this is not to exclude the more difficult area of adult education. The failure of the Australian health system to focus more on behavioural change through impacting on child socialisation—something that is needed if the Indigenous health differential is to be tackled head on—is due significantly to an illness of another kind: the disease of politicisation.

The Disease of Politicisation

In 2004 the prestigious international medical journal, *The Lancet*, contained a paper by Ian Anderson, an academic physician of Aboriginal identity, and Bebe Loff, a legally trained medical ethicist, entitled 'Voices lost: Indigenous health and human rights in Australia' (Anderson and Loff 2004, pp. 1281–1282). It began by referring to the statistic that Aboriginal people's life expectancy was then about twenty years less than that of Australians as a whole (men: 56 years versus 77, women: 63 years versus 82), and that Indigenous rates of disease were also greater. It also mentioned that more money was spent per capita on Indigenous health than on non-Indigenous health per annum, but not enough to cope with the greater needs of Indigenous people.

Their discussion then suddenly turned to the federal government's then recent abolition of ATSIC (the Aboriginal and Torres Strait Islander Commission), which since 1989 had been an elected Indigenous body responsible for the allocation of various resources, policy development, and oversight of federal government

Indigenous programs. This was a body that, by 2004, had lost credibility and support very widely, not only among many Indigenous people but also on a bipartisan basis in federal politics. One of the chief reasons for this loss of credibility was the ATSIC leadership's obsessive concern with what is known in Australia as 'the rights agenda', especially with heavily symbolic political issues such as the national treaty proposal, a government apology for past mistreatment, and native title. Together with its neglect of some very pressing on-the-ground issues such as violence, especially by men against women, sexual abuse of minors, and child neglect, this reduction of the major issues to largely political and symbolic ones undermined ATSIC's standing badly. Given this, and the fact that ATSIC had long been relieved of the Indigenous health budget (since 1995), it was not clear why its demise was relevant to Anderson and Loff, other than as evidence of a federal government they wished to portray as hostile.

Anderson and Loff said, and many would agree, that increasing primary health care services to Indigenous people—part of what they called 'the practical agenda'—was unlikely of itself to yield substantial improvement in people's health. But they then followed this, not by any mention of bringing about a shift in health-related cultural practices by means of socialisation or education, but by the claim that:

> If Aboriginal people have no voice, if there is no capacity for self-government, if there is no means for coming together to identify and address problems, there cannot be any hope of progress in addressing the appalling disparities between the health of Indigenous and non-Indigenous Australians. A so-called practical agenda will come to nought. It is remarkable that this simple fact continues to be ignored. (Anderson and Loff 2004, p. 1281)

Here was the reduction of a serious medical, social, and cultural issue to the politics of 'voice', and a racial separatist appeal to the aim of 'self-government'. That a journal with the historic reputation of *The Lancet* would stoop to publishing propaganda like this was incredible. Such statements always carry with them an underlying message about cause and effect. What this statement told the world was that the Aboriginal health differential was primarily caused by insufficient political representation and talk. There is typically no room in such an argument for tackling the role of culturally embedded behaviours that have a direct impact on health. This was no exception. These behaviours include absolutely basic things like domestic sanitation and personal hygiene, housing density, diet, the care of children and the elderly, gender relationships, alcohol and drug use, conflict resolution, the social acceptability of violence, cultural norms to do with expression of the emotions, the relative value placed on physical wellbeing, attitudes to learning new information, and attitudes to making changes in health-related behaviour. These were always going to be central factors in closing the notorious Australian health gap. When accounts of the gap leave them out, what is going on? Are these basics regarded as being in the too-hard basket?

The Anderson and Loff approach, like so many politicised accounts of the Indigenous health gap, ignored several ethnographically fine-grained explorations of the role of cultural factors in the generation of Indigenous health problems. Maggie Brady's works on the drivers of alcohol abuse and petrol sniffing were exemplary and well known (Brady 1992, 2004; Brady and Palmer 1984). Another good example was Jon Willis's account of barriers to men's use of safe sex technologies in a particular region of Central Australia. His paper was called 'Condoms are for whitefellas' (Willis 2003). Of thirteen such barriers identified by Willis, most were based on cultural values and psychological reactions which were traditional or at least long conventional in the region. Given similarly conventional attitudes to having multiple sexual partners in the same region, these barriers to protection were a key element in the prevalence rates for major sexually transmitted infections (STIs). It was no surprise that the prevalence rates for gonorrhoea, chlamydia and syphilis in the relevant nearby Nganampa Health Service survey region in 1996 were 841, 157 and 106 times the national notification rates respectively (Willis 2003, p. 210). A comprehensive control program and aggressive STI screening and treatment, including annual population-wide screening, resulted in a dramatic reduction in gonorrhoea and chlamydia in the Nganampa region from 1996–2003. Syphilis, less prevalent, was in gradual decline from 1996–2006. From 2003–2006 there was a dramatic resurgence in gonorrhoea almost to the 1996 levels.

Researchers concluded that a core group travelling to or coming from regions with poorer STI programs had failed to be impacted by health promotion campaigns. A large ceremonial event in 2004, which attracted over 1,000 non-residents, coincided with an immediate doubling of the gonorrhoea rate in the region (Huang et al. 2008). This negative health event was not due to any lack of ostensible local self-governance by the regional health authority. Nganampa had taken over from the government health services in 1985.

If the answer to criticisms of the kind I make here is that Indigenous self-government and voice-power will deliver improvements by some kind of automatic rule, there is an obvious reply: conditions in remote Aboriginal communities, especially, but also in urban ghettos like Redfern in Sydney, have generally become worse, not better, since the transfer of power from church and government to locally elected bodies in the 1970s and 1980s. There is no practical evidence for racial separatist politics as a cure for extreme rates of renal failure, ischaemic heart disease, high infant mortality and extreme rates of domestic homicide. Those who suggest this usually do so out of raw political self-interest. They thus become part of the problem.

There is, however, a more solid argument that relates the governmental order to Indigenous health, namely Stephen Kunitz's 1994 work, *Disease and Social Diversity: The European Impact on the Health of Non-Europeans*, a study of the provision of special health service entitlements to Indigenous people as against universal entitlements. In 1987 American Indians without health insurance were covered by the Indian Health Service, while 22% of African Americans were without insurance. In the same year, maternal mortality was 7.1 per 100,000 live births for Indians and Alaska natives, 6.6 for all races, but 12.0 for all races other than white. Infant mortality was similar: 9.3 per 1,000 live births for Indians, 14.6 among Alaska natives, 10.1 among all races, 15.4 for all non-whites, and 17.9 for African Americans (Kunitz 1994, p. 181).

But what Kunitz drew from such figures was not some kind of magical relationship between the transference of political control and health, but between targeted funding and the health of populations with special needs (Kunitz 1994, p. 182). In a number of cases the Indians had secured a 'medicine chest' provision in treaties agreed with the colonists, as well as reservations of land. Indeed, in all Kunitz's Fourth World case studies (the United States, Canada, New Zealand, Australia), there was only one country where treaties were not made, and that was Australia (Kunitz 1994, p. 25). He regarded the fact that Aboriginal people were at the bottom of the life expectancy table when compared with American Indians (and Alaska natives), Canadian Indians, and New Zealand Maori, as being a consequence of this absence of treaties (Kunitz 1994, pp. 26–27).

That there was a correlation that led him to this view I do not doubt. But I think one has to consider the possibility that both parts of the correlation arise from a third factor or group of factors, particularly differences between the pre-existing social and economic organisation of the peoples concerned. Australia was the exception here on other relevant grounds as well: it was the only sample made up entirely of recent ex–hunter-gatherers. Comparisons between Aboriginal Australians and village peoples who had devised sanitation measures for the settled life, and who lived in stratified societies with quite highly formalised arrangements for suppressing internal conflict and conducting warfare during external conflict, are comparisons between very different kinds of peoples. The selection of Fourth World peoples for medical comparisons is not one based on historical and cultural commonalities in the subject populations but on a common post-colonial political condition as victims. The scientific relevance of this basis of selection has never been justified. Recently nomadic ex–hunter-gatherers within the English-speaking New World nation states should be compared with each other, and then with those of pastoral and, separately, sedentary horticultural and agricultural indigenous peoples. It may be that the indigenous health difference between Australia and the rest of the New World can be accounted for other than by suggesting a poorer government performance in Australia's case. The latter has been a common view but the evidence is lacking.

Kunitz himself argued that health differences between indigenous peoples who have been subject to the same historical, environmental and governmental conditions, such as those distinguishing Navajo from Hopi Native Americans, could basically be accounted for on the basis of their cultural differences (Kunitz 1994, pp. 129–132). The Navajo were semi-sedentary pastoralists and the Hopi were sedentary agriculturalists living in socially stratified villages (Kunitz 1994, pp. 121, 124). It was the Navajo who enjoyed greater freedom from epidemics and endemic infectious disease and whose population survived colonisation more robustly, in the numerical sense, than any other American tribe (Kunitz 1994, pp. 134, 142). 'Different living conditions' accounted for mortality differences, with the Navajo moving seasonally, being sparsely distributed, and living away from water sources so that the latter remained uncontaminated. Although they defecated not far from their houses, their mobility and sparseness reduced the health dangers of doing so. Hopi, by contrast, lived permanently in crowded quarters and excreta were often deposited in narrow streets and passages between houses (Kunitz 1994, pp. 133, 134). In general, however, Kunitz did not foreground pre-existing health-related cultural practices as a major factor in how colonisation events were experienced differently by indigenous peoples internationally, although he later agreed he could well have done so (Kunitz, personal communication, 2004).

So where should our focus of attention be here—with the political imperatives of 'voice' raised by people like Anderson and Loff, or Gillian Cowlishaw? (Anderson and Loff 2004; Cowlishaw 2003) On getting to understand and give air time to Hopi 'discourse' about the 'meanings' of defecating in the nearest laneway? Or on understanding how this customary practice is learned by children, is reproduced through socialisation, has whatever meanings are attributed to it, interacts with the life cycle of micro-organisms to produce suffering and possible death, and can be removed by appropriate interventions?

Kunitz's book ended with a discussion of causality. Science, he said, transcends culture in the sense that smallpox vaccine is effective, regardless of how a society is organised (Kunitz 1994, pp. 187, 188). Science is democratic, in the sense that antibiotics can cure serious diseases, regardless of the social standing or skin colour of the patient (Kunitz 1994, p. 188). But there are also many health problems that are not susceptible to explanations based on the idea of necessary cause. (Necessary cause is something whose absence always ensures the absence of the particular medical condition.) Many illnesses are 'still best explained by multiple weakly sufficient causes, and may always be, and understanding their incidence, prevalence and distribution, as well as their prevention and treatment, may require intimate understanding of particular people and settings' (Kunitz 1994).

This means, he argued, that the biomedical model of understanding causation, and the anthropological approach, ideally should cross-fertilise each other. But because they belong to different professional interest groups, they are more likely to be used as "ideological weapons with which different groups may bash one another in a fight over whose way of knowing is most 'fundamental'". Disease and mortality, he said, are products not only of 'pathophysiological processes and the life cycles of parasites but also [of] the many ways in which human beings live on the land and with each other. That is what is fundamental' (Kunitz 1994).

Disease and Conquest

The simple and often vague attribution of the cause of Fourth World health and other problems to colonisation and subsequent 'disadvantage' stands in striking contrast to more fact-based, and therefore more complex, models of the process. These are accounts of the kind put forward by Alan Cass and others for end-stage renal disease among Indigenous Australians, or Ernest Hunter's schema for relating precursors and consequences of Aboriginal alcohol misuse (Cass et al. 2004; Hunter 1993, p. 197). It is incumbent on those who put forward largely historical and political causal explanations of Indigenous health problems to show us the mechanics of the chain of events. This is not just for the sake of historical accuracy, but because the past can teach us a lot about what is going on in the present, as Maggie Brady's historical work on drinking has so cogently shown (Brady 2008). One problem here is that the pre-contact health baseline for Indigenous Australians is not plentifully described. The most positive scientific assessment of pre-colonial Aboriginal general health which I have come across is Stephen Webb's, namely that it was 'very good anywhere on the continent', (Webb 1995, p. 293). although he also said it varied regionally and lacked effective means of treatment for many diseases (Webb 1995, pp. 293–294). But his preferred yardstick was mainly the health of the first European settlers in 1788. A comparison with modern post-industrial Indigenous and non-Indigenous health would be far starker. For example, Lauriston Sharp's unique survey of bush groups in the Mitchell River region in 1933–1935 yielded an infant mortality rate (death in the first year) of 412 per 1,000 live births (Sharp 1940). In the period 1947–1972 the rate for the same groups, who by then had largely settled at what is now Kowanyama, where medical assistance was available, had dropped to 95 per 1,000 (Taylor 1975, p. 23).

Kunitz has presented one of the more complex general models of colonial impacts on Indigenous health, and it is noticeable that many of its elements continue to be active causes of post-colonial problems. He identifies the following basic elements:

Disease ecology (Kunitz 1994, p. 6): Major parts of the Old World, especially the warm tropics, had their own diseases to which European would-be colonisers had little immunity, whereas in most of the New World the situation was reversed (Kunitz 1994, p. 11). It follows that colonisers in the Australian case met little real challenge in the way of disease ecology upon their arrival.

Biological background of population (Kunitz 1994, p. 7): Immunological status was a vital factor in creating differences between the colonisation experiences of the Indigenous peoples of large parts of Eurasia and parts of Africa as against those of the peoples of the New World. Smallpox, measles and other diseases to which New World populations had no history of exposure were demographically devastating, wrecking subsistence production (Kunitz 1994, p. 8) and causing demoralisation and 'social collapse'. (Kunitz 1994, p. 9)

Physical conflict: This includes warfare but also small-scale conflicts. (Kunitz 1994, p. 12)

Mode of economic colonisation: Where labour and land were both wanted, as in the case of the Hawaiians, the people were integrated into capitalist society. Where only land was wanted, as with most Aborigines and American Indians, isolation and encapsulation on reservations and missions occurred (the dispossession factor). Where labour was wanted, but not land, as in Samoa, a planter class evolved, with the indigenous people continuing to live and work in their villages. (Kunitz 1994, p. 5)

Political and institutional factors: Policy-related causes of both failure and success (Kunitz 1994), including whether or not central government as opposed to regional or state government has taken responsibility for indigenous health, and whether or not treaties were signed between indigenous peoples and colonisers. (Kunitz 1994, p. 6)

Harder to define: 'Epidemic-induced panic, social disorganization, and demoralization'. (Kunitz 1994, p. 12)

Pre-existing social organisation and culture: For example, sedentary agricultural people such as the Pueblo Indians had institutionalised mechanisms for socialising children in ways that reduced resorting to violence during conflict, whereas hunter-gatherers traditionally make more use of dispersal. Hunter-gatherers also place more emphasis on personal autonomy so that others are less willing to intervene to stop abusive drinking or violence than is the case of other societies. (Kunitz 1994, p. 186)

A number of these immediate consequences in turn also themselves became drivers of change:

Population collapse: This seems to vary very widely, ranging apparently from 53–95% in the Americas. (Kunitz 1994, pp. 13, 129)
Economic collapse: For example, where the healthy population fell below that adequate to feed everyone. (Kunitz 1994, p. 12)
Ideological collapse: Religious colonisation could also lead to demoralisation because the religion of the invaders was often thought by both Europeans and natives to be the more powerful. (Kunitz 1994, p. 9)

When it comes to examining the role of pre-existing cultural factors it is important to recognise that, after colonisation, these factors were no longer operating in the same environmental and cultural contexts as in the past, and they became applied to new foods and drugs, new diseases, and new relationships. In that sense, they were no longer 'pre-existing cultural factors' in quite the same sense, but often they remained in a transforming line of direct descent back to the ancient past.

To cite one example, the camping patterns of semi-nomadic Aboriginal residential groups of the past are quite well documented in the ethnographic literature. Camps of fifteen, thirty-five, even fifty people were not uncommon (Peterson and Long 1986). The main functional reasons for camps being of such a size were economic: to provide sufficient able-bodied people of sufficient skill to supply the needs of the camp members; and defensive: to have sufficient people to keep watch and defend the members of the group against revenge-attack or wife-raiding parties, for example. Translated in a modified way into modern settlement house occupation, co-residence of ten or twenty relatives is likely to be officially described as 'crowding', whether it is the residents' preference or not. Overcrowded and unhygienic sleeping arrangements are associated with scabies, one of the most important skin infections in Central and northern Australia and one which leads to streptococcal infections that are statistically associated with end-stage renal disease.[2]

[2] Cass et al. (2004). On the similar experience of Inuit, who have moved 'from the clean, open spaces of the tundra to squalid prefabricated villages', see (Shephard and Rode 1996, p. 257).

Crowded House

Relationships between Indigenous people and their houses have figured frequently in Australian public debates and media revelations. In the 2000s there was much talk, yet again, of a shortage of housing, and increased public funding was once again dedicated to tackling the problem. There was, as in the past, recognition of the relationship between household conditions and health problems. The summary of the Royal Australian Institute of Architects policy on Indigenous housing says in part:

> There is clear evidence that the failure of governments to provide a reasonable standard of housing design, construction and maintenance has direct and immediate consequences for the health and well-being of Indigenous people. The inadequate supply of housing, which leads to overcrowding, aggravates these problems. (Royal Australian Institute of Architects 2008)

There has also been a dawning public recognition that the average life expectancy of a house in many specifically Indigenous communities is extraordinarily short, often about seven years. Partly as a response to this rate of attrition on public housing, there has been a push to increase Indigenous rates of home ownership, and a lot of hope has been placed in altered tenure arrangements as a means to this end. The theory is that preservation and maintenance of housing will be better when it is privately owned rather than public housing. New tenure arrangements themselves have attracted a great deal of criticism and debate. At the heart of the debate, for some people, is the question of 'assimilation', and allied to this is the issue of 'mainstreaming' of service delivery and governance.

Many of the assumptions in these cases have been well-meaning but ethnocentric in their portrait of the home occupiers being talked about. 'Crowded houses' are consistently misrepresented in the media simply as cases of building shortages and of Indigenous poverty. Both factors are important. But houses with fifteen or twenty overnight inhabitants need to be understood, in the context of these discussions, as culturally and socially generated ways of dwelling, and of doing so not only within the constraints of what is available, but also within the constraints of where people put their social priorities and their spending priorities. People often have to weigh the positive aspect of living with high numbers against the negative aspects. Those at the heart of a household frequently have to weigh up the consequences of rejecting the claims of their relatives on a house, as against accepting them. Houses are often focal points in networks of demand sharing (Peterson 1993), where the nature of relationships is both employed and reinforced and also tested by the making of requests for goods and also for shelter. 'Do you still love me?' So what are called 'crowded houses' are not, in general, simply the outcomes of high demand and inadequate supply. They are also built on the economy of kinship, of claims on others, on the avoidance of rejection, and on considerations of physical security.

What is crowded for some people might not be so crowded for others. Before the colonial and post-colonial age of settlement, and typically at outstations away from settlements in recent times, Aboriginal people have generally opted to camp closely together by night and to spend their sitting-down time even more closely together in the daytime and evenings, when not out and about. Many times I have been with people sitting in bush camps in remote places, many often within touching distance of each other, in a wide open, vast, and largely unpeopled landscape. Camp sizes in the past varied considerably, in relation to the seasons and to ceremonial meetings. There were patterns of aggregation followed by dispersal. But very frequently observers noted camp sizes of between about fifteen and thirty-five people. (Peterson and Long 1986).

These bush camps consisted of relatives and were, in significant part, exercises in cohesion and co-operation with people one could more or less trust. Their members were economically productive of most of their group's needs, and these camps also provided protection for their members in case of feuding or raiding with members of other groups. But they had no fully constant memberships and could split into two or more groups, such as when members peeled off to visit a different set of relatives, or as a means of dealing with tensions and conflicts between members of a camp. They could also amalgamate with or camp next to other groups to share the proceeds of a mass harvest, such as flying foxes or swamp roots, for example, to perform collective ceremonies, or to make a show of common force at times of warfare.

Flexibility was traditionally the keynote of Aboriginal societies in relation to living arrangements, and it still is to a significant extent. The shelters people built in the bush were made from renewable and locally available materials, and were usually quickly created, without a large amount of labour. Shelters other than those built for extended wet or cold seasons could be quickly added to, joined up or divided (Memmott 2007). Residents built their own shelters, often co-operatively, and the skills required would have been present in every group. A shelter was thus typically a product of the labour of at least some of those who lived in it. It was not 'public' property or the property of an absent 'government'. This gave it the kind of ownership that accrued to other artefacts such as canoes, baskets or spears. This was neither communal nor exclusively individual. That is, those other than the primary owner could have structured claims over it. A person's camp might be, and frequently was, on someone else's land, but residents had specific rights over their domestic space nonetheless. If a shelter had to be abandoned or burned as a result of a death, the burden of its replacement was not high. If a person in a state of rage were to smash up a shelter as a way of displaying the depth of their grief or anger, again, its repair or replacement was not very onerous, although the consequences of smashing up one's own shelter were very different from those of smashing up someone else's. To smash up the built environment was, and in many places remains, a way of legitimately venting feelings while avoiding assaulting other persons. It thus has its uses in managing rage, one that has deep continuity with the deep past.

These and other long-established cultural practices remain relevant to understanding how people often relate to their housing today. For example, some settlements are dangerous places at night, and it pays to have an overnight household of sufficient size to defend its inhabitants and deal with troublemakers should they arrive. But is the solution to this particular motivation for so-called 'crowding' the redesign of dwellings as something like long-houses, designed to fit twenty people, or barricaded houses? Or is it more important to create community security and better housing availability and then see what happens to household size? In some settlements a short-term solution to security problems has been to enclose houses with high cyclone wire fences and provide them with padlocked gates. At Aurukun, in my own observation, the effect of this kind of fencing, in spite of its benefits, has also been very negative in terms of social life. Before grog there were no fences and one could safely go visiting after sunset. At the height of its troubles in the 1990s this palisaded suburbia at Aurukun was often likened to Port Moresby.

It can be a mistake to argue that domestic architecture should be designed simply to fit in with a people's current practices of household density or house use, because we should not assume that every feature of a people's current practice is there simply because people want it to be there. Lack of security can hardly be described as a chosen way of life. Choice can play a part in household size but so also do the constraints of necessity, and deeply embedded ways of relating to, and dwelling with, other people, such those I have just discussed. One alternative to more houses has been bigger houses, designed to accommodate the numbers often found in conventional-sized dwellings, but there can be a catch here. Certainly Helen Ross found at Halls Creek, Western Australia, that 'the use and abuse of kinship norms ensures that household sizes increase to fill the space available' (Ross 1987, p. 110). We should not assume these tendencies are constants. They may be in rapid flux, with different generations living in the same community having different expectations of and uses for housing, and different attitudes to maintaining a house.

For most Aboriginal people, the ending of their old pre-colonial economic system, which was based on semi-nomadic or nomadic foraging, coincided also with a very new experience, one for which their former cultures, inevitably, did not prepare them. The move to fixed housing brought a loss of control—of siting, of distance from others, of size, adjustability, ability to see others, and so on. But most importantly, in the present context, people suffered a degree of loss of control over occupancy. As Joe Reser said:

> Living in a European house entails an equal, if not greater, loss of control over one's social environment. In addition to the fact that the house dweller has little choice over his neighbours, and the general social and physical organisation of space about him, he also exercises considerably less control over who uses and lives in the house. (There are really no proscriptive norms nor developed institutions for dealing with European houses—though there are very clear mandates in the camp situation. The question of rights and ownership is usually very unclear and diffuse, and hence it is difficult to exercise any control as nominal head of house or signer of lease.) (Reser 1979, p. 68)

Concentrations of kin in fixed dwellings have also created major health problems. Under the classical Aboriginal regime, clothing was absent or minimal, there were no woven blankets or sheets that needed washing, and the waste products of preparing food, as well as human waste products usually buried in the nearby bush, were left behind with each shift of camp to a fresh place. In the arid zone changes of camp location were more frequent than in better watered regions such as the lower Murray River or the wetlands of the monsoon belt. In maximally rich areas camps could last up to a few months, but no camps anywhere were permanent. The curtailing or ending of this old mobility, whether by coercion or by choice, meant the spending of much more time, even the whole year, in one place, usually a place where there were 'permanent' shelters or houses provided for people to live in.

This dramatic shift of circumstances created living environments that were now biologically hazardous in a very new way, unless there was also at the same time a cultural shift towards the sort of domestic and public health regimes practised by most of the world's settled populations in recent centuries. It was many centuries before people in Western Europe, for example, came to understand and accept the measures needed to minimise infectious diseases that formerly wiped out large populations through epidemics. This entailed far more than the acquisition of information. It entailed a deep cultural shift, one that incorporated modern understandings of the causes of disease, so that germs and parasites, rather than miasmas, hot winds, sins or supernatural forces, became understood as causative agents of typhoid, tuberculosis, cholera, and many other devastating illnesses. Millions of lives were saved as a result.[3]

Under the older, more interventionist Indigenous governance regimes in Australia, such as the church missions and government settlements, not only were health measures taught at school but hygiene inspections of housing carried out by a matron or other health officer were routine. The weekly boiling of sheets and blankets and clothes was often a requirement of those who controlled the settlements and, most importantly, the rations. This level of coercion and surveillance would be repugnant to us now. That was, of course, in what we tend now to call the 'assimilation era'. In this case, assimilation to the procedures required for any healthy settled society was imposed from outside. It reinforced and reflected the position of Indigenous Australians as a subject people. Still, many Indigenous people absorbed these practices and made them their own, reaping the health benefits they entailed. That is, they assimilated the health needs of living in a house in a settled fashion. On health grounds one would have to say that whether imposed from outside, or adopted as people's own practice, this kind of assimilation, given the biological facts of the settled life, was not a calamity; it was a necessity.

But many other people did not undergo this same kind of internalised cultural change, so that when the coercive hygiene regimes of the old system were lifted—mainly in the late 1960s and early 1970s—many people, especially in remote Australia, continued to practise a modified form of mobile forager hygiene and sanitation in their new, settled circumstances and housing. Especially when combined with high household densities, the health consequences of this are well known. There is still a tendency in Australian debates for some to associate Aboriginal cultural adaptations to urban and settled living as 'going white'. This is to falsely racialise an adaptation that peoples all over the world, regardless of ethnic origin or appearance, have been making for thousands of years. We were all nomadic hunter-gatherers once.

---

[3] Anderson (2002) traces in detail these scientific/cultural shifts among English-speaking settlers through Australian colonial and immediate post-colonial history.

Many Aboriginal people want more control over their households and over who can live in them. Too many complain that the burden of a house's rent and food and cleaning and washing and cooking falls on the shoulders of too few household members, often older women. The wider society needs to be open to the possibility that some such people will want to opt for the privatisation of tenure over these properties as a means to improving their bargaining position and their quality of life. The household head who has the rent book is often in need of a better bargaining chip when it comes to exercising control over how many can be accommodated, especially with those who do not contribute financially. Ironically, private home ownership can be understood not so much as a departure from communal Aboriginal tradition as a reincarnation of the traditional rights of householders. Campers had customary rights to their own surface improvements, while at the same time an undisturbed communal title, possibly not held by the occupant, persisted in the land underneath. In 2007–2008 the Northern Territory Intervention's provision for increasing people's private stakes in housing was mischievously trumpeted by some as an attempt to steal Aboriginal land. It was only one strand in the barrage of disinformation flying about at the time. The number of people who welcomed the move in the bush showed that this particular intervention, at least, had appeal. When external intervention appeals, or works, we should perhaps recognise that it may be connected with traditional Aboriginal values.

Brief Interventions

The simple idea that people drink heavily because of cultural loss or territorial dispossession will not stand up to scrutiny. Some of the heaviest drinkers I have ever encountered have been people who had the privilege of a bush upbringing, had never been deprived of their land, had a rich grasp of classical High Culture, including the holding of vast religious knowledge, and who were multilinguals of enviable facility. They have also included some of the least miserable and best-adjusted people I've met. Like other bush drinkers, they could move quickly into fighting mode once 'full-spark', sometimes when only 'half-spark'.[4]

Maggie Brady has presented cogent evidence that brief verbal interventions by doctors with individual Aboriginal problem drinkers could be an effective technique for enabling them to give up the grog (Brady 1995a, b, 2000). She found this outside intervention was influential at a late stage in the drinking careers of some individuals. Knowledge in 'mainstream' Australia concerning the impact of a doctor's advice earlier than this had been around since at least the 1980s. It had largely been neglected by the Aboriginal medical services, Brady argues, for three main reasons: structural, political and ideological.

The structural reasons were 'associated with federalism, the roles of DAA [Department of Aboriginal Affairs] and later ATSIC in managing substance abuse, and

[4] Aurukun English for stages of drunkenness.

the insulation of Aboriginal programs from outside influences'.[5] The political reasons were 'associated with a long-standing separation of Aboriginal health services from Aboriginal alcohol services' (Brady 2000, p. 11). The ideological reasons were:

> … associated with Aboriginal constructions of difference, and of 'difference' in alcohol dependence. There was a shift to theories of cultural loss, and the disease model and long term treatment were reinforced by the arrival of Indigenous alcohol treatment activists from America and Canada.
>
> The prevalence of these constructions of drinking has led to the development of new 'healing programs', and to an emphasis on 'culture' as a form of treatment. This often romanticised and idealised notion fails to explore honestly the ways in which ideas of 'culture' are manipulated, distorted and exploited by drinkers—something that Merv Gibson … from Hope Vale … articulated in 1987. In many cases, the manifestations of 'culture in treatment' seem to be simply new variations on the old theme of residential and end-stage treatment programs. (Brady 2000, pp. 11, 2. For a detailed critique of 'culture' based treatment programs see Brady 1995. Gibson and Pearson (1987) was actually co-written with Noel Pearson (Pearson, personal communication, 2006))

Any intervention, even one that appeals to what are asserted to be the healing properties of traditional culture, presupposes a belief in improvability, if not perfectibility. At the deepest cultural level, where people's world views and primary presuppositions lie, for many at least in remote Australia a belief in the improvability of life should not be assumed. Talk in offices may be of progress, but private and community action or inaction often reflects what Stanner called a 'mood of assent' to the tragic terms of life, a view—not of pessimism—but of acceptance that reality is 'a joyous thing with maggots at the centre' (Stanner 1963, p. 37). The chasm between liberal democratic progressivist official thinking and the reality of the traditional Aboriginal culture it promotes in glittering international art shows is made ruthlessly apparent in these instances. Stanner deserves quoting in more detail:

> The Murinbata [of Port Keats area, now also Wadeye] themselves make a kind of picture of the articulation of the segmental groups. They use sticks or stones in such a way that what emerges looks a little like a branching tree or a flung fish-net. But it is not a picture of sociality. That picture exists in the dramatization given by *Punj* [public name of higher men's ceremony] in complex symbolisms of mime, song, dance and rite. The ontological reality stated there is not reducible to points of force on a network. A 'theory' of that reality would have to be a rationalization of a reality which, if my account is correct, the Murinbata put to themselves as a joyous thing with maggots at the centre. It takes considerable temerity to try to improve on this imagery. (Stanner 1963)
>
> [I]t is consistent [with earlier discussion] that a people in a hard environment, with a poor material culture and little detached knowledge, should develop a religion around the inexorable. (Stanner 1963, p. 167)
>
> Much evidence points, not to decadence, but to a lively and developing life on the plateau. (Stanner 1963, p. 85, 57, pp. 151–152; see also Tonkinson 1991, p. 33; Dussart 2000, pp. 22–23)

This is not, of course, to ignore what T.G.H. Strehlow called 'the sustaining ideals of Aboriginal societies' (Strehlow 1956) and an edifice of 'right ways' such as those

[5] Brady (2000, p. 11). DAA=Department of Aboriginal Affairs, later more or less replaced by ATSIC.

enjoined upon novices during initiation. But the grounding of these ideals was continuity with the past, not departure from it for a new and improved condition. The idea of social progress comes from outside Aboriginal tradition.

What seems to be at the root of the success of the doctor-patient alcohol intervention technique described by Brady is the fact that the doctor is from beyond the patient's world of kin, the intervention is private, doctors are on the whole trusted, respected, and considered knowledgeable, the advice is personalised. Further, 'perhaps most importantly, a doctor can legitimise a change in a patient's behaviour. He or she can give an Aboriginal patient an "excuse", a solid reason, from an authorising "other", a person who is outside of the person's immediate social network' (Brady 2000, p. 8).

Ironically, the doctor's intervention is for these very reasons 'culturally appropriate', to use the post-1970 jargon, or at least culturally effective, by reason of his or her status as *non-kin*. It is not because of any imitation of traditional culture in the doctor's method, but because of the way the intervention actually works in relation to some key culturally conservative Aboriginal values and practices that it seems to be so successful.

The basic point of this medical example is that it is not legitimate to reject interventionist strategies as culturally invasive when it is demonstrable that some of them may be 'culturally appropriate' from an Indigenous point of view. The services of a uniformed police presence that are so often in demand from members of Aboriginal communities is another example. As non-kin, the police owe no obligations to disputing parties or to assailants and victims. I was once invited by the NPY (Ngaanyatjara Pitjantjatjara Yankunytjatjara) Women's Council to take part in a meeting between them and senior police officers in Alice Springs. When the need for increased police presence on the remote settlements came up one of the officers promised more positions for local Aboriginal police aides. This aroused the fury of a fair number at the meeting. One senior woman from Kaltukatjara (Docker River) harangued him in Pitjantjatjara. Didn't he understand that local police were beholden to kin obligations? Were his ears shut when they insisted on having *piranpa* (white) police in the remote settlements? A modestly increased *piranpa* police presence in the region was welcomed not long afterwards. This example, like the alcohol one, reflects a general principle: Indigenous Australians frequently recognise that their own social and cultural resources are not enough to enable them to cope with the problems with which they are confronted in a post-colonial world, yet they can hardly be accused of blaming the victim.

Blaming the Victim?

The central area of disagreement over the causes of the Indigenous/non-Indigenous health gap in Australia seems to be between what Emma Kowal and Yin Paradies have called 'structural' explanations and those that stress 'agency'. In their study of participants in a public health practitioner workshop, Kowal and Paradies found that there was a clear tendency towards structural attributions of cause grouped under items such as the *health system*, *historical context*, *culture*, *financial situation*, and residential *remoteness*. They found participants were uncomfortable with explanations that stressed agency—that is, effects attributable to acts by Indigenous people themselves. Nearly all the causal factors the participants identified as 'politically incorrect' were within the individual behaviour category (Kowal and Paradies 2005, pp. 1347–1357). 'That is, participants were more likely to blame the system, and were reluctant to nominate Indigenous people's choices or actions as a cause of their ill-health … This ethos of political-correctness is clearly a response to *victim-blaming*, a term given to expressions of Indigenous agency that are generally seen as racist (for instance, blaming Indigenous ill-health on their cultural practices)' (Kowal and Paradies 2005, p. 1352). Kowal and Paradies concluded that the culture of the Indigenous public health industry in Australia had resulted in an overstructuration of Indigenous ill health and a de-emphasising of Indigenous people's agency. I would add that causation and blame are much more easily confused with each other if the subject itself has become a primary arena for displays of moral politics.

It is important to make a distinction, albeit a problematical one, between individual voluntary and conscious agency and what are often called 'culturally embedded practices'. The scope and the effectiveness of individual decision-making, in any society, are always constrained by the wider cultural and social contexts people live in. An apparently rational personal choice based on health outcomes can often be blocked, for example, by a need to enjoy solidarity with others, or to follow traditional practices as defined by figures of authority, or to avoid ostracism arising from appearing to be different or from appearing to be like a member of an out-group. Even the existence of choice itself, including the conceivability of choosing to do something other than what is usually done, or the acceptability of being open to learning new health-related information and new practices, can be denied to individuals by their social world. It is quite a common observation that in Aboriginal classical practice the asking of questions about serious matters is discouraged among the young, information is often given to them only in piecemeal and fragmentary ways, innovation is denigrated as contrary to the law, and the law (ideally at least) never changes, whether to accommodate new circumstances, new knowledge or for any other reason.[6]

There is widespread agreement that many Indigenous health and social problems stem ultimately from the after-effects of colonisation, but no agreement at all that this has been the only cause.[7] When people say that attributing causes of ill health to cultural practices, or even to personal choices, is 'blaming the victim', they are suggesting that an attribution of this kind is making some kind of statement about moral culpability. This is usually quite untrue. What interests me about the accusation is why some people should feel so strongly attracted by it.

[6] On the discouragement of rapid or comprehensive factual learning by young people and the cryptic imparting of knowledge to them by elders, see, for example: Strehlow (1947, pp. 5–6, 110, note 32; 1971, pp. 70, 197–198, note 37); Hale (1984); Keen (1994, pp. 244–249); Sutton (1998, p. 365).

[7] I reject monolithic causal accounts typified by that in Mathews (1996, pp. 29–38).

One of its attractions may be that it disrupts the scientific discussion of causality and replaces it with a moral contest in which the author of the politicisation can leap to take the high ground. To that extent it is an exercise in domination. When enough people of a similar political persuasion take the same leap they often make it pretty clear that they are also defending the solidarity of their group and its comforting assurance of correct thinking. When it is the dominant opinion group, this defence is also of the group's domination. Such a group is identified by Kowal and Paradies as 'the mainstream left/progressives/liberals'. These people, they add, are threatened by the possibility that they do not, in fact, share similar health aspirations with Indigenous people (Kowal and Paradies 2005, pp. 1351, 1354).

To observe that this has been a dominant set of attitudes in the helping professions is not to ignore the many exceptions to it. There are people who have been saying that culturally transmitted behaviours and attitudes lie at the centre of the huge differences between Indigenous and non-Indigenous health outcomes, and here I include both classical patterns that pre-date colonisation, and the many patterns of behaviour that have emerged since then. The critical point in all this, once again, is child socialisation.

For example, Gary Robinson, then of the Menzies School of Health Research in Darwin, wrote in 1996:

> … reduction in mortality requires the transmission of improvements in key indicators over generations; these improvements cannot solely be produced by direct medical intervention, but may only be sustained on the basis of significantly changed environments, patterns of activity and consumption and household patterns which influence childcare and development. Even in the short term, the capacity of individuals and their families to alter aspects of 'lifestyle' may be decisive in achieving any degree of effect in treatment. These patterns are deeply sedimented aspects of local cultures and environments, including patterns of household, family and community life, with their systems of exchange, obligation and dependence. These the individual cannot 'rationally' influence in the interests of his or her own health, and they are not directly amenable to medical or public health interventions without assaults on culture, tradition and lifestyle which would be ineffectual or incur strong resistance. (Robinson 1995, p. 3)

Robinson ended that paper on what sounded like a note of resignation, saying that 'the researcher's consciousness of certain lines of causation and of the effects of social change on health and illness does not provide a recipe for change in the interests of better health' (Robinson 1995, p. 7). This was because social change was unpredictable and could not simply be engineered, and because to raise the need for social change was also to suggest removal of power from Indigenous people, and a decline in their autonomy and self-determination.

I think there is another way to look at these last points. For a start, major social change of a predictable kind was in fact generated historically by the creation of holding and training institutions for Indigenous people under mission and government policies of the colonial era and afterwards. That was social engineering on a grand scale and, in addition to its harmful effects, it had clearly visible positive effects on things like the protection of inmates from frontier ruffians and their drugs and diseases; on the isolation and treatment of infectious disease cases; on the administration of inoculations such as for hookworm; on the use of violence between family members; on the suppression of blood-feuding, and so on. But it was also a major suppression of people's autonomy. While people will say, and so will I, that it is unthinkable to argue for that kind of social engineering and intervention any more, it is arguable that the maintenance of racially separate communities via state funding constitutes a massive continuation of that intervention, and one that results, in many cases, in rapid cultural change. This kind of change is not automatically one that moves towards non-Indigenous culture in any representative sense. So often it has been into the culture of welfare dependency and the insular culture of the ghetto.[8]

If people want a typically modern health profile they need to adopt a typically modern set of health practices, whether as an addition to their existing health culture or in significant replacement of it. Health service providers should be encouraging this kind of cultural addition and change if they really want to see better outcomes as defined in their own medical terms.

Curiously, hospitals that employ Aboriginal traditional doctors are in the 2000s encouraging the perpetuation of traditional beliefs about disease causation and the use of mystification in producing alleged cures. This places the medical service providers in an impossibly self-contradictory position if they are serious about behavioural change as preventative medicine. If they are serious, then use of traditional doctors should not be official hospital business, but should be left to private arrangements between patients and their communities.[9]

Traditional Aboriginal healers have valued status and roles in many Indigenous communities. They may also publicly oppose surgery and blood transfusions and teach that injections do not work. They may deny the germ theory of disease and thus effectively proclaim the safety of squalor. They may encourage delay in hydration treatment for infants suffering severe diarrhoea, and they may advertise their own treatments as being highly efficacious in the face of evidence of massive ill health among their own people. Despite this, in remoter parts of Australia such healers are at times employed by a government-funded health delivery system that is based on science and succeeds in great part because of medicine's reliance on testable evidence and methodological doubt. Such traditional doctors are working not just with bush medicines, but, in their own understanding, are also working under Aboriginal law, *ngangkaṟiku Tjukurpa* (doctors' law) as it is known, for example, in Pitjantjatjara. They can be quite open about the fact that they are in a power struggle with Western-style medical practitioners for recognized 'doctor' status, for wages, and for motor vehicles.[10]

Well-meaning Whitefellas who support traditional doctors as part of their own mission to peel back the post-colonial power differential have to face the fact that, with the likely exceptions of palliative care and possibly mental health care,

[8] For example, for Mornington Island, see McKnight (2002, pp. 53–65).

[9] See, for example, Tonkinson (1982, pp. 225–241); Reid (1983, pp. 57–91); Hunter (1993, pp. 54–57) on Aboriginal doctors in remote Australia.

[10] See statements by various ngangkaris in Ngaanyatjarra Pitjantjatjara Yankunytjatjara Women's Council Aboriginal Corporation (2003, pp. 20, 37, 43, 49, 54–55, 57, 62–63, 65, 70, 74–75, 83–84).

traditional healers who promote such views are likely overall to constitute more of a hindrance than a help to the already disastrous health of their communities. The issue I raise here is not, however, to question their existence but to question why agents of the state, whose primary brief is to improve health, should blur the distinction between traditional and interpersonal voluntary behaviour on the one hand, and state-sanctioned and funded services on the other. It is self-defeating. A parallel concern is with the way the Northern Territory Police have been used as peacekeepers and supervisors at leg-spearings. These confusing attempts at cultural appropriateness ironically seem to echo the traditional Aboriginal complaint that the Whitefellas' law is not predictably fixed and 'one-way', the way laws should be.

One of the more powerful traditional factors in preventing adaptation to contemporary living conditions is the instilling in many Aboriginal people, from an early age, of a belief that most serious illnesses and most deaths are due to the ill-will and sorcery of other people (Tonkinson 1982, p. 237; Reid 1983, pp. 35–44; Devitt and McMasters 1998, p. 92). This itself is a profound politicisation of disease and death. Systems of sorcery beliefs and practices are found widely around the world in traditional societies, and even in some not so traditional ones. In Christian Science, a religion founded in the United States in the nineteenth century, sorcery is known as Malicious Animal Magnetism. Most sorcery belief systems are primarily concerned with blame rather than objective causation. Blaming makes sense in its own way, as it rationalises what has happened, and externalises causes in a way that is not easily challengeable on the grounds of scientific evidence. Sorcery beliefs have had great durability in Aboriginal societies.

The evidence is heavily stacked against the rose-coloured expectation that Aboriginal people with a traditional orientation will simply adopt foreign causal theories, living conditions and health practices with alacrity, on the basis that they are good for their health. So it is not realistic to assume that the kind of cultural change I refer to here is going to occur quickly and simply as a result of education or persuasion of adults. The cycle of childhood socialisation needs to be re-geared if specific behaviours to do with things like hygiene and sanitation, the legitimation of violence, the degree of priority placed on physical wellbeing itself, and openness to preventative health measures, are to change more quickly.[11]

There is no evidence from the past that suggests that these highly desired changes are going to be achieved by further indigenising the health bureaucracy. Whether that kind of racialisation of an essential public service is desirable or not, after more than three decades of development in that area, it seems so far to have had a much more beneficial effect on the careers of health politicians than on Indigenous health.

One notable feature of Aboriginal life, as I have seen it in the remoter and many less remote parts of Australia over the decades, has been its stoicism, especially among traditionally-oriented people. Endurance without complaint has long been highly valued, while over-frequent complaint about illness or pain has often been

[11] On Aboriginal child socialisation in this context, see for example Berndt and Berndt (1972, pp. 115–140); Cowlishaw (1982); Hamilton (1981, 1982, pp. 49–71); Hernandez (1941).

met with indifference or, occasionally, the disciplining anger that discourages the repetition of the complaining. This has also long been part of childhood socialisation in such places, where children are brought up to be tough, autonomous, and outward-focused. Nonetheless, in such places the chronically ill may be addressed and referred to as 'the sick one' (*Tjikbala* in creole), and recognition of their marked condition may be woven into how they are referred to in terms of kin status, as in *muk alpenh* ('your chronically sick mother's older brother', Wik-Ngathan). These are routine signs of compassion. They are also in recognition of the person's permanent nature, as is also the case with the weaving of left-handedness into the way people are referred to and addressed. In spite of these recognitions of flaws that cannot be fixed, compassion also traditionally led to assisting with bush medicine and treatment by bush doctors. Then there are those key words in Aboriginal languages that express sorrow for another's condition, usually translated as 'poor thing!', and in Creole as *pobaga* (from 'poor bugger'). There has been, in other words, the usual dialectic between the showing of sympathetic concern and the drawing of a line against over-indulgence of the complainant. But different societies draw this line in different places.

It remains true, then, that the threshold for recognising a state as one of real suffering was set very high in this mobile foraging society where hardiness and fitness were, in the past, the norm. This may be one of the most underestimated reasons why Aboriginal patients, especially in the bush, may seek treatment very late, and rate low in terms of compliance with treatment regimes, by global urban standards. They may also rate their health as good when by global standards it is not good.

Under a simplistic relativity argument one could say that much of what an urban modern would class as pain and suffering is not much more than an inconvenience and irritation to someone from a remote and bush-toughened Indigenous background, and for this reason each cultural group member should just be left to define the seriousness of their morbidities in their own terms. What may then flow from this laissez-faire position is a critique of interventionist medical thinking, and a rejection of the idea that general practitioners are there to learn and to serve, but not to be change agents, in the communities where they work.

The problem many of us have with this argument, which is ostensibly on the side of the less powerful and against the interfering hand of government, is that it focuses on adults of competence and political adulthood and leaves the truly powerless to their fate. Foetuses, babies, infants, children, and the disabled and infirm are protected from neglect by Australian law. The state itself is an intervention. This legal apparatus translates into administrative practice and criminal law the modern liberal political philosophy that regards the wellbeing of all members of the society as the business of the whole community. It also reflects global, post-industrial standards of what constitutes levels of suffering that demand voluntary and, where required, obligatory interventionist treatment, as with notifiable diseases or children starved or killed by neglect. It is a cheap shot to call this paternalism, or, shifting genders here, a case of over-fussing by the nanny state. As is becoming increasingly clear, the most effective interventions of the kind I refer to here are arising from collaborative efforts by local community health workers, Aboriginal and not, and the professionals of the medical services, whose ranks increasingly include GPs of Indigenous ancestry.

Bibliography

Anderson, Warwick. 2002. *The cultivation of whiteness: Science, health and racial destiny in Australia.* Melbourne: Melbourne University Press.

Anderson, Ian, and Bebe Loff. 2004. Voices lost: Indigenous health and human rights in Australia. *The Lancet* 364:1281–1282.

Berndt, Ronald M., and Catherine H. Berndt. 1972. Aborigines. In *Socialization in Australia*, ed. F. J. Hunt, 155–140. Sydney: Angus & Robertson.

Brady, Maggie. 1992. *Heavy metal: The social meaning of petrol sniffing in Australia.* Canberra: Aboriginal Studies Press.

Brady, Maggie. 1995a. *Broadening the base of interventions for Aboriginal people with alcohol problems.* (Technical Report No. 29). Sydney, National Drug and Alcohol Research Centre: University of New South Wales.

Brady, Maggie. 1995b. Culture in treatment, culture as treatment. A critical appraisal of developments in addictions programs for Indigenous North Americans and Australians. *Social Science and Medicine* 41:1487–1498.

Brady, Maggie. 2000. Introducing brief interventions for indigenous alcohol misuse: Can doctors make a difference? Paper presented at Australian Institute of Aboriginal and Torres Strait Islander Studies Seminar, 18 Sept 2000.

Brady, Maggie. 2004. *Indigenous Australia and alcohol policy: Meeting difference with indifference.* Sydney: University of New South Wales Press.

Brady, Maggie. 2008. *First taste: How Indigenous Australians learned about grog* (a series of six pamphlets). Canberra: The Alcohol Education & Rehabilitation Foundation.

Brady, Maggie and Kingsley Palmer. 1984. *Alcohol in the outback: Two studies of drinking.* Darwin: North Australia Research Unit.

Cass, A., J. Cunningham, P. Snelling, Z. Wang, and W. Hoy. 2004. Exploring the pathways leading from disadvantage to end-stage renal disease for Indigenous Australians. *Social Science and Medicine* 58:767–785.

Cowlishaw, Gillian. 1982. Socialisation and subordination among Australian Aborigines. *Man* 17:492–507.

Cowlishaw, Gillian. 2003. Euphemism, banality, propaganda: Anthropology, public debate and indigenous communities. *Australian Aboriginal studies* 1:2–18.

Devitt, Jeannie, and Anthony McMasters. 1998. *Living on medicine: A Cultural study of end-stage renal disease among Aboriginal people.* Alice Springs: IAD Press.

Dussart, Françoise. 2000. *The politics of ritual in an Aboriginal settlement: Kinship, gender, and the currency of knowledge.* Washington: Smithsonian Institution Press.

Gibson, Merv, and Noel Pearson. 1987. Anthropology and tradition: A contemporary Aboriginal viewpoint, paper presented at the Australian and New Zealand Association for the Advancement of Science conference. Townsville: Peoples of the North, Canberra, AIATSIS Library.

Hale, Kenneth. 1984. Remarks on creativity in Aboriginal verse. In *Problems and solutions: Occasional essays in musicology presented to Alice M. Moyle*, eds. J. C. Kassler and J. Stubington, 258–259. Sydney: Hale & Iremonger.

Hamilton, Annette. 1981. *Nature and nurture: Aboriginal child-rearing in North-Central Arnhem Land.* Canberra: Australian Institute of Aboriginal Studies.

Hamilton, Annette. 1982. Child health and child care in a desert community, 1970–1971. In *Body, land and spirit: Health and healing in Aboriginal society*, ed. J. Reid. St Lucia: University of Queensland Press.

Hernandez, T. 1941. Children among the Drysdale River tribes. *Oceania* 12:122–133.

Huang, Rae-Lin, Paul J. Torzillo, Vivian A. Hammond, Stephanie T. Coulter, and Adrienne C. Kirby. 2008. Epidemiology of sexually transmitted infections on the Anangu Pitjantjatjara Yankunytjatjara lands: Results of a comprehensive control program. *Medical Journal of Australia* 189:442–445.

Hunter, Ernest. 1993. *Aboriginal health and history: Power and prejudice in remote Australia*. Cambridge: Cambridge University Press.

Keen, Ian. 1994. *Knowledge and secrecy in an Aboriginal religion*. Oxford: Clarendon Press.

Kowal, Emma. 2008. The politics of the gap: Indigenous Australians, liberal multiculturalism, and the end of the self-determination era. *American anthropologist* 110:338–348.

Kowal, Emma, and Yin Paradies. 2005. Ambivalent helpers and unhealthy choices: Public health practitioners' narratives of indigenous ill-health. *Social Science & Medicine* 60:1347–1357.

Kunitz, Stephen J. 1994. *Disease and social diversity: The European impact on the health of non-Europeans*. Oxford: Oxford University Press.

Mathews, John D. 1996. Aboriginal health: Historical, social and cultural influences, in Aboriginal health: Social and cultural transitions. In *Proceedings of a conference at the northern territory university*, Darwin, 29–31 Sept 1995, ed. Gary Robinson. Darwin: Northern Territory University Press.

McKnight, David. 2002. *From hunting to drinking: The devastating effects of alcohol on an Australian Aboriginal community*. London: Routledge.

Memmott, Paul. 2007. *Gunyah, Goondie + Wurley: The Aboriginal architecture of Australia*. St Lucia: University of Queensland Press.

Ngaanyatjarra Pitjantjatjara Yankunytjatjara Women's Council Aboriginal Corporation. 2003. *Ngangkari work: Anangu way. Traditional healers of Central Australia*. Alice Springs: Ngaanyatjarra Pitjantjatjara Yankunytjatjara Women's Council Aboriginal Corporation.

Peterson, Nicolas. 1993. Demand sharing: Reciprocity and the pressure for generosity among foragers. *American Anthropologist* 95:860–874.

Peterson, Nicolas, and Jeremy Long. 1986. *Australian territorial organization: A band perspective* (Oceania Monograph 30). Sydney: University of Sydney.

Reid, Janice. 1983. *Sorcerers and healing spirits. Continuity and change in an Aboriginal medical system*. Canberra: Australian National University Press.

Reser, Joseph P. 1979. A matter of control: Aboriginal housing circumstances in remote communities and settlements. In *A black reality: Aboriginal camps and housing in remote Australia*, ed. M. Heppell. Canberra: Australian Institute of Aboriginal Studies.

Robinson, Gary. 1995. Introduction. Aboriginal health: Social and cultural transitions, *Proceedings of a conference at the Northern Territory University,* Darwin, 29–31 Sept 1995.

Ross, Helen. 1987. *Just for living: Aboriginal perceptions of housing in Northwest Australia*. Canberra: Aboriginal Studies Press.

Royal Australian Institute of Architects, Indigenous Housing Policy, 2008, http://www.architecture.com.au/policy/pages/ih/summary.php. Accessed Nov 2008.

Sharp, R. Lauriston. 1940. An Australian Aboriginal population. *Human Biology* 12:481–507.

Shephard, Ray J. and Andris Rode. 1996. *The health consequences of 'Modernization': Evidence from circumpolar peoples*. Cambridge: Cambridge University Press.

Stanner, W.E.H. 1963. *On Aboriginal religion*. Sydney: Oceania Monographs.

Strehlow, T.G.H. 1947. *Aranda traditions*. Melbourne: Melbourne University Press.

Strehlow, T.G.H. 1956. *The sustaining ideals of Australian aboriginal societies*. Adelaide: Aboriginal Advancement League of South Australia.

Strehlow, T.G.H. 1971. *Songs of Central Australia*. Sydney: Angus & Robertson.

Sutton, Peter. 1998. Icons of country: Topographic representations in classical Aboriginal traditions. In *The history of cartography, vol 2: Cartography in the traditional African, American, Arctic, Australian, and Pacific societies,* eds. David Woodward and Malcolm Lewis. Chicago: Chicago University Press.

Sutton, Peter. 2009. *The politics of suffering: Indigenous Australia and the end of the liberal consensus*. Melbourne: Melbourne University Press.

Taylor, J.C. 1975. Aboriginal child health: anthropologist's report. *Queensland institute of medical research 30th annual report.* Brisbane: Government Printer.

Tonkinson, Myrna. 1982. The mabarn and the hospital: The selection of treatment in a remote Aboriginal community. In *Body, land and spirit: Health and healing in Aboriginal society*, ed. J. Reid. St Lucia: University of Queensland Press.

Tonkinson, Robert. 1991. *The mardu Aborigines: Living the dream in Australia's Desert.* 2nd ed. New York: Holt, Rinehart and Winston.

Webb, Stephen. 1995. *Palaeopathology of Aboriginal Australians: Health and disease across a hunter-gatherer continent.* Cambridge: Cambridge University Press.

Willis, Jon. 2003. Condoms are for whitefellas: Barriers to Pitjantjatjara men's use of safe sex technologies. *Culture, Health & Sexuality* 5:203–217.

Part III
Legal, Medical and Therapeutic Contexts

Chapter 16
Some Aspects of Human Suffering and the Criminal Law

Guy Green

This discussion deals with the criminal law as administered in systems which have their origins in the common law tradition such as Australia, the United Kingdom and the United States, but the wider issues which are raised are relevant to most developed legal systems.

The criminal law does not have what might be called a jurisprudence of suffering: there is no single informing principle relating to suffering which permeates the whole of the criminal law. However, human suffering is relevant in various ways to the definition of some crimes, sentencing, the operation of the criminal justice system and the issue of the limits of the punitive or coercive powers of the state.

The Definition of Crimes

The history of the development of the criminal law suggests that preventing the infliction of suffering as such has never been the primary rationale of the criminal law. However, although the definitions of most crimes against the person do not explicitly include causing suffering as a necessary ingredient, they do include conduct which usually causes suffering. That is particularly so in the case of crimes such as wounding or causing grievous bodily harm which, as well as an assault, include the additional element that the victim must have suffered a particular kind of injury which would almost invariably cause suffering or distress. But even that indirect proscription of causing suffering to others is a relatively recent development in the law. Broadly speaking, in earlier times the law was more concerned with preventing behavior which might give rise to breaches of the peace or protecting property than it was concerned with protecting individuals from suffering or harm. '(T)he extraordinary lenity of the English Criminal Law towards the most atrocious acts of personal violence', observed Sir James Fitzjames Stephen about the early common

G. Green (✉)
13 Marine Terrace, Battery Point, Tasmania, Australia 7004
e-mail: ggre0119@bigpond.net.au

J. Malpas, N. Lickiss (eds.), *Perspectives on Human Suffering*,
DOI 10.1007/978-94-007-2795-3_16,

law, 'forms a remarkable contrast to its extraordinary severity with regard to offences against property' (Stephen 1996, p. 109). It was not until as recently as the beginning of the nineteenth century that legislation was enacted in Britain which created a comprehensive code of offences against the person.

Sentencing

Every system of criminal law has a sentencing regime which includes penalties which may cause suffering. Leaving aside the death penalty, which is not dealt with in this discussion, of the penalties which are imposed in the majority of western systems today, the only one which is likely to cause suffering to any significant degree is a sentence of imprisonment.

Suffering can also be relevant to sentencing in other ways. In the case of offences against the person, the suffering of the victim is a factor relevant to the exercise of the sentencing discretion although, as with the definition of crimes, a court is more likely to place emphasis upon the nature of the violence used or the extent of the victim's injuries than upon the suffering of the victim *per se*. In some cases the suffering of the offender as a result of the crime can also be relevant. That may sound odd but that can be the case when the crime does not involve any animosity towards the victim such as manslaughter where death is caused by gross negligence. In such cases the offender's suffering and remorse can be very intense and, although it is only one factor, it is taken into account in the sentencing process.

The Operation of the Criminal Justice System

Suffering can flow from the operation of the processes of the criminal justice system itself. Despite the presumption of innocence, it is accepted as a practical necessity that defendants have to be brought under the control of the court until the verdict and that that may entail coercive measures and deprivation of liberty which can cause distress and suffering. It is also accepted that persons suspected of committing a crime need to be interrogated by investigating or prosecuting officers. There are strong constraints upon the way in which such interrogations may be conducted but prompted in part by the advent of international terrorism and large scale organised crime there are pressures to relax those constraints to the point where it is suggested that strong duress or even what borders on torture should be permitted.

Defendants are not the only persons who are subject to the court's authority in the criminal justice system. Witnesses can also be compelled to appear and will be subject to penalties if they do not. And once in the witness box they are required to answer questions put to them. This can be very disturbing especially when it entails their having to relive a bad experience or be strongly cross examined. This presents a difficult problem for the law. Witnesses should be protected especially when, as is often the case, they are witnesses through circumstances not of their own making. However, grave injustice could be done if witnesses were not subject to the authority of the law: it would be unthinkable that the outcome of a trial could be dependent upon whether or not a witness chose to appear and answer questions. It must also be recognized that some witnesses lie while others are unreliable or mistaken, so it is essential that their evidence be tested by cross examination. Steps have been taken in an attempt to reconcile those competing considerations. The law has tried to make the experience of appearing as a witness less disturbing by, for example, empowering courts to allow especially vulnerable witnesses to have a support person nearby while they give evidence, or to direct that their evidence be given by audio visual link.

In some ways jurors present an even more intractable problem. If juries are to be truly representative and if the burden of jury duty is not to be borne only by conscientious citizens, then jury service has to be compulsory. But this can entail jurors having their liberty curtailed for what may be very long periods and having to be exposed to proceedings and evidence which some jurors find disturbing or even traumatic.

Another way in which the processes of the law can cause suffering is when they are abused or applied improperly. Isolated cases where officials within the criminal justice system act improperly or unlawfully and cause suffering to individuals are not being referred to: they cannot be said to be part of the operation of the legal system at all. But there are instances where such conduct, although improper or unlawful, is so widespread and accepted that it can be said to be institutionalized. For example, there is evidence that in some systems police or prison officers have routinely used informally sanctioned violence, sometimes causing great suffering in the questioning of suspects or the treatment of prisoners (Nagle 1978).

Constraints on the Powers of the State

Every society regards the exercise of powers of investigation, coercion and sentencing as justified for the maintenance of order and the protection of individuals, property and the security of the state even though they might involve the infliction of suffering. Are there limits to those powers and, if so, what are they? This is not merely a question of reconciling the competing values involved. In the sort of societies being discussed here it is broadly accepted that there is a point beyond which society should not go in the exercise of those powers, no matter how serious the crime or how great is the threat to order or security. The issue is what principles should inform the definition of those limits. That issue is most crucially raised in connection with sentencing so that will be the main vehicle for this discussion.

Over the years a marked ambivalence towards that issue has been evident. For example, in the eighteenth century, what was described as the 'doctrine of enhanced severity' emerged. This doctrine was founded on the view that, as crime was increasing, the penalties which were being imposed under the appallingly harsh sentencing regime which was already in place should be progressively made even more brutal until the crime rate started to drop. But the proponents of that doctrine also recognized that it would be difficult to implement because of the 'compassionate nature of the English people' and because 'inhuman punishments are contrary to the spirit of Christianity and the progress of civilization' (Radzinowicz 1948, p. 232). One can still see that tension and ambivalence between compassion and vengeful feelings in the public's response to crime and sentencing today.

A number of systems have constitutional provisions which prohibit the infliction of 'cruel and unusual' or 'inhuman or degrading' punishment. For example, such prohibitions are found in the United Kingdom Bill of Rights 1689, the Eighth Amendment to the United States Constitution, the Universal Declaration of Human Rights adopted by the United Nations and the Charter of Fundamental rights of the European Union.

There have been many cases where courts have had to define 'cruel and unusual punishment' but it is not easy to extract an intellectually satisfying guiding principle from them. Some judgments assert that the prohibition 'was intended to prohibit torture and agonizing punishment' (Words and phrases 1940-onwards, p. 299). That is useful as identifying two forms of punishment which are included in the prohibition but does not provide a general principle. Other judgments refer to punishment which 'outrages public standards of decency' or 'offends fundamental notions of human dignity.' But such tests are often qualified by the addition of a reference to whether the punishment is disproportionate to the crime. For example, a frequently cited test is whether a punishment is 'so disproportionate to the crime for which it is inflicted that it shocks the conscience and offends fundamental notions of human dignity' (Reyes v. The Queen 2002; Words and Phrases 1993-updated, p. 890 ff.). That qualification is significant. So expressed, that test does not create an absolute standard which forbids punishments which society regards as being such that no human being should be subjected to them whatever crimes they have committed. Under that test, punishment is not prohibited because the punishment *per se* shocks the conscience or offends fundamental notions of human dignity, but because its lack of proportion to the crime does so. Under that test, in the case of horrific crimes horrific punishments could be permitted, the only limit being that they must not be disproportionate to the crime.

Another constraint which is a necessary incident of the principles of the rule of law is that persons who are subject to the exercise of the state's punitive or coercive powers are not outlawed: the state continues to owe them a duty of care and they may not lawfully be subject to any penalty or indignity other than that which is expressly authorised by law. But the principles of the rule of law alone do not place any limits upon what coercive or punitive powers may be conferred on the state.

In most systems it is at least implicitly accepted that, in addition to constitutional constraints or those which are implicit in the principles of the rule of law, there are limits upon the punishments which may be imposed upon persons convicted of crimes which are derived from the basic values upon which the society and its legal system are founded.

Suffering in some form is an inevitable part of the human condition and includes forms which are so minor as to be insignificant. But are there qualitative differences, as opposed to merely differences in degree, between different kinds or degrees of suffering? In other words, is there a non arbitrary criterion for determining the point at which it could be said that the nature of suffering is qualitatively transformed? Defining that point will inform our determination of the limits beyond which the state should not go in the exercise of its powers.

The religious and secular humanist traditions upon which our society and its legal system are founded hold that individuals have unique significance and absolute value and an entitlement to have their essential dignity as human beings preserved. I would argue that, regardless of the crime which has been committed and regardless of the threat faced by society, those values entail propositions along the lines advanced by a distinguished scholar in the field, Professor Andrew Von Hirsch, that the point at which punishment becomes unacceptable in a civilized society is when it denies offenders their status as members of the moral community who remain persons whatever they have done; when it is dehumanizing, when it involves degradation as opposed to merely censure or when it causes suffering which entails destruction of the human personality (Andrew 1993, p. 82–83).

Bibliography

Andrew von Hirsch. 1993. *Censure and sanctions*. Oxford: Clarendon Press.

Nagle, Justice J. F. Royal Commissioner. 1978. *Report of the royal commission into new south wales prisons*. Sydney: Government Printer.

Radzinowicz, Leon Sir. 1948. *A history of English criminal law and its administration from 1750*. vol. 1, 232. London: Stevens.

Reyes v. The Queen. 2002. 2 Appeal cases 235 (Law reports of decisions of the Judicial Committee of the Privy Council).

Stephen, James Fitzjames Sir. 1996. *A history of the criminal law of England.* Abingdon: Routledge (reprint of 1883 edn.).

Words and phrases. 1940-onwards. *Words and phrases*. vol. 10A. St Paul, Minneapolis: West Publishing Co.

Words and phrases. 1993-updated. *Words and phrases*. vol. 2. Scarborough: Carswell.

Chapter 17
Suffering: A Perspective From Law

Norchaya Talib

Introduction

The uniqueness of each person necessarily means that every person is different and has different needs. Yet the similarities in all human beings and so between one person and another also mean that each person has the ability to understand the needs of another or a group of others. The similarities referred to in this essay lie in the broader and perhaps more abstract areas of need, often described as 'fundamental rights' in legal language, whereas the differences lie in the detailed and specific needs of a person at any particular time. I write from the perspective of an academic working within the framework of Malaysian law. I also write on the premise that law deals with suffering based on the similarities between individual persons. This is not an assertion of fact based on any empirical evidence, but more my own reflections on law's treatment or legal response to human suffering.

A comparison with the medical viewpoint on suffering, seen primarily through the work of Eric Cassell, will show how divergent are law and medicine's perspectives on suffering. It is hoped that the source of the differences may be better understood by both disciplines and at the same time narrowed so that a more meaningful contribution may be made by both disciplines for the alleviation of human suffering. An understanding of the limitations within each discipline and the different outlook of the other could further lead to the lessening of the suffering of plaintiff-patients in medico-legal litigations who may be subject to both law and medicine and to the attendant processes within both disciplines.

By its very nature, law provides a structure upon which the detailed needs of persons may be met. The structure may be abstract in nature, presented in the form of principles, an example being fundamental principles embodied in a written constitution or it could be less abstract and more practicable such as specific

N. Talib (✉)
Faculty of Law, University of Malaya, Kuala Lumpur, Malaysia
e-mail: norchaya@gmail.com

J. Malpas, N. Lickiss (eds.), *Perspectives on Human Suffering*,
DOI 10.1007/978-94-007-2795-3_17, © Springer Science+Business Media B.V. 2012

rules within which specified community activities or institutions may be run or set up, for instance, rules on the setting up of corporations which provide means of employment. Whether abstract or practical, law or legal rules is said to be 'one of the great civilizing forces in human society, and that the growth of civilization has generally been linked with the gradual development of a system of legal rules, together with machinery for their regular and effective enforcement (Lloyd 1976).'

Seen from this perspective, it is not difficult to understand why law's purpose is often described as being the regulation of human affairs. 'Regulation of human affairs' however, is a phrase that can be interpreted simply or may be one surrounded by uncertainty. Much depends on the perspective one takes. For instance, to explain it as the regulation of currently recognized 'interests' or 'rights' would perhaps be a common understanding of the role of laws in any legal system. There is, however, a further question that can be asked, namely, why would we need to regulate rights, for what purpose, and which rights should be regulated and which to be discarded in order to meet this purpose? If this question is posed, then the answers open up into many possibilities. They range from the extremely practical, that it is the function of law to decide which interests to give priority to between competing interests or rights with the policy factors behind each choice to be evaluated and decisions made on that basis, to the higher ideal or spiritual, that in and through the regulation of rights the focus and objective is the attainment of truth.

It is against this background of the possible range of meanings and purposes of the law that the concept of suffering may be explored. This essay does not attempt to unravel the breadth and depth of such an inquiry. Instead a more literal approach to how law views suffering will be examined, and will perhaps provide an impetus to other explorations in future works of the connection between law and human suffering. There will be areas of discussion in this essay in which law appears to offer responses that are crystal-clear, but there will also be areas in which, from a legal perspective, there is no clear understanding of what the questions at issue may mean.

Suffering: Perspectives and a Working Definition

Suffering is a state that is to be observed and described rather than defined. This is not only because suffering is subjective in a way that varies from person to person, but because a person's own suffering undergoes permutations and changes, and may be alleviated or become more pronounced over time and in relation to different circumstances and experiences. Despite the elusiveness of capturing the full breadth of what suffering means and the restrictive nature of definitions, a working definition will nonetheless tentatively be offered as to the meaning of suffering.

In conventional terms, suffering is often quite generally understood as a state of being miserable or unhappy or *a state of severe pain or agony*. It is a state of extreme anguish and privation, the bearing of pain or distress as a result of psychological suffering.[1] States of mind that accompany and are associated with suffering are misery, woe and wretchedness (the antonyms of which are happiness, health or joy). In this characterisation, it is the emotions connected with suffering that are the focus of attention more so than any physical injury of the sufferer.

Law views suffering rather differently in this respect. Legal definitions of suffering are more cause-specific. Suffering is described as the pain, inconvenience, embarrassment and inability to perform normal activities *as a result of injury* caused by another's negligence or wrongdoing, for which the person injured may recover general damages. General damages are monetary compensation, the amount of which is unspecified and not based on specific calculation. It is based on the empathy of the one who tries the case—the judge.[2] Suffering also seems to be more clearly identifiable in law, described as follows—the physical and mental distress suffered from an injury, including actual broken bones and internal ruptures, the aches, pain, temporary and permanent limitations on activity, potential shortening of life, depression, and embarrassment from scarring, all of which form part of the 'general damages' recoverable by someone injured by another's negligence or intentional attack. [3] This idea that suffering is compensable has been directly attacked by various academics, and the suitability of the legal approach in awarding compensatory damages for pain and suffering will be further considered here.

From the medical perspective, Cassell presents suffering as follows:

> Suffering occurs when an impending destruction of the person is perceived, and it continues until the threat of disintegration has passed or until the integrity of the person is restored in some manner. Suffering extends beyond the physical. Generally suffering may be defined as the state of severe distress associated with events that threaten the intactness of the person. (Cassell 2004, Chap. 3, p. 32)

In an article 'On Dying and Human Suffering', Kellehear describes suffering from a social scientific perspective (Kellehear 2009). He characterizes it as a condition having some element of physical pain that is as much an event (injury) as an action (response). It is also often an unspeakable experience, associated with grief and loss. The emphasis on suffering as connected with loss and the consequences of loss is something also evident in the work of Arthur Frank (2001). Suffering is thereby understood in terms of an 'absence', a thing that is 'missed', 'unrecoverable' and a 'wound' that will never heal. Suffering has also been treated as a social state, as a means by which others in society are labeled, yet it is the association of suffering with grief and loss that seems to be more fundamental.

[1] wordnetweb.princeton.edu/perl/webwn. See also webster-dictionary.net.

[2] See http://legal-dictionary.thefreedictionary.com/

[3] See http://legal-dictionary.thefreedictionary.com/

Law and Suffering

This essay is particularly concerned with suffering as it arises in relation to the law, and especially with respect to one branch of civil law, namely medical law. The focus within medical law is limited to the doctor-patient relationship, and selected issues governing and surrounding that relationship. Suffering from the perspective of criminal law is not examined, although a brief overview of the different approaches between the two branches of law is given. Unlike medicine whose approach to suffering focuses on the patient-sufferer, law's approach to suffering shifts the focus from the sufferer to include other members of society. The degree and distribution of attention given to the plaintiff-patient sufferer and to other members of society differs depending on which area, and so which perspective of law, one takes as one's starting point.

In its most primary and basic function in attempting to regulate human behaviour, both civil and criminal law imposes punishment as a deterrent on those who inflict pain and suffering unjustifiably upon others. In civil law pain and suffering is acknowledged and recognized as a component of the probable consequence of a wrongful conduct. The injured party who is successful in claiming redress from the wrongdoer is also compensated for the pain and suffering undergone. The suffering of the injured party is therefore addressed. In criminal law, whose main aim is to prevent the infliction of pain and suffering to another, the law usually responds by inflicting further pain and suffering as punishment to the offender. The degree of pain and suffering inflicted as punishment depends on the gravity of the offence committed whilst taking into account the rationale or underlying principle of sentencing for that particular offence. The suffering of the victim of the crime is not the focus of criminal law, which focuses instead on sanctioning the offender and so preventing the future suffering of other members of the society by meting out consequences aimed at preventing both the offender and others from engaging in similar behaviour.

Whereas the civil law aims to restore the individual to his original position before the injury through the award of compensatory damages (which at the same time is intended to achieve the distributive justice objective of the law), the criminal law imposes punishment on the offender, whether retributive, deterrent, or rehabilitative in nature, and this infliction of suffering has the wider objective of securing both present and future peacekeeping in the society.

Law seeks to regulate human conduct in order to achieve its central purpose, the attainment of justice. Rules are enacted and implemented in order to limit the boundaries of acceptable and unacceptable behaviour in order that no individual is unfairly treated and social equilibrium is maintained. Yet conflicts are natural and unavoidable, given differences in interest on the part of individuals and communities, and ever-changing desires. Law plays a crucial role in the resolution of conflicts. While law might be described as having the albeit limited, role of attempting to relieve suffering through monetary compensation paid to the wrongly injured party, law also attempts to relieve the wider fear, apprehension, and suffering of a community wronged by a criminal offence, and to do so through the imposition of pain and suffering on the wrongdoer. The role of law in human suffering is never more obvious than in the sphere of criminal law where the suffering of the victim becomes a justification for law's imposition of suffering on the offender.

The Law on Damages

When suffering occurs as a result of a proven legal wrong the person injured has recourse to remedies, the primary one being an award of damages or monetary compensation (Lim 1995, pp. 10–11).

In law, suffering is generally synonymous with pain, or more specifically with the physical pain, hurt, inconvenience, or inability to perform normal activities that may result from an injury caused by the negligence or wrongdoing of another. The person injured may recover 'general damages'—an amount not based on specific calculation that is subjective and based on the empathy of the judge. The monetary value of damages for pain and suffering is subjective, as distinguished from medical bills, future medicals, and lost wages which can be calculated, called 'special damages'.

In Malaysia the assessment of damages is governed by statute (*Civil Law Act* 1956; *Civil Law (Amendment) Act* 1975, 1984; Rutter 1993). Damages are divided into two broad categories, namely pecuniary and non-pecuniary losses. Damages for pain and suffering fall under the latter category.

Although the degree of physical disability caused by wrongful conduct may be assessed medically by a physician, the monetary value attached to it cannot be logically assessed, and neither is the sorrow, grief or sense of loss experienced by either the victim or, if death results, of the next-of-kin of the deceased. Yet the law is only able to offer consolation to the person in the form of monetary compensation. It might be argued that financial compensation constitutes a fair, appropriate and practical response or, conversely, that the unsuitability of providing financial awards for emotional losses simply means that the law on damages for non-pecuniary losses rests on fiction.

The principle in awarding damages is that the plaintiff is entitled to an award which is fair and adequate, commensurate to the loss or injury suffered (*Pickett v British Rail Engineering Ltd* 1980). The amount should also not be excessive as this would unfairly burden the wrongdoer.

What amounts to fair and reasonable compensation? Firstly according to the law, the court implies and assumes intangible losses such as pain and suffering, life expectancy and loss of amenities, including future loss of earnings and loss of earning capacity. Loss of amenities, for instance, is awarded on the basis of a deprivation that the law considers to be a substantial loss, regardless of whether the injured party is aware of it (Lord Scarman 1980). Pain and suffering depends on the individual's personal awareness of pain and his or her capacity for suffering (perhaps providing an analogue to Cassell's view that suffering is personal to the sufferer).

Emotional suffering such as distress, fear, anxiety and worry caused by the injuries inflicted are also taken into account, and so is embarrassment and loss of confidence as a result of disfigurement and scarring (*Seah Yit Chen v Singapore Bus Service* 1990). In assessing damages the court directs its mind to the harm, injury, damage or loss which the plaintiff has incurred. The most relevant consideration is the nature of the harmful consequences suffered by the plaintiff and not the nature of the wrongdoer's acts or omissions (Lim 1995, p. 12).

It seems that the law does not study 'actual' suffering but does presume it from the nature of the injury sustained. As it is impossible for the law to accurately determine and quantify the gravity of the loss in monetary terms the sum awarded is often based on what the society deems fair, usually reflected in earlier decisions. This in turn depends on existing policies, resources and ultimately, the values, operative within the society with regard to the type of loss suffered. It might thus be concluded that the law does formally acknowledge suffering, yet it understands it only in terms of the assistance and relief that can be assessed in compensation.

Adequacy of Compensation

The law does not alleviate suffering by attempting to remove the cause of suffering.[4] It is difficult to assess whether, and to what extent, this compensatory approach is adequate, since, in any particular case, only the sufferer can determine the adequacy of monetary compensation in relieving his or her suffering.

A real hurdle facing individuals undergoing litigation is the lengthy legal process involved in settling a claim. A case may take many years before the court arrives at a judgment. The uncertainty in the outcome of litigation may cause added suffering. The law gives rise to a hope or expectation that there will be fair monetary compensation, but in the end, when this expectation is unmet either because the award is too small or the delay had cumulatively caused overwhelming anxiety, it can actually cause more suffering. The merits of retaining pain and suffering damages in tort law have been the subject of continuous debates (Sugarman 1985; Avraham 2003).

Purpose of Compensation

It bears repeating that the primary response of the law towards suffering is to provide for compensatory damages based on the principle of *restitutio in integrum*—restoring the injured person to a state as close as possible to the state that would have obtained had the wrong not been committed. The aim is thus to make the victim 'whole' again. Herein lies the fiction inherent in the law—that of law awarding

[4] Although there may be cases in which suffering is caused by continuing activity on the part of the offender that distresses the sufferer.

monetary compensation for pain and suffering which has no monetary dimension (Rabin 2006).

If the focus shifts, however, from the incommensurability between the character of legal compensation and the actual emotional loss, then an argument may be made for the adequacy of the present system, not from the adequacy of monetary compensation, but rather on the basis of the utility offered by the legal process of hearing. Apart from financial compensation, and sometimes other than for financial compensation, victims often have other reasons for taking legal action. The narrative element of legal proceedings may offer some partial alleviation of the suffering incurred, as it allows the sufferer's grief to be heard, for public recognition of the wrongdoing or injustice that has occurred, and may also offer the victim an opportunity to regain dignity and respect (Mulder 2008). The process of litigation may thus allow for some relief from suffering. Through the evidence tendered, victims may express their perception of themselves as human beings and how they are perceived by others. The reaffirmation of self this may enable can itself be seen as a form of emotional compensation. Legal proceedings may also address innate psychological needs for self-determination, in particular, three key needs of self-expression—autonomy, relatedness and competence (Mulder 2008). Thus legal procedures may contribute overall to individual well-being, and in this way become a source of healing, aside from any monetary outcome awarded by the court.

A Case of Justice, Suffering and Suffering for Justice?

At the end of December 2006, the Federal Court in Malaysia in the case of *Foo Fio Na v. Dr SooFookMun and Anor* (2007) delivered a much-awaited judgment governing the standard of care of physicians. The plaintiff, a 24 year old lady suffered some injuries when the car she was travelling in hit a tree. She was admitted into hospital and at the time of admission had some pain on her neck. When conventional treatment did not relieve the pain the surgeon recommended her to undergo surgery. After the surgery she found she could not move her body and limbs. She was informed that the paralysis was temporary and that she would be able to move her limbs in two weeks' time. Two weeks passed and there was no improvement. She was operated on again and after the second surgery she could move her hands although her legs remained paralyzed. Despite being told that the paralysis was temporary she never regained use of her legs. She discharged herself from the hospital eleven months later. She subsequently sued the surgeon for negligence, for failure to obtain her consent for both procedures.

The case was heard in three different courts, first in the High Court which found the surgeon to be negligent. The surgeon appealed. The Court of Appeal reversed the earlier finding and held that the surgeon did not breach his duty of care. The plaintiff appealed to the Federal Court which restored the High Court decision and found the surgeon negligent. Ms Foo who is a quadriplegic was awarded a total of about RM 500,000 as damages.

The Federal Court judgment was handed down a little over twenty-four years from the date of the accident in question, and just under twenty years from the initial filing of the suit in the High Court in January 1987.

The judgment had ended much speculation on whether the standard of care of physicians in Malaysia would remain the same as it had been for the past fifty years or whether the pro-patient test as applicable in Australia would be adopted. The latter test prevailed and this currently forms binding precedent. The pro-patient test frees the patient from paternal decision-making by the physician on matters pertaining to his, the patient's health. This emancipation is arguably a development that adds to the sense of individuality, of making 'whole' and so in theory at least, this change in the law ought to have the effect of reducing patients' suffering, if any, arising from the exercise of paternalism (Lois 2009).[5]

However, this case is also an example of how the length of the legal process may be extremely relevant in either exacerbating or alleviating suffering. Although no direct finding has been recorded that the plaintiff in this case objected or suffered additionally due to the length of the entire legal process, it seems self-evident that the length of the legal process may well have had a negative effect, and that, in general, the length of a legal process is relevant in considerations of suffering endured. If the length of a process is too great, as in this case, what initially began as an expression of self and the preservation of dignity and respect may erode and lessen with time, and may interfere with the overall well-being of the plaintiff. In this regard, each particular system has the responsibility to ensure that the legal process relieves or reduces suffering and not the other way round.

Medicine and Suffering

Eliminating the causes of suffering is the common goal of both doctors and patients. Yet there exists a paradox here in that patients often suffer from their treatment as well as their disease. Cassell asserts that this paradox arises due to the inadequate view of the ends of medicine (Cassell 2004, Chap. 3, p. 31)—a view that tends toward a focus more on the disease than the human experience. Suffering, however, is not just a matter of bodily disease or bodily affliction, but something that affects the person (Cassell 2004, Chap. 3, p. 224). One indication of this is the way in which persons assign meaning to their illness and pain, no matter what the cause, and in doing so, they can contribute to an increase in their own anxiety and fear which then leads to further suffering (Cassell 2004, Chap. 15). Although suffering may arise from physical illness and symptoms, it is not just a matter of physical distress alone. Indeed, on Cassell's account, suffering is typically associated with a sense of threat to the integrity of the person, and this must be addressed, rather than any underlying

[5] However Shepherd Lois argues for limited autonomy—see Lois (2009). The context of Lois' article concerns advance directives, but the treatment may be extended to informed consent, particularly in societies where shared decision-making among family members has always been the norm.

disease or physical condition alone, if the suffering itself is to be adequately dealt with (Cassell 2004, Chap. 15). Cassell emphasises that suffering is something that relates first to the person, and the fact of suffering is only to be decided by the person who suffers, even though suffering takes on significance in a wider interpersonal content (Cassell 2004, Chap. 15, pp. 33–34). Patients can be in pain, and yet not be suffering because they 'know what it is'. In contrast when they do not know the nature or source of pain, people may report considerable suffering even from apparently minor trauma. This reinforces the complex nature of suffering, and its intimate connection to the character of the person.

Comparing Legal and Medical Perspectives on Suffering

Law and medicine each understand suffering in different terms. Whereas law takes suffering to consist in the pain and inconvenience arising from a physical injury, medicine treats suffering as pain in mind and spirit arising from a loss which need not be physical in nature. The law compensates for suffering. It proceeds on the legal fiction that suffering is somehow quantifiable—there is an assumption that monetary compensation can somehow replace what has been lost (Mulder 2008). Moreover, while the real effectiveness of damages in alleviating pain and suffering is uncertain, it ought to be acknowledged that the financial benefit arising from the payment of damages may nevertheless assist in fulfilling the material needs of the person wronged. Inasmuch as the legal response to suffering seems to be to address just that aspect of the person's life that relates to their financial circumstance, the medical response, on the other hand, is to attempt to address matters in a much broader fashion—in the eyes of an author such as Cassell, it must involve an attempt to address the situation of the person as a whole, and, as far as possible, restore the person as a whole.

There are a number of other respects in which suffering understood from a legal as opposed to medical perspective can be contrasted. Sometimes one finds points of similarity: for instance, just as patients suffer from their disease, but may also suffer as a result of their treatment, a person who seeks justice from law may suffer from the legal processes and outcomes from the application of those rules. Yet in general, the differences seem to outweigh the similarities. Thus, in addition to those already noted, it is worth observing, for instance, that while suffering seems to be an essential 'tool' for the law, especially when the purpose is punishment as opposed to restoration, suffering does not function as a tool in medicine in the same way; while fault is a requirement in law before compensation is meted out, fault functions in medicine not at all (although it might be said that some doctors have taken fault to be an issue in cases of disease that result from the actions of the patient—most notably in the case of smoking). The differences at issue here reflect the fact that medicine and law have different aims and objectives, but also address different needs and aspects of the person—and so, one might say, each conceptualizes the person differently. Thus the personal suffering of one person is never the sole focus of the law, since the law adopts a broader perspective of well-being, that of the community as a whole—and the person appears only in that larger context. Any imbalance within the community is addressed by monetary compensation as a practical means of restoration. The situation is quite different in medicine, since although general healthcare strategies operate from the broader perspective of community well-being, still medicine aims more directly, and in more encompassing fashion, to address personal distress, and so to attend to the personal situation of the individual.

The differences explored above may be tabled as follows:

Law's perspective on suffering	Medicine's perspective on suffering
Law compensates for suffering	Medicine treats the whole person
The purpose of (monetary) compensation is to restore the person	The purpose of treatment is to restore the person
Fault must be established before compensation for suffering is meted out	Fault is irrelevant to medicine
Suffering is intentionally inflicted as a method of punishment	Punishment is irrelevant to medicine
Law's outlook is more diffused, not focused on the suffering of one person. Means of redress is practical and economically oriented	Medicine's outlook is more patient-centred. Means of redress is personal and emotionally oriented

Given these differences, and given also the way in which sometimes medicine and law may overlap (particularly inasmuch as legal decisions, at least in regard to damages, may sometimes draw on medical considerations, while medical practice must often be mindful of legal complications as they affect practice), then whether each discipline might not benefit from a consideration of the differences between their respective approaches is an issue that deserves further attention.

Summary and Conclusion

Cassell proposes that the alleviation of suffering through medicine should be achieved by treating the person and not merely the disease or the body. The parallel for law would perhaps be that law needs to consider whether the legal system and individual laws as a whole address the 'person' (which may have both individual and collective implications) or merely the (altered) body or interest consequent on the wrong. This would be one area in which legal and medical practice may perhaps enter into some greater dialogue, and in which the law may be asked to address the wider question of the extent to which it is genuinely 'humane' in its own practices.

The focus of law is typically on the legal principles and other relevant legal rules that are applicable in any particular case. This emphasis on principles has no necessary connection to issues of personal well-being in practical terms. The case law discussed above demonstrates that although a decision may make for advancement in legal principle, a lengthy legal process may itself contribute to suffering, and thereby give rise to injustice. Rules and principles are by themselves meaningless unless they are given effect without causing undue harm to individuals—and without attention to the suffering that may be inflicted rules and principles cannot contribute to justice. Moreover, even while law as well as medicine can be seen to have a broader concern with the promotion of socially beneficial outcomes in different ways, it is only through the engagement with individuals that this is possible. Consequently, both law and medicine must retain a significant focus on the matter of individual well-being.

Cassell gives a significant role to interpersonal engagement—talking and 'active listening' to patients—as an element in the control of suffering. This engagement involves three different points of focus: first the patient; second the body; and third the relationship with the physician (Mulder 2008, p. 290). The analogy that might be drawn here with law might be the engagement with the interests of the individual (whether as a patient or other injured group member); the engagement with the law as a whole in both its substantive and procedural aspects; and the engagement in the wider relationship between the law-makers and the people in addressing changes in the law. For instance, in the enactment of laws on medical and bioethical issues such as organ transplantation, surrogacy, abortion and euthanasia, one might adopt a more holistic approach that would encompass all of these aspects in evaluating the issues, and especially the suffering, at stake: the benefits and dangers to individuals, the potential of abuse in the wording of legislation, and larger questions concerning whether these practices enhance the quality of life, would all need to be addressed and reflected upon.

There have been no empirical studies that could help shed light on whether applying Cassell's recommendation of 'active listening' as an aid in the alleviation of suffering would have a positive effect in the law—whether it might contribute to a lessening of suffering or greater justice. It could be argued, however, that some form of 'listening' is already embedded in the process of law-making, in parliamentary and public debate, at least in principle and in theory, if not always in practice. Yet in the actual application of law, once legislation has been enacted, it seems that this process of listening is often disrupted. Many factors may lead to legislation taking on a different character once it is enacted, or may result in law becoming disengaged from the original concerns and contexts that motivated it—including disengagement from individual cases, and instances of individual suffering, that may have prompted the legislation. Perhaps the problem here reflects the institutional character of legal practice, which, it may be argued, is necessarily distanced from individual concerns, no matter how strongly they may have motivated law-makers in the first instance.

As much as it is essential to address suffering on a subjective and personal level, however, and to emphasise the need for law to perhaps focus more on the individual, the tension between private and public rights and interests will always be present. Law would not be fulfilling its function if it were to only focus on select individuals or groups of individuals. A balance needs to be struck at all times, and as more competing interests arise, the individual might have to make way for the interests of the collective. Law may perhaps distribute its role in the alleviation of suffering by playing a more effective role at the initial stage of both policy and law-making, with the aim of preventing or minimizing foreseeable suffering rather than intervening only after the fact through the imposition of punishment or an award of compensation (unless of course, punishment is the only way to prevent or minimize suffering in the future). The medical objective of 'restoration of the person' post-injury, as law is at present, is arguably not achievable, and cannot itself be construed as a relevant goal in legal process.

The way law relates to suffering is, as we have already seen, complex, and while it may overlap with aspects of medicine also diverges from it in many ways. While one may view law as aiming to reduce or to redress suffering, it is also clear that law can itself be a source of suffering—and not only through the use of punishment or through the rigours of the legal process. Legal systems can institutionalize forms of inequality and oppression, they can lead to the imposition of forms of judgment that are prejudicial or discriminatory—forms of judgment that fail to take account of different collective as well as individual interests—they may ignore suffering in some forms while they give undue recognition to others. No legal system can be perfect, and law, unlike medicine, cannot focus solely on the individual person alone. Still, it seems we may still expect law to do more to address, and to acknowledge, the human figure that is at the centre of almost every legal process, and to find ways better to take account of this human element. In doing so, we will also need to find ways better to address the question of suffering as something that does indeed pertain to the individual—even the individual as appearing in relation to the law.

Bibliography

Avraham, Ronen. 2003. *Pain-and-suffering damages in tort law: Revisiting the theoretical framework and the empirical evidence*, University of Michigan John M. Olin Centre for Law & Economics, Working Paper Series, Feb 2003.

Cassell, E. J. 2004. *The nature of suffering and the goals of medicine*, 2nd edn. New York: Oxford University Press.

Civil Law Act. 1956. (Rev 1972). Malaysia. Act 67.

Civil Law (Amendment) Act. 1975. Malaysia. Act A308.

Civil Law (Amendment) Act. 1984. Malaysia. Act A602.

Foo Fio Na v Dr Soo Fook Mun and Anor. 2007. 1 Malayan Law Journal 593.

Frank, A. W. 2001. Can we research suffering? *Qualitative Health Research* 11:353–362.

Kellehear, A. 2009. On dying and human suffering. *Palliative Medicine* 23:388–397. http://pmj.sagepub.com/cgi/content/refs/23/5/388.

Lim, Heng Seng. 1995. *Assessment of damages in personal injury and fatal accident claims: Principles and practice*. Kuala Lumpur: Marsden Law Books Sdn Bhd.

Lloyd, D. 1976. *The idea of law*. Harmondsworth: Penguin.

Lois, Shepherd. 2009. Asking too much: Autonomy and responsibility at the end of life. *Journal of Contemporary Health Law and Policy* 72:72–81. http://ssrn.com/abstract=1553228

Mulder, J. D. W. E. 2008. Compensation is not just about money and neither should its economic assessment be. Tilburg Law and Economic Centre (Tilec), Discussion paper, March 2008. http://ssrn.com/abstract=1099865.

Pickett v British Rail Engineering Ltd. 1980. Appeal Cases 136.

Rabin, Robert L. 2006. Pain and suffering and beyond: Some thoughts on recovery for intangible loss. *DePaul Law Review* 55:359–377.
Rutter, Michael F. 1993. *Handbook on damages for personal injuries and death in Singapore and Malaysia*, 2nd edn. Singapore: Butterworths Asia.
Scarman, Lord. (1980) *Lim Poh Choo v Camden and Islington* Area Health Authority AC 174.
Seah Yit Chen v Singapore Bus Service (1978) Ltd. 1990. 3 Malayan Law Journal 144.
Sugarman, Stephen D. 1985. Doing away with Tort Law. *California Law Review* 73:555–564.

Chapter 18
To Suffer With: The Poetry of Compassion

Jack Coulehan

In medicine the words 'pain' and 'suffering' are so frequently in tandem that for many physicians pain-and-suffering glides off the tongue as a single concept. Suffering tends to be treated as merely the psychological or personal dimension of pain. It follows, then, that since pain and other unpleasant symptoms *cause* the suffering, this negative psychological reaction should be eliminated by treating pain or, better yet, curing the disease. Thus, the primary focus of research and teaching about pain-and-suffering is on nocireceptors and pharmacology. However, physicians who maintain this *professional* belief system about suffering are not necessarily insensitive to the existential or spiritual dimension of suffering. They merely separate their concept of an appropriate professional response to suffering in patients from their beliefs about suffering that touches them personally.

A quarter of a century ago, Eric Cassell argued that physicians do, in fact, have a professional responsibility to understand and treat suffering at an existential level, especially in the care of seriously ill and dying patients. In his famous *New England Journal* article, 'The nature of suffering and the goals of medicine,' and later in his book of the same name, Cassell defined suffering as 'a specific state of severe distress induced by the loss of integrity, intactness, cohesiveness, or wholeness of the person, or by a threat that the person believes will result in the dissolution of his or her integrity' (Cassell 1982, 1995, 2004). This definition identifies an end state ('severe distress'), operative conditions ('loss' or 'threat of loss'), and substantive qualities ('integrity, intactness, cohesiveness, or wholeness'). Michael Kearney, an Irish internist and hospice physician provided a synergistic definition of 'soul pain' (his term for suffering) as 'the experience of an individual who has become disconnected and alienated from the deepest and most fundamental aspects of him or

---

This chapter is a revised and expanded version of J. Coulehan, 'Compassionate Solidarity: Suffering, Poetry, and Medicine,' originally published in *Perspectives in Biology and Medicine,* 52(2009):585–603.

J. Coulehan (✉)
Center for Medical Humanities, Compassionate Care, and Bioethics, Stony Brook University, Stony Brook, USA
e-mail: jcoulehan@notes.cc.sunysb.edu

J. Malpas, N. Lickiss (eds.), *Perspectives on Human Suffering,*
DOI 10.1007/978-94-007-2795-3_18, © Springer Science+Business Media B.V. 2012

herself' (Kearney 1996, p. 60). The psychiatrist Victor Frankl specified 'the deepest and most fundamental aspects' as the matrix of beliefs and expectations that give meaning to life. He wrote, 'Man is not destroyed by suffering, he is destroyed by suffering without meaning' (Frankl 1997).

These two opposing views—that physicians should address suffering only indirectly by treating disease, and that physicians should get close enough to patients to understand their existential suffering—reflect different radically beliefs about the nature and mechanisms of healing. Nonetheless, most physicians incorporate elements of both sets of beliefs in their professional lives, although they often do not appreciate the resultant incompatibility. In this essay I explore these different therapeutic responses to suffering. First, I look more carefully at the experience of suffering as expressed by creative writers, as well as presenting a patient case history that illustrates the central role of symbols in healing. In the following sections, I analyze in turn the doctrine of objectivity and detachment in medicine and the doctrine of compassionate solidarity, which preserves a form of objectivity, while promoting the formation of empathic relationships with patients. Through compassionate solidarity physicians may become healers as well as treaters. Finally, I argue that poetry (and other creative writing) is a useful adjunct for helping physicians to understand suffering, solidarity, and healing; and also for developing the self-awareness needed to become effective healers.

The Experience of Suffering

Suffering as Disharmony

Sarah Mailcarrier was an elderly Navajo woman who lived at Cornfields on the Navajo Reservation. The dirt road to Cornfields ended at a trading post in a clump of cottonwood trees along a dry arroyo in Beautiful Valley. Rutted tracks led from the trading post to scattered camps in the surrounding desert. At the time I was a Public Health Service physician at Greasewood Clinic, about 20 miles south of Cornfields. Sarah Mailcarrier was the matriarch of a camp with five or six homes where her daughters and their families lived. A daughter had asked me to come and see her because of pain and swelling in her legs. When I examined Sarah, who was lying on a mat in her *hoghan*, cachectic and groaning in pain, I was sure she was terminally ill.

Our clinic driver took Mrs. Mailcarrier to Fort Defiance Hospital, some 50 miles east of Cornfields. Sure enough, she suffered from cancer of the cervix that had spread throughout her pelvis and abdomen, blocking lymphatic ducts and causing massive edema. The cancer was also threatening her kidneys, her ureters already partially obstructed. The only available treatment was radiation, which might shrink the tumor and extend the patient's life. But radiation therapy wasn't available at the small reservation hospital, so Sarah would have to travel another 40 miles to a larger regional hospital in Gallup, New Mexico.

In fact, the patient and her family declined further medical intervention. Rather, they carried her home in the bed of a pickup truck, never stopping at the hospital pharmacy to fill her morphine prescription. The family then hired a medicine man or *ha'atali* to conduct a Blessingway, a nine day healing ceremony, in their camp later that month. The Blessingway was a major event that attracted relatives and friends from settlements over the mesa and down the valley. In addition to ritual chants, dances, and sand paintings, participants enjoyed several evenings of feasting and socializing. The ceremony was expensive. Mrs. Mailcarrier's family had to slaughter quite a few sheep, in addition to raising money to pay the *ha'atali* and his assistants. Fortunately, however, the Blessingway was a great success. Mrs. Mailcarrier's pain disappeared, her energy increased, and she was able to continue in her role as family matriarch for several months. When I visited her, she appeared serene. Eventually, she drifted into a coma and died.

When I first met Sarah Mailcarrier, she was suffering terribly. I could see it in her face and eyes, as well as those of her children. Her groans were unmoored and disoriented. They were soul-groans. We usually translate the Navajo term for suffering as 'disharmony,' meaning that the sufferer has lost his or her way; more generally, the Navajo Way, which gives structure and meaning to Navajo life. As an Anglo doctor, I couldn't do anything to address this existential problem, which had been precipitated by her illness. However, the traditional healing ceremony could and did relieve her suffering. During the final months, when I visited her frequently, Sarah didn't seem to suffer, even though she must have had severe symptoms from her cancer. It seems paradoxical that while her cancer got worse, her suffering diminished.

Sarah Mailcarrier's successful treatment neither extended her life nor cured her cancer. Her world had been knocked off kilter by a radical threat to her internal harmony. By manipulating meaningful symbols and narratives, the *ha'atali* helped her to restore that harmony; i.e. alleviate her suffering. In some ways we are less surprised that a Navajo woman 'got better' from symbolic healing than we would be at the same response in a middle-class Anglo. Westerners have little trouble accepting that traditional healing practices can be effective in non-Western cultures (Morris 1998; Coulehan 1991). However, it is more difficult for us to appreciate the same dynamics taking place in Western culture; i.e. that the patient's beliefs about the meaning of illness and his or her interaction with the healer influence whether—and how much—the patient suffers.

The other important lesson from Mrs. Mailcarrier's Blessingway ceremony is that traditional Navajo medicine consists primarily of poetry (spoken, chanted, and danced to), in association with other artistic practices, like sandpainting and storytelling. In Western medicine we speak of the art of healing as one aspect or dimension of scientific practice. However, in Navajo culture medicine is literally and quite obviously an art form (Coulehan 1992a). Thus, the Navajo case serves to introduce the concept that poetry provides us with deep insight into both the experience and the relief of suffering (Coulehan and Clary 2005).

Creative Expression of Suffering

The late nineteenth century French novelist and playwright Alphonse Daudet wrote a series of notes about his experience of tabes dorsalis, a form of tertiary syphilis. These notes were recently translated and published by Julian Barnes as a collection called *In the Land of Pain*. Here are three examples of Daudet's reflections:

> Very strange, the fear that pain inspires these days—or rather, this pain of mine. It's bearable, and yet I cannot bear it. It's sheer dread: and my resort to anesthetics is like a cry for help, the squeal of a woman before danger actually strikes. (Daudet 2002, p. 9)

> Pain in the country: a veil over the horizon. Those roads, with their pretty little bends—all they provoke in me now is the desire to flee. To run away, to escape my sickness. (Daudet 2002, p. 45)

> I've passed the stage where illness brings any advantage, or helps you understand things; also the stage where it sours your life, puts a harshness in your voice, makes every cogwheel shriek. Now there's only a hard, stagnant, painful torpor, and an indifference to everything. Nada! Nada! (Daudet 2002, p. 65)

Daudet illustrate three aspects or stages of suffering: the cry for help, the desire to flee, and, finally, the indifference and immobilization.

Anna Akhmatova, the great twentieth century Russian poet, spent most of her life laboring under official Soviet disapproval. Her husband was killed, her son imprisoned, and she endured a marginal hand to mouth existence for decades, her poems suppressed by the government. After her son Lev was arrested in 1938, Akhmatova waited every week in line at the prison gates for 17 months, hoping that she would be allowed to give him some food or warm clothes. Dozens, perhaps hundreds, of other women waited with her, hoping for word of their husbands, sons, or fathers. Akhmatova later wrote 'Requiem' to express her suffering during that period:

> Today there's so much I must do:
> Must smash my memories to bits,
> Must turn my heart to stone all through,
> And must relearn how one must live. (Akhmatova 2004, vol. VII, p. 137)

> Admit it—fighting back's absurd,
> My own will just a hollow joke,
> I hear my broken babbling words
> As if some other person spoke. (Akhmatova 2004, vol. IX, p. 140)

> Do what you please, take any shape that comes to mind,
> Burst on me like a shell of poison gas,
> Or creep up like a mugger, club me from behind,
> Or let the fog of typhus do the task. (Akhmatova 2004, vol. VIII, p. 139)

In this case the first excerpt communicates the poet's recognition that she must change her life in response to suffering. She must act—smash her memories, turn her heart, relearn how to live—rather than remain passive. In the next segment, however, the poet has become passive and cynical. Finally, she appears to welcome annihilation. Her numbness is transformed into a strong, but confrontational, desire for nothingness.

As poet and novelist D. H. Lawrence was dying of tuberculosis in late 1929 and early 1930, he wrote 'The Ship of Death',and a number of related poems. 'The Ship of Death' is an explicit articulation of suffering, unified by two major metaphors, the body as a piece of decaying fruit and a ship setting out on the sea. For Lawrence the process of creating these works, which he drafted again and again, was a form of *arsmoriendi*, a poet's way of coming to terms with his inevitable dissolution:

> Now it is autumn and the falling fruit
> and the long journey towards oblivion.
> Already our bodies are fallen, bruised, badly bruised,
> already our souls are oozing through the exit
> of the cruel bruise.

We encounter a grove of fruit trees in autumn. Overripe fruit has already fallen. Vital juices ooze into the ground. Our souls leak from wounds in our damaged bodies. The souls are frightened by the cold, uncertain world they encounter as they leave the body.

> We are dying, we are dying, piecemeal our bodies are dying
> and our strength leaves us,
> and our soul cowers naked in the dark rain over the flood,
> cowering in the last branches of the tree of our life. (Lawrence 1947, vol. VI, pp. 138–140)

D. H. Lawrence's second metaphor imagines death as a voyage to an unknown and inexplicable shore. Human beings can 'redeem' themselves from suffering by maintaining their integrity in the face of the 'dark flight down oblivion':

> O build your ship of death, your little ark
> and furnish it with food, with little cakes, and wine
> for the dark flight down oblivion. (Lawrence 1947, vol. V)

> Now launch the small ship, now as the body dies
> and life departs, launch out, the fragile soul
> in the fragile ship of courage, the ark of faith
> with its store of food and little cooking pans
> and change of clothes,
> upon the flood's black waste,
> upon the waters of the end
> upon the sea of death, where still we sail
> darkly, for we cannot steer, and have no port. (Lawrence 1947, vol. VII)

One may overcomes suffering by building a 'ship of death,' thus imposing order on the experience and making it comprehensible; by supplying food and small cakes, which is to say, by incorporating one's own death into a meaningful belief system.

It is instructive to consider these literary excerpts in the light of the three phases of suffering described by Reich (1989, pp. 83–108). When a person is first confronted by catastrophic illness or loss, he or she responds with silence and immobilization. The sufferer is not only struck dumb, but he or she cannot make informed decisions—or sometimes any decisions at all—because the sense of loss overwhelms agency. Autonomy is diminished. And imagination gives out; it is not up to the task of creating meaningful images. Reich calls this stage *mute suffering*, the experience of being speechless in the face of one's own suffering. Obviously, mute sufferers are unable to express their experience in poetry, prose, visual arts, or any form of imaginative communication.

Expressive suffering is the second phase, in which the sufferer seeks to understand the experience by finding a language to express it. Daudet does this by writing personal journal entries, while Akhmatova and Lawrence go through the more structured process of creating poems that are intended to communicate with a larger audience. This poetic process parallels the sufferer's internal process of finding an expressive voice, which in itself can exercise some control over suffering. For example, the cancer patient may learn to articulate her deepest fears and sense of loss to family members, or to a chaplain or health professional, in a way that encourages conversation. The expressive sufferer can also respond in his own style, using his own habits of coping. Akhmatova chooses to speak to her suffering, 'Do what you please, take any shape that comes to mind.' In context, these sentiments are not submissive. They are spoken with attitude—Akhmatova was a tough woman who survived decades of persecution. Daudet, on the other hand, describes his reaction to syphilitic pain by creating a finely wrought image: 'the squeal of a woman before danger actually strikes.' In this he distances himself from dissolution by implying that his cries are premature, even though his actual pain is severe. Lawrence's rotting fruit metaphor acknowledges that he is now cut off from the tree of life. His soul has begun to disperse ('oozing through the exit/of the cruel bruise'), but finds itself terrified and presumably trying to re-enter the world of the living ('cowers naked… in the last branches of the tree of life.')

Reich's third and final phase is called *new identity in suffering,* where the sufferer discovers a new self, or a new understanding of self, that in essence overcomes suffering by preserving personal integrity. The old self may have been destroyed, but a new self, a new character, has emerged. According to Reich, this process requires solidarity with others. In fact, even the second stage, expressive suffering, requires the participation of others, if only as listeners (Reich 1989, pp. 86–91). Gregory Orr's poem 'Tin Cup' illustrates the adoption of a new identity in suffering:

> Here's a tin cup
> furred with rust.
> Here's a bad heart
> I've lugged this far.
> Begging? No.
> Hauling with me
> all a mortal has.
> You think I'm grim
> and thin, wisened
> as a dry stick.
> You think I've come
> to bore you
> with a long story
> of torment.
> And yet I swear
> I love this earth
> that scars and scalds,
> that burns my feet.
> And even hell is holy. (Orr 2002, p. 9)

Detachment: Keeping Suffering at Arm's Length

What is the physician's appropriate response to her patient's experience of suffering? What professional stance should he adopt when confronted by the suffering of seriously ill and dying patients? More concisely: Is there a type of professional response that in itself tends to relieve suffering (i.e. is therapeutic)? Medical philosophy and practice provide us with at least two conflicting answers to these questions. The most widely accepted and institutionalized answer is that medical professionals should respond to suffering with objectivity and detachment (Becker et al. 1961; Bloom 1989; Hafferty and Franks 1994; Hunnert 1996; Inui 2003; Kassirer 1998; Manson 1994; Zoloth-Dorfman and Rubin 1995). The other answer tends to be less well-articulated, but is nonetheless highly valued by many practitioners; i.e. physicians should respond to their patients' suffering by forming bonds of compassionate solidarity with them (Coulehan 1995, 2002; Farber et al. 1997; Novack et al. 1997; Suchman et al. 1997; Zinn 1993; Bennett 2001; Charon 2001; Connelly 1998; Petersdorf 1992).

Detached Concern

In both theory and practice, modern medicine focuses primarily on detachment as the proper response to suffering. The terms 'clinical distance' and 'detached concern' are also used, especially the latter. 'Detached concern' is of particular interest because it has evolved from being a non-value laden descriptive term to being a highly valued prescriptive term over the last 50 years. Medical sociologists created 'detached concern' in the 1950s to describe the sense of detachment they had observed in their studies of medical students and patients (Lief and Fox 1963; Becker et al. 1961). Later, medical philosophers and educators seized upon the term, endowing it with orthodoxy: medical students and young doctors were right to demonstrate emotional detachment from their patients (Petersdorf 1992). They identified two reasons for this. First, detachment protects the physician from being overwhelmed and paralyzed by pain and suffering. The lay person who faints at the sight of blood may, with proper training, become an accomplished surgeon, at least in part by learning to disconnect from the emotional side of the experience. The process of disconnecting begins with human dissection in the gross anatomy laboratory and develops over many years as the trainee is socialized into the culture of medicine. According to these beliefs, doctors who stay 'soft' tend to get depressed and burn out.

The second reason for detachment is to protect the patient. Medical decisions ought not to be influenced by feelings and biases. Blumgart, for example, writes that detachment is necessary to prevent 'loss of objectivity and perspective' (Blumgart 1964). An emotional response may lead to biases in clinical judgment that compromise patient care. Hence, the tradition that physicians ought not treat their loved ones. Emotional vulnerability impairs medical performance. Strong attachment (or repulsion) greatly impairs doctoring. To this way of thinking, even the doctor's day-to-day emotional life (disregarding relationships with patients) should be looked upon skeptically, because emotions are intrinsically irrational and, at least to some extent, compromise the ideal of objectivity.

There is no empirical support for these claims, but they are widely accepted because they reflect today's prevalent model of disease and medical intervention. In this model disease is considered an insult or process that disrupts the body and can, in principle, be completely understood in anatomical, physiological, biochemical, or even molecular terms. Existential and spiritual suffering that results from disease (or trauma) is expected to resolve when the disease is cured, alleviated, or controlled. If a physician restores the patient to a satisfactory level of physical and emotional functioning, the patient's suffering diminishes. If restoration is not possible, then medicine can't address the suffering.

Detachment Is Not Enough

One important result of these ideas is that they limit the scope of medical concern to those aspects of suffering considered 'fixable' (Gunderman 2002). They also imply that, from a human perspective at least, disease is—or ought to be—meaningless. Disease equals invasion, error, decay, and chaos; the doctor's role is to fix these problems. But ideally they are problems without intrinsic personal or moral meaning. To believe that illness represents punishment, reward, romance, or some part of a pattern of meaning, is wrong. Attributions of meaning are only liable to increase one's suffering, as Susan Sontag argued in *Illness as Metaphor* and *AIDS as Metaphor* (Sontag 1978, 1988). Sontag insisted that the healthiest way of dealing with illness is to strip it of meaning. Or as the theologian Stanley Hauerwas writes, 'The ideology... institutionalized in modern medicine requires that we interpret all illness as pointless' (Hauerwas 1990, p. 69).[1]

This set of concepts is often called the *biomedical model* (Engel 1977). Its demand for objective observation and measurement, coupled with the belief that simpler systems ultimately cause complex phenomena, means that medicine seeks its *deepest* explanations in the *simplest* observable systems. According to detached concern advocates, the objectivity requirement means that emotional connection with patients is dangerous and usually damaging. Critics, however, claim that precisely because of this requirement modern medicine is inhumane, rather than patient-centered. However, this is an unwarranted overgeneralization: physicians who

[1] These orthodox beliefs have recently been challenged by an upsurge of moralization that tends to blame patients for their illnesses. In the pre-scientific era, diseases were often attributed to moral depravity. This theme has reemerged in the recent tendency to blame patients for the 'bad' behavior that causes, or contributes to, their disease (e.g. smoking, drinking alcohol, eating trans-fats, not exercising).

are firmly committed to these reductionistic ideas are generally still motivated by a desire to help their patients as persons. They don't consider themselves technicians and, surprisingly, many still endorse the idea of the 'art of medicine.'

The 'concern' in 'detached concern' is intended to preserve not only the physician's motivation to relieve suffering, but some level of personal involvement with patients. 'Concern' is a weaker and more ambiguous word than 'care' or 'compassion.' The originators of the concept no doubt intended this. To say 'I am concerned about you' may be interpreted either positively (looking out for her welfare) or negatively (questioning her behavior). In either case the phrase distances the speaker, while the alternate 'I care for you' implies connection. Thus, as a modifier of detachment, 'concern' doesn't contribute much to our understanding. It leaves medicine open to Cynthia Ozick's indictment in 'Metaphor and Memory,' where she wrote that physicians cultivate detachment from their patients because they are afraid of finding themselves 'too frail… to enter into psychological twinship with the even frailer souls of the sick' (Ozick 1989, pp. 265–283).

This, however, is only one approach to suffering patients in medicine. Despite a perceived need for detachment, physicians almost universally agree that relationships are part of medical practice. They believe the art of medicine includes compassion, responsiveness, rapport, and 'bedside manner.' They believe that doctors should be concerned about their patients as individuals. In other words, physicians should connect, as well as being detached.

Compassion: Getting Close to Suffering

As an Anglo intruder, I was unable to share Sarah Mailcarrier's symbolic world. She had symptoms—severe pain, nausea, vomiting, anorexia, edema, weakness, and shortness of breath—that could be relieved by medications, but she didn't seem to need them. How was I to understand her condition? How did she understand it? What did the condition mean to her? I had no clue. Nonetheless, I *could* connect with Mrs. Mailcarrier at a more visceral level; i.e. empathize with her as a fellow human being.

We communicated by expression, gesture, touch, and tone. I acted respectfully (for example, by not making direct eye contact, which is taboo, especially when talking with an elder, in Navajo society), while making somewhat comical use of my limited Navajo vocabulary. As a result, my visits may have made Sarah Mailcarrier feel a little better, although my help was minimal in comparison with her traditional ceremony. While this Navajo experience is unrepresentative of ordinary medical practice, in which doctor and patient share many cultural beliefs and expectations, Sarah's case is useful because it allows me to focus on the therapeutic power of empathy and compassion as manifested in behavior. The effect of empathy is generic and not culturally specific. In *The Healer's Calling,* Daniel Sulmasy says that 'true healing' requires three simple human elements: compassion, touch, and conversation (Sulmasy 1997, p. 17). He writes that 'Health care is about being there with people in their finitude and doubt, in their pain and uncertainty, respecting each one and saying that one cares, and showing by one's deeds that one really does care in all the ways one can' (Sulmasy 1997, p. 35).

From Empathy to Compassion

The words 'patience' and 'compassion' both derive from the Latin stem *pass-*, 'to suffer.' One of the meanings of patience is the calm endurance of inconvenience, pain, or suffering. A patient is a person who endures suffering (although with no requirement to do it calmly or patiently!) Compassion means to suffer with. When we identify compassion as a medical virtue, the etymological meaning is that to be a good doctor, or other health care professional, one ought to suffer with the patient. This concept is a far cry from detached concern.

Warren Reich defines compassion as 'the virtue by which we have a sympathetic consciousness of sharing the distress or suffering of another person and on that basis are inclined to offer assistance in alleviating and/or living through that suffering' (Reich 1989, p. 35). Leonard Blum offers a second, synergistic definition that sheds more light on processes that occur inside the compassionate person. He writes that compassion is 'a complex emotional attitude toward another, characteristically involving imaginative dwelling on the condition of the other person, an active regard for his good, a view of him as a fellow human being, and emotional responses of a certain degree of intensity' (Blum 1980, p. 509). It's clear from these definitions that compassion involves (a) a sympathetic awareness of the other's distress, (b) a sense of sharing that distress in some manner; and (c) an inclination to offer assistance. The latter feature motivates some persons to become helping professionals. Writing specifically about medicine, Sulmasy contends that a compassionate physician engages patient suffering at three levels: (a) the objective, by recognizing suffering, (b) the subjective, by internally responding to suffering, and (c) the operative, by performing concrete healing actions (Zinn 1993).

The first step (a) may at first suggest the objectivity so highly valued in detached concern. However, in the case of compassion, the observing instrument (i.e. the physician) is sensitive to a wider spectrum of data. He or she is able to identify symptoms and signs of suffering-as-suffering, in addition to symptoms and signs of disease processes. To accomplish compassionate objectivity, one must develop the communication skills associated with clinical empathy. Empathy is a process by which one comes to understand another's total 'message,' cognitive and affective; words, feelings, and gestures (Coulehan and Block 2006, pp. 29–44; Spiro 1992). To put it metaphorically, empathy means getting onto the patient's wavelength, figuring out where she is coming from, or walking a mile in his moccasins. Moreover, attainment of *clinical* empathy also requires the physician to let the patient know that he or she has actually *heard* (i.e. understood) the message (Basch 1983; Coulehan et al. 2001; Halpern 1993, pp. 160–173; Hoffman 1984, pp. 103–131;

Wispe 1986). It is a positive feedback loop in which the physician titrates his or her understanding by checking back with the patient in an iterative process.

From Self-Awareness to Compassion

Self-awareness is a prerequisite for Sulmasy's second step (b), the subjective or internal response to suffering. Many commentators stress the need for physicians to better understand their own beliefs, feelings, attitudes, and response patterns (Charon 2001; Connelly 1998; Novack et al. 1997; Coulehan et al. 2003; Frankel et al. 2003; Pololi et al. 2000; Bolton 1999). One of the earliest proponents of this view was the British psychiatrist Michael Balint, who focused attention of the therapeutic power of the physician-patient interaction with his aphorism, 'The doctor is the drug' (Balint 1972). Balint encouraged physicians to meet regularly in small groups to discuss their difficulties with patients and their personal reactions to patients (Balint 1972). Physicians are particularly vulnerable to feelings of anxiety, loneliness, frustration, anger, depression, and helplessness when caring for chronically, seriously, and terminally ill patients (Connelly 1998; Meier 2001; Novack et al. 1997). The common technique of changing feelings into 'affects' leads physicians to trivialize emotions, including their own responses, and thereby to distance themselves from their patients (Coulehan et al. 2003).

The more physicians try to reverse this process by developing an understanding of their own beliefs, attitudes, and feelings, the more likely they will be able to connect with, and respond to, their patients' experience. To quote a poem by Rumi:

> We are the mirror as well as the face in it.
> We are tasting the taste this minute
> of eternity. We are pain
> and what cures pain, both. We are
> the sweet cold water and the jar that pours. (Rumi 1995)

Translated into more pedestrian words, Rumi says that only by developing the ability to see ourselves in others are we able to understand them. Psychiatrist Robert Coles uses the term *moral imagination* for this process of empathic understanding, (Coles 1989, p. 179) and in *The Call of Stories* he demonstrates how the study of creative literature can serve as a way of enhancing the moral imagination.

As in the excerpt from Rumi, the late twentieth century poet Denise Levertov explores the dynamic of empathic understanding in her poem 'When We Look Up':

> He had not looked,
> pitiful man whom none
> pity, whom all
> must pity if they look
> into their own face (given
> only by glass, steel, water
> barely known) all
> who look up

to see-how many
faces? How many
seen in a lifetime? (Not those that flash by, but those
into which the gaze wanders
and is lost
and returns to tell
Here is a mystery,
a person, an
other, an I? (Levertov 2003, p. 27)

In this poem Levertov uses the words 'pitiful' and 'pity' in a way that preserves her poetic meaning, but ignores an important distinction, at least with regard to the common usage of these words. Experiencing another person's suffering by means of empathy and the moral imagination leads to an experiential bond that is quite different from the attitude of pity, which carries the connotation of separateness and condescension. Even detached concern allows physicians to pity some of their patients; after all, who wouldn't be moved to pity by such unfortunate human degradation? In fact, the word 'unfortunate' is often used in medicine as a code word to indicate which patients are deserving of pity, as in the following: 'This unfortunate 47 year old man with anaplastic adenocarcinoma of unknown origin…' Or, 'This unfortunate 16 year old girl with Down's syndrome and acute leukemia…' In such cases, the speaker indicates to her colleagues that it is appropriate for them to look down with pity upon the patient.

However, Denise Levertov means something quite different when she associates 'pity' with 'Here is a mystery, /a person, an/other, an I?' Like Rumi's poem, 'When We Look Up' is about compassion, rather than pity. It captures the concept of compassionate solidarity in a more imaginative way than prose description. As Leonard Blum concludes in A.O. Rorty's *Explaining Emotions,* '… expanding our powers of imagination expands our capacity for compassion' (Blum 1980, p. 510).

To Relieve Suffering

Compassionate Solidarity

The objective and subjective steps or components of compassion find their fulfillment in action. But does this action necessarily have to be directed toward a specific source of suffering, e.g. curing the disease, suppressing the symptoms, or directly engaging (as the Navajo *ha'atali* did) the patient's belief system? Does this mean that I could not demonstrate compassion for Sarah Mailcarrier unless I were a Navajo? Or at least that my Anglo compassion would be ineffective?

On the contrary, the creation of an empathic connection is in itself a healing action; being present to, listening, affirming, and witnessing are actions that can be accomplished, at least to some degree, prior to and independent of understanding the patient's cultural beliefs and expectations. There are various names for this type of relationship, but the one I prefer is *compassionate solidarity.* Unlike detached concern, its focus is on the patient as a person, rather than on the disease, even though it remains systematic and objective. The American physician-poet William Carlos Williams, and the English general practitioner John Sassall provide us with two literary examples of compassionate solidarity. In his *Autobiography* Williams writes that he often began his evening office hours feeling totally exhausted, but as soon as he began seeing his patients, 'I lost myself in the very properties of their minds: for the moment at least I actually became them, whoever they should be, so that when I detached myself from them… it was as though I were awakening from a sleep' (Williams 1951, p. 356). Williams describes a state of immersion in which the 'I' perspective remains intact (e.g. 'in a flash the details of the case would begin to formulate themselves into a recognizable outline'), but stays in the background. He is entirely present to the situation, thus bridging the gap between subject and object. Williams' experience is similar to that of English general practitioner John Sassall, as recorded in John Berger's photographic essay, *A Fortunate Man*. Berger observes that Sassall is a good doctor 'because he meets the deep but unformulated expectation of the sick for a sense of fraternity' (Berger and Mohr 1967, pp. 75–77). In fact, Sassall 'does not believe in maintaining his imaginative distance: he must come close enough to *recognize* the patient fully.' He believes that if the patient 'can begin to feel recognized… the hopeless nature of his unhappiness will have been changed' (Berger and Mohr 1967, pp. 75–77).

Beyond Solidarity

In the excerpts presented above, compassionate action was accompanied by a *self-less* experience. Note, however, that selflessness was self-limited: when office hours ended, Williams' ego emerged and he reflected with detachment on what had happened during his state of immersion. Immersion in this sense is not the same as submersion in, or identification with, the patients' suffering. Rather, the experience of being out-of-myself corresponds to an empathic connection that validates the patients' suffering. While compassionate solidarity is therapeutic in itself, it also serves as an avenue for deep communication about meaningful images and symbols, when this next step is culturally possible and appropriate. In a broad sense, all therapeutic interactions with conscious patients have a symbolic dimension. Surely, Mrs. Mailcarrier had created a symbolic niche for Western medicine (e.g. the magic 'shot' that relieves symptoms), but that niche was unrelated to 'the deepest and most fundamental aspects' of her identity. Alternatively, the Blessingway ceremony directly addressed the source and effects of suffering on her interior life. The poetry of the *ha'atali's* actions was meaningful to her in a way that might be approximated by the poetry of a priest's, counselor's, and/or physician's actions in ordinary health care situations. Since suffering persons cannot help but interpret medical intervention in light of their personal beliefs, which are almost always much broader than evidence-based medicine would dictate, medical acts have a symbolic dimension. There is, in this sense, a deep relationship between medicine and poetry:

> Medicine cannot be stripped of metaphor, image, symbol, meaning and interpretation. Ill persons experience meaning in their lives and illnesses, they (like all of us) experiences themselves as characters in a life narrative, and they find in medicine a vast network of healing symbols. Physicians (like poets) manipulate those culturally important symbols. They speak in metaphor. They tell stories. They conduct ceremonies. (Coulehan 1992b, p. 517)

In addition to enhancing empathy and self-awareness, poetry also provides a language with which to express healing by image, metaphor, and symbol. This language can be important to physicians and other health professionals because it permits them to process difficult feelings and conflicts they experience when caring for suffering patients. By means of such imaginative self-expression, health professionals may engage in healing themselves and, thus, become more effective healers of others.

Two late poems by William Carlos Williams illustrate the step from compassionate solidarity to a self-conscious understanding of symbolic healing. In 'To a dog injured in the street' (1954), Williams writes:

> It is myself,
> not the poor beast lying there
> yelping with pain
> that brings me to myself with a start—
> as at the explosion
> of a bomb, a bomb that has laid
> all the world waste.
> I can do nothing
> but sing about it
> and so I am assuaged
> from my pain.
> to believe it.

First, there is the flash of self-awareness. The ability to recognize suffering in others requires the imaginative leap of seeing oneself as vulnerable to suffering and, therefore, as being connected to the other. Second, the internalization of this insight in some way serves to lessen the writer's own pain; even though 'I can do nothing/ but sing about it… I am assuaged.' (Granted, this is a poem about empathy with a dog, but the point is obviously even more powerful when a human being is 'yelping with pain.) In 'The Yellow Flower' (1954), Williams continues:

> What shall I say, because talk I must?
> That I have found a cure
> for the sick?
> I have found no cure
> for the sick
> but this crooked flower
> which only to look upon
> all men
> are cured. This
> is that flower
> for which all men

sing secretly their hymns
of praise. This
is that sacred
flower! (Clark 2004)

Here, once again, the poet acknowledges his inability to cure the sick. However, in addition to compassionate solidarity, he also offers an imaginative leap, a 'crooked flower' by which 'all men/are cured.' The crooked flower is what everyone longs for, each of us in his or her own way.

Summary and Conclusion

Suffering is the experience of distress or disharmony caused by the loss, or threatened loss, of what we most cherish. Such losses may strip away the beliefs and symbols by which we construct a meaningful narrative of human life in general and our own in particular. The vocation of physicians and other health professionals is, insofar as is possible, to relieve suffering caused by illness, trauma, and bodily degeneration. However, since suffering is an existential state that does not necessarily parallel physical or emotional states, to relieve suffering physicians cannot rely solely on knowledge and skills that address physiological dysfunction. Rather, they must learn to engage the patient at an existential level.

However, the standard teaching in medical pedagogy is that physicians should relate to their patients with 'detached concern.' This term was initially invented by medical sociologists to characterize physicians' observed detachment from patients as persons, and their inclination to treat patients as objects rather than subjects of experience. Later, detached concern was adopted by medical educators as normative because they believed it captured the necessity of detachment in medical practice, as well as medicine's beneficent motivation (concern). However, in reality, contemporary medical education and practice favor a process of progressive detachment from patients that devalues subjectivity, emotion, solidarity, and relationship as both irrelevant and harmful. Such sought-after detachment (although fortunately not achieved by most physicians) almost ensures that practitioners are unable fully to appreciate and respond to human suffering.

The term 'compassionate solidarity' summarizes an alternate model of the physician's response to patients and their suffering. Compassionate solidarity begins with empathic listening and responding, which facilitate objective assessment of the other's subjective state; requires the physician to develop reflectivity and self-understanding; and is in itself a healing act. Going beyond compassionate solidarity, the physician may in some cases also understand the disharmony in the patient's symbolic world and, thus, be able to further relieve suffering through symbolic healing.

Reading and writing poetry, along with other imaginative writing, may help physicians and other health professionals grow in self-awareness and gain deeper understanding of suffering, empathy, compassion, solidarity, and symbolic healing.

Bibliography

Akhmatova, Anna. 2004. *The word that causes death's defeat. Poems of Memory*. Trans. N.K. Anderson. New Haven: Yale University Press.

Balint, Michael. 1972. *The doctor, his patient and the illness*. New York: International Universities Press.

Basch M. F. 1983. Empathic understanding: A review of the concept and some theoretical considerations'. *Journal of the American Psychoanalytic Association* 31:101–126.

Becker, Howard Saul, Blanche Geer, Everett C Hughes, Anselm Strauss. 1961. *Boys in white: Student culture in medical school*. Chicago: Chicago University Press.

Bennett, M. J. 2001. *The empathic healer: An endangered species?* New York: Academic Press.

Berger, John, and Jean Mohr. 1967. *A fortunate man*. New York: Pantheon Books.

Bloom, S. W. 1989. The medical school as a social organization: The sources of resistance to change. *Medical Education* 23:228–241.

Blum, L. 1980. Compassion. In *Explaining emotions*, ed. Amélie Oskenberg Rorty. Berkeley: University of California Press.

Blumgart, H. L. 1964. Caring for the patient. *New England Journal of Medicine* 270:449–456.

Bolton, G. 1999. Stories at work: Reflective writing for practitioners. *The Lancet* 354:243–245.

Cassell, E. J. 1982. The nature of suffering and the goals of medicine. *New England Journal of Medicine* 306:639–645.

Cassell, E. J. 1991. *The nature of suffering and the goals of medicine*, 1st ed. New York: Oxford University Press.

Cassell, E. J. 1995. Pain and suffering. In *Encyclopedia of Bioethics*, ed. W. T. Reich, 2nd ed. New York: Simon & Schuster.

Cassell, E. J. 2004. *The nature of suffering and the goals of medicine*, 2nd edn. New York: Oxford University Press.

Charon, Rita. 2001. Narrative medicine. A model for empathy, reflection, profession, and trust. *Journal of the American Medical Association* 286:1897–1902.

Clark, M. M. 2004. Art and suffering in two late poems by William Carlos Williams. *Literature and Medicine* 23:226–240.

Coles, R. 1989. *The call of stories: Teaching and the moral imagination*. Boston: Houghton Mifflin.

Connelly, J. 1998. Emotions, ethics, and decisions in primary care. *Journal of Clinical Ethics* 9:225–234.

Coulehan, J. 1991. The word as an instrument of healing. *Literature and Medicine* 18:111–129.

Coulehan, J. 1992a. May I walk in beauty. *Humane Medicine* 8:65–69.

Coulehan, J. 1992b. On medicine and poetry. In *Life on the line: Selections on words and healing*, eds. S. B. Walker and R. D. Roffman. Mobile: Negative Capability Press.

Coulehan, J. 1995. Tenderness and steadiness: Emotions in medical practice. *Literature and Medicine* 14:222–236.

Coulehan, J. 2002. Being a physician. In *Fundamentals of clinical practice. A textbook on the patient, doctor, and society*, eds. M. B. Mengel and W. Holleman, 2nd ed. New York: Plenum Medical Book Company.

Coulehan, J. 2009. Compassionate solidarity: Suffering, poetry, and medicine. *Perspectives in biology and medicine* 52:585–603.

Coulehan, J., and P. Clary. 2005. Healing the healer: Poetry in palliative care. *Journal of Palliative Care* 8:382–389.

Coulehan, J., and M. R. Block. 2006. *The medical interview: Mastering skills for clinical practice*, 5th ed. Philadelphia: F.A. Davis Company.

Coulehan, J., F. W. Platt, R. Frankl, W. Salazar, B. Lown, and L. Fox. 2001. Let me see if I have this right: Words that build empathy. *Annals of Internal Medicine* 135:221–227.

Coulehan, J., P. W. Williams, S. V. McCrary, C. Belling. 2003. The best lack all conviction: Biomedical ethics, professionalism, and social responsibility. *Cambridge Quarterly of Healthcare Ethics* 12:21–38.

Daudet, Alphonse. 2002. *In the land of pain,* ed. Julian Barnes. New York: Knopf.

Engel, G. L. 1977. The need for a new medical model: A challenge for biomedicine. *Science* 196:129–136.

Farber, N. J., D. H. Novack, M. K. O'Brien. 1997. Love, boundaries, and the patient physician relationship. *Archives of Internal Medicine* 157:2291–2294.

Frankel, R. M., T. E. Quill, and S. H. McDaniel, eds. 2003. *The biopsychosocial approach: Past, present, future.* Rochester: University of Rochester Press.

Frankl, Viktor. 1997. *Man's search for meaning*, rev. ed. New York: Washington Square Press.

Gunderman, R. B. 2002. Is suffering the enemy? *Hastings Center Report* 32:40–44.

Hafferty, F. W., R. Franks. 1994. The hidden curriculum, ethics teaching, and the structure of medical education. *Academic Medicine* 68:861–871.

Halpern, J. 1993. Empathy: Using resonance emotions in the service of curiosity. In *Empathy and the practice of medicine,* eds. H. Spiro, M. Curnen, E. Peschel and D. St. James. New Haven: Yale University Press.

Hauerwas, Stanley. 1990. *God, medicine, and suffering.* Grand Rapids: Eerdmans.

Hoffman, M. L. 1984. Interaction of affect and cognition in empathy. *Emotions, cognitions, and behavior,* eds. C. E. Izard, J. Kagan and R. B. Zajonc. Cambridge: Cambridge University Press.

Hunnert E. M. 1996. Characteristics of the informal curriculum and trainee's ethical choices. *Academic Medicine* 71:624–633.

Inui, T. S. 2003. *A flag in the wind: Educating for professionalism in medicine.* Washington: Association of American Medical Colleges.

Kassirer, J. P. 1998. Managing care—Should we adopt a new ethic? *New England Journal of Medicine* 339:397–398.

Kearney, Michael K. 1996. *Mortally wounded. Stories of soul pain, death and healing.* Dublin: Marino Books.

Lawrence, D. H. 1947. *Selected poems*, introduction by Kenneth Rexroth. New York: New Directions.

Levertov, D. 2003. *Selected poems.* New York: W.W. Norton.

Lief, H. I., and R. Fox. 1963. Training for 'detached concern' in medical students. In *The psychological basis for medical practice,* eds. H. I. Lief and N. R. Lief. New York: Harper & Row.

Manson, A. 1994. The fate of idealism in modern medicine. *Journal of the Medical Humanities* 15:153–162.

Meier, Diane, Anthony L. Back, and R. Sean Morrison. 2001. The inner life of physicians and care of the seriously ill. *Journal of the American Medical Association* 286:3007–3014.

Morris, D. B. 1998. *Illness and culture in the postmodern age.* Berkeley: University of California Press.

Novack, Dennis H., Anthony L. Suchman, William Clark, Ronald M. Epstein, Eva Najberg, and Craig Kaplan. 1997. Calibrating the physician: Personal awareness and effective patient care. *Journal of the American Medical Association* 278:502–509.

Novack, Dennis H., Roland M. Epstein, and Randall H. Paulsen. 1999. Toward creating physician-healers: Fostering medical student's self-awareness, personal growth, and well-being. *Academic Medicine* 74:516–520.

Orr, G. 2002. *The caged owl: New and selected poems*. Fort Townsend: Copper Canyon Press.

Ozick, C. 1989. *Metaphor and memory: Essays.* New York: Knopf.

Petersdorf, R. G. 1992. Are we educating a medical professional who cares? *American Journal of Diseases of Children* 146:1338–1341.

Pololi, L., R. M. Frankel, M. Clay, and A. Jobe. 2000. One year's experience with a program to facilitate personal and professional development in medical students using reflection groups. *Education for Health* 14:36–49.

Reich, W. T. 1989. Speaking of suffering. A moral account of compassion. *Soundings* 72: 83–108.

Rumi, J. 1995. *The Essential Rumi*. Trans. C. Barks and J. Moyn. San Francisco: Harper.
Sulmasy, Daniel. 1997. *The healer's calling. Spirituality for physicians and other health care professionals*. New York: Paulist Press.
Sontag, Susan. 1978. *Illness as metaphor.* New York: Farrar, Straus and Giroux.
Sontag, Susan. 1988. *AIDS as metaphor.* New York: Farrar, Straus and Giroux.
Spiro, H. 1992. What is empathy and can it be taught? *Annals of Internal Medicine* 116:843–846.
Suchman, A. L., K. Markakis, H. B. Beckman, R. Frankel. 1997. A model of empathic communication in the medical interview. *Journal of the American Medical Association* 277:678–682.
Williams, William Carlos. 1951. *The autobiography of William Carlos Williams.* New York: New Directions.
Wispe, L. 1986. The distinction between sympathy and empathy: To call forth a concept, a word is needed. *Journal of Personal and Social Psychology* 50:314–321.
Zinn, W. 1993. The empathic physician. *Arch Intern Medicine* 153:306–312.
Zoloth-Dorfman, L., and S. Rubin. 1995. The patient as commodity: Managed care and the question of ethics. *Journal of Clinical Ethics* 6:339–356.

Chapter 19
On Facing Human Suffering

Norelle Lickiss

I. Why stare at the sun? Why stare down the Gorgon? Why stare down or gaze at human suffering? Irvin Yalom would insist that staring at death is a means to face death-related anxiety (which takes on so many guises) and reduces fear of death (Yalom 2008). And we humans may fear suffering rather more than we fear death. Yet suffering is an intrinsic part of the human condition: we are both contingent and fragile—we need not be, and will not be forever, and we are aware of this: this may be not only the marks of our humanity, but also our suffering as a universal feature of our condition, yet particularized in each person.

Suffering, rooted in this intrinsic contingency, fragility and awareness of it (and interpretations of it all), has influenced the human record since the beginning: art, writings, philosophy, and the earliest traces of medicine. Mary Rawlinson, in our own times, offered a philosophical analysis concerning human suffering—what sort of phenomenon is it? She noted that 'a tradition extending from Plato to Kant through Christian Platonism proves inappropriate for the treatment of suffering insofar as it fails to locate suffering with respect to the purposive activity of the human subject, identifying it instead with distance or alienation from an ideal order' (Rawlinson 1986).

Maybe all that we can know or understand about human suffering has been said or written, but there appears an imperative in every age, and our times, to enter into an exploratory relationship with it; especially is this true for physicians, since the relief of suffering is the traditional goal of medical practice. This essay explores some dimensions of human suffering as encountered especially in the course of clinical practice, and the ponderings engendered by such personal encounters. Persons, suffering persons in their particularity, are the unseen presence in this writing.

II. The issue of suffering and its relief is central to the medical tradition. Early Greco-Roman philosophers wrestled with human distress and suffering, and how to deal

N. Lickiss (✉)
School of Philosophy, University of Tasmania, Hobart 7001, Tasmania, Australia

Sydney Medical School, University of Sydney, Sydney 2006, NSW, Australia
e-mail: norelle.lickiss@gmail.com

J. Malpas, N. Lickiss (eds.), *Perspectives on Human Suffering*,
DOI 10.1007/978-94-007-2795-3_19,

Table 1 Hippocratic tradition and Asklepian Healing. (After Kearney 2000)

Hippocratic tradition	Asklepian healing
Draws on objective evidence	Draws on subjective evidence
Calls for clinical objectivity	Calls for clinical subjectivity
Treats pain and lessens suffering by Intervening from without	Concerned with healing from within
Works as *opus contra naturam*	Works with nature
Primary training involves knowledge and skills	Primary training involves self knowledge
(Hippocrates b 560 BCE)	(Asklepios—Greek God of Healing)

with it, usually by more adequate knowledge, but it is noteworthy, as Nussbaum points out, that the philosophers often used medical metaphors or analogy, when discussing philosophy's potential to relieve suffering (Nussbaum 1994). Nussbaum quotes Epicurus (341–271 BCE), from among the Greeks, and Cicero (106–43 BCE), from among the Romans: 'Empty is that philosopher's argument by which no human suffering is therapeutically treated', writes Epicurus, 'for just as there is no use for a medical art that does not cast out the sicknesses of bodies, so too there is no use in philosophy, unless it casts out the suffering of the soul'; and Cicero tells us that, 'there is, I assure you, a medical art for the soul. It is philosophy, whose aid need not be sought, as in bodily diseases, from outside ourselves. We must endeavour with all our resources and all our strength to become capable of doctoring ourselves.'[1]

Early medical traditions are documented by medical historians such as Sigerist (1951, 1987)—notable is the ancient Greek tradition which has been critical for Western medicine (Conrad et al. 1995; Porter 1998). Michael Kearney, in his recent studies of healing, has emphasized the dual traditions of Hippocratic Medicine (which flourished in 5C BCE) with its stress on the understanding and treating of disease wherever possible, and the later Asklepian cult (which flourished 500 BCE to 500 CE), with its focus on healing the whole person especially when cure was no longer possible (Kearney 2000). Kearney contrasts the two streams of activity (see Table 1 derived from Kearney), but it needs to be noted that the Hippocratic tradition also recognized that there was a time when what we would call 'comfort care' should prevail. Recently there have been significant conceptual advances relevant to suffering in a medical context, although writing by practicing clinicians is sparse. Physicians in clinical practice have the personal role in society to relieve human suffering amenable to medical measures, to be present to it, to share it, not to talk or write about it. Writing about matters such as human dignity is challenging but not painful. Articulating words about human suffering may evoke, for a physician, complex emotions, memories, personal pain, regret, maybe the reliving of close-to-the-brink experiences embedded deep in memory, even the opening up of personal fracture lines, or mild aversive responses to 'mere' writing, so central to the professional lives of others. Yet the strange, particular perspective of the relatively inarticulate physician may be a necessary ingredient of an interdisciplinary amalgam concerning human suffering.

[1] Ibid.

Historians paint the backdrop to clinical perspectives. Sigerist, already mentioned above, noted that: ‘medical theories always represent one aspect of the general civilization of a period, and in order to understand them fully, we must be familiar with other manifestations of that civilization, its philosophy, literature, art, music’ (Sigerist 1951, p. 11). It is therefore not surprising that Porter, as his final contribution to medical history, raised the question of how the soul or spirit, or *psyche* indeed, can be understood in contemporary culture: the implications of such conceptions not only for life and suffering, but also human death, are considerable (Porter 2003). Sydenham (1624–1689), sometimes styled the British Hippocrates, could write: ‘How my soul, which I look on to be an immortal Being in me, that is the Principle of thinking, should extinguish with my Body, I cannot in any reasonable way of thinking conceive’;[2] such may not ground a medical consensus in twenty-first century, or figure in the writings of clinicians on human suffering, however such matters find place in late night musings.

In 2003, Cherny contributed a review of the problem of human suffering in the Third Edition of the prestigious *Oxford Textbook of Palliative Medicine* (Cherny 2003). The review mentioned that, on the basis of a consideration of the extensive clinical and psychosocial research undertaken with cancer patients, Cherny and colleagues defined suffering as ‘an aversive experience characterized by the perception of personal distress that is generated by adverse factors that undermine quality of life’ (Cherny et al. 1994). Others have sought to offer definitions from other perspectives.

Eric Cassell has contributed much to the medical literature on human suffering. In a landmark paper (Cassell 1982). Cassell differentiated ‘suffering’ from ‘distress’—and introduced an operational definition of suffering as ‘a sense of impending personal disintegration’. Cassell’s portrayal of the perception of suffering may be rendered in common parlance as ‘a sense of being about to go to pieces’. An unpublished project undertaken in Sydney in the early 1990s, indicated that patients could readily recognize whether or not they had, in the course of a serious illness, ever felt ‘about to go to pieces’, and if so what were the circumstances.[3] It was clear that such an experience was readily identifiable, and that the trigger for such a feeling could arise in one or more of several personal fields: loss of a relationship with persons, place, things, role, cultural matters—or concerning only the self (for example, perception of loss of some aspect of dignity, intrapersonal conflict, realization of guilt). The language of breakage was often used—such and such event ‘broke my spirit’. Maybe the event was so fraught that speech failed—a possible trigger for fracture, as Shakespeare noted in Macbeth (Shakespeare 2007): ‘Give sorrow words: the grief that does not speak/Whispers the o’er fraught heart, and bids it break’ (*Macbeth,* Act 1, V Scene 3). It was clear over decades of practice that the trigger for intense suffering could also be the witnessing of the suffering of another, or the memory of the suffering of another, a memory often prompted by another event: com-passion is surely a manifestation of our radical connectedness.

[2] Ibid, p. 28.

[3] Undertaken by M. Best, N. Lickiss, C. McCosker, Prince Alfred Hospital, Sydney.

Pain is recognized as a source of distress; it may or may not, on Cassell's model, be associated with of suffering. Chapman and Gavrin considered both pain and suffering, including the neurological bases of each, and noting the current range of definitions of suffering—they preferred to define suffering as 'a complex negative affective and cognitive state characterized by a perceived threat to the integrity of the self, perceived helplessness in the face of that threat, and exhaustion of psychosocial and personal resources for coping' (Chapman and Gavrin 1993).

Although suffering is quintessentially subjective, research related to suffering in health care contexts is undertaken, despite some concern that such research is not justified or possible (Frank 2001). The research undertaken on all continents has to take into account the primacy of the subjective in the face of a regrettable tendency to objectify that which is intrinsically subjective (and less easily quantifiable), with qualitative studies the most usual approach. Daneault and colleagues, in studies of patients experiencing cancer, concluded that the core dimensions of suffering are: (i) feeling subjected to violence, (ii) being deprived and/or overwhelmed, and (iii) living in apprehension (Daneault et al. 2004). Janice Morse and colleagues from Edmonton have in the last decade further enriched understanding on the basis of extensive research relating to persons in very distressing situations, notably differentiating a phase of endurance and then a phase of emotional release: in the first phase, 'holding' techniques (not touch or comfort) are needed to help the person to endure, whilst in the second, comforting and empathic techniques including touch, are appropriate (Morse 2001). On Cassell's model (as well as in practice) the distinction may be relevant to prevent a distressed person from reaching breaking point. Such considerations point to the complexity of human suffering, and the need to conceptualize it as clearly as possible.

III. Suffering is an inevitable companion in the lives of most clinicians in many disciplines: their perceptions, their interpretations and their responses are all worthy of consideration. The focus here is medical for pragmatic reasons; nursing literature is rich in relevant matters. Distress and, at times, suffering, will be part of the life of a conscientious physician, because of (a) the witnessing of great suffering, (b) experiencing the inevitable failure of treatments to control disease and to relieve all distress, (c) being present at, or bearing, the death of patients, and (d) noting personal failings, including errors of judgment, in the exercise of high levels of responsibility, and (e) increasing awareness of the limits of what one may bear, noting with T. S. Eliot that 'Man cannot bear too much reality' (Eliot 1943, 'Burnt Norton').

How is the place of suffering in the human condition understood by doctors? How do contemporary physicians, junior doctors, medical students view human suffering? Or an individual who is suffering? Apart from acute matters, possibly obvious at a glance, and fortunately open to a well-recognized and available remedy, and immediate action mandated—the delight of junior doctors, there is need to consider what meaning is given to the scene. In the presence of a person who is grossly distressed, and almost certainly suffering or clearly distraught, maybe even dying thus, how does the physician conceptualize or interpret this situation? Or simply respond? It is well known (and well-remembered by some of us) that a rapid exit either physically or emotionally is a common response. It is rare to find a physician who can truly 'stare down the sun', and stay with the suffering person whilst seeking how best to alleviate the distress, yet this is what is mandated. It is tempting to suggest that doctors may sometimes act like the friends of Job with suggestions of blame, of information withheld, or uncommonly even of a masked theodicy, but in the end there may be a wise matter-of-factness (maybe accompanied, despite the appearance of almost mandated traditional medical equanimity, by distress and disquiet because of profound compassion), that such is the case. As a consequence, the colleagues of doctors, especially nurses, bear a large proportion of the clinical burden of suffering—staying there, present, when the busy doctor is drawn away by other duties, sometimes conveniently—but the patient may be the one most bereft of succour.

Physicians speak little of this. Shaerer, reporting on the response of French family doctors to patient deaths wrote:

> Human suffering does not amount to a physical or moral pain or a difficulty. Suffering is something like crossing a desert; it is an experience in which a person will experience evil, and yet at the same time, will be led to discover the deepest meaning of one's own life. This is true of the suffering of a doctor. (Schaerer 1993, pp. 27–37)

Yalom would recognize the experience Shearer describes as an 'awakening' experience, which may move the doctor from an 'everyday' mode to a more 'existential' mode of living, concerned, not with *how* but *that* things are (including oneself). Nevertheless, most physicians would reject notions (often associated with traditional religions) that 'suffering is good for you', whilst recognizing that human response to extreme suffering can reveal nobility and potential for growth beyond expectations, even in themselves. The well-known 'tears on the staircase' of junior doctors may be matched by the tears of very experienced consultants experiencing, in the raw, the tragedy and grandeur of the human condition as lived out in the suffering of individuals. It is increasingly recognized that strategies need to be in place to ensure the personal sustainability and flourishing of the physician immersed in care of distressed patients (Meier et al. 2001): what is not certain is whether or not there is benefit to the patients cared for by doctors committed to those practices, but it is likely to be so.

Cassell has expressed regret recently that we are still failing in the West (his focus) to relieve suffering, despite decades of 'talk' (Cassell 2004). At a global level the inequities are so serious, unjust, immoral, and almost beyond the comprehension of most in the West—despite readily available information—that this will not be further considered at present. In the affluent West there is no lack of technology, intelligence, commitment or even funds (prescinding from issues of fair intra-national distribution), nor of compassion; however, there is evidence of unsustainability, despite serious warnings for decades (Enthoven 1978), with inadequate attention to cost/ benefit ratio, especially from the point of view of the patient—of relevance to the genesis and relief of suffering. The quality of clinical decision-making, especially with respect to severely ill patients, likely to be enmeshed in a sea of suffering, is often questionable, despite widespread attempts to facilitate the exercise of clinical wisdom. The rising interest in advance directives/decisions/care plans is promising and overdue—and yet there are complex and deep problems: for example, there are suggestions that such approaches are not encouraged by oncologists lest the slightest possibility for temporary prolongation of life be lost, and death not be delayed. How can such love of and respect for life be balanced by the appropriate acceptance of death? King Lear had difficulty in being allowed to die (as noted below), as do many of our fellows (fear of which is surely contributing to the requests for physician intervention to cause death directly). The traditional Talmudic principle, 'Affirm life, but do not obstruct death', says it all, but is not always heard, it seems even in centres of excellence. Sensitive understanding is called for—and the deficiencies of medical respect for life in the past, even in the twentieth-century, weigh may heavily on the medical mind.

IV. What is at the root of all of this? Cassell offers a twenty-first century analysis:

> I believe that there are two things that continue to hold back an appreciation of suffering and its relief. The first is a continuing failure to accord subjective knowledge and subjectivity the same status as objective knowledge and objectivity. The second is an increasing denial of the inevitable uncertainties in medicine and a quest for certainty'. (Cassell 2004, p. xii)

It can be contended that the problems in contemporary medicine are in fact philosophical—with conceptual bases unable to sustain the weight of current practice. Inadequate understanding of human suffering is surely playing a part, but the difficulty may rest on deeper deficiencies. The phenomenon of medical burnout in the West, and now being reported in Japan (termed 'catastrophic collapse of morale') would alone suggest that something is seriously lacking at a profound level, recently discussed by Cole and Carlin (2009). These authors stress that 'there are no quick fixes for the suffering of physicians, just as there are no quick fixes for the suffering of patients,' and insist that medicine needs to be 'rehumanized'. They conclude their analysis with the telling words: 'humanizing medicine depends in no small part on recovering the humanity of physicians'. How should this be conceived?

Is it worth asking again, what does medical practice require to relieve suffering more effectively, if that be its goal? Why do medical practitioners, sometimes in the highest places, fail to comprehend the calculus of human suffering, or be paralyzed by being present as witness to suffering? What does an individual physician need to be more effective? Can any matters be specified (or learned or taught)? There are many possible approaches to an examination of why contemporary medical practitioners in affluent Western contexts is, in the eyes of many, frequently failing in the core business of relieving human suffering. Phenomenological or sociological modes of enquiry with new dimensions of research? More detailed historical analysis? Or a renewed search for meaning—in case the 'terrible beauty' of the recent past may point out the need for a new Enlightenment, built on surer foundations?

Central is the need for a more adequate concept of person, and of the processes of personal development, as the foundation for much of the rest, for suffering is an essentially subjective personal reality. Jacob Needleman, some decades ago, in a discourse (New York Academy of Sciences) concerning mortality noted that, 'what medicine lacks is any fundamental notion of the nature of man and any remotely adequate understanding of that to which we refer as a person' (Needleman 1969). Cassell, in the preface to the first edition of his major book appears to support such comment:

> The job of the twenty first century is the discovery of the person – finding the sources of illness and suffering within the person, and with that knowledge developing methods for their relief, while at the same time revealing the power within the person as the nineteenth and twentieth centuries have revealed the power of the body. (Cassell 1991, p. x)

It may also be true that the vast experience of physicians of persons in limit situations should be harnessed by thinkers to enrich our understanding of the human. A reconsideration of what we mean by 'person', and the closely related matter of the processes of personal development, may serve as a point of departure.

V. Ancient writers wrote much of the human predicament, and ways of consolation, though with little attempt to analyze the person. The writer of the drama of Job portrayed threats to personal integrity, but the drama was focused on other matters than exploring personhood. Renaissance writers glorified human dignity, highlighting the status of the human in the universe. Shakespeare was innovative in that Shakespearian dramas explored human interiority, portraying often the conversation of persons with themselves (Bloom 1998, p. xvii); the changes wrought by this intrapersonal dialogue foreshadowed some contemporary philosophical thought. But, over the last century or so, for divers reasons, including dramatic changes in health care possibilities, there has been much relevant writing on the nature of personhood, some emphasizing that 'person' is a concept which extends beyond the confines of the individual. Several examples from North America may be noted.

Henry James wrote, in a rather dated and quaint way of stressing the complexity of person (from 1892), with a focus on the relationship of 'possession': 'A man's me is the sum total of all that he can call his, not only his body and his mind, but his clothes and his house, his wife and his children, his ancestors and his friends, his reputation and his works, his lands and his horses, his yacht and his bank account.'[4] Whitman expressed it otherwise: 'I am not contained between my hat and my boots', inviting further thought.[5] Charles Taylor, as philosopher, stressed cognate points, though moving between the terms 'self' and 'person':

> I am a self only in relation to certain interlocutors: in relation to those conversation partners who were essential to my achieving self-definition... A self exists only within 'webs of interlocution'... To ask what a person is, in abstraction, from his or her self interpretations, is to ask a fundamentally misguided question...We are only selves insofar as we move in a certain space of questions, as we seek and find orientation to the good. (Taylor 1989, p. 36)

Cassell, in the course of his deliberations on human suffering already mentioned, sketched the areas in personal 'topography' which may engender suffering. He listed those parts which constitute 'person': roles, relationships, actions, behaviours, as

[4] H. James, quoted in Becker (1971, p. 43).

[5] Whitman (1891), 'Song of Myself'.

well as a body, dreams and a transcendent dimension—'a life of the spirit, however expressed or known'. But Cassell stressed that persons cannot be reduced to their parts. He noted further that:

> all the aspects of personhood – the lived past, the family's lived past, culture and society, roles, the instrumental dimension, associations and relationships, the body, the unconscious mind, the political being, the secret life, the perceived future, and the transcendent being – dimension – are susceptible to damage and loss. (Cassell 1982, p. 643)

This portrayal of human complexity is in the tradition of a relational concept of 'person'. The observations of the unpublished research of Best, McCosker and Lickiss, already mentioned, were clearly in accord with Cassell's 'topography' of persons.

From my own perspective, I have found useful a cognate, schematic, ecological model of a person, stressing that 'person' is a relational reality, a web as it were, of relationships in a dynamic whole: stressing that relationships constitute, rather than add to, personhood. We are, as it were, webs—constituted by interrelating realities, and constantly in flux. A diagram may be an aid to consideration.

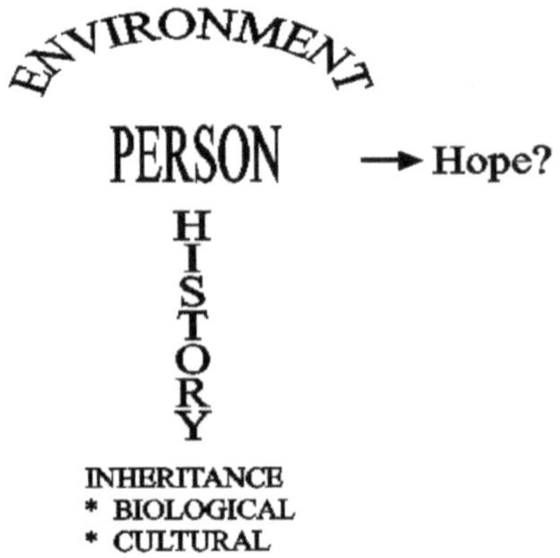

From an ecological point of view a person is a relational reality with respect to the present life situation, but also to the personal past (what is done and also experienced), not only the facts regarding the past but how the past is interpreted and incorporated into the present. The inheritance (biological and cultural) of a person provides the platform, as it were, on which the personal history has been constructed and interpreted, and must continue to influence the present. Intrapersonal dialogue fits readily into this schema. The way out of what might otherwise be conceived as a closed system appears to be offered by the vector of hope. In clinical practice over decades it became clear that what a patient hoped for was difficult (sometimes painful) to articulate—and also unpredictable. It will be noted on this model, that all elements are in dynamic relationship articulated in action, apparent or not to the observer; the personal process is complex and each person is unique.

We know what may cause breakage—the shattering of a fragile web. But what holds these notional elements together? The issue of coherence invites deeper exploration. In order to consider further, and at another level of enquiry, what is a/the principle of coherence, or even what it can be named, it may be wise to return to our earliest human sources.

The earliest Hebrew scriptures give a powerful (mythical) portrayal of the formation of man and woman (Genesis), attracting continuing profound analysis (Zornberg 1995, p. 14). Two components are delineated—dust of the earth, and breath from elsewhere—and these together form a living man; woman, being constituted as the same as man, also has these two components, and is radically connected with man, as he with her. Death, for both man and woman, is seen as the loss of whatever is from elsewhere, allowing what came from the earth to disintegrate and return to earth. Philosophers have tried to codify these profound human realities, but it remains our human experience that there is in us that which is of the material universe, and something other—the latter being what which we may call by the generic name, 'spirit', and which during our lifetime defies entropy. The principle or source of personal coherence, whereby the complex relationships which constitute as persons (as well as our material components) are held together, may surely be radically 'spirit', or bear this name. Spirit, the form of the material, may also serve as that which binds the whole as one. Such considerations are redolent of the remarks of Sydenham, already mentioned—it may be that a radical humanism needs far more focus on human origins as a means of better conceptualizing human capacities as well as the shattering that is possible in the realization of human possibility.

This statement does not take away the problem—but merely gives a name in response to a question. The shape of what Shakespeare portrayed as the inner self must surely relate to this principle. This concept does not address the notion that the form may endure on dissolution of the material—maybe the ephemeral is of its essence, maybe not: this matter is not at issue at this juncture (although it is clear what position Sydenham held). Shakespeare's King Lear (Shakespeare 2007) offers one of the most poignant portrayals in literature of human death as the time to yield up that which is the principle of coherence, or rather to allow it to be yielded up:

> Edgar: He faints. My Lord! My lord!
> Lear: Break, heart, I prithee break.
> Edgar: Look up, my lord!
> Kent: Vex not his ghost: O let him pass! He hateth much
> That would upon the rack of this rough world
> Stretch him out longer. (*King Lear*, Act V, Scene 3)

Whether the principle of coherence, which may be named 'spirit', is powerful enough to prevent personal disintegration under extreme onslaught—or in fact, cannot assist the centre to hold even under what might to other persons be minor provocation, may require an examination of the effect, not only of physical threats to survival, but also of all the constitutive relationships (other persons, place, past, culture, personal history) on the inner/interior life; we could postulates two way dynamic. But how the material affects or effects change in what is non-material appears beyond (my) present analysis, and has been a challenge to philosophers in the past. Maybe it is worth noting that there are examples of personal reality appearing changed from within. Was Shakespeare hinting at something like this when offering what Bloom calls 'self-overhearing' as a means for core (interior) personal change? The question remains however at another level—what determines or at least influences the shape of one's core or spirit? Of one's capacity not to yield to forces which threaten personal disintegration? Does a continuing awareness (despite all) of a Pattern inhering in Being prove to be a bulwark against personal disintegration? Psychologists, neurophysiologists, philosophers, theologians—all may address such questions: others of us may simply describe events, and sometimes experience them.

Reference should be made to the seminal concepts of Antonovsky concerning a 'sense of coherence' based on extensive sociological research. He wrote that: 'The sense of coherence explicitly and unequivocally is a generalized, long-lasting way of seeing the world and one's life in it.... It is ... a crucial element in the basic personality structure of an individual and in the ambience of a subculture, culture or historical period.' He related social networks to the 'sense of coherence', and expressed the view that 'social supports enhance the ability of the individual to obtain meaningful information, or in my terms, enhance the sense of coherence' (Antonovsky 1979). Such a concept is in accord with the stress on person as a relational reality. In his later writing Antonovsky outlined how the sense of coherence develops over the life span and laid the foundations for decades of research on these themes (Antonovsky 1988, pp. 89–127).

Personal change does occur. Erikson, in a series of writings in the last quarter of the twentieth century, portrayed a way of considering personal development over a lifetime, and his concepts have stood the test of time (Erikson 1968, 1982). Erikson (from a psychoanalytic perspective) stressed the role of psychosocial crises, occurring at various stages throughout life, as triggers for choice of a path in the face of two distinct options. He saw personal growth as taking place by negotiation of developmental tasks through the resolution of crises. The growing human person is continually faced by options, each life stage being characterized by its own options which, whilst they confront one through life, do come to ascendancy in a given stage. For example, the favourable outcome of infancy is an attitude of basic trust rather than basic distrust, and on this basis the child goes on to be faced with the next choice—that of autonomy or fear of decision. Where the life process is characterized by the embracing of favourable options, the personality becomes characterized by trust, reasonable autonomy, initiative, capacity for effort, a sense of identity (to be and share oneself) rather than confusion, capacity for intimate personal relationships rather than isolation, fruitfulness rather than stagnation, and finally a sense of wholeness of life (what Erikson calls integrity) rather than despair. In the course of the negotiation of these developmental tasks personal relationships are inevitably involved. Change is driven from the interior, but (as in the case of a growing orchid) ingredients of the environment are also critical. Actions of persons leave marks in the actor as well as others. Life cycles, as Erikson called them, are interlocked, cog-wheeled, as it were, welding the human community into a matrix in continuous flux. It may be worth noting that the interlocking 'cogs' in the wheel differ necessarily from each other, whilst in intimate connection. Some persons will be grappling with fear, weakness, loss, even despair, whilst others are in the bloom of happiness, impelled by love and realistic hope, and dreams. But the connections between all sustain all, and form the human pattern.

Despair, on Erikson's model, is one of the two options in the last phase of life—at any age: the favourable option being rather the development of a sense of wholeness (which Erikson calls 'integrity') being at one with one's place and time, and life pattern. Authentic living with frailty or dying, as authentic living, is surely embedded not in falsehood but in truth. Certainly no lie can be justified to separate a person from his or her own truth—depriving him or her of becoming what is possible. The matter of the personal significance of the last phase of life, at any age, needs far more focus: failure to appreciate it may be a potent source of deep distress. Cassell stressed that a goal of medicine is the relief of suffering (and the obverse of that notion is surely the facilitation of human flourishing in no matter what circumstances) by assisting the subject cohere (helping the 'centre to hold')—a precious service indeed, not within the capacity of all physicians, but respected by all.

The shape of the final task needs to be understood in general terms by those in contact with patients approaching death—at any age. Such patients may well vacillate between wholeness and despair, before the way is clear. They may long to express their internal states, explore the threat of despair through dialogue with others—but to participate in such dialogue is so very difficult for the interlocutor—and to reach out towards what wholeness is possible, to round out the symphony of one's life. If it is surely the task of each person to explore the limits of one's possibilities (which involve in the end the going out from oneself, as the highest exercise of autonomy) then it is surely the task of a doctor to free patients from obstacles (such as pain) to such an exploration. Furthermore, no person should die in iatrogenic despair. No person should die with the dominant perception of self as a 'therapeutic failure', nor disillusioned after being sustained by unrealistic hope, recognized as such even by the physician engendering it, conceiving it as an act of compassion. The physician, whilst emphasizing a realistic range of possibilities as a way of indicating prognosis, should assist the patient to center hope not on what will in the end probably fail in a situation of eventually fatal illness (such as anti-disease therapies), but it what should not fail—the commitment to care, the relief of pain, and in the intrinsic value of the patient as a unique irreplaceable subject of existence. These matters call for much pondering if we are not to add to the despair of those living with complex chronic diseases or dying in 'high tech' contexts—or anywhere.

VI. On the basis of such considerations, are there ways of looking again at our approach to the relief of suffering in clinical contexts? It may be possible to categorize the various generic means for relief of suffering (of relevance to medicine) simply as follows:

1. Ameliorate a definable 'cause' of suffering, or trigger which is precipitating the sense of being 'about to go to pieces.'
2. Strengthen the principle of coherence.

Amelioration of an identified contributory factor implies that there has been a diligent search to identify whether or not the patient is suffering, what has been the trigger, and what this patient usually (historically) does if coherence is so threatened. The story told of the past, as well as the present, the narrative, will give a guide also to the patient's capacity for withholding major threats to cohesion, and may give clues also to explanations for change in that capacity, for good or ill. All gives a portrait of what the patient is suffering (literally 'undergoing'), and how best to assist. Sometimes the telling is the beginning of a sense of recovery ('I feel better now') without any removal of the 'trigger'—a pointer to the subtlety both of the dynamic of suffering, and the processes of human reconstruction. Recovery from a state of suffering should not be thought of as a process of adaptation to circumstances, but of personal growth, of the realization of new possibilities—a manner of thinking which needs to be central in the conceptualization and practice of clinical psychology.

Removal of factors threatening personal cohesion is the stuff of much medical practice, especially (but not only) in the field of palliative medicine, whether practiced in the general health system or in very specialized contexts. Pain, a feature of cancer for some patients—whether due to disease or its treatment, is relievable (even if not wholly removed) in most instances, applying contemporary principles—yet cancer-related pain is still problematic, globally and locally—for various reasons. Relief of other major symptoms is also usually possible. But no level of symptom relief can obviate all suffering—for suffering is not intrinsically medical but personal. What is sometimes called existential suffering may remain—with overwhelming grief in the face of losses or coherence unable to be restored. In such circumstances it is strengthening of the principle of coherence which offers the only possibility. Restoration of personal integrity in the face of irremediable stressors, remains the human task—and the means are not new. Interpersonal solidarity remains the lynch pin.

There are frequently, in ordinary everyday life, not only in the horrors of war, circumstances in which it is not possible to remove the stressor, but need to help persons to endure. The work of Morse, already mentioned, warning of the need for holding techniques, not touch, until the stressor is gone, and emotions can be given full rein, is of critical importance, yet may be hard to remember in the rush of emotion felt by those responding to disaster (in an emergency department or earthquake). Attending to persons trapped in rubble in natural disasters, while rescue efforts are being made, or even failing, are also examples. Such careful research and reflection is critical and reflects in a practical and teachable way what has been long known.

The maintenance or restoration of a sense of coherence will require different means in diverse circumstances, but normally rests in the restoration of relationships, in the place of fracture. The relationships to be restored may be:

a. intrapersonal—re-engagement with a self thought lost, by removal of horrendous pain, or refreshing sleep, or release from constraint, or interior renewal, and rebirth of hope,

b. interpersonal, involving the agency of another person, whether stranger or not, as simply a proximate human ('lending strength'), or involving a pre-existing significant but broken relationship (one sees this in forgiveness/reconciliation as well as a reunion, through collocation or telephone or vision),
c. with place as critical to identity—for example, returning home,
d. through restoration of something else central to sense of self or self worth—a capacity or an object,
e. through acknowledgement, once again, of lost or disparaged spiritual tradition, history or cultural affinity,
f. through discovery or construction of meaning in the face of incomprehension or absurdity.

This restoration—wrought through changes in any of these domains, is close to a recovery of human dignity, but with a critical additional notion. Human dignity may be present in the midst of suffering, since fundamentally radical human dignity is best regarded as intrinsic and not lost even by damage to relationships constitutive of the person: the trace of what is there suffices to make human dignity present—even though not readily perceived by the person or beholder, if unmindful that dignity is in the order of being, not attributes, nor merely possibility. The relationships between human dignity and human suffering are subtle, but recent philosophical discussion has stressed that the aesthetic dimension of life needs to be kept in focus: 'the ongoing moral challenge in the face of pain and suffering is to ensure that our various expressions of the beautiful life continue to preserve and enhance the dignity we all share' (Pullman 2002). Moreover, it has been said by a professor of anatomy, 'it is the task of medicine is to emancipate man's interior splendour' (Mortimer 1974), and this may be never more poignant than in the face of human suffering. And the nature of that splendour may remain a riddle for the mind. All this is matter for reflection—and the stuff of radical humanism indeed. It will be noted that there is considerable affinity between such notions and the philosophical frame of Rawlinson.

VII. Human suffering is uniquely personal—the universal is particularized in each individual. Communitarian suffering is radically personal and individual, though unquantifiable. Can one compute the total sum of the human suffering(s) of two World Wars, of the Shoah, of Hiroshima, of the Rwanda massacre, of recent tsunamis or earthquakes, of any natural disaster? It makes little sense to try to think in such ways. What is true is that every community is made up of persons, that the experience of each is unique, that the suffering of each is unique, however strong the attempts by tyrants or torturers to depersonalize (and usually by attacking precisely the relationships which are constitutive of the person), and however common are the external factors directed at breaking the spirit. And it is necessary but painful to recognize also that physicians have been the source of deliberately intended unspeakable human suffering—and in our own times: the Nazi doctors were not alone in this betrayal but their place has been an unforgettable blight on the history of medicine. Alexander, observer at the Nuremberg trials, tried to analyze the roots of the egregious moral collapse of some of the most eminent German medical academic leaders, and pinned the beginning on a 'shift in attitude to the non-rehabilitatable sick' (Alexander 1949)—a caution for our own times and forever.

Reflection on the human condition is difficult, and especially in the context of contemporary medical practice, and articulating such reflections even more difficult, at least for those outside the humanities and the arts. Medical practitioners may have largely drawn back from reflection, lest such be a distraction from the pursuit of the biological basis of disease and the means to 'conquer' it, and to continue to bear the onerous burdens of practice. But a tipping point may be close. Reflection is essential, and this reflection may need to go back to ancient portrayals of the human, to Genesis, to the Greeks, to the high philosophers of the middle ages (including Maimonides and Aquinas), to the renaissance thinkers, to Shakespeare, to the struggling enlightenment philosophers, to those seeking to salvage Western thought after the catastrophes of the twentieth-century, to the scientists bringing new perspectives, to non-Western traditions, and to those working to explore and harness new ideas concerning the human and the human good.

Medicine surely cannot be considered any longer as merely a natural science, nor medical practice merely the application of empirical science or technology. Illness (the subjective experience of a deficit of well-being, which may be codified into a 'disease') is a critical part of a human life, to be considered and alleviated in the perspective of that person's whole life, even glimpsed for just a few moments in time, to assist the 'centre to hold'. It could be that there needs to be a renewed focus on the thought of Dilthey, the nineteenth century German philosopher, in his careful analysis of the basis of the 'human sciences', as he pointed out the limits of the methodology and philosophical basis of the 'natural sciences'—it would appear that there could be value in the recognition of medical science as a 'human science' in Dilthey's terms, or at the very least to be considered as a bridge between the human sciences and the natural sciences.; it may be truly the synthesis of these, if adequately understood (Dilthey 1923). Foucault would surely agree (Foucault 1973).

At the very least, the significance of the historical and the subjective, and the dimensions of human values and experience (and narratives concerning these things) may begin to gain a status equal to quantifiable objective biological tests as tools for diagnosis and of evaluation of the worth of clinical intervention. Nothing less may be necessary to begin to relieve some of the regrettable suffering being experienced by persons in halls of clinical excellence, even where there is a perceived (but maybe inadequately conceived) commitment to the human good, as well as by so many of the human community, everywhere.

The obligation to care for each other is not rooted in law or in contract, but, as Levinas has stressed, is rooted in the call of the other in need (Levinas 1989, pp. 75–87). Kafka reminded us in the early twentieth-century: 'You can hold yourself back from the sufferings of the world; this is something you are free to do and is in accord with your nature, but precisely the holding back is the only suffering that you might be able to avoid' (Kafka 1973). Such counsel has to be more poignant in the already troubled twenty-first century. Not to care is not a human option, and for a physician, betrayal.

Bibliography

Alexander, L. 1949. Medical science under dictatorship. *New England Journal of Medicine*. 241:39–47.

Antonovsky, Aaron. 1979. *Health, stress and coping*. San Francisco: Jossey Bass.

Antonovsky, Aaron. 1988. *Unravelling the mystery of health: How people manage stress and stay well*. San Francisco: Jossey Bass.

Becker, Ernest. 1971. *The birth and death of meaning: an interdisciplinary perspective on the problem of man*, 2nd edn. Harmondsworth: Penguin Books.

Bloom, Harold. 1998. *Shakespeare: The invention of the human*. New York: Riverhead Books.

Buber, Martin. 1949. *The prophetic faith*. New York: Macmillan.

Camus, Albert. 1960. *The Plague*. Trans. S. Gilbert. Harmondsworth: Penguin.

Carson, Ronald A. 1997. Medical ethics as reflective practice. In *Philosophy of medicine and bioethics*, eds. Ronald A. Carson and Chester Burns. Boston: Kluwer.

Cassell, E.J. 1982. The nature of suffering and the goals of medicine. *New England Journal of Medicine* 306: 639–645.

Cassell, E.J. 1991. *The nature of suffering and the goals of medicine*, 1st ed. New York: Oxford University Press.

Cassell, E.J. 2004. *The nature of suffering and the goals of medicine*, 2nd ed. New York: Oxford University Press.

Chapman, R., and J. Gavrin. 1993. Suffering and its relationship to pain. *Journal of Palliative Care* 9:5–13.

Cherny, N. 2003. The problem of suffering. In *Oxford textbook of palliative medicine*, ed. D. Doyle, G.W. Hanks, N. Cherny and K Calman, 3rd ed. Oxford: Oxford University Press.

Cherny, N., N. Coyle, and K.M. Foley. 1994. Suffering in the advanced cancer patient: A definition and taxonomy. *Journal of Palliative Care* 10:57–70.

Chochinov, Harvey M. 2007. Dignity and the essence of medicine: The A, B, C & D of dignity-conserving care. *British Medical Journal* 334:184–187.

Cole, Thomas R., and Nathan Carlin. 2009. The suffering of physicians. *The Lancet* 374:1414–1415.

Coles, R. 1989. *The call of stories: Teaching and the moral imagination*. Boston: Houghton Mifflin.

Conrad, L.I., M. Neve, V. Nutton, R. Porter, and A. Wear. 1995. *The western medical tradition*. Cambridge: Cambridge University Press.

Daneault, S., V. Lussier, and S. Mongeau et al. 2004. The nature of suffering and its relief in the terminally: A qualitative study. *Journal of Palliative Care* 20:7–11.

Dilthey, Wilhelm. 1923. *Introduction to the Human Sciences*. Trans. R.J. Betanzos. Detroit: Wayne State University Press.

Eliot, T.S. 1943. *Four quartets*. London: Faber and Faber.

Enthoven, A.C. 1978. Cutting cost without cutting the quality of care (Shattuck Lecture). *New England Journal of Medicine* 298:1229–1238.

Erikson, E.H. 1968. *Identity and the life cycle, psychological issues monograph*. New York: International Universities Press.

Erikson, E.H. 1982. *The life cycle completed: A review*. New York: W. W. Norton.

Foucault, M. 1973. *Birth of the Clinic*. Trans. A.M. Sheridan Smith. London: Tavistock.

Foucault, Michel. 1994. *The birth of the clinic: An archaeology of medical perception*. New York: Vintage.

Frank, A.W. 2001. Can we research suffering? *Qualitative Health Research*, 11:353–362.

Kafka, Franz. 1973. The collected aphorisms, no. 103 (Oct 1917–Feb 1918). In *Shorter Works*, vol 1. Trans. M. Pasley. London: Secker & Warburg.

Kearney, Michael K. 2000. *A place of healing: Working with suffering in living and dying*. Oxford: Oxford University Press.

Kearney, Michael K., Radhule B. Weininger, Mary L.S. Vachon, Balfour M. Mount, and Richard L. Harrison. 2009. Self-care of physicians caring for patients at the end of life: "Being Connected… a key to my survival". *Journal of the American Medical Association* 301:1155–1164.
Levinas, Emmanuel. 1989. *The Levinas reader*, ed. Sean Hand. Oxford: Blackwell.
Malpas, Jeff, and Norelle Lickiss, eds. 2007. *Perspectives on human dignity*. Dordrecht: Springer.
Meier, Diane, Anthony L. Back, and R. Sean Morrison. 2001. The inner life of physicians and care of the seriously ill. *Journal of the American Medical Association* 286:3007–3014.
Morse, J.M. 2001. Towards a praxis theory of suffering. *Advanced Nursing Science* 24:47–59.
Mortimer, K. 1974. The impossible profession: The doctor–priest relationship. *Proceedings of the Australian Association of Gerontology* 2:81–82.
Needleman, J. 1969. The perception of mortality. *Annals New York Academy of Sciences* 164:733–738.
Nussbaum, Martha C. 1994. *The therapy of desire: Theory and practice in Hellenistic ethics*. Princeton: University Press.
Porter, Roy. 1998. *The greatest benefit to mankind: A medical history of humanity*. New York: W. W. Norton.
Porter, Roy. 2003. *Flesh in the age of reason*. New York: W. W. Norton.
Pullman, Daryl. 2002. Human dignity and the ethics and aesthetics of pain and suffering. *Theoretical Medicine* 23:75–94.
Rawlinson, M. 1986. The sense of suffering. *The Journal of Medicine and Philosophy* 11:39–62.
Schaerer, R. 1993. Suffering of the doctor linked with the death of patients. *Palliative Medicine* 7 (Sup. 1): 27–37.
Shakespeare, William. 2007. *Complete Works* (*The RSC Shakespeare*), eds Jonathan Bate and Eric Rasmussen. Basingstoke: Macmillan.
Sigerist, H.E. 1951. *History of medicine, vol 1: Primitive and archaic medicine*. New York: Oxford University Press.
Sigerist, H.E. 1987. *History of medicine, vol II: Early Greek, Hindu, and Persian medicine*. New York: Oxford University Press.
Taylor, Charles. 1989. *Sources of the self: the making of modern identity*. Cambridge: Harvard University Press.
Whitman, Walt. 1891. *Leaves of grass, 1891–1892 edition*. Philadelphia: David McKay.
Whitman, Walt. 1986. *Leaves of grass, the first (1855) edition*. New York: Penguin Books.
Yalom, Irvin D. 2008. *Staring at the Sun: Overcoming the dread of death*. Melbourne: Scribe.
Zornberg, A.G. 1995. *The beginning of desire: Reflections on genesis*. New York: Double Day.

Chapter 20
Suffering Seeks a Voice

Frank Brennan

> *A kind of serenity is one of the rewards that come from having learned to just stand and stare. You don't have to discover God or Nature. What you are doing is looking at things for their own sake*
>
> *Donald Horne, Dying: A Memoir*

Standing and staring at suffering is shockingly hard. Like looking at the sun our natural instinct is to turn away. We may stare at the suffering in ourselves or others but deflect it, rationalise it, obliterate it or deny it. Suffering is natural but never welcome. At its best it is momentary and we are saved. At its worst it collapses the house of self. All equanimity, all composure, all coping is overborne. We are alone and naked and our life has become a foreign place.

Suffering is a powerful subjective experience. It is also a witnessed event. Simplistically, the challenge and mystery of suffering has two perspectives—the person who suffers and the person who witnesses that suffering in others. The themes of this paper are dual. Firstly, that suffering searches for a voice. Secondly, that one of our defining challenges as humans is our response to the suffering of others. I shall begin by describing the nature of suffering in the context of serious illness, how health professionals respond to that suffering and move on to consider suffering in a collective sense.

Illness and Suffering

When a person becomes seriously ill, life can contort into a different shape altogether. It removes the security of health, it exposes one's vulnerability, it threatens all imagined futures. It is that disjunction that is disorienting. It may be the first crack in the veneer of inviolability. It is the beginning of suffering.

F. Brennan (✉)
Calvary Hospital, 91 Rocky Point Road, Kogarah 2217, NSW, Australia
e-mail: fpbrennan@ozemail.com.au

J. Malpas, N. Lickiss (eds.), *Perspectives on Human Suffering*,
DOI 10.1007/978-94-007-2795-3_20, © Springer Science+Business Media B.V. 2012

> Invariably a serious illness comes unwanted, unexpected, a house guest to tolerate. The house guest may stay and then it is to be endured. The house guest will scrawl on your calendar. Appointments, treatments, tests. One morning, the guest comes down to the breakfast table and says 'No more.' (Brennan 2009, p. 53)

The person with a serious illness may experience all manner of suffering—physical, emotional, spiritual. Often those dimensions are interconnected. Indeed, to see them in strict isolation is to miss the point of this interconnectedness. The experience of pain or fatigue may be seen through the prism of the frustration of dependence, unresolved family issues, a growing grief of a life circumscribed or fears of how your spouse and children will cope when you have died. Anger and regret may add to the burden of pain. Mysteries abound—why some people who are physically comfortable suffer greatly and others who remain troubled by physical symptoms are tranquil. Why people of life-long religious faith may begin to question that faith. One person's perspective on suffering can shift: what was once intolerable is now tolerable, what was once a violation of their equanimity, indeed a threat to their very soul, may with time be viewed differently. Inexplicable things may occur—even in the context of the same events—a return to calm, a more balanced view on things, an acceptance, indeed a spiritual growth.

The Role of the Health Professional

> A stranger also sits at the table. They seem concerned. They appear friendly. They introduce themselves as a health professional. They say: 'Yes, sadly, the guest is right. We will do our best. But you may not be able to stay. Indeed, you may not have a say.' (Brennan 2009, p. 53)

Given the complexity of suffering and its endlessly changing topography, health professionals entering into this territory are challenged travelers. As health professionals we observe the suffering of our patients but cannot truly feel it. We respond but we cannot know.

We are left with what we need and what we have.

What we need is the discipline of observation. We need to look upon our patients with the eyes of a poet. We must observe the physical, certainly, but also all the subtle undercurrents beneath. We must hear the unuttered cry. And we must do so with a sensibility born out of compassion.

What we have are our professional skills. Medically we are not mute. We do not come to our patients with empty hands. We have the capacity to significantly improve physical symptoms and, in combination with a multi-disciplinary team, help to deal with other psychological, social and spiritual issues. That is the foundation of the discipline of palliative care. Those skills, however, are not universal. The extent of education of undergraduates in the care of people with life-limiting illnesses and the dying varies considerably. Where deficits lie, they remain an indictment of the professions of medicine and nursing. Without knowledge and skills, how can doctors and nurses respond to the suffering of others? With these skills there is at least a foundation upon which to build.

Occasionally, even with the highest professional skills, all the very best we do is not enough. A patient may be pitched to the farthest point of endurance and then beyond. What is our response then? There are no easy answers. Quite the contrary: we are all on the rapids together (Dawe 2007, pp. 18–19). Understanding this may be the first step:

> I am defenceless utterly—Francis Thompson, *The Hound of Heaven* (Thompson 1929, p. 52)

> We should be in mourning,
> we should be in tears
> our blinds should be permanently drawn—John Harriot, *Our World*

All concerned—patients, families and health professionals—are stripped bare in the face of such suffering. At this point, for patients and health professionals, two things remain: their worth and our presence. It is important through these dark days to state to our patients that while this illness has stripped away so much and continues to do so, it can never take away who the patient is, their beautiful uniqueness, their inner core, their inherent dignity. That is untouchable. The second response is at once simple and complex: ourselves. Our presence. Our commitment to continue with that patient. It may not be enough but, at its most sustained, it may help to fill the interstices between suffering, at its most egregious, and annihilation. One of the greatest challenges in palliative medicine, in these circumstances, is to not allow our sense of professional impotence stand in the way of the centrality of our presence.

In order to occupy that centrality comfortably, the physician needs to be ready and open to the suffering of the patient. If our presence is to be central—and our patients invariably expect this from us—we must have the capacity to bring ourselves coherently to the relationship. If we arrive damaged, broken or impaired we are not truly present. As health professionals we must attend to the harmony of self before we can attend to the disharmony of others.

If the physician is inattentive, jaded, exhausted or so desensitized by constant exposure to suffering they may well miss its signs. Or worse, they may recognize it and turn away. How often do physicians sense suffering but do not ask the question for fear of the answer? These are vital issues for clinicians. A clinician who has not been taught to respond, who chooses to perpetually distance themselves from the suffering of others may spend their entire professional careers never seeking, seldom asking and rarely responding.

Suffering and Meaning

With suffering the yawning, open question is why? Why is this happening? The search for meaning is universal. The search for meaning in suffering is eternal. And through human existence countless explanations have been proffered.

It is the mystery of meaning. And perhaps if the experience of suffering is personal so is the meaning of suffering.

Throughout recorded time that question of meaning is addressed to God. Why do the innocent suffer? If you exist and love us why do you allow this to occur? As Job found there are all answers and no answers. And as Annie Dillard so succinctly put it: 'Who are we to demand explanations from God? (And what monsters of perfection should we be if we did not?)' (Dillard 1994). These two questions permanently challenge mankind.

When walking across the terrain of suffering there are several fault lines that may entrap us. One is despair, the other glorification. One response to suffering is annihilation, to feel that all light or consolation has been banished. Another is to glorify suffering, to see it as, and of itself, ennobling or redeeming. Both approaches attempt to wrestle from the mystery of suffering two landfalls—meaninglessness at one point and meaning at another. Permanent and intractable despair pitches suffering beyond ourselves. Glorification denies its awfulness (Cassidy 1991, p. 85).

It may be that the first step in this process is the simple acknowledgment of mystery. That suffering propels us on a quest for meaning but denies a final answer. That attempting to wrestle meaning from suffering is the universal response, but there may be no universal solution. There is a tremendous irony here: at the very moment when we are most vulnerable our most intense search for meaning occurs. The focus of our gaze is intense. We exhaust our spirits looking. We seek but we may not find. Holding that in balance—this instinctive search and the recognition that no satisfactory answer may be found—is one of the most exquisite challenges of the sufferer and those who care for them.

Collective Suffering

Suffering is commonly seen as a burden endured by the individual. Suffering can also be a collective experience. Wars, pandemics, natural disasters, famine and civil unrest can all contribute to national, continental or indeed global suffering. The whole of mankind can feel cast adrift. Adrift in an empty and uncaring universe.

Suffering is not inconvenience. Suffering is not irritation. To lose a set of keys is inconvenience. To lose a child is to suffer. There is a major difference and it is important that our response to events is proportional and not catastrophizing. Equally it is good for us, in western countries, to remember that what we may experience as suffering may be mild or temporary compared to the sufferings endured daily, permanently and unremittingly in countries where securing the barest preconditions for life are an endless struggle.

Some years ago I worked in South Africa. I witnessed all manner of suffering. Widespread infant malnutrition. The legacy of a major measles epidemic with hundreds of children dead within weeks. State sanctioned racism. Constant political unrest. Upon returning to Australia I began working shifts in an emergency department. One evening a man presented in great distress over a minor cut to his finger. I recall an active sense of anger: this is not distressing; how can you think that? do you have any idea in your comfortable suburban existence what true suffering looks like?

I did not articulate those thoughts and immediately thought them through. It was an important moment in my re-entry back to Australia. Equally, it was an important lesson in the subjectivity of suffering. Yes, as an observer I could enumerate all manner of suffering to this man but it wouldn't alter *the subjective fact* of his own suffering.

Suffering Seeks a Voice

Suffering seeks a voice; whether at the bedside of a patient, in the home of a grieving relative or for a whole people cowered into silence. It is the crying plea of a patient for more time, it is the fear of what will happen to the children, it is the deep sadness of leaving this earth when this earth still holds such promise. Suffering seeks a voice.

That voice may be an instinctive cry through the most systematic crushing of life and hope. During the Yezhov Terror (1937–1938), one of the worst of Stalin's purges, there were mass arrests throughout the USSR. People waited outside the prisons hoping to learn any information about the fate of their loved ones. The son of one of the greatest Russian poets, Anna Akhmatova, was arrested. Later Akhmatova wrote:

> I spent seventeen months waiting in line outside the prison in Leningrad. One day somebody in the crowd identified me. Standing behind me was a woman, with lips blue from the cold.… Now she started out of the torpor common to us all and asked me in a whisper (everyone whispered there):
> 'Can you describe this?'
> And I said: 'Yes I can.'
> Then something like a smile passed fleetingly over what had once been her face. (Akhamtova 1993, p. 180)

Akhmatova fulfilled her promise and, amongst many writers, voiced the suffering of her people. In *Requiem*[1] she became the 'mouth through which a hundred million scream' (Figes 2002):

> This was when the ones who smiled
> Were the dead, glad to be at rest.
> And the sign, the soul, of Leningrad
> Swung from its prisons.
> And when, senseless from torment
> Regiments of convicts marched
> And the short songs of farewell
> Were sung by locomotive whistles
> The stars of death stood above us
> And innocent Russia writhed
> Under bloody boots
> And under the tires of Black Marias

[1] I have combined two translations: Akhamtova 1992, 1993.

This impulse to express suffering is deep, visceral, implacable. It is expressed beautifully in Derek Mahon's poem, *A Disused Shed in Co. Wexford* (Mahon 1999, pp. 89–90). Written at the time of the Troubles in Northern Ireland, he uses the image of the opening of a shed door after years of darkness and the mushrooms that lie there, to express a deeper truth:

A half century, without visitors, in the dark—
Poor preparation for the cracking lock
And creak of hinges. Magi, moonmen,
Powdery prisoners of the old regime,
Web-throated, stalked like triffids, racked by drought
And insomnia, only the ghost of a scream
At the flash-bulb firing squad we wake them with
Shows there is life yet in their feverish forms.
Grown beyond nature now, soft food for worms,
They lift frail heads in gravity and good faith.

They are begging us, you see, in their wordless way,
To do something, to speak on their behalf
Or at least not to close the door again.
Lost people of Treblinka and Pompeii!
'Save us, save us,' they seem to say,
'Let the god not abandon us
Who have come so far in darkness and in pain.
We too had our lives to live.
You with your light meter and relaxed itinerary,
Let not our naïve labours have been in vain!'

And that voice of suffering may rise and continue to rise. In apartheid South Africa it came in songs of protest. After the transition to a democratic South Africa it came through the myriad voices that testified before the Truth and Reconciliation Commission. The enormous outpouring of individual and collective grief that emerged from those hearings did much to heal the wounds of that country. In South Africa in the time of the HIV/AIDS pandemic it continues. Witness this gathering I attended in Kwazakele in the city of Port Elizabeth:

The bells of Kwazakele (Brennan 2007)

I am being driven out to a community centre in Kwazakele. There nurses gather each week, to provide their patients with a meal, HIV/AIDS counseling, anti-retroviral medication. Today is a special day—it is the annual Christmas party. A nurse explains that because of the poverty in the area, this may be the last substantial meal they have until the clinic reopens in the New Year.

In a street with few vehicles, I am surprised to see a white stretched limousine pull out into the road in front of us. The nurse explains that the richest business in Kwazakele is the undertakers. I look more carefully. It is a hearse.

We drive past the cemetery. In the brilliant glare, I see an ocean of crosses stretched out, some flowers moving in the wispy breeze, ribbons, photos, mounds of earth.

The nurses at the centre greet me warmly. They are formidably well informed: statistics on prevalence, the care of opportunistic infections and symptom control.

One nurse leads me into another room. About 15 adults are there. Some standing, most sitting. All have AIDS. The nurse asks each their CD4 count. All know. The speak Xhosa, the local African language. It is Nelson Mandela's mother tongue. The nurses translate for me. I thank them for having me this day. I wish them a Happy Christmas.

We are ushered into an adjoining hall. At one end is a mural of African village scenes. A large table was set with Christmas decorations. The group arranges themselves behind the chairs. With the barest hum as a prelude, the group begins to sing. I had forgotten the power of this—the harmonies, the effortless melody, the surging sound of a group in perfect synchronicity. Of course, I had heard this singing before, but never this close—to pick the individual voices, to sense it like a moving thing. This close, I feel I have been drenched in sound.

They sat down. The senior nurse said a prayer. She thanked me for attending. She turned to the group and invited anyone to speak about the meaning of Christmas to them. At one end of the table, a woman stood and leaned on her walking frame. She lowered her head and moaned. She spoke words that began like a chant and ended like a wail. There was no need for translation. Another woman stood and said that this Christmas especially would be hard, that her daughter had died of AIDS on Christmas Eve last year. She herself was alive, but the disease was making her weaker. I looked around the table. All the women were crying, heads bowed, some burying them in their hands, one with fingers stretched over her closed eyes. Along the seated line, the nurses walked, placing tissues into each hand. A woman rose and stood. She was in her late twenties. 'Last year,' she said 'I couldn't move. I was in bed all the time. Now I can walk. I hope I have more Christmases.'

The weeping continued, deepened. Now the whole table is crying, men and women. The nurses came to comfort them, holding them around their shoulders, touching their faces, their hands. The weeping goes on like a torrent. Of course, it is individual but it is also collective. There is an African word—Ubuntu. The people as a group. We, together. The sense of the collective. The tears of each are now one. Cry the group. Cry Kwazakele. Cry the Beloved Country.

It goes on. The sobbing now sounds like a storm, soaking us all. It rises, dips and pauses, then is caught in the draught of the sound of crying from each end of the table. I feel I am being lowered into a well of sorrow. I can see the sides, but cannot touch them. The light is fading. The sound of the crying sounds like a choir.

Throughout, the nurses are dry eyed. Having worked here, I know that there is a strong professional convention, as a nurse, not to cry in front of patients. I turn and see the eldest nurse in the kitchen behind us, near the wall, out of vision of the group, with a tissue in her hand. It was this sight of this tall woman, sitting on a small stool, quietly, secretly, crying beyond the view of the group. She composed herself. She stood and re-entered the room, calm, a small smile upon her face. She walked over and let out a long call, stamped one foot, raised her hands over her head and clapped them twice. It was a signal. They stood as one and, following her start, began singing again. Oh the beauty. The beauty of their song. Their faces lifted, their eyes closed.

Suffering seeks a voice. In the above example the patients voice theirs individually and as a collective. More usually that voice may find its time privately and often unexpectedly. The smallest comment may trigger it. And once released it may rage like a torrent:

The Woman from County Meath (Brennan 2006)

The warmth of the Dublin day caught everyone by surprise. Through the window I could see children playing in the garden. We had walked into the visitors' room. The family was waiting. They were from County Meath. He was a farmer, only 54, she a teacher. They had seven children. It was clear that he was dying. He had battled seemingly intractable pain, but now over the past few days was much more settled.

I spoke about these days and what to expect from this point onwards. I then concentrated on the family themselves and recommended, as we do, the usual things: that they each take turns in being with him, that they try to eat and sleep, that they talk to each other; in short to look after themselves through this vigil. I turned to the patient's wife and said, 'I know you've been here all the time. It might be good to go and have a rest, even just for a little while.'

There was a long silence. She looked at me as though down a passage. She turned her head to one side, looked out the window, then towards me again and said, 'No, I will not be leaving him.'

She spoke tenderly of their first meeting at age 17, of their courting and their wedding day, of their marriage and the birth of their children. She spoke in soft beautiful phrases, then sentences that began plainly, but became brilliant, each seemingly more evocative than the last. And with every memory of their life together, each reflection she would end by saying 'No, I will not be leaving him,' until that phrase repeated became the tolling of a distant bell. And then she said something that I have never heard expressed in the same way before. She said that from their wedding day they were united; that they were, as the prayer states, one body and that as he had fallen ill so had she, that as he was buffeted by the storms of pain, so was she, that as he was suffering, so was she, and that as he lay dying so was she. No James Joyce, no Oscar Wilde, no Samuel Beckett could have put it so powerfully. As Angela Murphy, the palliative care nurse with me in the room that day said later. 'She was saying what he was feeling.'

In many ways of course she wasn't talking to us. She was speaking across the vast sea of their lives. I had spoken at a practical level about rest. The response I received was from a person adrift on that sea, not wanting to leave or soften the fate. Too often, as doctors, we speak practically and are heard emotionally. And, perhaps, that is our role.

Angela and I left the room and walked back onto the ward. We were both too moved to say much. Later that day Angela rang me and said, 'Frank, we may never hear the like of that again.' When I returned to Australia I was asked to present some memories from Ireland. I contacted Angela. Without prompting she said, 'Of course, you'll talk about the woman from Meath.'

And in distant years if I ever were to encounter Angela Murphy again walking down O'Connell Street in Dublin or perhaps George Street in Sydney, we would stop and, no doubt, remember the woman from Meath who spoke to us of a love that was boundless, a union that was indissolvable and who gave us a momentary glimpse into the mystery at the heart of it all.

Listening as Healing

Suffering may seek a voice but a concomitant aspect of suffering is equally valid: that listening to that voice can play a part in healing. It may never take away the cause of the suffering. That may be impossible but a mystery unfolds every time a person or a people are listened to by others. A critical part of the practice of Palliative Medicine is listening. Certainly we could practice without truly listening—garnering a constellation of physical symptoms and addressing those meticulously. But that would represent a flawed practice. It would miss the significance of the breadth and depth of suffering. A patient's pathology is one part of that only. The response to that pathology stretches out beyond that point in all directions. Without listening a health professional comes ill-equipped to that terrain. With it, all may be possible, even in the worst of suffering. As Marie Murray states:

> Listening is more than hearing. It is heeding. It is concentration. It is paying attention.… Listening is silencing one's own voice to hear someone else. It is wanting to know rather than wishing to inform. It is suspension of self in the service of other. It is not giving advice, providing solutions or solving problems. It is silent. It is unselfish. It is reverential. It is healing. (Murray 2007)

Without that attention the person may feel they are alone in a cavernous universe, deaf to their voice of suffering. Deaf and potentially even callous. Suffering is then magnified by loneliness. Now they are not only cast upon a shore of suffering but fated to endure this on their own.

In this narrative drawn from my work observe not only the articulation of suffering but also the response of people around the patient and how crucial that response is to the experience of the suffering.

Pieta

By now the story was familiar. The familiarity did not ease the sorrow. That such a thing could be, was inexplicable. And in that inexplicability lay the depth of sorrow. He was 28 years old. A new man. Forming. His origins were Macedonian. He was a serious man. He was married; no children. His father had died only a few months before. Suddenly. The family was still reeling in their grief.

His admission to the hospital had been long. Multiple investigations, surgery, sepsis, prolonged courses of antibiotics. The last scan was bitter news. The tide of any hope for cure had gone out. He was becoming much weaker.

Each day the women sat by his bed. Their eyes down. His wife, his mother and his mother-in-law. In mourning for her husband, his mother was always dressed in black. She rarely looked up. One day when I asked them whether they had any questions for me, his mother sighed, looked at me directly and asked: 'Why?'

With the ultimate aim of home in mind he was transferred to the Hospice to gain some time and, possibly, some strength. At first he and his family were disoriented—no intravenous fluids, no regular checks on his temperature, blood pressure and pulse. A scene of quiet compared to the hospital months. With explanation they settled.

One morning I was asked to see him urgently. He was distressed. Two senior nurses accompanied me. When we entered his room I could sense a change. He had deteriorated since I'd last seen him. His mother sat beside his bed, her hand resting on his, her head down. I sat next to him. We talked about what he was feeling—emotional, anxious, even bewildered. He spoke in a whisper. He paused and, turning to look at me, asked me what I thought. As gently as I could I reflected on the change in his condition. We could all see this. I said that things were becoming harder. I said that I thought that his time was coming. He looked up at the ceiling, then towards me and asked: 'What do you mean by that?'

I replied: 'Soon, Paul, you are going to die.'

Immediately his mother, as though stung, leapt up from her chair turned in a small circle screamed out and flung herself on him. 'No, Paul, you won't die. Your father's gone and not this. You will live until you are 86 years old.' She sat sobbing, her head on his hand, kissing his fingers, whispering over and over, 'You can't go… you will live until you are 86.…'

Paul looked up and quietly said: 'Comfort her.'

One of the senior nurses immediately came over to hold her.

I placed my right hand on his chest. I said I knew how much he had gone through and that we would do our best to keep him comfortable and support him. I said that I did not think that he would die today or tomorrow, but that it would be soon.

I could see him thinking about what I had said. He whispered: 'I want you all to pray with me.' He began the Our Father and by the end everyone in the room had joined. On the dresser was a beautiful icon from the Orthodox Church.

Paul looked at me and said: 'Doctor, do you think God will look after me with what I am going through.… Do you think He will love me?'

I answered: 'I'm sure God loves you… He loves you, Paul, now and forever.' My mouth was dry. My hand lay on his chest. My voice was barely audible and now as much to myself as him repeated: 'Now and forever.'

A peace came. The nurses left the room. I stood up to leave. Paul reached for my hand along the edge of the bed and said: 'Doctor I want you to stay.' I held his hand. Paul and his mother then began a long conversation in Macedonian. Later she explained that he had tried to reassure her, settle her and talk of the mystery of God's will.

When he finished he closed his eyes and, exhausted by the encounter, fell asleep. I stood up and said slowly to his mother: 'You… have a good son.'

Later I spoke with the nurses. All of us were struck by the similarity of what we had witnessed to that of another occasion. Another young man, thousands of years ago, dying in front of his mother who, turning to one of his closest friends, uttered the words: 'Comfort her.'

Listening to the person suffering may be the first step away from the precipice. As Eric Cassell observed: 'Suffering occurs when an impending destruction of the person is perceived; it continues until the threat of disintegration has passed or until the integrity of the person can be restored in some other manner' (Cassell 1982). Listening—deeply, humbly, stripped bare of all but the most instinctive response—may be our greatest gift.

At its worst the price of suffering is our humanity. Our aliveness echoes down the years but the echo becomes faint. We are no longer our well selves. We are vulnerable. But even in that vulnerability, that sheer brokenness, another part of ourselves may call us to a different plane:

Thalassa
Run out the boat, my broken comrades;
Let the old seaweed crack, the surge
Burgeon oblivious of the last
Embarkation of feckless men,
Let every adverse force converge—
Here we must needs embark again.

Run up the sail, my heartsick comrades;
Let each horizon tilt and lurch—
You know the worst; your wills are fickle,
Your values blurred, your hearts impure
And your past life a ruined church—
But let your poison be your cure.

Put out to sea, ignoble comrades,
Whose record shall be noble yet;
Butting through scarps of moving marble
The narwhal dares us to be free;
By a high star our course is set,
Our end is life. Put out to sea. (MacNeice 2007)

We are flawed creatures. We shall all die. But the manner and nature of our suffering, individual or collective, is only one part of our humanity. Another is our response to the suffering of ourselves and others. Do we retreat from the heat embarrassed, threatened, appalled? Or do we turn and try to face the sun of suffering with each other and, together, put out to sea?

Bibliography

Akhmatova, Anna. 1992. *The complete poems of Anna Akhmatova,* ed. Roberta Reeder. Trans. J. Hemschemeyer. Edinburgh: Canongate Press.

Akhmatova, Anna. 1993. Requiem. In *Twentieth-century Russian poetry,* eds. A.C. Todd and M. Hayward. London: Fourth Estate.

Brennan, F. P. 2006. The woman from County Meath. *Annals of Internal Medicine* 114 (11): 864.

Brennan, F. P. 2007. The bells of Kwazakele. *The Griffith Review- Spring 2007*. Sydney: ABC Books.

Brennan, F. P. 2009. *Standing on the platform—stories and reflection from palliative care*. Kogarah: Vision Media.

Cassell, E. J. 1982. The nature of suffering and the goals of medicine. *New England Journal of Medicine* 306:639–645.
Cassidy, S. 1991. *Good Friday people*. London: Longman and Todd.
Dawe, B. 2007. White-water rafting and palliative care. In *The best Australian poems of 2007*, ed. Peter Rose. Melbourne: Black Inc.
Dillard, A. 1994. *Holy the firm*. New York: Collins.
Figes, Orlando. 2002. Purging of the poets. *BBC History Magazine*, Nov 30–34.
MacNeice, Louis. 2007. Thalassa. In *The collected works of Louis MacNeice,* ed. P. MacDonald. London: Faber and Faber.
Mahon, D. 1999. *Collected poems*. Oldcastle: Gallery Press.
Murray, M. 2007. The art of good listening. *Irish Times*.
Thompson, Francis. 1929. The hound of heaven. *Selected poems of Francis Thompson*. London: Cape.

Chapter 21
Technological Efficiency, Human Dignity, and the Meaning of Suffering

Daryl Pullman

Introduction

As I write this essay I'm preparing for a meeting with representatives of the senior administration of our local health authority, members of the hospital's ethics service, and clinicians from the hospital's obstetrics and gynecology unit. Among the issues to be discussed is a request by the clinicians to amend the hospital policy on termination of pregnancy to allow the practice of inter-cardiac injection of potassium chloride (KCL) or a similar lethal agent, in order to terminate the life of a fetus in utero prior to extracting it from its mother's womb. The practice would be restricted to fetuses determined to be afflicted with serious anomalies that usually result in death within the first year of life. The anomalies under consideration are generally discovered near the time of viability through antenatal testing. Although many of these fetuses would progress to full term in the absence of this intervention, the clinicians are concerned this will cause needless suffering for both the prospective parents and for the newborn child. Why permit a damaged fetus to continue to full term when we have the technological means and the opportunity to terminate it? What would be the point of such needless suffering?

This essay explores some elements of the problem of human suffering as it is experienced in health care settings. The focus of this discussion, however, is not the patients who are ostensibly the primary sufferers in these illness narratives, but rather the care-providers and other individuals who are either by choice or circumstance implicated in this suffering. The terms 'compassion' and 'sympathy' connote the shared nature of human suffering, and it is this aspect of the phenomenon that is examined here.

The manner in which we experience suffering and hence the meanings we attach to it, are influenced by a variety of socially and culturally mediated phenomena. Technologies in general and medical technologies in particular are especially influential in this regard, as they often dictate the manner in which we relate to one

D. Pullman (✉)
Faculty of Medicine, Memorial University, Newfoundland, Canada
e-mail: dpullman@mun.ca

J. Malpas, N. Lickiss (eds.), *Perspectives on Human Suffering*,
DOI 10.1007/978-94-007-2795-3_21,

another as human beings. As such they can have a profound influence on how we think about pain and suffering, can affect the manner in which we express sympathy and compassion, and can in turn shape our understanding of what our shared dignity requires of us.

In what follows I begin with some general observations about the nature of pain and suffering and how the manner in which we experience these phenomena—both individually and corporately—contributes to our individual and communal sense of self. Here I summarize some earlier work in which I liken our attempts to come to grips with human suffering to a kind of aesthetic project in which we strive together to construct and maintain a life narrative that is both morally good and aesthetically beautiful (Pullman 2002). Suffering as such is a shared human phenomenon that must be incorporated into the stories we all share. The main focus of the present essay, however, is the role that technology plays both in mediating our intra and inter-personal relationships, and in shaping the manner in which we respond to our shared suffering. A notion of technological efficiency is outlined, which, it is argued, often transforms the nature of our roles and relationships in the illness narratives in which we participate, thus altering our perceptions and understanding of the nature of pain and suffering, even as it transforms or truncates our capacity to express sympathy and compassion.

Often the most vexing cases of human suffering in the medical context happen at the margins of life, when life is just beginning, as in the case outlined above, or at the end of life when death is either imminent or hoped for. In other cases we struggle to comprehend the seemingly interminable suffering experienced by those with chronic illness that occurs over many years. It is situations such as these that cause us to question our shared dignity as human beings. The essay concludes with some reflections on how technologically mediated suffering can undermine our understanding and expression of this shared dignity.

Narrative Construction and the Meanings of Suffering

Humans are by nature meaning conferring beings; we are hard-wired to impose structure upon and to make sense of the world as we experience it. It is through an on-going process of constructing and restructuring our personal and communal narratives that we weave the various aspects of our existence into a coherent whole. We are all, as such, inveterate story tellers. 'Stories do not simply describe the self,' says sociologist Arthur Frank, 'they are the self's medium of being' (Frank 1995, p. 53).

Human suffering constitutes a significant challenge for any story teller who must somehow weave this all too common phenomenon into the on-going narratives we construct in order to cope with the world as we experience it. Of course, not every story serves the same purpose, and hence the existence of pain and suffering represent different challenges depending upon the nature and purpose of the narrative being constructed. For philosophers and theologians, pain and suffering represent intellectual challenges that must somehow be incorporated into the grand stories they construct in order to account for reality in all of its dimensions, be they ontological, epistemological, moral, or otherwise. Thus in a recent paper philosopher John Ozolins asks if suffering is valuable, or just useless pain (Ozolins 2003). For while pain *simpliciter* can be explained as nature's way of alerting us to avoid various physical dangers such as the heat of the stove, or of the need to seek medical attention when we injure a limb and so forth, it is more difficult to make sense of the on-going suffering occasioned by the unremitting pain of a cancer patient, or of the human suffering that follows in the wake of a major natural catastrophe such as an earth quake, flood, or famine.

For health professionals in general and physicians in particular, pain and suffering represent a kind of practical challenge that is somewhat unique to those in the healing professions. This is because the stories they construct to make sense of the on-going reality of suffering as they confront it, casts them in the key role of healer. As such, they are tasked with attending to the pain and suffering of others on a daily basis in a manner that is somewhat foreign to those of us who do not fill those particular roles. 'My story is broken: Can you help me fix it?' is the title of an article by physician-ethicist Howard Brody (1994). Brody argues for a particular conception of the physician-patient relationship in which physicians take on the somewhat unique task of what might be described as 'narrative repair.' We will return to this metaphor later when we consider how medical technologies can affect the manner in which clinicians identify where and how the patient's story has gone wrong, and then shapes the nature of their responses to it.

The vast majority of us generally need not attend to (or account for) the pain and suffering of others in quite the same manner as do health professionals whose life's work (i.e. their *raison d'etre* cum health professional) is in some sense defined by the need to attend to and ideally, to eliminate the pain and suffering of others. This is not to ignore the fact that many non-health professionals spend significant portions of their lives attending to the pain and suffering of others. However, in most instances these latter caregivers have had that role forced upon them because of circumstances beyond their control such as when a parent, partner or child falls ill. Thus the illness narratives they construct in an attempt to make sense of the pain of their loved ones and the suffering they share with them are qualitatively different from those of professional caregivers who have chosen to define themselves in this way. The qualitative difference arises primarily from the nature and quality of the relationships they share with those who are in pain or are otherwise suffering, and for whom they often find themselves responsible. Dealing with suffering in this very visceral sense is more than an intellectual endeavor or a practical problem; it is very much an existential challenge that can tax all of our resources—intellectual, emotional, spiritual, and otherwise—as we struggle individually and corporately to come to grips with this phenomenon.

To this point we have been discussing pain and suffering concurrently as the two often occur simultaneously, especially in the context of health care. However, in order to fully appreciate the existential challenge occasioned by human suffering, we must distinguish it from the pain which may or may not be the occasion for it. Although pain and suffering are closely related, the concepts are phenomenologically distinct. Physician Eric Cassell summarizes some aspects of this distinction as follows:

> … people in pain frequently report suffering from the pain when they feel out of control, when the pain is overwhelming, when the source of the pain is unknown, when the meaning of the pain is dire, or when the pain is chronic. In all these situations, persons perceive pain as a threat to their continued existence—not merely to their lives but to their integrity as persons. That this is the relation of pain to suffering is strongly suggested by the fact that suffering can be relieved, in the presence of continued pain, by making the source of the pain known, changing its meaning, and demonstrating that it can be controlled and that an end is in sight. (Cassell 1982)

Notice, first, that suffering is experienced by persons, not bodies: 'Suffering is a consequence of personhood,' states Cassell, 'bodies do not suffer, persons do' (Cassell 1992, p. 3). Second, the critical link between pain and suffering is primarily epistemic. What does the pain mean? Persons in pain suffer when they cannot make sense of their experiences. The meaning attached to the pain experience is crucial to a clearer understanding of the nature of suffering. But as noted already, suffering need not be confined only to those whose bodies are in pain. By virtue of their relationships to those who are in pain, others become characters in the illness narrative in which that pain and suffering is manifest. As such they also struggle to make sense of the illness experience of their loved one; in so doing they suffer along with them: 'The loss that accompanies illness,' writes Frank 'begins in the body, as pain does, then moves out until it affects the relationships connecting that body with others' (Frank 1991, p. 36). Suffering thus threatens the aesthetic integrity of the life narrative of both those in pain and of those who suffer with them, as it threatens to disrupt the unity of their shared story:

> Suffering is experienced when some crucial aspect of one's own self, being, or existence is threatened. The meaningfulness of such threat is to the integrity of one's own experience of personal identity…. Whether suffering is invoked by pain depends more on the meaning the individual gives to the pain in relation to the integrity of personal identity than it does on the amount, degree, or type of pain. (Kahn and Steeves 1986)

As noted previously, terms like 'sympathy' and 'compassion' describe the process of 'suffering with'. Clearly sympathy and compassion serve an important existential function as a means of psychological and social support. But they can be viewed as well as part of an epistemic process by which we strive together to make sense of the pain endured by those whose lives we share. Ideally, 'making sense' of such experiences involves an attempt to weave them into a coherent whole that maintains the integrity of the lives of not only those who are in pain but of the sympathetic and compassionate ones who suffer along with them. It is this process of weaving these experiences into a coherent and meaningful story that is described here as an aesthetic project.

Reflective consciousness is a condition of personhood. It is also the basis of our capacity to suffer. Conscious reflection enables human beings to form a sense of self, an essential condition of personhood. Conscious reflection also enables persons to reflect upon the goals and projects that are constitutive of their selves, and to recognize when such goals and projects are frustrated or rendered impossible. The self (i.e. ego) has the capacity to step outside of particular experiences and to find meaning in (or to provide meaning to) those experiences.

Many of our experiences are constitutive of our sense of self as they serve to define who and what we are as persons. Pain and suffering can disrupt the integrity of the self. 'To suffer,' states Cassell, 'is to be diminished or threatened in one's personhood' (Cassell 1991, p. 52). However, our sense of self has an inter-subjective dimension evidenced in the shared meanings we construct in social space. It is this inter-subjectivity that makes possible shared suffering and serves as the very basis of compassion. Kleinman captures these points nicely:

> Illness narratives edify us about how life problems are created, controlled, made meaningful. They also tell us about the way cultural values and social relations shape how we perceive and monitor our bodies, label and categorize bodily symptoms, interpret complaints in the particular context of our life situation; we express our distress through bodily idioms that are both peculiar to distinctive cultural worlds and constrained by our shared human condition. (Kleinman 1988, p. xiii)

Self-constituting projects are often frustrated by disease. Pain can rob persons of the physical capacity to pursue meaning conferring endeavors. But suffering can also be the product of psycho-social, economic, or other factors that frustrate an individual in the pursuit of significant life projects. This illustrates the possibility of suffering in the absence of physical pain. The sphere of suffering radiates out beyond individual pain to affect the lives of all those involved in the narrative, aesthetic project we call life. 'Suffering,' writes van Hooft, 'is a spiritual phenomenon, an event that strikes at the faith we can have in life. The role of suffering in our lives is contested at the level of discourse at which cultural meanings and visions of life are negotiated' (van Hooft 1988).

Maintaining a unified and meaningful life narrative is thus both a moral and an aesthetic project. Suffering occurs when any aspect of the person is threatened or is perceived as undergoing disintegration. Such aesthetic upheaval is often referred to as a loss of dignity. Alan Radley captures the point this way:

> … dignity is something worked out between people, an idea that makes its appearance in the practices of sufferers and observers. It is therefore contingent upon social relationships, both between medical professionals and patients, and between sufferers and carers. (Radley 2004)

Persons, as such, are fragile creatures. Any number of social, physical or other contingent events can impinge upon a person's sense of self. The loss of a loved one or other valued relationship might upset the integrity of the person. When physical injury or disease robs the patient of the capacity to pursue projects that provide a sense of meaning and purpose, the patient suffers.

Although the patient is ostensibly the focal point of any illness narrative (i.e. it wouldn't be an 'illness narrative' if someone wasn't ill), it is nevertheless a narrative that is constructed jointly by those involved in the patient's life and care. As noted earlier, however, narratives serve a variety of purposes, and not everyone involved in any given narrative experiences the phenomenon of suffering in the same way. Thus while the pain of the patient and the shared suffering of her loved ones represents an existential crisis that must somehow be incorporated into their shared life-story, this same pain and suffering often represents a more pragmatic and practical challenge for the physician vis-à-vis his or her role as healer. Physicians, as Brody suggests, are in the business of fixing stories, described earlier as 'narrative repair.' This is not to suggest that physicians and other professional healers lack sympathy and compassion; the vast majority of professional care-givers are compassionate and caring human beings. It is only to acknowledge once again that their relationship with the patient and concomitantly, their perception of the patient's pain and suffering, is qualitatively different from that of those whose identities are intimately connected with that of the patient.

Physicians are invited into a particular narrative at a particular time and for a particular purpose; they are there because a life story has now become an illness narrative. As such, they play a particular kind of role in ameliorating the pain and suffering of their patients. In modern medicine the physician's relative success in this regard is often contingent upon the availability of and their skill in utilizing the expanding variety of technological interventions at their disposal. As such, the medical professional's role within any particular illness narrative could be characterized as that of a technician. Again, and this point must be emphasized, there is no suggestion here that health care professionals and physicians in particular are distant or uncaring individuals. Most are genuinely concerned about the pain and suffering of their patients, and they experience a certain amount of moral distress when unable to adequately manage them. Nevertheless, the reality of modern medicine is that the primary tools at the disposal of the health care professional, the ones that the bulk of their training focuses upon and hence the ones to which they most naturally turn when faced with their patients' suffering, are generally technological in nature. Whether it is diagnostic imaging, surgical intervention, or the ever expanding regimen of chemo-therapeutic and other pharmaceutical agents, modern medicine provides technologically mediated care. It is the nature of such technological interventions and the manner in which they shape our understanding of and responses to pain and suffering, that we want to examine now.

Technological Efficiency and the Commodification of Suffering

The role of technology in contemporary life has long been a central topic for philosophers, social theorists, and novelists alike. The dominant ideology has generally been one of technological progress in which technology is seen as an instrument to meet universal human needs, overcoming various obstacles for the betterment of humankind. Thus we characterize ancient history in terms of the materials used to make tools (stone, bronze and iron ages respectively), and more contemporary advances in terms of energy sources to power our machines (steam, oil, electrical, nuclear, solar, etc.), or by the advances in the technological means by which we communicate with one another (telegraph, telephone, internet, wifi), and so forth.

This positive perception of technological progress is largely the view represented by philosophers like Marcuse (1964) and Habermas (1970), for example. On the other hand, there has long been a parallel discourse characterized by ambivalence for technology's role, and full of dire warnings about technology run amok. The novels of Mary Wollstonecroft Shelley, Charles Dickens, and John Steinbeck are but a small representative sample of this literary genre. Ellul (1964), Winner (1977), and Borgmann (1984, pp. 44 ff.) represent general philosophical critiques of this dominant ideology, and Foucault (1994), in his various works, has offered perspicuous insights into the role of technology in medicine.

Our purpose here is not to offer a critique of the notion of progress as it pertains to medical technology, or to even suggest that medical technologies are in some sense inherently bad. Indeed it would be difficult to deny that on a wide variety of measures in terms of pain and symptom management, cures for previously debilitating or lethal conditions, lower infant mortality rates, longer life expectancy, and so forth, medical science and technology have made tremendous strides over the past decades. Our interest here, however, is in appreciating something of the manner in which the roles of professional caregivers are shaped in large part by such technologies, and how this in turn affects the manner in which these caregivers are inserted into the illness narratives of their patients and of those sympathetic and compassionate others who suffer along with them. Given the manner in which modern medical technologies dominate contemporary medicine and the central role physicians in particular play as practitioners of these technologies, they wield tremendous influence both in shaping our understanding of the nature of human suffering and in affecting our responses to it.

Foucault's conception of the 'medical gaze' is by now a familiar post-modern conception of the manner in which the objects of our experience are in some sense actively constructed rather than merely apprehended by us. The medicalized body that results from this gaze is reduced by the intellectual apparata of medicine (anatomy, physiology, biochemistry) to produce a biomedical conception of disease processes. The body, as such, is anatomized as the site or manifestation of problems that need to be fixed (recall the notion of 'narrative repair'). Martyn Evans contrasts the medicalized body which is introduced to the medical student in her training and which then becomes familiar to the experienced physician, with the individual body with which each of us is familiar in everyday life:

> Scientific medicine is concerned—as it must be—with the general, the repeatable, the universalizable, hence… the *general* nature of the medical body, in contrast with the individual identity of the body familiar to us in everyday life. Medical practice seeks to locate each individualized patient within the disease categories provided by specialized medicine; the doctor searches for correspondences between the actual patient in front of her and an 'idealised' presentation of a disease, available in textbooks but far less commonly encountered in the surgery… By complete contrast the body familiar to us in everyday life is not standardized. Instead… it is *absolutely* individuated as the principal ground of our identity in terms of which we recognize and acknowledge each other [his emphasis]. (Evans 2001)

Three key insights are relevant here. First, the medicalized body reduces the person to the physical components and processes which constitute the medical entity.

Second, in reducing persons to bodies the distinction between pain and suffering disappears. Suffering becomes synonymous with the physical or psychic pain experienced by the physical entity. Ideally the source of this suffering *cum* pain is first identified by diagnostic medical technologies; once isolated it is efficiently eradicated or managed by therapeutic technological interventions. We will return to this paradigm of medical technological efficiency momentarily. The third key insight pertains to the manner in which the medicalized body is no longer the principal ground of our identity.

Our personal identity is a social phenomenon that is contingent upon the relationships we have with other human beings, especially with those close intimates with whom we share our life's story. Identity, as such, arises out of our shared relationships, values and experiences, and the meanings we attach to them in social space. This notion of social identity is central to our capacity to demonstrate sympathy and compassion vis-à-vis our shared suffering. However, the medicalized body and the concomitant model of technological efficiency that underwrites the notion of medical progress, systematically transforms the patient's identity, reducing it to the physical processes and constituent parts that comprise the physical body that is isolated in medical space. In so doing the medical gaze transforms our illness narratives as it reshapes our understanding of pain and suffering and our perceived roles in attending to them.

Physicist Ursula Franklin has assessed the impact that technologies in general have had on contemporary society by distinguishing between technologies of growth and technologies of production. The growth model captures our common experience that entities in the world are made of different but appropriate sizes. Size and scale are given relative to any particular growing organism. Relative size is a natural outcome of growth, 'but growth itself cannot be commandeered; it can only be nurtured and encouraged by providing a suitable environment. Growth occurs; it is not made' (Franklin 1990, p. 26).

The production model of technology, on the other hand, entails a systematic process of reducing a complex system to its component parts and then managing the parts and processes accordingly. It is this model of technology that has dominated contemporary society since the industrial revolution, and it is the contemporary paradigm for medical technology as well. A production model assumes that in principle things are completely controllable, and if in practice control is incomplete, further improvements in knowledge, design, or organization will bring all essential parameters under control. It is this process that explains the medical practitioner's tendency to first conflate pain and suffering and then to treat them as in principle completely controllable through a technological fix. Pain and suffering as such are a technical problem to be solved or eradicated rather than an existential human crisis that must somehow be managed.

Philosopher Albert Borgmann has provided a useful critique of the production model of technology under what he describes as the 'Device Paradigm' (Borgmann 1984). Although Borgmann is not writing about medical technology *per se*, his insights are instructive as he outlines a notion of technological efficiency that captures certain elements of contemporary medicine and provides some insights about the technological management of pain and suffering. Borgmann argues that the production model treats various technologies or technological processes as devices that are designed to produce commodities. Ideal technological devices provide commodities in a manner that is instantaneous, ubiquitous, safe, and easy. When a deficiency in any one of these areas is identified the technological process can be adjusted to correct for it.

Borgmann's model of technological efficiency and its inherent deficiencies can be illustrated by comparing two technologies, a wood stove and a modern central heating system. Which of these technologies is more efficient? The commodity a wood stove and central heating are each designed to produce is heat, and when assessed against the criteria outlined here central heating is clearly a more efficient technology. A wood stove does not provide its commodity instantaneously, ubiquitously, safely or easily as there is a great deal of labour and risk involved in cutting wood, starting a fire, and waiting for a room to warm. Central heating, by comparison, provides the commodity heat at the touch of a button or the turn of a thermostat, quickly, safely and easily. Clearly, on the production model of technological development, central heating is a more efficient technology.

At this point, however, Borgmann asks us to consider the wood stove once again, but now we should think of it not as a simple technological device to produce a particular commodity, but rather as a focal point for a variety of social practices. What other social functions might a wood stove provide that would be lost with the conversion to central heating? Among the things to consider here are the skills one needs to acquire in order to handle an axe or other wood cutting instruments, and the associated skills in setting and maintaining a fire. When a wood stove is the only source of heat for the home, someone will have the responsibility to attend to these tasks which brings with it a certain degree of social accountability. On a cold winter night in a home heated by a wood stove the family members do not disperse throughout the house to attend to their respective interests in isolation; rather they congregate in the room that is heated thus making social interaction a necessity rather than an option. This model of technology comports more closely to what Franklin describes as a 'growth model.' On this view the wood stove is much more than a device to produce a simple commodity; it becomes the focal point for a broad range of social practices that require the development and expression of a variety of practical and social skills, none of which are completely under our control.

Clearly we cannot predict whether social relationships will flourish around a wood stove; it is possible that family members would instead quarrel endlessly and bitterly. But on this view the measure of efficiency is not the relative ease with which a product or commodity is produced (instantaneously, safely, easily, ubiquitously), but rather the nature of the environment in which growth can occur. As Franklin notes, growth cannot be controlled; we can only provide the environment and opportunity for it to flourish. Thus if technological efficiency were measured not by a device's capacity to produce a simple commodity like heat, but rather by the manner in which it becomes a focal point for social practices, the wood stove could quite conceivably be judged as more efficient than central heating.

Borgmann's device paradigm can be applied to an analysis of modern medical technologies, and the problem of human suffering. The commodity that modern medicine aims to produce is a healthy patient, free from pain and suffering. Technological devices, whether diagnostic processes or therapeutic interventions, are designed to isolate the problem of pain and suffering and to produce health, the desired commodity, in a technologically efficient manner. In so doing the machinery of medicine and the technological experts (read physicians) who manage it assume a central role in the illness narrative as the pain and associated suffering that hinder the production of the commodity (a healthy, pain free patient) are systematically eliminated.

As in the case of the wood stove, however, this model of technological efficiency can be re-evaluated from another perspective. Think of illness now and the associated pain and suffering that accompany it, not merely as a technical problem to be solved but as a focal point for a variety of social practices. On this view pain and suffering are again treated as separate phenomena. Dealing with the patient's pain and associated suffering provide an opportunity to bring the patient back into the foreground and to surround her with those sympathetic and compassionate companions who are writing this part of her illness narrative with her. The device paradigm and the production model of technological efficiency it supports focuses our attention only on the commodity to be produced (ideally, a healthy, pain free patient). As such it ignores the role of the compassionate and sympathetic others who are in some sense superfluous to the technologically medicated production. The growth model, by contrast, emphasizes the role of these compassionate and caring others as integral to the environment in which meanings are constructed and in which healing can occur. "Healing" as such, does not necessarily equate with a physically well, and pain-free patient, but rather with a shared life narrative that makes sense of the experience of suffering despite potential on-going pain and loss. In entering into this mutual suffering those constructing this chapter in an on-going illness narrative may have opportunities to mine the depths of their common humanity that might otherwise have remained buried deep below the surface.

The aim of the foregoing is neither to romanticize human suffering nor to trivialize modern medicine and those dedicated professionals who practice it. Pain and suffering remain devastating realities of contemporary life despite all the advances of modern medicine; no one wishes to suffer personally or to see others suffer so that they can thus have the opportunity to practice sympathy and compassion. Indeed, anyone who has had the misfortune of experiencing a devastating illness or of suffering with loved ones who are in deep pain and despair will be thankful for the relief that modern medicine and its skilled practitioners can provide. The point, instead, is to alert us to the potential we all face, whether health care professional, patient, or compassionate companion or loved one, to be overwhelmed by the modern medical technological juggernaut that tends to foreground technology and technicians while pushing the patient and especially her compassionate loved ones to the wings. The aim is not to reject modern medicine but to recognize its limitations as an instrument for human sympathy and compassion.

Human Dignity and the Aesthetics of Suffering

This chapter opened with reference to an evolving situation in my institution's obstetrical unit involving a discussion of the appropriate manner in which to attend to the potential suffering of damaged fetuses. Our dedicated clinicians see themselves as advocating for their patients in this regard: 'Why permit a damaged fetus to continue to full term when we have the technological means and the opportunity to terminate it?' they ask. 'What would be the point of such needless suffering?'

It is not my intention to pass judgment on my clinician colleagues as I have the deepest respect for them as individual persons and as professional caregivers. I know they do not approach this issue lightly, and I have no doubt that they are genuinely vexed by what they perceive to be their limited options in this regard. Neither do I want to suggest that every such instance of late termination is necessarily problematic ethically. The point here is that the technological milieu of contemporary medicine and the model of efficiency it dictates, shapes the manner in which this illness narrative unfolds for physicians, patients, and for those others who are part of the story alike. These physicians are faced with a moral dilemma. They have discovered a damaged fetus. There is no way to repair it. To allow it to proceed to term will cause suffering both for the newborn and for the parents. Termination seems clearly to be the lesser of two evils. It is the most *efficient* manner in which to deal with this pain and suffering. This is the illness narrative as told from the clinician's perspective.

Given the foregoing discussion we can now evaluate some key elements of this narrative as viewed through the medico-technological lens, and consider alternative scenarios that might cast this potential suffering in a different light. The key elements of this medicalized story map nicely onto the production model of technology and to the device paradigm of technological efficiency which informs it. The commodity to be produced is a healthy child. The primary means of production is the obstetrical unit supported by antenatal screening and testing. Notice here that the mother's womb is in a certain sense subsumed by the technological machinery, and we might even describe the potential mother as a customer who seeks a high quality product. When quality control identifies an inferior product in the system the natural response is to eliminate it, adjust the machinery, and try again.

Although this rather glib characterization borders on hyperbole, it does so to make a point about the nature of pain and suffering when viewed from this perspective. Pain and suffering on this view serve no purpose whatsoever; they are simply the unwanted and unnecessary by-products of an inefficient system. There is no room for shared suffering in this scenario other than perhaps the shared disappointment others might feel if the pregnancy were to proceed unhindered and the parents were then presented with an inferior product. Neither is there any dignity to be found in this technologically determined process.

Again, this is not a matter of romanticizing human suffering. Indeed, there are many health care contexts in which the prolongation of suffering seems futile and unwarranted. One of the cruel ironies of my role as a clinical ethics consultant is that while I wrestle with our obstetricians about the ethics of terminating otherwise viable (though admittedly 'damaged') fetuses on the one hand, on the other hand I at times struggle openly with our neo-natal intensivists about the wisdom of on-going aggressive treatment of severely compromised newborns. It is worth noting that in either case the fragile lives under consideration are often at a similar gestational age. In the latter case the neo-natal intensive care unit (NICU) serves as the device, although in this scenario the commodity to be produced is not a perfect infant, but rather an infant that survives the NICU (the *efficient* NICU is measured quantitatively by a high survival rate). In the high tech environment of the NICU those not involved in the direct management of the machinery are often pushed to the margins in terms of compassionate caring. There is little opportunity for parental engagement in holding and loving their struggling child, let alone for the extended family and community. Here the supporting cast is often relegated to cameo appearances as this tragic narrative unfolds.

If the suffering occasioned by illness narratives such as these is to have any meaning at all, if there is any dignity to be salvaged, expressed, or enhanced, it will have to come from an alternative reading. Franklin's notion of a 'growth model' of technological progress in contradistinction to the dominant 'production model' provides such a perspective. On this reading the developing fetus or compromised newborn is viewed not as a damaged product to be discarded or otherwise managed, but as an opportunity for growth. As the illness narrative unfolds this tenuous life becomes a focal point for a variety of social practices. Clearly, the news that a developing fetus is afflicted with a terminal condition or that a premature newborn is struggling for its life constitutes a tragedy for all involved; parents, other family members, and clinicians alike. But it presents an opportunity for growth as well, as we draw upon those positive qualities that make us distinctly human, and strive together to express our common dignity. Our dignity as such is not a private matter; it is rather a shared expression of who we are and what we aspire to be as a caring community. It is this expressive aspect of our shared dignity that I've described elsewhere as an aesthetic project (Pullman 2002).

Conclusion

Suffering is a constant feature of our human situation even as the need to respond to it is a matter of the human condition. How we choose to respond will in turn be both expressive of who and what we are, even as it shapes to some degree what we can become. All of this has implications for our shared dignity.

Human dignity is a dynamic normative concept that encompasses both moral and aesthetic dimensions. Both dimensions are relevant to how we understand our roles and the expectations we have of one another in the on-going narratives that constitute our shared life stories, and in how we embrace, understand, and respond to human suffering. Dignity in the basic moral sense recognizes that each several human being is worthy of respect irrespective of any contingent features of a life situation. It is the aesthetic dimension of human dignity, however, that is most relevant here, as it focuses specifically on those contingent features of our shared life situations that we strive to weave together into a coherent whole. Human suffering is just such a contingent feature, and as such it presents both and existential and an aesthetic challenge and opportunity.

Of course beauty, they say, is in the eye of the beholder, and not all will be convinced that the compassionate embrace of human suffering will lead to a meaningful and aesthetically satisfying narrative account. As Franklin has noted, growth cannot be commandeered; it can only be encouraged and nurtured by providing an appropriate environment. We cannot predict how any individual will respond when faced with human suffering, whether it is his own, a kindred other's, or of others more remote. Hence we cannot predict whether any particular illness narrative will be aesthetically satisfying. In this respect the production model of technological efficiency that dominates contemporary health care offers a certain degree of predictability by virtue of its simplicity, and some may find this latter account more aesthetically appealing. The challenge to each of us is to reflect on these competing narratives, and to recognize the implications of each for the kind of people we want to be.

Bibliography

Borgmann, Albert. 1984. *Technology and the character of contemporary life*. Chicago: University of Chicago Press.

Brody, H. 1994. My story is broken; Can you help me fix it? Medical ethics and the joint construction of narrative. *Literature and Medicine*, 13:79–92.

Cassell, E.J. 1982. The nature of suffering and the goals of medicine. *New England Journal of Medicine*, 306:639–645.

Cassell, E.J. 1991. *The nature of suffering*. New York: Oxford University Press.

Cassell, E.J. 1992. The nature of suffering: Physical, psychological, social, and spiritual aspects. In The hidden dimension of illness: Human suffering, 1–10, eds. P.L. Starck and J.P. McGovern. New York: National League for Nursing.

Cassell, E.J. 2004. *The nature of suffering and the goals of medicine*, 2nd ed. New York: Oxford University Press.

Ellul, Jacques. 1964. *The Technological Society*. Trans. J. Wilkinson. New York: Knopf.

Evans, M. 2001. The 'medical body' as philosophy's arena. *Theoretical Medicine*, 22:19–20.

Foucault, Michel. 1994. *The birth of the clinic: An archaeology of medical perception*. New York: Vintage.

Frank, A.W. 1991. *At the will of the body: Reflections on illness*. Boston: Houghton Mifflin.

Frank, A.W. 1995. *The wounded storyteller: Body, illness, and ethics*. Chicago: University of Chicago Press.

Franklin, Ursula. 1990. *The real world of technology*. Montreal: CBC Enterprises.

Habermas, Jürgen. 1970. *Toward a rational society*. Boston: Beacon Press.

Kahn, D.L., and R.H. Steeves. 1986. The experience of suffering: Conceptual clarification and theoretical definition. *Journal of Advanced Nursing* 11:623–631.

Kleinman, Arthur. 1988. *The Illness Narratives*. New York: Basic Books.

Marcuse, Herbert. 1964. *One-dimensional man: Studies in the ideology of advanced industrial society*. Boston: Beacon Press.

Ozolins, John. 2003. Suffering: Valuable or just useless pain. *Sophia,* 42:53–77.
Pullman, Daryl. 2002. Human dignity and the ethics and aesthetics of pain and suffering. *Theoretical Medicine*, 23:75–94.
Radley, Alan. 2004. Pity, modernity and the spectacle of suffering. *Journal of Palliative Care*, 20 (3): 179–184.
van Hooft, Stan. 1988. The meanings of suffering. *Hastings Center Report* 28 (5): 14.
Winner, Langdon. 1977. *Autonomous technology: Technics-out-of-control as a theme in political thought*. Cambridge: MIT Press.

Chapter 22
Suffering and the Sleeplessness of Clinicians

Matthew Hamilton and Grant Gillett

The primary focus of modern medicine is on the biology and patho-physiology of physical disease such that the patient's experience of illness and the many forms of pain and suffering arising in it are often recognized only as indicators of the reality with which we have to deal in treating the physical body. Evidence based medicine may aim at the relief of suffering as the primary end of medicine, but it constructs what should be done in quite other terms. Patients and the public often do not understand these terms or why there is a gap between their distress and the imperatives that guide their treatment (Cassell 1999). The gap reflects the conflict between the patient's lived experience and the series of dichotomies forming the deep binary logic of the culture of biomedicine: mind-body, physiological-psychological, body-soul, objective-subjective and real-unreal (Kleinman 1994, pp. 169–198). As a person encounters the real-unreal world of the clinic their experience is often alienated from them as their narrative is colonized by a medical narrative beyond their control (Frank 1995, pp. 12–15). In this encounter, the patient is expected to be compliant with those who are responsible for their recovery, with the physician both assuming responsibility for that recovery, and even for determining what counts as recovery (Frank 1995, p. 29). The patient is therefore a passive character in their own illness story and the professionals in control may not appreciate what is important to the patient, and become frustrated that their indices of success and failure do not fit the lived reality of the patient's suffering. In such an encounter the ability to recognize the patient's true suffering can disappear, however accurately and efficiently the patient's ('objective') disease is diagnosed and treated.

However the patient's suffering will not disappear, it is the spur to the clinical enterprise and therefore brings patient and doctor back to the point where the biomedical construction fails in relation to the real illness. We will use the Lacanian concept of repetition to show how this unresolved suffering represents a *tuche* or

G. Gillett (✉)
Bioethics Centre of the Medical School, University of Otago, Dunedin, New Zealand
e-mail: grant.gillett@otago.ac.nz

M. Hamilton
Dunedin School of Medicine, University of Otago, Dunedin, New Zealand

J. Malpas, N. Lickiss (eds.), *Perspectives on Human Suffering*,
DOI 10.1007/978-94-007-2795-3_22,

trauma, a residue that escapes scientific signification, drawing the physician back to 'the wound' (in his/her clinical persona) resulting from an inability to respond to the patient's suffering. We will then identify a pathway for engaging with the patient's unresolved suffering through understanding the cycles of integration and signification by which a person constructs their Imago. Through the Imago we see the illness and can begin the healing process with both patient and physician being able to address that which causes the suffering.

Suffering and the Trauma of Illness

The doctor is entangled in the complex relationship between pain and suffering because the patient is the sole final indicator of the success of the regimen of treatment being used. In the discourse of the clinic we construct medical truth by configuring the human suffering that presents itself in the language that structures our clinical response to it. Thus we go from 'tummy ache' to abdominal pain, and perhaps appendicitis, the truth behind the tummy ache. We go from chronic and unrelieved jabs of pain in the face, to neurogenic facial pain, to *tic doloreux*. We go from anorexia to … where? Suffering, when it is refractory to the regimen of treatment, acts like a 'trauma' which, just as in the psyche, causes *repetition* and keeps drawing the doctor back to attend to it (Gillett 2006).

The trauma, for Lacan, represents a point where the *cogito*—the thinking self—does not adequately cope with the real. The medical cogito creates its own objects of thought—illnesses as understood in medical discourse—and the trauma is a mismatch between the real (the lived suffering of the patient) and the object of the medical cogito (the medical description or encoding of the condition). Medicine is, however, redeemed in part from being lost in its own misconstruals because it is not merely a system of thought but also a praxis.

Any praxis produces a field of activity in which its practitioners work and its concepts enable one to cognitively locate, interact with, and exploit the objects constituting that field. But discursive features (such as legitimation and power) do not totally define experience in a praxis, and the trauma—the encounter with the real, is particularly relevant to the development of clinical knowledge and our understanding of suffering. The trauma that escapes our encoding and provokes repetition (being drawn back to that which is unassimilated) happens when 'the clinic' cannot find meanings adequate to deal with the encounter. Clinical 'repetition' occurs when practitioners are attuned to suffering but the cognitive tools of medical science do not properly disclose and make comprehensible the nature and causes of that suffering.

Foucault acknowledges that not all sciences are on an equal footing in their vulnerability to 'social forces' and argues that sciences such as theoretical physics and organic chemistry are relatively immune to such influences. Medicine, however, is inherently bio-psycho-social. It provokes the question, 'What makes a science restlessly search for truth and unable to be subjagated to power relations shaping its discourses of validation?'

Medicine is an interesting case: on the one hand it is practical and has palpable results so that the cycle of conceptualization, intervention, monitoring of results, and refinement of theory can be kept in touch with real world events at the 'coal-face.' Stephen Toulmin (invoking Wittgenstein's concept 'form of life') speaks of 'different substantive enterprises that have survived the pragmatic tests to which they were subjected in the evolution of those enterprises' comprising a medical *Lebenswelt* (life-world, after Husserl) (Toulmin 1997, p. 53). The Hippocratic foundations of medicine arise in a praxis that engages with suffering so that its core concern is with something that may prove resistant to theorization and provide a reality check (suffering as the touch or trauma of the real world) on the medical form of life and the meanings and truth it generates.

On the other hand, there is the discursive regime dominating contemporary biomedical science that fosters a biological, reductive, modernist (in terms of *data* and *theory*) and relatively objective (or object-like) conception of human function. It exerts invisible but palpable control of the medical research industry and over many facets of clinical life, including guidelines for best practice which, therefore, tend to track technology rather than a real concern with suffering (so that evidence of efficacy is factored in theory-driven terms). Given the interests converging at the point where medicine meets power, the political process, and economics, there is now a growing voice claiming that medicine itself is more prone than other branches of science to ideological and axiomatic distortion because the focus on evidence can serve as a convenient and effective means by which orthodoxy cements its hold on the profession and thereby on the human population suffering various maladies.

Notice the structure of the argument:

1. Truth is a product of language and the encounter with the real.
2. Language and thought are products of culture (here the culture of the clinic).
3. The encounter with the real may demand more from the clinician than medical language and thought can provide for.
4. It particularly does so where the clinician is attuned to suffering.
5. A Hippocratic praxis is motivated to provide an adequate response to suffering.
6. Doctrinaire medicine may not be able to potentiate such a response.
7. Hippocratic practice is driven to go beyond current clinical orthodoxy and find new truths to be engaged with and given articulate form.

We therefore have an impasse: biomedicine is a culture closely tied to scientific objectivity and biomedical theory (part of an episteme in which the bio-medical industries and health care bureaucracy both figure) and is therefore on a fast-track to a highly technologized and objective view of human function but suffering is inescapably human and situated in the complex milieu where souls are formed and then undergo various trials and tribulations (the basis of our pain and distress). In the face of the currents created by these forces, where can we find our footing and affirm (or even defend) the human face of clinical practice?

Orthodoxy, Trauma, and Repetition

Foucault's challenge to any human praxis (replete with structures of power and governance) and its claims to knowledge disturbs those who believe that medicine should resist ideological fashions and remain true to its calling. Can we, as clinicians, anchor ourselves so as to resist political and ideological currents and their processes of legitimation (in service of power/knowledge)?

Two related features of medicine are highly important here:

1. Medicine is a *techne,* (Aristotle's term for an art informed by technical knowledge and reflection) showing a dynamic interplay between praxis and conceptualization.
2. The art involved is healing—making people whole by addressing the disruption to their being that is suffering.

A pragmatic analysis of knowledge and medical knowledge in particular reveals an integrated structure of categorization, thought, and activity arising in a form of life where we are engaged with some aspect of the world that has its own reality beyond our thoughts about it—in clinical life that is the suffering of the patient. The patient's suffering does not defer to attempts to fit it into any theory and therefore clinical knowledge outstrips purely theoretical enterprises and their kind of truth.

Purely theoretical discourses posit a relation between two independent terms—the world and the system of thought where we know about the world only through the theory (and its system of theoretically informed observations and devices). A *life-world is* different, especially when it aims to take seriously something as complex and multifaceted as human suffering. A suffering patient cannot be forgotten and clinical life with its repeated encounters does not allow a clinician who aspires to be a healer to ignore the patient and take refuge in theory. Clinical medicine is therefore a kind of institutional or vocational neurosis structuring an entire life-world whereby suffering repetitively demands that we attend to it. Any other response is impure, uncaring, or immoral, not in tune with the Hippocratic ethos, so that it compromises the whole proceedings.

Pragmatist approaches therefore direct our attention toward the purposes and interests driving knowledge and implicitly critique the claim that science reveals the world *sub specie aeternitatis*, or without bias by historical and cultural particularities. But they do not undermine the idea that we can discover important things about what is 'out there' (or 'in there,' as the case may be), they merely remind us that any truth is related to certain purposes and reveals those features of the world that we have devised ways of dealing with. This perfectly general point has particular relevance to clinicians who try to understand and make an adequate response to the suffering of patients, in that the cognitive tools they use are constrained by what medicine is good at and has under control as part of its world of (knowledge driven) activities and techniques, the life-world of the medical *techne*.

Truth arises in a life-world (*Lebenswelt*) when you know how to negotiate it by making connections between intersecting (and sometimes irreconcilable) concepts and constructions. Each true thought fits well into some way of thinking or acting and therefore the more widely we cast the net to inform and enhance our system of thinking, the more adequate our knowledge in the face of the contingencies of life. The divergence between a map derived from the experience of the patient and the scientific map constructed by medical discourse is created by just such intersecting cognitive constructions. Many features of suffering are not well charted in terms of bio-medical categories and techniques but that intersection means that the tension between the two might be creative. Scientists confront exactly this creative tension when they encounter a phenomenon that forces them to re-think the way they have structured or imaged reality (as constantly happens in the exciting world of quantum experimentation). Clinical thought is similar, problematic phenomena cause us to rethink our approach so that, for instance, we might need to think about the meaning of an illness event in the whole context of a person's life to understand that person's untreatable suffering.

We have claimed that a clinician with the appropriate attitude towards medical truth is troubled by human suffering especially if medical science finds itself struggling to understand that suffering. Ethical sensitivity of the right kind, we could say, potentiates a *tuche*—a touch or residue in experience that may escape scientific signification—and a properly attuned healer returns again and again to the 'wound in the clinical psyche' left by this 'touch' and his or her inability to respond to the suffering of the patient (all very post-Freudian or Lacanian).

Therefore, in the clinic at least (and perhaps more generally) moral virtue and epistemic virtue are intertwined. It takes a certain kind of person (one with what Frank might call 'an attuned sense of the patient's lived narrative' or an eye for the *somebody* who presents as *somebody* to be diagnosed and treated) to achieve the relevant openness to experience. And it takes not only a certain kind of cognitive skill to conceptualize what is happening but also an ability to 'look awry,' (Žižek 1991) to deconstruct the validated links that are created and legitimated by an area of discourse. Thus, to review where we have got to, clinical praxis involves subjective bodies and their intersecting trajectories, a reality that engages a clinician with patients, and the suffering of the patient can provoke ways of thinking about what is going on that throws up leads that are worth pursuing (Carson 1997) to produce Hippocratic knowledge (a multifaceted set of skills honed in response to suffering despite an imperfect framework of theory at any given point in that enterprise)

Truth, Virtue, and Discovery

Attempts to understand pain, suffering, the stories of patients, and their relation to the knowledge of doctors take us back towards the epistemic and practical values of an age when medicine did not know the causes of health and disease. The term 'epistemic virtue' suggests not only that one should be guided by reason, science, and a clear view of the facts but that knowledge and a kind of good or excellent function are different facets of the same jewel. But is that view naïve given Foucault's critiques of the clinic, bio-medical science, power, the political legitimation of clinical praxis by interested parties and our current evidence about the devious practices creating medical knowledge (Elliot 2004)?

Foucault argues that power and its intricate (socio-politico-epistemic) workings control the legitimation of statements within any given discourse as is clearly seen in contemporary bio-medical discourse where an exalted status is given to a range of theory-driven judgments in accordance with orthodox views of health and disease. Doctors should decide 'what is really going on,' 'the good of the patient,' 'good evidence for this or that,' 'a reasonable therapeutic option,' and so on in a way that obeys certain (evidence based or scientific) canons (sometimes serving interests other than those of the patient). The story of the patient may not be visible in these terms and, even more radically, the patient's opinion as to whether the medical story actually does fit his illness as he experiences it may have no standing whatsoever. But Foucault and the postmodernists teach us we should reveal and deconstruct power imbalances by tracing their motivations, allegiances, and provenance. This implies a moral constraint whereby knowledge liberates practitioners from the epistemic regime put in place by a power group (such as the biomedical industry) so that it no longer obscures lived reality. Such liberation, one might think, could then begin to allow clinical knowledge to be owned equally by the sufferer and the healer (in accordance with the ideal of partnership and therapeutic alliance).

Therefore, the moral commitments of good doctors, including the willingness to share information and power, are inseparable from the ability to grasp the truth of suffering rather than ignoring or sublimating it (within objective theory). Lacan's remark that a science is such because of the purity of the soul of the operator (Lacan 1981, p. 9) is reflected *par excellence* in the close relation between *the good* (the demand that we address suffering with compassion and skill) and *the true* (the actual resonances of suffering) in the clinic (but is not always so apparent in other areas of scientific endeavour).

Hippocrates also thought that medicine is a great example to science in general because it methodically and sensitively charts the accumulated wisdom that comes from engaging with the realities of the human condition. In fact it engages with reality because it is concerned with human suffering and it cannot abandon science and good practice because that is our way of analyzing the fact that we are fearfully and wonderfully made. Truth in medicine reflects the encounter with the real that is (Hippocratic) care for human suffering.

Care is an ethical concept and contemporary medical ethics regards it as something beyond mere provision of orthodox remedies because illness is a 'biocultural' phenomenon (Morris 1998) confronting us with suffering or distress that is, in part, determined by the meanings that inform a person's life. Thus the dynamic encounter between the patient, the doctor, and the real may have to straddle the gap between objective bio-medical knowledge and the clinical heart of medicine.

Mind the Gap

We see the gap between the patient's experience of their illness and its medical 'reality' when patients continue to suffer despite proper biomedical treatment. The gap and the *tuche* or trauma both reflect an inability to understand or articulate the source of the patient's suffering. We can explore this gap by looking at two ways in which experience and its components can be excluded from articulation and therefore understanding: the first extends Lacan's concept of the trauma and the second arises from phenomenology.

The first source of exclusion is approached by pursuing Lacan's *tuche* or trauma (Lacan 1981, p. 129) (that aspect of an encounter with the real world that the conscious self does not adequately cope with). Uncharacterizable malaise may occur precisely because its significance eludes the subject. Lacan observes that any event, whether interpersonal or otherwise, affects us in ways that are signifiable but also in other ways that go beyond those meanings. These latter effects are inarticulate (indeed may not be articulable) but can affect us quite deeply despite that and when they do, emotional work may be required to accommodate them within a livable life story.

The second source of exclusion is best appreciated when we notice that consciousness is selective and focuses on some aspects of or patterns in experience at the expense of others. The patient may focus on certain aspects of their illness as important while other events made no impression, as they do not fit with the story that the patient is shaping and living. This selective consciousness becomes problematic where the patient attributes their illness to a complex network of events that are difficult to relate to the illness at hand. When the patient's explanation for their illness and their biomedical illness are quite different we may need to find the deeper level of the patient's illness that needs to be resolved so as to close the gap and respond adequately to the patient's suffering.

For a physician these two sources of exclusion are seen when aspects of the patient's suffering do not appear in 'the history of the presenting complaint' that details the patient's symptoms When the suffering of the patient is not able to be articulated in a way suited to the 'objective or documentable' discourse of the clinic that is conducted in the terms understood and used in professional care, the clinician may miss something quite important. Katherine Montgomery Hunter notices the special nature of medical knowledge:

> At its source in a medical center, medicine is practiced by means of a series of narrative accounts of illness told in a relatively self-enclosed dialect and according to strict rules that define the genre. (Hunter 1991, p. 8)

> Reinterpreted as a diagnosis, however preliminary, the transformed and medicalized narrative may be alien to the patient; strange, depersonalized, unlived and unlivable, incomprehensible or terrifyingly clear. (Hunter 1991, p. 13)

Foucault relates clinical discourse to the medical gaze that fixes the patient in a biomedical system of concepts and may not reveal what is really causing the patient's suffering (Foucault 1963). If the strict rules of the medical narrative do not account for the patient's continued suffering, they can leave the physician without the ability to explain the illness either professionally to other health care providers or personally to the patient. That inability should provoke the physician to ongoing reflection or perhaps even dissatisfaction with the conceptual tools available in orthodox medicine.

Exclusion by non-signification and selective consciousness underlies three situations commonly encountered by patients when they feel their experiences *ought not be spoken*, or *cannot be spoken* or that they do not have the *words to speak of them*. By selectively focusing on certain events or symptoms over others and creating the illness in an approved clinical form some types of patient suffering cannot be pinpointed. In each of the three situations, the patient is silenced by a disempowering structure of knowledge that makes them incapable of speaking their narrative.

Patient experiences that *ought not to be spoken* show the boundary between patient and physician created by significantly different networks of meaning and legitimation accessed by the patient and the medical system. The patient may realize that their illness experience does not translate into the medical framework and be too embarrassed to explain their experiences in their own 'language.' The embarrassment erects a boundary in the therapeutic relationship, for instance, when the patient is reluctant to tell the doctor that he has used alternative therapy out of fear that he will be alienated from the mainstay of his medical care. The embarrassment, intolerance, or discomfort that may be felt by the doctor when the alternative treatment is mentioned is usually readily apparent to the patient and signals the discursive boundary. But in addition to things of which the patient could speak if he did not sense that a transgression is involved there are things which cannot be spoken.

Patient experiences that *cannot be spoken* arise from aspects of the self about which a person does not know how to talk. For instance, the patient may be troubled by suffering which he or she cannot put into words in any adequate way. 'I don't know, I just don't feel like doing anything, what's the point?' might indicate an ongoing no-win situation experienced by someone unable to cope with their complex bio-psycho-social problem. It may reflect the lack of any realistic opportunities to 'get a life,' and chronic physical malaise perhaps due to poor nutrition or fatigue. This may well appear in the case record as 'depression' (P_X Prozac, Amitryptiline) or 'does not want to go to work' both texts that obscure rather than illuminate the real suffering of the patient. The discourse of medicine contributes to this kind of silence when it does not legitimate accounts of illness that may be so real to the patient that it is debilitating. The *ennui* and strength-sapping drain of a chronic problem such as cervicogenic pain may make every little achievement in the day a major battle against the reluctance of mind and body. This struggle is not evident in the phrase 'axial pain'—with a very low weighting on most [New Zealand] ranking systems for elective spinal surgery. In fact, surgery may not be the right response to the problem but such measures convey a lot about the importance of suffering of this kind in medical thinking.

Patients who find that there are *no words to speak* in relation to some of the things afflicting them may arise because those things are not captured by any of the discourses framing their experience of illness. When a patient cannot find, words that signify their experience in a way that captures the meaning of their illness, the resulting cognitive and emotional paralysis can also be profoundly debilitating and alienating. This situation becomes particularly apparent when a patient needs to come back for treatment of multitudinous minor complaints arising because they do not understand their illness. The medical system, seeking biomedical indices of the suffering may be quite unable to provide the understanding needed to address the problem. The suffering of a patient that has *no words to speak about it* may be difficult to identify but, again, show itself in the silences during a clinical interview. The physician then needs to step outside the biomedical framework and search for alternative discourses that enable the patient to articulate their suffering (and by naming it begin to deal with it). The patient may, for instance, feel that they have committed some deep and dark spiritual offence and long to speak about it to some trusted person unconnected with the structure of condemnation that would otherwise be involved and a doctor may be able to bring a perspective to bear which is less fraught.

A patient's continued suffering despite 'competent medical treatment' may reveal a gap arising from an ongoing trauma that is invisible, therefore incomprehensible and untreatable. The clinician may be profoundly dissatisfied by the tools and discourses available within accepted medical understandings of disease when that happens. The conceptual tools of biomedicine then need to be transformed by partnership so that together the clinician and the patient can explore the (unsignified) suffering by searching the patient's phenomenal world for what is of significance there and a wise doctor asks the patient for help in exploring that world so as to try and understand what is happening in ways that the techniques of care can engage with.

Pain

The complexities of signification and integration of lived experiences into a person's Imago can be seen in the human experience of pain (Gillett 1991). Pain resists signification and integration into a lived experience because it is organismic and biological and its reality transcends language and symbolization; it occurs on the level of bodily experience which language encounters, attempts to express, and then fails to encompass leaving a residual need that demands attention (Kleinman 1994, p. 178). Through complex socio-somatic and unconscious processes, bodily events and external stimuli inscribe the person's history and social relations onto their body in ways that may be largely unknown to the person him or herself, so that the personal meaning of the pain cannot be reduced to biological terminology. This personal meaning of pain is developed through symbolic processes, mapping the body and the self onto a world of stories, of heroism, resilience, illness, and death. The complex connection between personal experience and its articulation and the importance for an individual of the way that others respond to their pain by themselves invoking certain stories and images mean that the experience of pain is not only personal but it is made and remade in ways that resist any simple definition.

These difficulties in perception and integration of pain into a lived experience lead a person to a variety of possible significations for the same event each of which affects the suffering of the individual in a distinctive way as can be seen in cases where the perceived meaning of pain influences the amount of medication required to control it. For instance, if the pain is believed to be due to an acute problem that will pass and leave no permanent damage, there is much less pain relief required as compared to when it is attributed to malignant disease that is killing the person. Even experiences of severe pain can be considered uplifting in certain circumstances as in some childbirths, whereas for others, in different circumstances, apparently minor troubles can be experienced as severely distressing (Danzer et al. 2002). Ultimately, if the suffering is beyond the person's ability to comprehend, the result can be uncharacterizable and unrelenting malaise or disability and the highly personal story that is woven around the pain can mean that two individuals with the 'same pathology' may develop vastly different disabilities. Thus the whole person needs to be addressed if we want to comprehend an individual's pain and suffering (Kleinman 1994, p. 183).

Pain and Suffering—Distinct

Understanding the process of signification through the Lacanian concept of the touch of the real and the self-understanding (or *Imago*) of the patient leads us towards addressing the patient's unresolved suffering and allowing us to engage in the healing process. The *Imago* is a notional image of oneself distilled from the reactions of others and crafted in certain ways to meet their expectations in order present oneself as someone who fits a recognizable mode of being-in-the-world-with-others. A person enters into a cyclical process of signification and integration directed by the *Imago* and in-forming it. The *Imago* is then a point from which the person views events, guiding him or her to focus on aspects of the world and ultimately determining how they should be signified and accommodated into one's story (of life and illness). The relationship between *Imago*, integration and signification therefore provides the framework for understanding a patient's suffering and the gap that exists between recognized or realistic sources of pain and the actual suffering of the patient.

That pain and suffering are distinct is evident in the gap between a cause of pain and its integration into the person's story as an experience of suffering. That the two are related but quite distinct is evident when pain does not necessarily cause suffering and suffering occurs without pain. Pain without suffering can be seen when somebody decides to be staunch during a dental procedure or the care of a wound and suffering that is not pain is seen in the suffering of the loved ones of a patient who, although not experiencing physical pain, may well be suffering. Therefore, a patient's suffering can, on occasion, be relieved without biomedical relief of pain through understanding its source, showing that it can be controlled (especially by the patient), and tracing the reasons why it will come to an end. Pain causes the most suffering when it is severe, uncontrolled, and unknown and discovering the meaning of pain to the patient can transform the related suffering because the recognition of one's pain by another is a hugely reassuring step towards the resolution of the problem causing it (Cassell 2004, p. 126). Thus the relationship between pain and suffering is not static or merely biological but dynamic and in part psychological. This gap between pain and suffering then provides a window into the processes of signification and integration and takes us one step closer to being able to engage with the patient's unsignified suffering when it occurs.

A further hurdle to resolving the patient's unsignified suffering is the medical framework's unstated but influential hangover from the Cartesian mind-body dichotomy. This dichotomy portrays certain varieties of suffering as not truly 'real,' a judgment that often leaves patients alienated from those caring for them because they both depersonalize the sick patient and disconnect the patient's distress and the medical case history. We need to see the person as a living embodied subject who has a story with its own integrity (or lack thereof) and who functions holistically as the subject of the narrative rather than as an object. Medicine can, however, signify holistic functions through new approaches such as psycho-neuro-immunology which, although firmly rooted in biomedicine, can encompass more of the person (Ader et al. 1995).

Suffering and Whole Persons

The whole person, who makes sense of their experience and lives their life story, is impinged upon and suffers in a way that draws our attention to the complexity of his or her life. We are all complex in that way; our lives are played out in terms of relationships (locating us in a culture and society), a series of roles, instrumental dimensions, associations, body habitus, political being, secret life, perceived future, and transcendental or spiritual being (Cassell 1999, p. 148). These various aspects of being are present in every person, woven together, interpenetrating each other, present *in continua*, and changing subtly or dramatically over time so as responsively to shape the person's lived experience. The complex quasi-stable balance that is achieved suffers when pain signals some threat or injury. Until the threat is understood, the signal then continues so that the person, like any other flesh and blood critter, is reminded, indeed compelled, to respond to it.

Signification and integration of experiences underpin a person's knowledge of themselves, the world and their relationship to that world—their *Imago*. This *Imago* then guides and signifies further experiences, gradually becoming more and more stable while being integrated into the person (Gillett 2008, p. 250). In this way, encounters with the 'real' and their integration into a person's life story and self conception contribute to the understanding through which a person can cope with suffering. The *Imago* and its characteristics, shaped by the life skills of the person, lie at the heart of the story so that it modifies symptoms by attributing significance to this or that feature of them, and a patient may have great trouble describing aspects of their suffering that, in fact, are deeply disturbing. Therefore, a clinician may have to be sensitively attuned and open a space to be spoken into from (and of) the person's whole being (Gillett 2004, p. 93).

The Meaning of Suffering

Personal meanings of an event are created by integrating it into a person's *Imago* through the use of social and historical narratives. Thus, the personal meaning of an illness, pain, or suffering, is more than a cognitive understanding of what is happening and reflects the affective meaning, bodily meaning, and spiritual meanings of an experience, aspects that may be in deep conflict at different levels. In fact many levels of significance are incorporated into a person's multifaceted orientations, reactions, and responses towards any event. The word 'chemotherapy', for instance, could elicit a cognitive understanding of the drug's mechanism of action, the emotion of fear, the body sensation of nausea and the spiritual feeling of transcendence or imminent mortality all jumbled together (Cassell 2004, p. 74).

Personal meaning frames the perception of events and the significance of any future loss as in the example of the patient whose suffering reduces significantly as the meaning of their pain becomes distanced from the thought of malignancy (Cassell 2004, p. 80). In cancer, for example, the patient's initial experience of pain is tied to the unknown but feared significance of the pain; it could mean anything from impending death to disability and the patient may think that it will never end but instead worsen inexorably toward death. As the possible meanings are delineated and discussed, the patient may become able to help devise strategies for dealing with the pain, recognizing it for what it is, and planning for their future. This process may not be best served by attacking the 'physical pain' with drugs but by a conversation (no matter how irrelevant some aspects of it may seem to be) that engages with the real meaning of the pain and explores its place in the patient's life story (thereby linking the subject to the truth, as in Foucault's conception of the real task of ethics). Health care professionals that are not receptive and informative companions on the journey of illness with the patient, but are instead fixated on their own understanding of a problem, often make the patient feel abandoned and alienated (because the way they see their own problem is not valid) and so contribute to the patient's suffering.

Any experience happens against a background of suffering for the person with two complementary and intertwined aspects, the patient's personal phenomenology as part of their life story and the socially recognized significance of what is happening. Chest pain for instance, may be fleeting and easily set aside or, if it is taken to signify heart disease, it may refuse to be ignored. The example is instantly understandable because life and death have universal significance, but other aspects of the pain depend closely on individual values and beliefs and the stories current in the *Lebenswelt* (life-world) of the patient. In this way the illness experience is interpreted and 'inscribes' the body as, in Foucault's terms, it is 'traced by language and dissolved by ideas.' The body, in the medical encounter may be 'a volume in perpetual disintegration' because of the multiple alienations separating the patient as a person from what is going on in it (Foucault 1984, p. 83). The *Imago,* as a reflection of the self as experienced (within society), is the locus of suffering based on the ordeals undergone by the body, and is both the frame from which the individual learns to see the world and the conveyor of values relating the person, their suffering, and their socio-cultural situation (a locus of *relations of power*), through the illness journey and its narrative.

The Social Nature of Suffering and a Trouble Shared

Experiences of pain and suffering are fundamentally inter-subjective resonating beyond the patient and affecting all who care for them, including. family, friends, coworkers, and clinical caregivers and these people in turn shape the experiential world of the sufferer. These other subjects bear witness to what is happening, offer personal and family support in the face of illness, and provide a framework of meaning for the patient's suffering (Kleinman 1994, p. 20). In this way we see the importance of a conversation which 'holds' the patient in personhood preserving them in the midst of their suffering and which, if lost, leaves a person socially isolated from their place of belonging (Nelson 2003). Such holding creates for the patient a circle of signification and transcendence of suffering that fosters the patient's healing in their illness (or wholeness as a person).

The social nature of suffering suggests that a social process is required for healing that can be obstructed or marginalized if the patient's story is colonized by their medical narrative so that they cannot find their voice and tell their story. Medicine's dominant narrative is that of the sick-role, a role that prescribes behavior the sick person expects from others and what they expect from him. The model sick role story includes restoration through medical intervention, the expectation that, with a series of (bio-medical) corrections, the person will be restored again to what they were (Frank 1995, p. 23). The sick-role, disease and illness intrude into the norms of social exchange and suspend any demands on the individual as part of properly functioning society. They also inscribe the body with stigmata associated with the role of the infirm (being wan or tired, not pursuing normal activities, and so on) (Kleinman 1994, p. 17). We see, in the sick role, *relations of power* at work that both affect the person's perspective of themselves and that shift the responsibility of restoration out of the hands of the patient and into the hands of the clinician in a way that can alienate the patient from the psycho-social process that healing (the recovery of wholeness) requires.

The process of narrative colonization is clearly seen when, despite the medical system taking over responsibility for the patient's restoration, that is not possible. The close link between the right of medicine to take control and the expected restoration narrative mean that, when a story of that kind becomes unsustainable, the patient him or herself is an affront to the order of things. The patient then becomes abject; there is no longer a place for them in the medical system yet the medical system, having delivered its verdict, retains responsibility, excluding the patient from being able to talk about their experiences in any way that rejects or subverts the medical narrative and restores the ownership of their life journey. Loss of one's voice as a contributor to the social fabric and the negotiated control of one's own life activity (or even the fear of that occurring) is a disempowering experience that itself adds to the suffering of many patients.

The expectation of recovery is tied to the modernist thought that for every suffering there is a remedy. Massive resources are expended to support the restoration motif which justifies the patient's story being colonized by the dominant medical narrative; who, after all, would not want to get better? (Frank 1995, p. 57) But suffering is intensified when the patient becomes abject and therefore fit only to be cast off. As abject, one is unable to be spoken about not only in the terms used by the doctors but, because of the dominance of medical discourse, also within one's own circle and even, at the extreme, useless to oneself, an inconvenience in the scheme of life accepted by 'right-thinking people (Frank 1995, p. 81).' The danger in dominant narratives of restoration is therefore that the very basis on which we justify our veneration of medicine and biomedical science, can leave a person who is unable to become 'good as new,' without a place in-the-world-with-others and also alienated from their illness. These alienations paralyze a person in the face of a petrifying contingency (hence the basilisk-like medical gaze) that robs one of one's life spirit on the face of an intimation of mortality (Gillett 2004, p. 127).

Medicine, Transcendence, and Stories of Suffering

Orthodox medicine has followed the Hippocratic model gaining knowledge from cumulative experience of the cases arising in clinical practice. We have then taken that relatively unstructured mass of clinical data and transformed it by developing systematic theories and modes of representation and explanation that feed into them. However, the intrinsic power of academic and institutional medicine has made the resulting knowledge theory-bound and paradigm-dominated, reinforcing its tendency to occupy the epistemic high ground and to appeal to its own demonstrated efficacy within the healing ethos. At this point, the idea of transcendence (in a philosophical rather than spooky sense) helps us to relate clinical knowledge to the suffering of the patient.

A patient lives the 'reality' of their illness, and tries to make meaning of the illness story, a meaning that can lead in either of two directions because the person can either be submerged by or transcend the losses and pain of their illness. Thus two kinds of transcendence are in play:

1. the fact that the illness transcends both the patient's experience of it and the clinical codification of it;
2. the fact that the patient him/her-self is more than the illness experience and brings resources from outside that narrow reality to try and deal with it.

When fear dominates, the illness story and the associated suffering threaten to submerge the patient and leave the medical care-givers in control, a process that alienates the patient from their illness. But if we find a way of integrating the encounter into the patient's life in a different way, transcendence, and with it a very different result in terms of healing, can be achieved. The story can be infused by hope springing from a recognition of the patient as a person and the journey s/he is on in a way that allows the patient to transcend the illness and achieve a new perspective on health, healing, and him/herself. This new perspective lifts the patient out from underneath the illness in a way that carries a hope of transcending the pain and suffering and resuming life as the person s/he actually is. The storytelling and the cloud of witnesses are crucial in this reframing. When it occurs, the illness narrative is subsumed within rather than dominating the real story of the patient and becomes itself part of the healing process.

Transcendence has many senses relevant to reflection on the human condition in general and illness in particular. First there is the fact that life, reality, the person and their suffering all transcend any story we can tell about them—the patient's story or the medical story—and, particularly when they do not fit into the stories we tell, they draw us insistently back to think again (through repeated encounters with the real). Second, there is the fact that the experience of the patient transcends the medical story in ways that incline towards being held in personhood. Third, there is the ability to lift oneself out from underneath one's suffering by encompassing or comprehending it and rendering it meaningful within the story of one's life. This last transcendence, as we have noted, is a necessary prelude to the restoring of a person to wholeness after an injury to their personhood (the reframing and re-integrating of life). It is also a subjective, personal process dependent on a person's context, narrative and sense of being, and each person reaches it in their own way by using different resources. For some, transcendence is the capacity to step outside the feeling of pain and to place that experience within a larger landscape of meaning and purpose (Pullman 2002). Others are able to enlarge, grow or redirect their inner force from one manifestation of their personhood to another; the pain does not destroy the person because the pain itself becomes a meaningful part of that person, a cross they have to bear on their journey and a reminder of the ordeal they are enduring (Cassell 2004, p. 192). In many cases, the sufferer is made whole by telling their own story and having it recognized by people who matter to them, which may include their doctors or nurses (Frank 1995, p. 132; Pullman 2002). The person whose story is heard and understood in this way can begin to be healed and to transcend their suffering through that witness. Transcendence transforms the experience of suffering into a meaningful passage as part of a story of being-with-others.

The converse is that wholeness is not always possible because the person has no adequate way of confronting the suffering and what it means. Two stories illustrate these often interwoven features of suffering.

1. *Anthea's case—the refractory spinal pain*
   Anthea was only 42 but already she had undergone a series of difficult and relatively unsuccessful operations to remove a prolapsed disc from her mid-thoracic spine. The disc was large, calcified and in part buried in the substance of the spinal cord, and removing it had caused some damage to the cord. In the background was lurking a tentative diagnosis of Multiple Sclerosis (MS) which could not be proven or disproven and may have been based on the presenting manifestations of the prolapsed mid-thoracic disc. A succession of increasingly debilitating drug regimes were tried and they proved inadequate to control her pain. Eventually Anthea decided that she herself would make some alterations to her regimen according to how she felt. In her next clinic appointment she reported that her pain was still there but that she was finding it much more bearable on a lower dose of medication than previously. She had also been told about the very real possibility that she did not have MS.

Anthea was affirmed in taking control of her pain and either that or the fact that a persistent worry about it was shifted slightly in a reassuring direction made her able to cope with it. She made it part of her life that she could think about and address as a problem rather than just be threatened by, in fear of, and alienated from so that it submerged her.

2. *Brian's case*
   Brian had a nagging pain in his side. He lived near a doctor and kept popping in for a prescription of pain relief, telling his (doctor) neighbor that it was just a tummy ache and he didn't want to bother his own doctor. Eventually his neighbor said that Brian must go to his own doctor so the problem could be investigated and dealt with in a regular and clinically sound way. His pain was diagnosed as pain from a stretched liver capsule because of metastases in the liver from an undetected pancreatic carcinoma. As his condition progressed, Brian's liver pain became uncontrollable and his need for pain relief escalated. He desperately sought more and more unconventional means to control his disease, culminating in the use of 'blessed handkerchiefs' that he had flown to him from a faith healer he had made contact with online. He wore the handkerchiefs around his neck until the day he died, in severe pain and deep yellow from the jaundice that he had begun to show when the cancer obstructed his hepatic pedicle.

Brian never came to any reconciliation with his own mortality and sought, until he died, desperately to escape the disease that assailed him. He died deeply distressed and wracked with pain. Clearly his caregivers could not find any way to enable him to transcend his suffering and find wholeness as a person as he approached his death.

In each of these cases we enter a domain in which the patient as a subjective body encounters the real and is not only touched, but both threatened and damaged in the fabric of their being by it. We find that we are drawn beyond the comfort of the framework of theory and observation created by scientific biomedical culture and realize that there are more things in heaven and earth than are conceptualized in our (biomedical) philosophy. We are then led to try and understand what it is that life has brought us into contact with. The clinician recognizes that s/he is 'in touch' with something real and cannot easily turn away from that touch, but is more usually drawn into a creative pursuit of what eludes clinical knowledge and has to find a path to truth in the face of the trauma that is human suffering.

Responding to Suffering—Regenerative Autonomy

Understanding a patient's encounter with the 'real' experience of their illness helps us to understand that suffering disrupts a person's autonomy, agency and their ability to imagine a livable future, all of which are essential for a person's ability to enact their lived story. With adequate personal and social support a person can transcend suffering in a creative way so as to find a meaningful response to their illness. Ethics sometimes does not serve patients well in the midst of suffering because an over-emphasis on autonomy (particularly constructed as legalistic non-interference) can leave patients alone without the resources to face difficult medical crises and without the ability to regain a sustainable way of living in the world with others. Where that happens, suffering can disrupt a patient's entire sense of personhood in such a way that, without acknowledgment and support, may lead to shame, disability, and depression (Halpern 2001, p. 36). A concept of regenerative autonomy (perhaps achieved in part by transcending one's suffering) acknowledges that when a patient's sense of personhood is disrupted through suffering and trauma they need support, recognition, and a witness to their story as they try to rebuild their wholeness.

Medical decisions require that patients choose between treatment options that may seriously affect their capacity for future functioning in the world. Wrong choices may leave them at the mercy of an illness of which their understanding is patchy and may even be mistaken in important ways. Many medical decisions require balancing of significant tradeoffs such as the risk of death, living with dysfunction, living with pain, and debilitating side effects (Halpern 2001, p. 42). Decisions of this sort involve choosing among different possible futures while in unfamiliar cognitive territory and under the duress of suffering. In making practical choices that will seriously affect the kind of life s/he will have, a patient must be helped to enact his/her conception of a worthwhile life but must also be given the assurance that comes from understanding the nature and course of their suffering (Halpern 2001, p. 58). The suffering patient's sense of personhood is often seriously impaired and with it their ability to conceive of their future and act in ways they would normally do. Autonomy as noninterference can therefore be a kind of abandonment, leaving the patient to make decisions that will have implications for the rest of their lives from a position where they have not yet been helped to integrate the trauma of the experience that they are suffering. Unrelieved suffering impairs the patient's ability to deliberate in a way that could confer value on any decisions s/he makes and re-integrate aspects of life that seem to be degenerating or fragmenting.

Autonomy as noninterference pays insufficient attention to the creation of autonomy (by developing agency and identity) through recognition and communication, starting in early infancy (Halpern 2001, p. 77). By contrast, the right kind of response to suffering recognizes a person and empowers them as part of an interpersonal process. In much the same way as parents, through nonverbal and verbal communication, help their children develop into full human beings (subjective agents who are somebody). By responding to their faltering initiatives so that they learn to find their way about in the world, health care professionals should realize that patients are finding their way in the land of *Clinicum* (Gillett 2004). Respect for autonomy as noninterference does not recognize these needs of suffering patients as they try to rebuild their autonomy (in a life world that is not their own) and therefore it does not empower them to do so.

If the patient is alienated from and not able to make meaning of their suffering, the doctor ends up doubly out of touch: out of touch with the patient who is out of touch with the suffering that is central in their illness. As the locus of the patient's suffering is not the body as a biological entity, but the person as an existential being facing a loss of meaning and purpose, (Cassell 2004, p. 14) the patient (the one who suffers) must be encountered and recognized before there can be any recovery of meaning and value sufficient to the significant decisions that have to be made and the significant passages that have to be traversed. As the doctor registers the reality of the patient's suffering and does not eclipse it (by imposing the medical gaze), he or she may have sleepless nights but, at least, they will not be because of an encounter with the elusive unknown of unexpressed or uncontrollable suffering that makes it impossible for the patient to achieve the wholeness they need. When a patient is encountered in the midst of the suffering, because the suffering itself is in the midst of the clinical encounter and not marginalized from it, the result can be quite different. A problem that is confronted by patient and doctor working in partnership can be faced for what it is, and medicine can come to terms with its own shortfalls in a way that leads towards the truth. That is why ethics links, in a certain way, subjects to the truth (as Foucault claims) even where the truth is full of pain and ordeals that have to be undergone. Through making that link, clinicians become ethically responsive to suffering and the patient's story can take a form that is able to be affirmed and lived in (by both patient and doctor).

Bibliography

Ader, R., N. Cohen, and D. Felton. 1995. Psychoneuroimmunology: Interactions between the nervous system and the immune system. *The Lancet* 345:99–103.

Carson, Ronald A. 1997. Medical ethics as reflective practice. In *Philosophy of medicine and bioethics,* eds. Ronald A. Carson and Chester Burns. Boston: Kluwer.

Cassell, E. J. 1999. Diagnosing suffering: A perspective. *Annals of Internal Medicine* 131:531–534.
Cassell, E. J. 2004. *The nature of suffering and the goals of medicine,* 2nd edn. Oxford: Oxford University Press.
Danzer, G., M. Rose, M. Walter, and B. F. Klapp. 2002. On the theory of individual health. *Journal of Medical Ethics* 28:17–19.
Elliot, C. 2004. Pharma goes to the laundry: Public relations and the business of medical education. *Hastings Center Report* 34:18–23.
Foucault, Michel. 1963. *The birth of the clinic: An archaeology of medical perception.* London: Routledge.
Foucault, Michel. 1984. *The Foucault reader*, ed. Paul Rabinow. New York: Pantheon Books.
Foucault, Michel. 1994. *The birth of the clinic: An archaeology of medical perception.* New York: Vintage.
Frank, A. W. 1995. *The wounded storyteller: Body, illness, and ethics*. Chicago: University of Chicago Press.
Gillett, Grant. 1991. The neurophilosophy of pain. *Philosophy* 66:191–206.
Gillett, Grant. 2004. *Bioethics in the clinic.* Baltimore: Johns Hopkins University Press.
Gillett, Grant. 2006. Medical science, culture and truth. *Philosophy, Humanities and Ethics in Medicine* 1:1–11.
Gillett, Grant. 2008. *Subjectivity and being somebody: Human identity and neuroethics.* Exeter: Imprint Academic.
Halpern, J. 2001. *From detached concern to empathy: Humanizing medical practice*. Oxford: Oxford University Press.
Hunter, K. Montgomery. 1991. *Doctors' stories*. Princeton: Princeton University Press.
Kleinman, A. 1994. Pain and resistance: The delegitimation and relegitimation of local worlds. In *Pain as human experience: An anthropological perspective,* eds. P. E. Brodwin and B. J. Good. Berkeley: University of California Press.
Lacan, Jacques. 1981. *The Four Fundamental Concepts of Psycho-analysis*. Trans. A. Sheridan. London: Penguin.
Morris, D. 1998. *Illness and culture*. Berkeley: University of California Press.
Nelson, H. Lindemann. 2003. Holding someone in personhood. *APA Newsletter* 3:92–94.
Pullman, Daryl. 2002. Human dignity and the ethics and aesthetics of pain and suffering. *Theoretical Medicine* 23:75–94.
Toulmin, Stephen. 1997. The primacy of practice: Medicine and post-modernism. In *Philosophy of medicine and bioethics*, eds. R. Carson and C. Burns. Dordrecht: Kluwer.
Žižek, Slavoj. 1991. *Looking awry.* Cambridge: MIT Press.

Chapter 23
The Selfsame Well: Human Suffering in Grief and Bereavement

Elizabeth A. Lobb

> *Your joy is your sorrow unmasked/And the self same well from which your laughter arises was oftentimes filled with your tears.*
>
> *Kahlil Gibran, The Prophet*

The death of a loved one or a significant person in one's life can be a painful event. The grief that can follow is a normal reaction to loss and represents a complex set of cognitive, emotional and social difficulties. Individuals vary enormously in the type of grief they experience, its intensity, its duration and their way of expressing it (Christ et al. 2003).

Is It Necessary for Everyone to Grieve?

The grief work perspective, based on Freudian theory, (Freud 1961) has dominated thinking about bereavement and grief for a number of years and states that it is necessary to bring the reality of the death into awareness to avoid complications in the course of grief (Stroebe 2001). Some theorists and researchers have suggested that the absence of empirical evidence in support of the grief work perspective has led to questioning of its effectiveness (Stroebe 2001; Stroebe et al. 2001a). For example, a study in 1989 found no empirical support for the five dominant ideas around grief work in the professional and lay literature at that time such as; (i) distress or depression is inevitable; (ii) distress is necessary, and failure to experience distress is indicative of pathology; (iii) the importance of working through loss; (iv) the expectation of recovery and (v) reaching a state of resolution (Wortman 1989).

Not only does current research suggest that there is little evidence that 'working through grief is a more effective process of coming to terms with loss than not working through it' (Stroebe and Stroebe 1991, p. 885) some studies argue further

E. A. Lobb (✉)
Palliative Care, Calvary Health Care Centre Sydney, Kogarah 2217, NSW, Australia
e-mail: Liz.Lobb@sesiahs.health.nsw.gov.au

J. Malpas, N. Lickiss (eds.), *Perspectives on Human Suffering*,
DOI 10.1007/978-94-007-2795-3_23,

that forcing individuals to focus on their grief may actually cause harm (Jordan and Neimeyer 2003). However, methodological issues in study designs make it difficult to conclude definitively that grief work is ineffective, and the assumption that the expression of distress and the experience of suffering is a critical aspect of adjustment following bereavement requires further research.

Whereas the traditional grief work perspective has emphasized the necessity of breaking the attachment bond with the deceased loved one, more recently, researchers have highlighted the important role played by maintaining a continued sense of attachment with the deceased (Klass et al. 1996; Stroebe 2001). They conclude that maintaining continuing psychological and emotional bonds with the deceased is not necessarily an indication of problematic grieving (Stroebe 2001; Stroebe et al. 2001a).

Hence, the wide range of grief patterns demonstrated in studies point to a need to re-evaluate common notions about what constitutes a normal response to a major loss (Wortman and Silver 2001). Views about normal grieving are not only prevalent among researchers and health providers, but are also held by the bereaved themselves and those around them. A lack of awareness can mean that they are unaware of the striking variability in response to loss, potential supporters are critical or judgmental of bereaved individuals who show too little or too much grief. Also the bereaved themselves may become concerned that their reaction to the loss is 'abnormal' and this may add to their distress.

What is clear is that individuals vary in the way they experience grief and suffering following the death of a significant other. Grief is a multidimensional concept with physical, behavioral and meaning/spiritual components and is characterized by a complex set of cognitive, emotional and social adjustments that follow the death of a loved one. Although individuals vary in the type of grief they experience, the intensity of their grief, its duration and the ways in which they express their grief, most grieving people show similar patterns of intense distress, anxiety, yearning, sadness and pre-occupation and find these symptoms gradually settle over time (Shear and Shair 2005).

A key factor in grief is that the individual brings their personal meaning to their experience of suffering. How grief is experienced can be influenced by a person's age, their stage of development, their gender, a previous history of loss and/or trauma, a history of a major depressive order, and the type of loss they have experienced, (whether it was anticipated, violent or traumatic). In addition, cultural norms and spiritual, religious and philosophical convictions need to be considered and addressed (Raphael 1983).

The nature of the death, whether it was anticipated or sudden can influence the grieving process. Typically, violent death is characterized by one of three unnatural modes of dying: suicide, homicide, or accident (Rynearson and McCready 1993). There is consensus that the death of a loved one by violent death is associated with poor recovery for many bereaved individuals. From a trauma perspective, losses from violent deaths are likely to promote reactions resembling post-traumatic stress disorder (PTSD). Some researchers suggest that psychological trauma involves a violation of basic assumptive worldviews connected with the individual's survival and that of the social group. Deaths by suicide, homicide, or accident are commonly conceptualized as a traumatic event that can lead to PTSD (Parkes 1998), thereby causing profound suffering, complications in grieving and difficulties with meaning-making (Rando 1992, 1996; Stroebe et al. 2001b; Neimeyer et al. 2002).

Violent, unexpected death can raise particularly painful questions such as 'why', and deaths that are perceived as preventable are seen as a risk factor for bereavement outcomes. It appears that this inability to make sense of the event or draw any meaning is a key factor in understanding the level of suffering the individual experiences.

'Meaning-making' or meaning reconstruction emphasizes responses to bereavement from the perspective of an individual striving 'to make sense of troubling events and which is often expressed in the organization of experiences into narrative form' (Rando 1996, p. 499). Meaning is sometimes framed in terms of the individual's interpretation, beliefs and self-statements. Individual consciousness 'represents one site for construction of meaning, which also resides and arises in language, cultural practices, spiritual traditions, and inter-personal conversations, all of which interact to shape the meaning of mourning for a given individual or group' (Neimeyer et al. 2002, p. 248).

Individuals are more often the best barometer of their grief. It is of no co-incidence that many people will come for bereavement counseling around 7 weeks after the death. Often by this time the flowers and cards have stopped arriving, cooked meals are no longer delivered to the door, people are expected to return to work or other activities and they are aware of the pressure from society to move on. However, the suffering and pain at this time is often more acute as the numbing effect from the endorphins in tears begins to wear off and the intense pain and suffering of separation can arise.

Is It Possible to Grieve too Much?

The majority of the population appears to cope effectively with bereavement-related distress and most people do not experience adverse bereavement-related health effects (Freud 1961; Stroebe 2001). However, more recently it has been suggested that prolonged grief does bring adverse health effects. In a recent review, the difference between normal grief and complicated grief (more recently defined as prolonged grief disorder) (Prigerson et al. 2009) has been described (Shear and Shair 2005).

Normal grief has been defined as the state that occurs when people 'are deeply saddened by the death of an attachment figure during a period of weeks or months of acute grief' (Shear and Shair 2005, p. 253). However, the person who typifies normal grief experiences 'an intense yearning, intrusive thoughts and images, and/or a range of dysphoric emotions' and these symptoms do not persist. The initial reaction subsides, interest but engagement in daily activities is renewed and the loss is integrated into the bereaved person's on-going life. 'As this integration occurs the suffering lessens and thoughts of the loved one cease to dominate the mind of the bereaved'.

However, for a minority of people, a normal grief adjustment does not occur. It is estimated that between 10 and 20% of people find coping painful and difficult

(Byrne and Raphael 1994; Prigerson and Jacobs 2001b; Middleton et al. 1996). It is proposed that for this small percentage of people, integration of the loss does not occur and acute grief is prolonged in the form of complicated grief (Kristjanson et al. 2006). The diagnostic term for 'complications that arise from grief' has been variably defined over the past 20 years, with a multitude of adjectives used to describe variations from normal grief. These adjectives include absent, abnormal, complicated, distorted, morbid, maladaptive, atypical, intensified and prolonged, unresolved, neurotic, dysfunctional, chronic, delayed, and inhibited (Prigerson and Jacobs 2001a).

Leading authors in the area of complicated grief suggest that symptoms of complicated grief fall into two categories: (a) symptoms of separation distress, such as longing and searching for the deceased, loneliness, preoccupation with thoughts of the deceased and (b) symptoms of traumatic distress, such as feelings of disbelief, mistrust, anger, shock, detachment from others, and experiencing somatic symptoms of the deceased (Prigerson and Jacobs 2001a). People who suffer from complicated grief experience a sense of 'persistent and disturbing disbelief regarding the death.' They typically experience feelings of anger, bitterness, and resistance to accepting the painful reality of the death for at least six months after the death to the point of functional impairment. Intense yearning and longing for the deceased continue, along with frequent pangs of intense, painful emotions. 'Thoughts of the loved one remain preoccupying often including distressing intrusive thoughts related to the death, and there is avoidance of a range of situations and activities that serve as a reminder of the painful loss. Interest and engagement in ongoing life is limited or absent' (Shear and Shair 2005, p. 253).

Historically, researchers have argued that complicated grief is an expression of a major depressive disorder or an anxiety-based disorder that has been triggered by the death (Brent et al. 1993; Kim and Jacobs 1991). More recently, researchers have concluded that grief symptoms only partially overlap with symptoms of depression and other Diagnostic and Statistical Manual (DSM) categories such as anxiety and post-traumatic stress disorder. Further, that although there may be some expected shared variance, complicated grief reactions do display sufficient unique variance to warrant separate consideration (Prigerson et al. 1995a, 1996; Boelen and van den Bout 2005). The distinction between complicated grief and bereavement-related depression or anxiety is made even more difficult by the tendency for the three syndromes to occur simultaneously. It is argued that depressed mood, psychomotor retardation, and damaged self-esteem are all depressive symptoms whereas symptoms of yearning, disbelief about the death, difficulty moving on/a sense of feeling stuck, feeling detached and bitter and agitated about the death are all specific indicators of complicated grief (Prigerson et al. 1995, 1996) .

Diagnosis of Complicated Grief

As a result of on-going research into this area a number of instruments have been developed and tested in an effort to measure grief responses and identify those who may be at risk for a more complicated grief response. Complicated grief can be reliably identified by using the Inventory of Complicated Grief (ICG) (Prigerson et al. 1995). It is indicated by a score >30 on the ICG at least six months after the death (Prigerson et al. 1995). There have also been moves to include complicated grief into the DSM-V (Prigerson et al. 2009; Lichtenthal et al. 2004). The DSM is a non-theoretical categorization system with an emphasis on phenomenology, etiology, and course as defining features of mental disorders. It offers guidance to mental health professionals with regard to what is pathological and what is normal (Lichtenthal et al. 2004). The existing DSM-IV-TR has recognized that grief symptoms may warrant clinical attention; however, they do not acknowledge complicated grief's unique set of symptoms (Lichtenthal et al. 2004). The DSM classifies bereavement as a normal stressor, but more severe pathology is classified in existing diagnostic categories (e.g., Major Depressive Disorder) (Bonanno and Kaltman 2001). However some disquiet has been expressed within both clinical and research circles associated with the potential DSM-V classification of complicated grief (Prolonged Grief Disorder). These include concerns about the pathologizing of grief, misuse of the term, fears regarding stigmatization and health insurance funding issues (Stroebe et al. 2000, 2001a).

Complicated Grief as a Risk Factor for Adverse Health Outcomes Complicated grief (CG) is receiving more attention in the research literature because although bereavement itself has been shown to pose an elevated risk for a variety of negative physical, mental and social outcomes, some studies have found that complicated grief among the bereaved is associated with heightened risk of physical and mental impairments. These include cancer, heart disease, high blood pressure, suicidal ideation, and changes in eating habits (Prigerson et al. 1997). Other studies found a significant decrease in mental health, a decreased sense of well-being, decreased functioning in life roles, more perceived additional life stressors and perceived less social support (Ott 2003).

Predictors of Complicated Grief

Cognitive behavioral conceptualizations of CG propose that negative cognition plays a core role in the development and persistence of emotional problems after bereavement. CG generates negative emotions which can lead mourners to engage in counterproductive attempts to avoid the implications and the pain of the loss. Cognitive variables such as negative beliefs about the self, life, and the future and threatening interpretations of grief reactions have been found to be strongly related to concurrent and prospective levels of complicated grief (Bonanno 2001). These findings support earlier work where cognitive variables such as global negative beliefs, negative world view (Boelen et al. 2006) and avoidance of emotional problems predicted CG (Boelen et al. 2003a, b, 2006). Additionally, individuals who are generally averse to lifestyle change were more vulnerable to CG (Beery et al. 1997). While these studies support the notion that negative interpretations of grief reactions in themselves do not indicate disturbance, they can, however, play a role in the development and maintenance of emotional problems after bereavement. As Bonnano and colleagues would argue, perhaps cognitive appraisals influence the degree to which these reactions are experienced as distressing (Bonanno et al. 2004). Consequently, they can then influence the degree to which mourners engage in avoidance strategies that are likely to impede recovery and may serve to exacerbate and prolong grief and suffering rather than ameliorate grief reactions.

Other predictors of complicated grief include adversities occurring in childhood such as death of a parent, childhood abuse (Silverman et al. 2001) or childhood separation anxiety (Vanderwerker et al. 2006). Gender was found to have a role (Chen et al. 1999), for example widowers with high levels of CG predicted hospitalization and having a physical event such as cancer, stroke, or heart attack. Widows had higher levels of CG than widowers and this predicted sleep changes, anxiety and depression (Chen et al. 1999). A clear predictor was found to be excessive dependency both as dependency on the spouse and as a more general personality (Bonanno et al. 2002) and having an insecure attachment style (van Doorn et al. 1998). Insomnia was also found to be a significant predicator of complicated grief along with the nature of the death (whether violent or not), the younger age of the deceased, levels of closeness with the deceased, recency of the death, relationship to the deceased and gender of the bereaved, with women showing greater grief (Hardison et al. 2005).

The suffering associated with complicated grief and the emerging evidence of long term emotional and physical suffering suggests the need for interventions for this small but vulnerable group. As discussed, traditionally, bereavement theorists have assumed that recovery from loss is based on the concentrated review and expression of the negative emotions brought about by grieving. This process, considered part of the work of mourning, is thought to foster acceptance of the finality of the death and aid in the necessary severing of attachment to the lost relationship. The social-functional perspective on grief and emotion has shifted attention away from an emphasis on the expression of negative emotions and hypothesises that recovery following the death of a loved one is made more likely when grief-related distress is minimized and positive emotion is activated or facilitated (Ott 2003, p. 493).

Interventions in Complicated Grief

In a recent systematic review on complicated grief different interventions were suggested by various authors for different bereavement patterns. For example, chronically depressed individuals might benefit from pharmacologic interventions (Kristjanson et al. 2006), whereas those struggling with complicated grief may benefit more from cognitive and behavioral interventions (Bonanno et al. 2002); bereaved elders who show a trajectory of chronic depression might benefit from a different intervention focus than those with a complicated grief pattern (Boerner et al. 2005); and that professional assessments and interventions should take into account the bereaved person's familial and/or social relationship to the deceased

(Mitchell et al. 2004). These findings highlight the importance of tailoring interventions, suggesting that the intervention may need to be as individual as the bereavement pattern.

Schut and colleagues reviewed and critically assessed grief and bereavement intervention efficacy studies at three levels: primary, secondary and tertiary (Schut et al. 2001, p. 731). Although the evidence is inconclusive, they reported that the timing of the intervention appears to play a role in efficacy for three reasons. Firstly, early intervention may disrupt the natural course of grieving, as emotional, social and practical consequences of the loss still need to take their natural course. Secondly, interventions could interfere with support networks triggering friends and family to withdraw and bereaved people may be prevented from finding their own solutions.

Jordan and Neimeyer postulate that there may be a critical window of time, neither too soon nor too long after a death, when mourners are most responsive to, and able to use, formal support services (Jordan and Neimeyer 2003). One possibility is that services may be most effective when delivered in a 6–18 month period following the death. 'This may be the time when complicated grief is both diagnosable and prognostic of later difficulties, but before problematic patterns of adjustment have become entrenched' (Jordan and Neimeyer 2003, p. 774). Further empirical work is needed to test this postulation. However, Schut and colleagues conclude that 'the more complicated the grief process appears to be or becomes, the better the chances of interventions leading to positive results' and that tertiary preventive interventions take place at longer durations from the death (Schut et al. 2001, pp. 705-737). Psychotropic medications and standard grief-focused supportive psychotherapies appear to have little impact. By contrast, a targeted intervention, complicated grief treatment (CGT) has recently been demonstrated to show significantly better outcomes than standard psychotherapy, 'CGT combines cognitive behavioral techniques with aspects of interpersonal psychotherapy and motivational interviewing' (Shear and Shair 2005, p. 70). It includes a dual focus on coming to terms with the loss and on finding a pathway to restoration.

Conclusion

Grief is thus, both a universal experience and a highly individual response. Perceptions of what constitutes normal responses and levels of suffering are changing. This paper suggests that suffering after the death of a significant other is not essential in the expression of grief. Some people may display minimal levels of distress or suffering and this is not necessarily detrimental. Most will experience some levels of physical, emotional, spiritual and existential pain. However, there is increasing evidence that a small percentage of people experience greater levels of distress and suffering in the form of complicated grief. As the outcomes of complicated grief can be physically, emotionally, psychologically and socially debilitating, early identification of those at risk and interventions to address the persisting levels of suffering are critical.

Bibliography

Beery, L. C., H. G. Prigerson, A. J. Bierhals, et al. 1997. Traumatic grief, depression and care giving in elderly spouses of the terminally ill. *Omega: Journal of Death and Dying* 35:261–279.

Boelen, P. A., J. Van Den Bout, and M. A. Van Den Hout. 2003a. The role of negative interpretations of grief reactions in emotional problems after bereavement. *Journal of Behavioural Therapy and Experimental Psychiatry* 34:225–238.

Boelen, P. A., J. Van Den Bout, and M. A. Van Den Hout. 2003b. The role of cognitive variables in psychological functioning after the death of a first degree relative. *Behaviour, Research and Therapy* 41:1123–1136.

Boelen, P. A., and J. Van Den Bout. 2005. Complicated grief, depression, and anxiety as distinct postloss syndromes: A confirmatory factor analysis study. *American Journal of Psychiatry* 162:2175–2177.

Boelen, P. A., J. Van Den Bout, and M. A. Van Den Hout. 2006. Negative cognitions and avoidance in emotional problems after bereavement. A prospective study. *Behaviour Research and Therapy* 44:1657–1672.

Boerner, K., C. B. Wortman, and G. A. Bonanno. 2005. Resilient or at risk? A 4-year study of older adults who initially showed high or low distress following conjugal loss. *The Journals of Gerontology* 60B:67–73.

Bonanno, G. A. 2001. Grief and emotion: A social-functional perspective. In *Handbook of bereavement: Consequences, coping, and care,* ed. M. S. Stroebe et al., 493–515. Washington: American Psychological Association Press.

Bonanno, G. A., and S. Kaltman. 2001. The varieties of grief experience. *Clinical Psychology Review* 21:705–734.

Bonanno, G. A., C. B. Wortman, D. R. Lehman, R. G. Tweed, M. Haring, J. Sonnega, D. Carr, and R. M. Nesse. 2002. Resilience to loss and chronic grief: A prospective study from preloss to 18-months postloss. *Journal of Personality and Social Psychology* 83:1150–1164.

Bonnanno, G. A., C. B. Wortman, and R. M. Nesse. 2004. Prospective patterns of resilience and maladjustment during widowhood. *Psychology and Aging* 19:260–271.

Brent, D. A., J. Perper, G. Moritz, C. Allman, J. Schweers, C. Roth, L. Balach, B. S. Canobbio, and L. Liotus. 1993. Bereavement or depression? The impact of the loss of a friend to suicide. *Journal of the American Academy of Child and Adolescent Psychiatry* 32:1189–1197.

Byrne, G. J., and B. Raphael. 1994. A longitudinal study of bereavement phenomena in recently widowed elderly men. *Psychological Medicine* 24:411–421.

Chen, J. H., A. J. Bierhals, H. G. Prigerson, S. V. Kasl, C. M. Mazure, S. Jacobs. 1999. Gender differences in the effects of bereavement-related psychological distress in health outcomes. *Psychological Medicine* 29:367–380.

Christ, G, G. A. Bonanno, R. Malkinson, and S. S. Rubin. 2003. Bereavement experiences after the death of a child. In *When children die: Improving palliative and end-of-life care for children and their families,* eds. M. Field and R. Berhman. Washington: National Academy Press.

Freud, Sigmund. 1961. Mourning and melancholia. In *The standard edition of the complete psychological works of Sigmund Freud,* ed. J. Strachey. New York: Basic Books.

Hardison, H. G., R. A. Neimeyer, and K. L. Lichstein. 2005. Insomnia and complicated grief symptoms in bereaved college students. *Behavioral Sleep Medicine* 3:99–111.

Jordan, J. R., and R. A. Neimeyer. 2003. Does grief counseling work? *Death Studies* 27:765–786.

Kim, K., and S. Jacobs. 1991. Pathologic grief and its relationship to other psychiatric disorders. *Journal of Affective Disorders* 21:257–263.

Klass, D., P. R. Silverman, and S. L. Nickman eds. 1996. *Continuing bonds: New understandings of grief.* Washington: Taylor & Francis.

Kristjanson, L. J., E. A. Lobb, S. Aoun, and L. Monterosso. 2006. *A systematic review of the literature on complicated grief.* Common wealth of Australia, Department of Health & Ageing.

Lichtenthal, W. G., D. G. Cruess, and H. G. Prigerson. 2004. A case for establishing complicated grief as a distinct mental disorder in DSM-V. *Clinical Psychology Review* 24:637–662.

Middleton, W., P. Burnett, B. Raphael, and N. Martinek. 1996. The bereavement response: A cluster analysis. *The British Journal of Psychiatry* 169:167–171.
Mitchell, A., Y. Kim, H. Prigerson, and M. Mortimer-Stephens. 2004. Complicated grief in survivors of suicide. *Crisis* 25:12–18.
Neimeyer, R. A., H. G. Prigerson, and B. Davies. 2002. Mourning and meaning. *American Behavioral Scientist* 46:235–251.
Ott, C. H. 2003. The impact of complicated grief on mental and physical health at various points in the bereavement process. *Death Studies* 27:249–272.
Parkes, C. 1998. Coping with loss: Bereavement in adult life. *BMJ* 316(7134):856–859.
Prigerson, H. G., and S. Jacobs. 2001a. Traumatic grief as a distinct disorder: A rationale, consensus criteria, and a preliminary empirical test. In *Handbook of bereavement: Consequences, coping, and care*, eds. M. S. Stroebe et al. Washington: American Psychological Association Press.
Prigerson, H. G., and S. Jacobs. 2001b. Caring for bereaved patients: "All the doctors just suddenly go". *Journal of the American Medical Association* 286:1369–1376.
Prigerson, H. G., E. Frank, S. V. Kasl, C. F. Reynolds, B. Anderson, G. S. Zubenko, P. R. Houck, C. J. George, and D. J. Kupfer. 1995a. Complicated grief and bereavement-related depression as distinct disorders: Preliminary empirical validation in elderly bereaved spouses. *American Journal of Psychiatry* 152:22–30.
Prigerson, H. G. P. Maciejewski, C. F. Reynolds, A. J. Bierhals, J. T. Newsom, A. Fasiczka, E. Frank, J. Doman, and M. Miller. 1995b. Inventory of complicated grief: A scale to measure maladaptive symptoms of loss. *Psychiatry Research* 59:65–79.
Prigerson, H. G., A. J. Bierhals, S. V. Kasl, C. F. Reynolds, K. Shear, J. T. Newsom, and S. Jacobs. 1996. Complicated grief as a disorder distinct from bereavement-related depression and anxiety: A replication study. *American Journal of Psychiatry* 153:1484–1486.
Prigerson, H. G., A. J. Bierhals, S. V. Kasl, C. F. Reynolds, M. K. Shear, N. Day, L. C. Beery, J. T. Newsom, and S. Jacobs. 1997. Traumatic grief as a risk factor for mental and physical morbidity. *American Journal of Psychiatry* 154:616–623.
Prigerson, H. G., M. J. Horowitz, S. C. Jacobs, C. M. Parkes, M. Aslan, K. Goodkin, B. Raphael, S. J. Marwit, C. Wortman, R. A. Neimeyer, G. Bonanno, S. D. Block, D. Kissane, P. Boelen, A. Maercker, B. T. Litz, J. G. Johnson, M. B. First, P. K. Maciejewski. 2009. Prolonged grief disorder: Psychometric validation of criteria proposed for DSM-V and ICD-11. *PLoS Medicine* 6:1–12.
Rando, T. 1992. The increasing prevalence of complicated mourning: The onslaught is just beginning. *Omega: Journal of Death and Dying* 26:43–59
Rando, T. 1996. Complications in mourning traumatic death. In *Living with grief after sudden loss: Suicide, homicide, accident, heart attack, stroke*, ed. K. Doka. Washington: Hospice Foundation of America.
Raphael, B. 1983. *The anatomy of bereavement*. New York: Basic Books.
Rynearson, E. K., and J. M. McCready. 1993. Bereavement after homicide: A synergism of trauma and loss. *American Journal of Psychiatry* 150:258–261.
Schut, H., M. S. Stroebe, J. Van Den Bout, and M. Terheggen. 2001. The efficacy of bereavement interventions: Determining who benefits. In *Handbook of bereavement research: Consequences, coping, and care*, eds. M. S. Stroebe and R. O. Hansson. Washington: American Psychological Association Press.
Shear, K., and H. Shair. 2005. Attachment, loss, and complicated grief. *Developmental Psychobiology* 47:253–267.
Shear, K., F. Frank, and P. R. Houck, et al. 2005. Treatment of complicated grief: A randomized controlled trial. *Journal of the American Medical Association* 292(21):2601–2608.
Silverman, G. K., J. G. Johnson, and H. G. Prigerson. 2001. Preliminary explorations of the effects of prior trauma and loss on risk for psychiatric disorders in recently widowed people. *The Israel Journal of Psychiatry and Related Sciences* 38:202–215.
Stroebe, M. 2001. Bereavement research and theory: Retrospective and prospective. *American Behavioral Scientist* 44:854–865.

Stroebe, M., and W. Stroebe. 1991. Does "grief work" work? *Journal of Consulting and Clinical Psychology* 59:855.

Stroebe, M., M. van Son, W. Stroebe, R. Kleber, H. Schut, and J. Van Den Bout. 2000. On the classification and diagnosis of pathological grief. *Clinical Psychology Review* 20:57–75.

Stroebe, M., H. Schut, and C. Finkenauer. 2001a. The traumatization of grief? A conceptual framework for understanding the trauma-bereavement interface. *The Israel Journal of Psychiatry and Related Sciences* 38:185–201.

Stroebe, W., M. Stroebe, and H. Schut. 2001b. Risk factors in bereavement outcome: A methodological and empirical review. In *Handbook of bereavement research,* eds. R. O. Hansson et al. Washington: American Psychological Association.

van Doorn, C., S. Kasl, L. C. Beery, S. Jacobs, and H. G. Prigerson. 1998. The influence of marital quality and attachment styles on traumatic grief and depressive symptoms. *Journal of Nervous and Mental Disease* 186:566–573.

Vanderwerker, L. C., S. C. Jacobs, C. Murray-Parkes, and H. G. Prigerson. 2006. An exploration of associations between separation anxiety in childhood and complicated grief in later-life. *The Journal of Nervous and Mental Diseases* 194(2):121–123.

Wortman, C. B., and R. C. Silver. 1989. The myths of coping with loss. *Journal of Consulting and Clinical Psychology* 57:349–357.

Wortman, C. B., and R. C. Silver. 2001. The myths of coping with loss revisited. In *Handbook of bereavement research: Consequences, coping, and care*, eds. M. S. Stroebe, R. O. Hansson, W. Stroebe and H. Schut. Washington: American Psychological Association Press.

Chapter 24
Reflections on Compassion, Suffering and Occupational Stress

Mary L. S. Vachon

Live with compassion
Work with compassion
Die with compassion
Meditate with compassion
Enjoy with compassion
When problems come,
Experience them with compassion

Lama Zopa Rinpoche,
A View on Buddhism: Compassion and Bodhicitta

Introduction

Caring for patients and their families can be both stressful and rewarding for the health care practitioner. Caregivers frequently feel that in their compassion they are suffering with patients and families and fear that the caregivers may become overwhelmed. Cassell (1982, pp. 693–645) has characterized suffering as both the human experience of physical distress and the emotive aspect of anything that threatens the intactness of the person. Kearney (2000), a hospice physician, writes that we may speak of curing another's pain, but an individual's suffering is beyond pain and is the experience that results from damage to the whole person. A Buddhist definition of compassion is 'wanting others to be free from suffering.' So compassion is the definition of the highest scope of motivation. It is said that to generate genuine compassion, one needs to realize that one's self is suffering, that an end to suffering is possible, and that other beings similarly want to be free from suffering (Rinpoche 2010).

In health care, some of the suffering caregivers experience comes from their witnessing the suffering of patients and families, and some comes from interactions with other colleagues and aspects of the health care system.

M. L. S. Vachon (✉)
Department of Psychiatry and Dalla Lana School of Public Health, University of Toronto, Toronto, Canada
e-mail: maryvachon@sympatico.ca

J. Malpas, N. Lickiss (eds.), *Perspectives on Human Suffering*,
DOI 10.1007/978-94-007-2795-3_24, © Springer Science+Business Media B.V. 2012

This chapter will review the concept of suffering and the experience of health care professionals, discuss the concept of compassion and review approaches being used that may serve to decrease the suffering of health care professionals, those who are called to serve others. Remen (2000) writes, 'Basically service is about taking life personally, letting the lives that touch yours touch you' (Remen 2000, p. 197). She contends that service is a relationship between equals. When you serve, the work itself keeps you from burnout. Unless you let the patients touch you, you will never last in this work (Remen 2000). Protecting ourselves from loss rather than grieving and healing our losses is one of the major causes of burnout (Remen 1996): 'We burn out not because we don't care but because we don't grieve. We burn out because we have allowed our hearts to become so filled with loss that we have no room left to care'.[1]

Suffering and Connectedness

Mount et al. (2007, pp. 372–388) write that life-threatening illness is an assault on the whole person—physical, psychological, social, and spiritual. It frequently presents caregiver and sufferer with a paradox—suffering does not correlate with physical well-being alone. They conducted a phenomenological study to explore the relevance of the existential and spiritual domains to suffering, healing and quality of life.

> The themes common to patients experiencing suffering and anguish include a sense of isolation and of being disconnected. In addition, these participants experienced an existential vacuum, a crisis of meaning and an inability to find solace or inner peace. They often expressed feelings of victimization and a need for control. Ruminations about unsettling issues of the past and anxieties about the uncertain future consistently removed them from the potential of the present moment. These coping patterns frequently had their roots in early childhood. (Mount et al. 2007, pp. 381–382).

Analysis across cases when the participants experienced integrity and wholeness yielded strikingly different themes from those with suffering and anguish. '[T]hese individuals tended to find a sense of meaning and connectedness in the context of their illness. They also tended to experience a greater acceptance of their illness. This might even be expressed as a degree of sympathetic connection to their disease' (Mount et al. 2007, p. 382). Mount and his colleagues note, 'Although healing connections may first be experienced at any one of the four levels (with Self, others, the phenomenal world, or ultimate meaning), it appears that openness to healing connections at one level fosters opening at others' (Mount et al. 2007, p. 383).

This openness to healing connections may take place not only in the patient, but in caregivers as well. Katz (2006, p. 3–12) speaks of the alchemical reaction which occurs when two individuals engage together at the most vulnerable time in human existence—the end of life. Alchemy is 'that space' that takes its own place in the poignant relationship between helper and patient. Both can be transformed through the experience. This chapter contends that, even in the midst of suffering,

[1] Remen (1996, p. 52), from Vachon (2006).

caregivers can have the option of healing connections that benefit both the caregiver and the patient/family member. However, in order to do this, caregivers need to engage in self-awareness practices and wellness strategies and be open to change (Kearney et al. 2009, pp. 1155–1164).

A recent palliative care consensus conference dealt with some of these issues in a document on improving the quality of spiritual care as a dimension of palliative care (Puchalski et al. 2009). The group developed the following definition: 'Spirituality is the aspect of humanity that refers to the way individuals seek and express meaning and purpose and the way they experience their connectedness to the moment, to self, to others, to nature, and to the significant or sacred' (Puchalski et al. 2009, p. 887). With relationship as the core of spirituality, one might infer that health care, by virtue of its relational quality, is inherently spiritual. As such, Puchalski and colleagues proposed a model of spiritual care reflected in the transformation occurring within professional-patient relationships. For this to occur, the health care professional 'must have an awareness of the spiritual dimensions of their own lives and then be supported in the practice of compassionate presence with patients through a reflective process' (Puchalski et al. 2009, p. 900). In developing self-awareness of one's personal values, beliefs and attitudes, a deeper more meaningful connection may take place between the professional and patient-family as well as enhanced coping[2]. 'Clinicians functioning with greater self-awareness may experience greater job engagement with less stress in interactions with their work environment, experience empathy as a mutually healing connection with their patients, and derive compassion satisfaction and vicarious posttraumatic growth. Self-awareness may both enhance self-care (Novack et al. 1999) and improve patient care and satisfaction' (Novack et al. 1997; Meier et al. 2001; Kearney et al. 2009).

The Cost of Suffering: Health Care Professionals and Care Providers

All too often, however, this ideal situation does not occur. Instead, clinicians experience suffering brought about by personal expectations, conflicts with colleagues and organizational demands. The physical distress and emotive experiences of suffering that may threaten a patient or client's sense of identity and intactness may also occur when health care professionals and care providers experience negative stress leading to suffering within the work situation.

A variety of terms have been applied in order to further the understanding of factors in the work situation that could lead to experiences of stress and potentially to caregiver suffering. Commonly used terms are burnout (Maslach et al. 2001; Maslach 2003), compassion fatigue (Figley 1995, 2002), vicarious traumatization (McCann and Pearlman 1990), moral distress (Jameton 1984; Rice et al. 2008; Liaschenko and Liaschenko 2004), and suffering (Boston and Mount 2006). Of these terms, burnout is the most widely researched, and the terms stress and burnout

[2] Puchalski et al. (2009), from Vachon (2011).

best researched.[3] Job engagement (Maslach et al. 2001), compassion satisfaction (Stamm 2002) and exquisite empathy (Harrison and Westwood 2009) are possible antidotes to burnout, compassion fatigue and vicarious traumatization, and may help to prevent suffering.

Burnout

Burnout is a form of mental distress manifested in individualswho experience decreased work performance resulting from negative attitudes and behaviors (Maslach and Leiter 2008). The characteristics of burnout are emotional exhaustion,depersonalization, or decreased empathy, and low personal accomplishment.Emotional exhaustion refers to feelings of being overextended and depleted of one's emotional and physical resources. Exhaustion prompts efforts to cope by distancing oneself emotionally and cognitively from work (Maslach and Leiter 2008). Depersonalization refers to negative, callous or excessively detached responses to various aspects of the job and is another distancing mechanism (Maslach and Leiter 2008). Lack of personal accomplishment refers to feelings of incompetence and underachievement at work. It may arise from a lack of resources (e.g., critical information, tools or time) to get the work done and may be directly related to emotional exhaustion and depersonalization or be independent of them (Maslach 2003; Kearney et al. 2009).

Burnout results from stresses that arise from the clinician's interaction with the work environment, including factors such as workload, control, reward, community, fairness and values, as well as emotional work variables, the requirement to display or suppress emotions in the work setting (Maslach et al. 2001). Job engagement is the opposite of burnout and is characterized by energy, involvement and efficacy in the workplace (Maslach 2003).

Burnout is a stronger predictor than depression for a lower satisfaction with career choice, and it is associated with poorer health (Kuerer et al. 2007). Burnout is also associated with suboptimal patient care practices and medical errors by physicians (West et al. 2006) and with lower satisfactionand longer post-discharge recovery by patients (Halbesleben and Rathert 2008). Medical residents who engaged in personal wellness strategies have higher mental wellbeing and more empathy towards patients (Shanafelt et al. 2005b).

Burnout arises from chronic mismatches between people and their work settings in some or all of these areas. The area of values may play a central mediating role for the other areas (Maslach et al. 2001); although, for individuals at risk of burnout, fairness in the work environment may be the tipping point determining whether people develop job engagement or burnout (Maslach and Leiter 2008). Some of the sources of suffering resulting in burnout may come from issues re-

[3] For a discussion of the research in stress and burnout in oncology and palliative care over the past 30 years, see Vachon and Sherwood (2007), Vachon (2010).

lated to community or relationships with colleagues, issues related to values and emotion-work variables.

Community and Relationships with Colleagues

Problems in team relationships have long been an issue in many areas of health care and have been documented elsewhere.[4] Although I have written for years about issues of staff conflict and team relations, my best understanding of the suffering involved with staff conflict, and the way in which it can reach to the core of one's sense of intactness as a human being, came when I was given a diagnosis of stage 4 non-Hodgkin's lymphoma. I was aware that my chances of survival were 25%, which certainly made me reflect on the things that I valued most dearly. My career has always been an important aspect of my identity. I decided that I could stay at home and reflect on dying while I had treatment, or I could go to work and attempt to be helpful to others.

My work situation at that time with one group of my colleagues had been challenging. I met with them saying that my work situation had been quite stressful, but that was not the source of my cancer, which I attributed to an underlying immunological deficiency. I asked that we move beyond the long-standing conflict and look to the future, either through talking about the issues or putting them aside. I told them I planned to work during treatment and that my oncologist had said that people who loved their work could usually work during treatment. I then left the meeting, inviting them to discuss their response to my request in my absence.

Three days after having my first chemotherapy treatment, I met with my administrator to discuss who should cover my patients if I was unable to work during treatment. I was on my way to lecture in Hong Kong and Shanghai on issues such as 'Breaking Bad News', 'Stress', 'Women with Cancer', 'Anticipatory Loss and Grief' and 'Anger', the latter two lectures I was giving with my son, who had been through a more than challenging adolescence and had just graduated with distinction from university. My thought was that if these were going to be the last set of lectures I would ever give, what could be better than to 'pass on the torch' to my son.

My administrator informed me that my colleagues had come to him asking that I not be allowed to work during my treatment as they felt it was a violation of professional ethics for someone on active treatment to work with patients receiving active treatment for cancer. I was later made aware that the group that had heard what I said did not discuss the issue as I had suggested. Instead, a number of the colleagues having challenges with me had met separately and felt that I had said my job stress had caused my cancer.

When I was told about this meeting by a colleague I said that was not what I said, she replied that was what they had heard and perhaps, since I had been going for

[4] For reviews of the topic, see Vachon (1987), Vachon (1995), Vachon and Sherwood (2007), Vachon and Müeller (2009), Sabo and Vachon (2011).

surgery the next day, I was anxious and not aware of what I was saying. I checked it out with others, who confirmed my position.

While in Hong Kong, I spoke with a leader in the psychosocial oncology field who was also lecturing. I said that I understood that when one had cancer one shouldn't have 'negative' thoughts, but I was having difficulty coping with the feelings I was having. He was quite clear that the issue needed to be discussed: 'These people are trying to destroy you and this must be brought into the light.' My image was that the oncologists and nurses were trying to save my life and my colleagues in supportive care wanted me, if not dead, at least to disappear from the work environment.

I had good support from a number of local, national and international colleagues in my desire to work, and did so, gaining many, many insights and certainly developing in self-awareness and learning a bit about compassion.

A source of suffering, most definitely; a fertile ground for developing considerable self-awareness and self-reflection, no question; a significant factor in my decision to leave my job and do my work in a private practice where my new found spiritual practices and beliefs can be practiced, without a doubt.

I enjoy the writings and teachings of Myss (2001, 2002), who suggests that when there are frequent signs in the workplace that one does not belong there, this is the universe trying to get one to recognize that it is time to move on. If one doesn't listen to the first message, the signals are increased until one finally tunes in. About three years later, I was going for foot surgery. I decided that if I was going to live it was time to get my feet fixed so that I could wear sandals. I was meditating prior to surgery, awakened in the recovery room in the middle of the meditative prayer that I was using, put up my feet and the idea of leaving my job came to me. I had no prior intention of leaving my job, but in the end I did and can now focus my attention on issues that are of interest rather than on political challenges. I thank my former colleagues for the push to move into the place where I am currently meant to be.

Conflicting Values and Emotion-Work Variables

Georges et al. (2002) quoted James and Field (1992), who said that when the originating ethics of palliative care are marginalized, the heart and soul of care are endangered. 'Expert' values based on medical technologies and psychosocial skills replace the compassionate help. Death is no longer a truth to confront, but a process that must be managed as efficiently as possible. Nurses on the academic palliative care unit who participated in this study (Georges et al. 2002) were encouraged in this context to acquire knowledge and skills, whereas development of the moral qualities necessary to care for those who are dying was not addressed. Therefore, they became less sensitive to the moral values in situations. They responded less to problems because their moral values were endangered, mainly because they conflicted with their professional norms and established rules. In situations of pain and suffering, these nurses mainly tried to overcome their powerlessness through a medical approach, overlooking the possibilities of alleviating suffering by an authentic caring attitude based on really meeting with patients.

Boston and colleagues (Boston et al. 2001) noted that dying persons experience disruption of the essence of day-to-day living and challenges to their perception of who they are. Through this process, they gain new wisdom and reshape their sense of meaning in life. A different way of knowing the world evolves, characterized by inner know-how and tacit knowledge that defines the self in relationship to others. Caregivers and others around them 'are perceived to be in another place, or don't seem to be there at all' (Boston et al. 2001, p. 248). Patients and caregivers may feel that they just don't connect. Boston and co-authors (Boston et al. 2001) speak of palliative care as taking caregivers into emotional realms that are neither easy nor comfortable. The caregiver may be permanently changed through this encounter.

Compassion Fatigue

Compassion fatigue has been described as the 'cost of caring' for others in emotional pain that has led helping professionalsto abandon their work with traumatized persons (Figley 1995). Compassion fatigue evolves specifically from the relationship between the clinician and the patient's traumatic experiences. Some researchers consider compassion fatigue to be similar to posttraumatic stress disorder (PTSD), except that it applies to those emotionallyaffected by the trauma of another (e.g., client or family member)rather than by one's own trauma (Figley 1995). Figley (1995, 2002) states that compassion fatigue is also known as secondary or vicarious traumatization (VT), although other researchers feel vicarious traumatization is different (McCann and Pearlman 1990). Compassion fatigue may lead to burnout (Figley 2002).

Symptoms of compassion fatigue parallel three domains of the classic symptomatology of PTSD: *hyperarousal*, disturbed sleep, irritability or outbursts of anger, and hypervigilance; *avoidance*, 'not wanting to go there again' and the desire to avoid thoughts, feelings and conversations associated with the patient's pain and suffering (Wright 2004); and *re-experiencing*, intrusive thoughts or dreams, and psychological or physiological distress in response to reminders of work with the dying (Figley 1995).

Compassion satisfaction—pleasure derived from the work of helping others—is a possible factor that counterbalances the risks of compassion fatigue (Stamm 2002).

Vicarious Traumatization

McCann and Pearlman (1990) first identified the problem of vicarious traumatization (VT), which they defined as the cumulative transformative effects upon therapists resulting from empathic engagement with traumatized clients (Harrison and

Westwood 2009). According to Harrison and Westwood (Harrison and Westwood 2009), there is consensus in the field that there is not enough empirical literature on the definitive factors that contribute to VT or the practices that may prevent or ameliorate its harmful effects. Their recent study of a small sample of six therapists showed that nine major themes were salient across clinicians' narratives of protective practices. 'These included: *countering isolation* (in professional, personal and spiritual realms); developing mindful self-awareness; consciously expanding perspective to embrace complexity; active optimism; holistic self-care; maintaining clear boundaries; exquisite empathy; professional satisfaction; and creating meaning' (Harrison and Westwood 2009, p 203).

Unlike previous studies, they found that empathic engagement with traumatized clients appeared to be a protective practice for clinicians working with traumatized clients. Clinicians who engaged in 'exquisite empathy' (a discerning, highly present, sensitively attuned, well-boundaried, heartfelt form of empathic engagement) described having been invigorated rather than depleted by their intimate professional connections with traumatized clients' (Harrison and Westwood 2009, p 213).

Moral Distress

Along the road leading to possible burnout, compassion fatigue and vicarious trauma, health care professionals may experience moral distress, which comes from confronting situations in conflict with one's ethical beliefs. These experiences can lead to profound suffering.

Moral distress in the workplace occurs when there is an experience of incoherence between one's beliefs and one's actions, and possibly also outcomes (i.e., between what one sincerely believes to be right, what one actually does and what eventually transpires). Jameton (1984, p. 6) describes moral distress as a situation where 'one knows the right thing to do, but institutional constraints make it nearly impossible to pursue the right course of action' (Jameton 1984). Webster and Baylis extend this definition and note that 'moral distress may also arise…for one or more of the following reasons: an error in judgment, some personal failing (for example, a weakness or crimp in one's character such as a pattern of 'systemic avoidance'), or other circumstances truly beyond one's control' (Webster and Baylis 2000, p. 218).

The concept of moral distress can be seen as being related to the issues of 'values,' 'fairness' and 'community' in burnout. Moral distress extends beyond compassion fatigue to involve issues that evolve from ethical conflicts in the treatment of patients and families, and may involve vicarious traumatization as caregivers imagine themselves in the value-laden, ethical and conflictual situations which their patients and family members are experiencing. These situations of moral distress often involve staff members being in conflict with one another. As Farsides notes (Farsides 2006, pp. 167–182), there may be ethical issues that arise specific to the very issue of team working that have received less attention than the broader field of ethics in health care. 'The starting point for the ethicist is that a team is a group of individuals with each individual a moral agent in their own right. As such, the individual practitioner will have beliefs, views, ideas and projects which in a substantial way track what they think about the world and how they categorize actions and events as right or wrong, morally acceptable or unacceptable, forbidden or allowed. A challenge facing the individual is to reconcile their personal moral views with those required by, or most readily identified with, their professional role and their membership of a larger moral unit—the team' (Farsides 2006, p. 168).

Oberle and Hughes (2001) did a qualitative study of seven doctors and fourteen nurses working in acute care adult medical-surgical areas, including intensive care. The respondents were asked to describe ethical problems that they frequently encountered in their clinical practice. All participants experienced ethical problems related to decision making at the end of life. The core problem for both doctors and nurses was witnessing suffering, which engendered a moral obligation to reduce that suffering. Uncertainty about the best course of action for the patient and family was a source of moral distress. Competing values, hierarchical processes, scarce resources and communication emerged as common themes. The key difference between the groups was that doctors are responsible for making decisions and nurses must live with those decisions.

Weissman (2009), a palliative care physician, notes that nurses have done the most work to explore the concept of moral distress in pediatric and adult intensive care units, oncology and psychiatry. He concludes that moral distress occurs around the same issues that exist in the daily practice of palliative care consultation: do-not-resuscitate (DNR) orders, excessive use of life-sustaining treatments (a.k.a. extraordinary care) and futility debates. In nursing, there seems to be strong link between moral distress, job dissatisfaction and burnout, so much so that the American Association of Critical Care Nurses (AACCN) has compiled a workbook to help nurses cope with their own moral distress (American Association of Critical-Care Nurses 2008).

Weissman (2009) notes that for the palliative care consultant there exists a constant tension between acceding to the values of the referring clinician versus providing care that honors the professional values of the consultant.

On the one hand, we want to be good colleagues and respect the values of our fellow physicians in a manner that acknowledges the limits of our role as consultants. Alienating the referring physician is the surest way to cut off the flow of future consultations, as many struggling palliative care programs have learned. On the other hand, in cases where our core beliefs and values as palliative care clinicians are challenged, where we see needless suffering, physical or emotional, our professional duty to the patient is clear, but may be impossible to operationalize. This is the point where moral distress occurs, which may manifest as individual or team feelings of inadequacy, anxiety, despair, or hopelessness. Palliative care clinicians, like nurses in ethically demanding specialties, take home the psychological burden of being witness to the sick and dying and the burden of moral distress. Either one alone would be sufficient to lead to compassion fatigue and burnout, the combination of both can be overwhelming (Weissman 2009, p. 865).

Weissman notes that many of the pioneers in palliative care were drawn into the field because of the gulf between the actual and ideal care of patients in their formative years of practice. He suggests that, at this point, 'moral distress for many of us has been our emotional 'baseline,' a state that has both positive and negative effects. The positive has been the continued motivation to work to improve the system of care; the negative being the emotional toll on ourselves and our families' (Weissman 2009, p. 866).

Compassion and Other Positive Emotions

Vaillant (2008), who is known for his pioneering work in adult development has written of the transformative power of positive emotion: 'Positive emotions—not only compassion, forgiveness, love and hope but also joy, faith/trust, awe, and gratitude—arise from our inborn mammalian capacity for unselfish parental love. They emanate from our feeling, limbic, mammalian brain and are thus grounded in our evolutionary heritage. All human beings are hardwired for positive emotions, and these positive emotions are a common denominator of all major faiths and of all human beings' (Vaillant 2008, p. 3).

Vaillant defines 'spirituality as the amalgam of the positive emotions that bind us to other human beings—and to our experience of 'God' as we may understand Her/Him' (Vaillant 2008, p. 5). He discusses the spiritually important emotions of love, hope, joy, forgiveness, compassion, faith, awe and gratitude. He speaks of the difference between negative emotions, such as fear and anger, which are 'all about me' and contrasts them with the positive emotions which have the power to free the self from the self. The emotions he chooses to discuss all involve human connection. Negative emotions are often crucial for survival, but in time present. Positive emotions:

> are more expansive and help us to build. They widen our tolerance, expand our moral compass, and enhance our creativity. They help us to survive in time future...while negative emotions narrow attention and miss the forest for the trees, positive emotions, especially joy, make thought patterns more flexible, creative, integrative and efficient...The effect of positive emotion on the automatic (visceral) nervous system has much in common with the relaxation response to meditation... In contrast to the metabolic and cardiac arousal that the fight-or-flight response of negative emotion induces in our *sympathetic* autonomic nervous system, positive emotion via our *parasympathetic* nervous system reduces basal metabolism, blood pressure, heart rate, respiratory rate, and muscle tension.[5]

Mount et al. (2007) study of dying patients referred to earlier showed that those in suffering and anguish were locked into what might be perceived as negative emotions and some of these were thought to have their origin in childhood. Those with a sense of integrity and wholeness tended to find a sense of meaning and connectedness in the context of their illness and tended to experience a greater acceptance

[5] Vaillant (2008), from Vachon and Huggard (2010). Emphasis was in the original.

of their illness. They can perhaps be seen to be living in the experience of positive emotions,[6] despite the fact that they are dying.

Perhaps, similarly to patients, the experience of caregivers and suffering can in part be reflective of their early childhood experiences and personalities. Factors such as resilience (Ablett and Jones 2007; Monroe and Oliviere 2007; Keeton et al. 2007; Kash et al. 2000), attachment style (Hawkins et al. 2007) and religious beliefs (Kash et al. 2000) have been shown to make a difference in perceptions of stressors and the experience of burnout.

Dr. Rachael Naomi Remen speaks of compassion, which, she says, 'begins with the acceptance of what is most human in ourselves, what is most capable of suffering. In attending to our own capacity to suffer, we can uncover a simple and profound connection between our own vulnerability and the vulnerability in all others. Experiencing this allows us to find an instinctive kindness toward life which is the foundation of all compassion and genuine service' (Remen 2000). This concept recognizes the reciprocity that is inherent in the caring relationship. Jean Watson, a nurse theoretician, states, 'When both care providers and care receiver are co-participants in caring, the release can allow the one who is cared for to be the one who cares, through the reflection of the human condition that in turn nourishes the humanness of the care provider. In such connectedness they are both capable of transcending self, time and space' (Watson 1989).

Compassion satisfaction has been defined as 'the pleasure you derive from being able to do your work well' (Stamm 2009, p. 12). It stands in sharp contrast to compassion fatigue, which pertains to the negative effects arising from one's work. Factors that have been identified as supporting compassion satisfaction range from positive affect and optimism to social support networks and work-life balance (Radley and Figley 2007). These same factors are reminiscent of factors associated with self-care strategies (Kearney et al. 2009; Keidel 2002; Vachon 1987; Shanafelt et al. 2005a, b). In a study of hospice workers, Alkema et al. (2008) found that compassion satisfaction was negatively correlated with burnout and compassion fatigue. At the same time, the researchers noted that self-care (excluding physical self-care) was negatively correlated with compassion fatigue, suggesting that health care professionals should integrate self-care strategies into their everyday life. Further, Alkema and colleagues found that emotional and spiritual self-care and personal-professional balance were predictive of higher levels of compassion satisfaction (Sabo and Vachon 2011).

Perry (1998a, b; 2008) used nursing narratives to explore exemplary nursing practice in palliative care and oncology nursing. She used the themes of the dialogue of silence, mutual touch and sharing the lighter side of life to illustrate aspects of exemplary nursing practice and identified joint transcendence as the essence of exemplary nursing practice. Most recently (Perry 2008), she did a phenomenological study of seven oncology nurses nominated by their colleagues as exemplary

[6] It is worth noting that Mount has himself been living with a serious, life-threatening illness for years while he has simultaneously been studying how others cope with their illnesses. See also Kearney et al. (2009).

caregivers. Three themes were identified: moments of connection, making moments matter and energizing moments.

Perry[7] speaks of the palliative care nursing experience as valuing each individual, experiencing the reciprocity of giving and receiving in relationships, a sense of interconnectedness and of mutual nurturing, being close to patients and sharing a part of one's self: the chance to make a difference in people's lives.

Boston and Mount (2006) interviewed caregivers in palliative care about their perceptions in attending to the spiritual and existential needs of palliative care patients. Eight themes were revealed: conceptualization of spirituality; creating openings; issues of transference and countertransference; cumulative grief; healing connections; the wounded healer; sustaining a healing environment for the caregiver; and challenges and strengths for the spiritual and existential domains of palliative care.

Decreasing Suffering in Caregivers

Meier et al. (2001) propose a model for increasing physician self-awareness, which includes identifying and working with emotions that may affect patient care. Kearney et al. (2009) have written of the need for physicians to be 'connected' to continue to practice end-of-life care.

In a study of well-being and personal wellness strategies of medical oncologists (Shanafelt et al. 2005a), half reported high overall well-being. Being aged 50 or younger, male, and working 60 hours or less per week were associated with increased overall well-being.

Ratings of the importance of a number of personal wellness promotion strategies differed for oncologists with high-well-being compared with those without high well-being. Developing an approach/philosophy to dealing with death and end-of-life care, using recreation/hobbies/exercise, taking a positive outlook and incorporating a philosophy of balance between personal and professional life were all rated as substantially more important wellness strategies by oncologists with high well-being…Oncologists with high overall well-being also reported greater career satisfaction (Shanafelt et al. 2005a, p. 23).

These coping strategies are similar to the top five coping strategies identified two decades ago (Vachon 1987): a sense of competence, control or pleasure in one's work; team philosophy, building and support; control over aspects of practice; lifestyle management; and a personal philosophy of illness, death and one's role in life.[8]

Chochinov (2007) has proposed the A, B, C and D of Dignity-Conserving Care. Using empirical evidence, he shows that kindness, humanity and respect, the core values and behaviors of medical professionalism, often relegated to the 'niceties' of care, embrace the true essence of medicine. These aspects of care variably re-

[7] Perry (1998b), from Vachon and Huggard (2010).

[8] This section adapted from Sabo and Vachon (2011).

ferred to as spiritual care, whole person care, or Dignity-Conserving Care, involve *attitude, behavior, compassion and dialogue.*

Spickard et al. (2002) note the best prevention for physician burnout is to promote personal and professional well-being on all levels: physical, emotional, psychological and spiritual. This must occur throughout the professional life-cycle of physicians, from medical school through retirement. It is a challenge not only for individual physicians in their own lives, but also for the profession of medicine and the organizations in which physicians work. Of course this concept applies equally well to all other professional caregivers.

Self-Awareness

The ability to respond to another with compassion and kindness requires a certain self-awareness and attention to our own hearts as well as attention to the suffering of others. This 'self-awareness,' or 'mindfulness,' lies at the heart of new therapeutic approaches to individual and communal stress and distress in the health care environment.

For example, in a recent article on the self-care of physicians, Kearney et al. note that 'a clinician who adopts a self-awareness-based approach to self-care may be able to remain emotionally available in even the most stressful clinical situations' (Kearney et al. 2009, p. 1160). They suggest that self-awareness is 'an innate psychological function' and in the study of physician self-care, it is suggested that enhanced clinician self-awareness may actually serve as a mitigating factor with respect to the development of compassion fatigue. Recall that 'compassion fatigue' has traditionally been defined as the inability to respond to another's suffering, distress or misfortune with compassion or empathy. It evolves from exposure to the traumatic experiences and suffering of others.

Harrison and Westwood that suggests that empathic engagement with traumatized patients and clients may actually serve as a 'protective practice' for clinicians and therapists. They (Harrison and Westwood 2009) refer to this empathic engagement with traumatized patients and clients as 'exquisite empathy.' They describe their research findings about 'exquisite empathy' as follows:

Most of the clinicians described how intimate empathic engagement with clients sustains them in their work. This finding surprised us, because we went into the research thinking that empathic engagement was a risk factor rather than a protective practice.

This study yielded the novel finding that empathic engagement can be a protective practice for clinicians who work with traumatized clients.

While this conclusion (that empathic engagement with traumatized patients and clients may actually serve as a 'protective practice' for clinicians and therapists) is contrary to the traditional understanding of 'compassion fatigue,' it holds great promise for clinicians working in many areas of health care and social services.

Mindfulness Meditation

An important and proven way to enhance personal self-awareness is mindfulness meditation. Mindfulness meditation practice has been around for hundreds, if not thousands, of years in many spiritual traditions, but this practice has only recently been explored in modern health care environments.

Jon Kabat-Zinn, who founded the Mindfulness Based Stress Reduction (MBSR) program at the University of Massachusetts Medical Center, describes mindfulness as 'moment to moment, non-judgmental awareness, cultivated by paying attention in a specific way, that is, in the present moment, and as non-reactively, as non-judgmentally, and as openheartedly as possible. …Mindfulness is none other than the capacity we all already have to know what is actually happening as it is happening' (Kabat-Zinn 2005, p. 108). Gonzalez and Byron have recently written on mindfulness meditation, based on their experiences with its use during the recent financial 'meltdown' (Gonzalez and Byron 2010). They use the terms *equanimity* (accepting 'what is' without resistance); *concentration* (the ability to maintain undivided attention on something, allowing distractions to remain in the background as you focus on the task at hand); and *clarity* (being clear and aware of what is going on, both internally and in the world at large). 'The greater your clarity the better you are able to make decisions, because you understand what drives you, including when you distract yourself because you are uncomfortable about what you become aware of or realize' (Gonzalez and Byron 2010, p. 15). *Purification* 'is a technical term referring to the clearing away of negative habitual patterns. We all have sources of unhappiness within us, and when you clear them away you can experience true freedom. As you observe what arises and do nothing to interfere, you experience purification' (Gonzalez and Byron 2010, p. 15). In the case of working with someone who is suffering, this would allow the caregiver to intervene with 'detached concern,' helping without being destroyed in the process. The MBSR program has now been implemented with great success in many health care facilities around the world (Shapiro et al. 2007; Grossman et al. 2004; Cohen-Katz et al. 2004).

MBSR has been found to successfully reduce stress and its symptoms in people with cancer, cardiovascular disease, pain and other conditions (Shapiro et al. 2003). There seems to be general agreement among many researching mindfulness that mindfulness meditation practice offers great promise and hope of therapeutic benefit for patients and clients, the healing professions and other care providers (Kearney et al. 2009; Shapiro et al. 2003, 2005; Cohen-Katz et al. 2004; Pipe et al. 2009).

The practice of mindfulness meditation simultaneously raises the consciousness of one's inner reality (physical, emotional and cognitive) and of the external reality with which individuals interact (Shapiro et al. 2005). The practice has begun to be utilized and researched in the workplace. Some organizations have used mindfulness meditation as part of a larger intervention. For example, an eight-week Mindfulness-Based Stress Reduction (MBSR) program for nurses in a hospital system was introduced and found to lower burnout and improve well-being (Cohen-Katz et al. 2004). The results of the study showed that the treatment group decreased scores on the Maslach Burnout Inventory and these changes lasted three months. Specifically, there was significantly decreased emotional exhaustion and depersonalization and a trend toward significance in personal accomplishment. In a matched, randomized controlled trial examining the effect of an eight-week mindfulness-based intervention program for medical students, the authors found that those participating in the intervention experienced less anxiety and depression and greater empathy than those in the control group (Rosenzweig et al. 2003).

Recently, the concept of compassionate silence has emerged as a component of the patient-clinician encounter in palliative care (Back et al. 2009). This ability may come from contemplative practices such as mindfulness-based meditation. Compassion requires active intention—that is, the health care professional not only gives attention, but maintains focus and clarity of perception. 'These compassionate silences arise spontaneously from the clinician who has developed the mental capacities of stable attention, emotional balance, along with pro-social mental qualities, such as naturally arising empathy and compassion' (Back et al. 2009, p. 14).

Writing in a reflective and emotionally expressive way is another form of self-care that enhances self-awareness. There are demonstrated somatic (Cepeda et al. 2008) and psychological benefits in patients (Morgan et al. 2008) to this practice, and it has been extended to promote reflection and empathic engagement in physicians (Charon 2001; Brady et al. 2002).

Conclusions

Burnout, compassion fatigue, moral distress and vicarious traumatization are concepts that have been used to understand aspects of occupational stress and suffering in professional caregivers. The suffering of caregivers, similarly to that of patients goes beyond pain and is the experience that results from damage to the whole person.

Buddhists define compassion as 'wanting others to be free from suffering.' Key to understanding the suffering of caregivers is to understand that in order to generate genuine compassion, one needs to realize that one's self is suffering, that an end to suffering is possible, and that other beings similarly want to be free from suffering (Rinpoche 2010).

The themes common to patients experiencing suffering and anguish include a sense of isolation and of being disconnected. Dying persons who were experiencing integrity and wholeness in their dying process tended to find a sense of meaning and connectedness in the context of their illness. They also tended to experience a greater acceptance of their illness (Mount et al. 2007). Mount and his colleagues note, 'Although healing connections may first be experienced at any one of the four levels (with Self, others, the phenomenal world, or ultimate meaning), it appears that openness to healing connections at one level fosters opening at others' (Mount et al. 2007, p. 383).

Caregivers also need to engage in these healing connections. Katz (2006) speaks of the alchemy that can occur between the patient and caregiver and suggests this is particularly apt to happen at the end of life. Spirituality has been defined as 'the aspect of humanity that refers to the way individuals seek and express meaning and purpose and the way they experience their connectedness to the moment, to self, to others, to nature, and to the significant or sacred' (Puchalski et al. 2009, p. 887). With relationship as the core of spirituality, one might infer that health care, by virtue of its relational quality, is inherently spiritual. A model of spiritual care reflected in the transformation occurring within professional-patient relationships was suggested by Puchalski and colleagues which requires the health care professional 'must have an awareness of the spiritual dimensions of their own lives and then be supported in the practice of compassionate presence with patients through a reflective process' (Puchalski et al. 2009, p. 900).

Professional caregivers can continue to work and even thrive in the context of providing service to those who are suffering. Job engagement, compassion satisfaction and exquisite empathy have been shown to sustain caregivers even in the midst of suffering. Caregivers who practice wellness strategies including aspects of self-care, relationships, work attitudes, religious/spiritual practice, personal philosophies, and strategies related to job-life balance have higher mental wellbeing and more empathy towards patients (Shanafelt et al. 2005b).

Positive emotions, including compassion can be transformative (Vaillant 2008). Recent research shows we 'hardwired for positive emotions, and these positive emotions are a common denominator of all major faiths and of all human beings' (Vaillant 2008, p. 3).

Self-awareness is crucial to the practice of compassionate presence with patients and their families as well as the ability to engage in compassionate silence. In developing self-awareness of one's personal values, beliefs and attitudes, a deeper more meaningful connection may take place between the professional and patient-family as well as enhanced coping (Sabo and Vachon 2011). Meditation and reflective journaling are two effective practices for developing self-awareness and compassion that allow caregivers to enter into situations of suffering, truly be present and helpful to patients and perhaps even be 'invigorated' by the encounters, rather than being overwhelmed.

Bibliography

Ablett, Janice, and R. S. P. Jones. 2007. Resilience and well-being in palliative care staff: A qualitative study of hospice nurses' experience of work. *Psycho-Oncology* 16:733–740.

Alkema, Karen, Jeremy M. Linton, and Randal Davies. 2008. A study of the relationship between self-care, compassion satisfaction, compassion fatigue, and burnout among hospice workers. *Journal of Social Work in End-of-Life & Palliative Care* 4:101–119.

American Association of Critical-Care Nurses, Ethics Work Group. 2008. *The 4As to rise above moral distress*, American Association of Critical-Care Nurses. www.aacn.org/WD/Practice/Docs/4As_to_Rise_Above_Moral_Distress.pdf. Accessed 6 Sept 2010.

Back, Anthony L., Susan M. Bauer-Wu, Cynda H. Rushton, and Joan Halifax. 2009. Compassionate silence in the patient-clinician encounter: A contemplative approach. *Journal of Palliative Medicine* 12:13–17.
Boston, Patricia A., Anna Towers, and David Barnard. 2001. Embracing vulnerability: Risk and empathy in palliative care. *Journal of Palliative Care* 17:248–253.
Boston, Patricia A., and Balfour M. Mount. 2006. The caregiver's perspective on existential and spiritual distress in palliative care. *Journal of Pain and Symptom Management* 32:13–26.
Brady, Donald W., Giselle Corbie-Smith, and William Branch. 2002. "What's important to you?": The use of narratives to promote self-reflection and to understand the experiences of medical residents. *Annals of Internal Medicine* 137 (3): 220–223.
Cassell, E. J. 1982. The nature of suffering and the goals of medicine. *New England Journal of Medicine* 306:639–645.
Cepeda, Soledad M., Richard Chapman, and Nelcy Miranda. 2008. Emotional disclosure through patient narrative may improve pain and well-being: Results of a randomized controlled trial in patients with cancer pain. *Journal of Pain and Symptom Management* 35 (6): 623–631.
Charon, Rita. 2001. Narrative medicine. A model for empathy, reflection, profession, and trust. *Journal of the American Medical Association* 286 (15): 1897–1902.
Chochinov, Harvey M. 2007. Dignity and the essence of medicine: The A, B, C & D of dignity-conserving Care. *British Medical Journal* 334:184–187.
Cohen-Katz, Joanne, Susan D. Wiley, Terry Capuano, Debra Baker, and Shauna Shapiro. 2004. The effects of mindfulness-based stress reduction on nurse stress and burnout: A quantitative and qualitative study. *Holistic Nursing Practice* 18:302–308.
Farsides, Bobbie. 2006. Ethical issues in multi-disciplinary team work in palliative care. In *Teamwork in palliative care: Fulfilling or frustrating?*, ed. Peter Speck. Oxford: Oxford University Press.
Figley, Charles R. ed. 1995. Compassion fatigue: Coping with secondary traumatic stress disorder. In *Those who treat the traumatized.* New York: Brunner.
Figley, Charles R. ed. 2002. *Treating compassion fatigue.* New York: Brunner-Routledge.
Georges, Jean-Jacques, Mieke Grypdonck, and Bernadette D. De Casterle. 2002. 'Being a palliative care nurse in an academic hospital: A qualitative study about nurses' perceptions of palliative care nursing. *Journal of Clinical Nursing* 11:785–793.
Gonzalez, Maria, and Graham Byron. 2010. *The mindful investor.* Ontario: Wiley.
Grossman, Paul, Ludger Niemann, Stefan Schmidt, and Harald Walach. 2004. Mindfulness-based stress reduction and health benefits: A meta-analysis. *Journal of Psychosomatic Research* 57 (1): 35–43.
Halbesleben, Jonathan R. B., and Cheryl Rathert. 2008. Linking physician burnout and patient outcomes: Exploring the dyadic relationship between physicians and patients. *Health Care Management Review* 33:29–39.
Harrison, Richard L., and Marvin J. Westwood. 2009. Preventing vicarious traumatization of mental health therapists: Identifying protective practices. *Psychotherapy Theory, Research, Practice, Training* 46:203–219.
Hawkins, Andrew C., Ruth A. Howard, and Jan R. Oyebode. 2007. Stress and coping in hospice nursing staff. The impact of attachment styles. *Psycho-oncology* 16:563–572.
James, Nicky, and David Field. 1992. The routinization of hospice: Charisma and bureaucracy. *Social Science and Medicine* 34:1363–1375.
Jameton, Andrew. 1984. *Nursing practice: The ethical issues.* Englewood Cliffs: Prentice Hall.
Kabat-Zinn, Jon. 2005. *Coming to our senses: Healing ourselves and the world through mindfulness.* New York: Hyperion.
Kash, Kathleen M., Jimmie C. Holland, William Breitbart, Susan Berenson, James Dougherty, Suzanne Ouelette-Kobasa, and Lynna Lesko. 2000. Stress and burnout in oncology. *Oncology* 14:1621–1637.
Katz, Renee S. 2006. When our personal selves influence our professional work: An introduction to emotions and countertransference in end-of-life care. In *When professionals weep:*

Emotional and countertransference responses in end-of-life care, eds. R. Katz and T. Johnson. New York: Routledge.
Kearney, Michael K. 2000. *A place of healing: Working with suffering in living and dying.* Oxford: Oxford University Press.
Kearney, Michael K., Radhule B. Weininger, Mary L. S. Vachon, Balfour M. Mount, and Richard L. Harrison. 2009. Self-care of physicians caring for patients at the end of life: "Being connected… a key to my survival". *Journal of the American Medical Association* 301:1155–1164.
Keeton, Kristie, Dee E. Fenner, Timothy R. B. Johnson, and Rodney A. Hayward. 2007. Predictors of physician career satisfaction, work-life balance, and burnout. *Obstetrics & Gynecology* 109:949–955.
Keidel, Gladys Catkins. 2002. Burnout and compassion fatigue among hospice caregivers. *American Journal of Hospice and Palliative Care* 19:200–205.
Kuerer, Henry M., Timothy J. Eberlein, Raphael E. Pollock, Mashele Huschka, Walter F. Baile, Monica Morrow, Fabrizio Michelassi, S. Eva Singletary, Paul Novotny, Jeff Sloan, and Tait D. Shanafelt. 2007. Career satisfaction, practice patterns and burnout among surgical oncologists: Report on the quality of life of members of the society of surgical oncology. *Annals of Surgical Oncology* 14:3043–3053.
Liaschenko, Peter E., and Joan Liaschenko. 2004. Perils of proximity: A spatiotemporal analysis of moral distress and moral ambiguity. *Nursing Inquiry* 11:218–225.
Maslach, Christina. 2003. Job burnout: New directions in research and intervention. *Current Directions in Psychological Science* 12:189–192.
Maslach, Christina, and Michael P. Leiter. 2008. Early predictors of job burnout and engagement. *Journal of Applied Psychology* 93:498–512.
Maslach, Christina, Wilmar B. Schaufeli, and Michael P. Leiter. 2001. Job burnout. *Annual Review of Psychology* 52:397–422.
McCann, I. Lisa, and Laurie Ann Pearlman. 1990. Vicarious traumatization: A contextual model for understanding the effects of trauma on helpers. *Journal of Traumatic Stress* 3:131–149.
Meier, Diane, Anthony L. Back, and R. Sean Morrison. 2001. The inner life of physicians and care of the seriously Ill. *Journal of the American Medical Association* 286:3007–3014.
Monroe, Barbara, and David Oliviere, eds. 2007. *Resilience in palliative care: Achievement in adversity.* Oxford: Oxford University Press.
Morgan, Nancy, Kristi Graves, Elizabeth Poggi, and Bruce Cheson. 2008. Implementing an expressive writing study in a cancer clinic. *Oncologist* 13 (2): 196–204.
Mount, Balfour M., Patricia H. Boston, and S. Robin Cohen. 2007. Healing connections: On moving from suffering to a sense of well-being. *Journal of Pain and Symptom Management* 33:372–388.
Myss, Caroline. 2001. *Advanced energy anatomy, CD-ROM.* Boulder: Sounds True.
Myss, Caroline. 2002. *Fundamentals of spiritual alchemy.* New York: HayHouse Audio.
Novack, Dennis H., Anthony L. Suchman, William Clark, Ronald M. Epstein, Eva Najberg, and Craig Kaplan. 1997. Calibrating the physician: Personal awareness and effective patient care. *Journal of the American Medical Association* 278:502–509.
Novack, Dennis H., Roland M. Epstein, and Randall H. Paulsen. 1999. Toward creating physician-healers: Fostering medical student's self-awareness, personal growth, and well-being. *Academic Medicine* 74:516–520.
Oberle, Kathleen, and Dorothy Hughes. 2001. Doctors' and nurses' perceptions of ethical problems in end-of-life decisions. *Journal of Advanced Nursing* 33:707–715.
Perry, Beth. 1998a. Beliefs of eight exemplary oncology nurses related to Watson's Nursing Theory. *Canadian Oncology Nursing Journal* 8:97–101.
Perry Beth. 1998b. *Moments in time: Images of exemplary nursing care.* Ottawa: Canadian Nurses Association.
Perry, Beth. 2008. Why exemplary oncology nurses seem to avoid compassion fatigue. *Canadian Oncology Nursing Journal* 18:87–92.

Pipe, Terri Britt, Jennifer J. Bortz, Amylou Dueck, Debra Pendergast, Vicki Buchda, and Jay Summers. 2009. Nurse leader mindfulness meditation program for stress management: A randomized controlled trial. *Journal of Nursing Administration* 39:130–137.

Puchalski, Christine, Betty Ferrell, Rose Virani, et al. 2009. Improving the quality of spiritual care as a dimension of palliative care: The report of the consensus conference. *Journal of Palliative Medicine* 12:885–904.

Radley, Melissa, and Charles R. Figley. 2007. The social psychology of compassion. *Clinical Social Work Journal* 35:207–214.

Remen, Rachael Naomi. 1996. *Kitchen table wisdom.* New York: Riverhead Books.

Remen, Rachael Naomi. 2000. *My grandfather's blessings.* New York: Riverhead Books.

Rice, Elizabeth M., Mohamed Y. Rady, Arreta Hamrick, Joseph. L. Verheijde, and Debra K. Pendergast. 2008. Determinants of moral distress in medical and surgical nurses at an adult acute tertiary care hospital. *Journal of Nursing Management* 16:360–373.

Rinpoche, Lama Zopa. 2010. A View on Buddhism: Compassion and Bodhicitta. www.viewonbuddhism.org. Accessed 27 Feb 2010.

Rosenzweig, Steven, Diane K. Reibel, Jeffrey M. Greeson, George C. Brainard, and Mohammadreza Hojat. 2003. Mindfulness-based stress reduction lowers psychological distress in medical students. *Teaching and Learning in Medicine* 15 (2): 88–92.

Sabo, Brenda, and Mary L. S. Vachon. 2011. Care of professional caregivers. In *Supportive oncology,* eds. Mellar P. Davis, Camilla Zimmermann, Petra Feyer and Petra Ortner. Philadelphia: Elsevier.

Shanafelt, Tait D., Paul Novotny, Mary E. Johnson, David P. Steensmaa, Martha Q. Lacy, Joseph Rubina, and Jeff Sloan. 2005a. The well-being and personal wellness promotion strategies of medical oncologists in the North Central Cancer Treatment Group. *Oncology* 68:23–32.

Shanafelt, Tait D., Colin West, Xinghua Zhao, Paul Novotny, Joseph Kolars, Thomas Habermann, and Jeff Sloan. 2005b. Relationship between increased personal well-being and enhanced empathy among internal medicine residents. *Journal of General Internal Medicine* 20:559–564.

Shapiro, Shauna L., Roger Walsh, and Willoughby B. Britton. 2003. An analysis of recent meditation research and suggestions for future directions. *Journal for Meditation and Meditation Research* 3:69–90.

Shapiro, Shauna L., J. Astin, S. Bishop, and M. Cordova. 2005. Mindfulness-based stress reduction for health care professionals: Results from a randomized trial. *International Journal of Stress Management* 12 (2): 164–176.

Shapiro, Shauna L., Kirk W. Brown, and Gina M. Biegel. 2007. Teaching self-care to caregivers: Effects of mindfulness-based stress reduction on the mental health of therapists in training. *Training, Education and Prof Psychology* 1 (2): 105–118.

Spickard, Anderson, Steven Gabbe, and John F. Christensen. 2002. Mid-career burnout in generalist and specialist physicians. *Journal of the American Medical Association* 288:1447–1450.

Stamm, Beth H. 2002. Measuring compassion satisfaction as well as fatigue: Developmental history of the compassion satisfaction and fatigue test. In *Treating compassion fatigue,* ed. C. F. Figley, 107–119. New York: Brunner-Routledge.

Stamm, Beth H. 2009. *The concise manual for the professional quality of life scale: The ProQOL.* Pocatello: ProQOL.org.

Vachon, Mary L. S. 1987. *Occupational stress in the care of the critically ill, dying and bereaved.* Washington: Hemisphere.

Vachon, Mary L. S. 1995. Staff stress in hospice/palliative care: A review. *Palliative Medicine* 9:91–122.

Vachon, Mary L. S. 2006. The experience of the nurse in end-of-life care in the 21st century. In *Textbook of palliative nursing,* eds. Betty R. Ferrell and Nessa Coyle, 2nd ed. Oxford: Oxford University Press.

Vachon, Mary L. S. 2010. Oncology staff stress and related interventions. In *Psycho-oncology,* eds. Jimmie C. Holland, William S. Breitbart, Paul B. Jacobsen, Marguerite S. Lederberg, Mathew J. Loscalzo and Ruth McCorkle, 2nd ed. New York: Oxford University Press.

Vachon, Mary L. S., and Christopher Sherwood. 2007. Staff stress and burnout. In *Principles and practice of palliative care and supportive oncology,* eds. Ann M. Berger, John L. Shuster and Jamie H. Von Roenn. Philadelphia: Lippincott.

Vachon, Mary L. S., and Monika Müeller. 2009. Burnout and symptoms of stress. In *Handbook of psychiatry in palliative medicine,* eds. William Breitbart and Harvey M. Chochinov. New York: Oxford University Press.

Vachon, Mary L. S., and Jayne Huggard. 2010. The experience of the nurse in-end-of-life care in the 21st century: Stressors, personal, professional, and organizational responsibilities. In *The Oxford textbook of palliative nursing,* eds. Betty Ferrell and Nessa Coyle. Oxford: Oxford University Press.

Vaillant, George E. 2008. *Spiritual evolution.* New York: Broadway Books.

Watson, Jean. 1989. Human caring and suffering: A subjective model for health sciences. In *They shall not hurt: Human suffering and human caring,* eds. R. L. Taylor and J. Watson. Boulder: Colorado Associated University Press.

Webster, George C., and Francoise E. Baylis. 2000. Moral residue. In *Margin of error: The ethics of mistakes in the practice of medicine,* eds. Susan B. Rubin and Laurie Zoloth. Hagerstown: University Publishing Group.

Weissman, David E. 2009. Moral distress in palliative care. *Journal of Palliative Medicine* 12:865–866.

West, Colin P., Mashele M. Huschka, Paul J. Novotny, Jeff A Sloan, Joseph C. Kolars, Thomas M. Habermann, and Tait D. Shanafelt. 2006. Association of perceived medical errors with resident distress and empathy: A prospective longitudinal study. *Journal of the American Medical Association* 296:1071–1078.

Wright, Bob. 2004. Compassion fatigue: How to avoid it. *Palliative Medicine* 18:4–5.

Chapter 25
Mental Suffering and the Brain: Insights from Neurology and Literature

Ross Mellick

Try as we may we cannot avoid either pain or suffering, propensities for both having been embedded in the neuronal pathways of the brain by a million years and more of Darwinian natural selection, guided by the nature/nurture process. Both are intrinsic to being human and whilst acknowledging the recurring horrors inflicted by powerful agencies on millions of individuals, generally in day-to-day experience suffering occurs because of the way the brain is, and is not caused by what the government, the boss, or some other individual does. It is an internal thing.

Suffering is determined by cellular mechanisms in the brain. Something of minimal significance in the outside world, a harsh word perhaps unintended, may be transmuted into intense suffering so that it becomes a life changing or life threatening event, whilst circumstances of intense suffering and imminent death, such as a death camp experience, might be completely overcome, even briefly. Suffering is a mental event, something private happening in the inner realm of thoughts and feelings generated by self and directed at self.

This is because self is not a discrete entity securely directing our conscious thoughts and activities, rather there are two selves in each brain. There is an inner double. Neuroscience has identified one in each hemisphere, two separate consciousnesses that may be in conflict. There is also a fault line, 'a.... fissure at the heart of our thinking'.[1] The fissure arises when we achieve self-consciousness and the ability to self-reflect. Each of us is therefore both an object in the world of other selves and things and also a subjective self with a unique mind, both an 'I' and an 'it', but never at the same time and therefore always divided.

Suffering occurs in many degrees of magnitude, for example: disapproval; unease; anxiety; distress; dread and terror. Events causing suffering in all degrees

[1] Shattuck (1997), Appendix.

R. Mellick (✉)
Institute of Neurological Sciences, Prince of Wales Hospital, University of New South Wales, Randwick 2031, NSW, Australia
e-mail: rossmellick123@optusnet.com.au

J. Malpas, N. Lickiss (eds.), *Perspectives on Human Suffering*,
DOI 10.1007/978-94-007-2795-3_25, © Springer Science+Business Media B.V. 2012

beset all of us in some form or other. It is not a mistake or accident. If we do not encounter it because of 'outside' agency then we are likely to create it from within.

Mental suffering is a final common pathway with unnumbered possible causes, from bodily pain, something we all know, to worldly day-to-day things involving the whole spectrum of feelings, fears and disappointments, like the intensity of unfulfilled desire and unrequited love, something most would experience, and also experiences in the creative and 'spiritual' realms which are less usual. Suffering is also attached like a shadow to our most valued and joyful experiences, and to life itself, because of the ever present threat of the loss of these good things.

Great advances in knowledge about the brain have occurred over the past 200 years, especially so in neurology and neuroscience, however there has been no meaningful advance in understanding suffering or the mental realm in general. Day-to-day human experience remains, for the most part, inaccessible because it is internal, in the mind. In the view of some, scientists and non-scientists alike, the objective nature of scientific enquiry permanently excludes it from the possibility of replicating in the mental realm the success it has achieved in understanding the body, physical illness and the natural world.

What follows will make reference to important research from cellular and behavioural neuroscience related to mental phenomena closely relevant to suffering, including free will, feelings and reason in decision making, empathy, the imagination[2] and, crucially, the nature of self, and will also provide insight into the mental realm and suffering which is not accessible to the current projects of science, and which is gleaned from literature.

The three thousand year-old traditions, oral and written, of the Hebraic and Hellenistic worlds, whose combined influence is foundational in the cultural evolution and development of the modern Western mind and world as we know it, placed self, suffering and the mental realm near to centre stage from earliest times. Something similar also has occurred in ancient texts from Asia. Any commonality is not surprising considering the causal role of brain structures on our humanness, no matter where we live or when.

The first example from these traditions is a Hebraic source, the story appearing in the Book of Genesis, concerning the great patriarch, Abraham, and his response to divine instruction to sacrifice his beloved son Isaac on Mount Moriah. We, of course, cannot know his state of mind in the situation that is recounted, but we can ponder his mental conflict. The instruction was contrary to everything he believed, this being a human sacrifice, and also additionally unthinkable because there was already a Covenant, a divine promise which depended upon the survival of Isaac. Very likely he had a strong commitment to obey the divine directive and also other

[2] The *Shorter Oxford English Dictionary*, (Oxford: Oxford University Press, 1986): free will—'the third way of bringing things to pass distinct from necessity and chance'; feelings—'the condition of being emotionally affected; reason, to think in a connected sensible or logical manner'; empathy—'the power of projecting one's personality into, and so fully understanding, the object of contemplation'; imagination—'the action of imagining, or forming, a mental concept of what is not actually present to the senses'.

co-existing strong feelings: love; trust; fear; perhaps horror, and possibly much else for which we may have no available vocabulary, not everything in the mental realm being necessarily capable of representation by words and modern language. Nevertheless, with this example we witness Abraham, and by implication other humans, in a circumstance when a decision has to be made with terrible competing alternatives as the human mind strains with things both mundane and beyond the mundane which in this day and age are represented by worldly, metaphysical and spiritual[3] realms. This event and its implications have, for millennia, engaged generation upon generation in endless written commentaries and discussion which continue to this day, irrespective of religious or spiritual orientation.

Abraham had previously demonstrated his free will effectively when he had argued successfully against the divine intention at Sodom and might have exerted his free will differently and perhaps argued again against the divine directive. He seemed, however, to have been motivated strongly by obedience and faith until the last minute when his hands were stayed by divine intervention. He had, however, demonstrated something unforgettable about the perimeters of human feeling, faith and obedience.

At about the same distant time in the Greek world, Homer in his great work *The Iliad*, writes also about mental suffering involving love, here between father and son, and also between Achilles and his beloved older friend Patroklos, but without a strong sense of crucial influence on human action from outside the mundane realm. Although the gods are involved, their role is secondary. My second example comes from this Greek source, and concerns Priam as he watches Achilles, in his unassuageable rage at the death of his friend Patroklos, drag his son Hector's dead body around the walls of his doomed city, desecrating the body in public view (Homer 1950). In Homer's work, we witness suffering contributed to by feelings of love, anger, revenge, sadness, and later, compassion and empathy.

Consider the action of free will in Priam's risky but insightful decision to face the fearsome Achilles directly, not as a king but as an old man, himself near to death and to simply request the return of his son's body. Here the dramatic events are framed and facilitated by shared awareness of the inescapable human fate of death. Achilles' rage is softened, he tells us, since as he gazed on Priam he remembered his father in advanced years. He is also aware of his own already foretold approaching death in battle. Rage and desire for revenge give way to a well of shared human emotion and empathy as he agrees to the request and he and Priam embrace.

The decision-making we witness in these two examples depends upon the interplay of many aspects of normal thinking, including reason, imagination, feeling, empathy and free will. In the above instances each of them appears to have made good decisions.

However, in day-to-day life, whether the choices we face are subtly or grossly different, we are not reliably good at exerting our free will and marshalling our cognitive skills with similar success. Often our free will leads us to wrong choices and

[3] Ibid, Spiritual—'concerning the spirit and high moral qualities, especially as regarded in a religious aspect.'

to considerable suffering for ourselves and others which may continue well beyond our lifetime. Good reasoning may also lead to conflicting choices because there may be more than one solution to a problem and the solutions may be contradictory. Also, everything we feel and do potentially engages the whole brain which may not be effectively governed by reason, which is only one possible way of thinking and making decisions.

The great seventeenth century philosopher René Déscartes had a broad understanding of thought and thinking which is similar to the meaning adopted here. Here he asks, and answers, the question: 'But what then am I? A thing which thinks. What is that? A thing that doubts, understands, affirms, denies, is willing, is unwilling, and also imagines and has sensory perceptions (Descartes 1999).' We will here also include thought which is neither willed nor conscious.

Some basic neuroscience will assist the understanding of what thinking means at the cellular level, because those cellular processes create all cognitive possibility without which we could neither reason, feel, be conscious of self or suffer. The insights that follow emphasize the vastness of the possibilities of the mental realm created by the brain, and also the limits determined by our genetic structure and our indivisible terrestrial nature which joins us like an invisible umbilical cord to the natural world.

The DNA in the first fertilized cell at the instant of our conception contains our parental inheritance and genetic data which includes an inner template of the world we will inhabit after birth, its temperature range, the content of the air and water, the force of gravity, the nutrients available and all manner of other essential information necessary for our individual survival. At a sub-cellular level we also contain vestigial living fossils of our biological past. Our mitochondria, the powerhouse of cells, represent the bacteria and the genes themselves join us to the protein chemistry of viruses. The great human genome project emphasizes our shared genetic similarity with other species, and also the essential link between our unexpectedly small number of genes and the way they are turned on and off by genetically anticipated environmental cues. For example, if we are not exposed to appropriate visual experience during specific windows of time, vision will not develop normally even though our eyes will appear normal.

The brain which we now have is not intrinsically a better organ than it was in ice-age times. However, we as individuals may be much better because each of us has a unique brain which we fashion by our individual experience. We also exist in a cultural setting and therefore may benefit or not from what has gone before as each epoch changes and possibly enriches the cultural environment: the Roman incorporated and added to the Greek, and the Northern Italian Renaissance embracing both, leading to the European Enlightenment of the eighteenth century, to the flowering of science, our modern age, and all else that forms our contemporary social environment in the Western world.

Spiritual traditions have also provided enrichment of the mental realm and although resting upon Judaic and Christian origins in the Western World these have been added to by ancient teachings of Original peoples, including Indigenous Australians.

The basic cellular unit of the brain is the neurone, of which there are estimated to be 10,000,000,000, each one having up to 10,000 connections (synapses) with other neurones. Each one communicates by electrical impulses and neurotransmitters. Some synapses facilitate transmission while others impede transmission. Thinking involves the play of both and their orchestration by feedback loops, producing dynamic and highly variable patterns of cellular recruitment and inter-reaction creating what we recognise as reasoning, feeling and all else that the brain is capable of in one vast integrated functioning unit. Different patterns of recruitment of neurones result in different cognitive events.

Tens of millions of neurones may be recruited in a unit of time measured in thousandths of a second enabling almost endless possibilities for permutations and combinations, cell with cell, cell with group, group with group, on both sides of the brain in all its many anatomical parts in ever changing, extremely fast ultramicroscopic electrical and neuro-chemical conversations.

Neuronal activity resulting from these processes can be seen in highly refined brain scans in the living human brain but is nevertheless only visible in very small degree despite the remarkable scanning techniques available which can perhaps be likened to snapshots of the lights of the city of New York seen from the moon, giving no idea of the countless millions of fast-as-a-flash electrical and chemical transactions occurring between all the various units that make up the whole great city in all directions at each instant. The almost unimaginable complexity is additionally multiplied because of the brain's capacity to change itself physically: new synaptic connections are formed and old ones eliminated as we engage in day to day life and embrace or put aside aspects of lived experience.

All information received from the outside world is transmuted through the five senses into electrical and chemical languages. The grass is not green out there nor the sky blue: the brain creates these experiences in our mental realm by translating from different wavelengths of light. The colours and the feelings we attached to them are made within the brain by neuronal activity. Self consciousness and all thought, memory, reasoning, feeling and imagining depends on neuronal activity in one configuration or another. Our feelings allow joy, happiness and also our ability to suffer.

The triumphs and follies of the entire expanse of human history, all the artifacts of human culture; the works of art in the museums of the world; the music; the literature, everything which has been produced by the human hand and mind from the beginning of human time has evolved from this process beginning with a thought, an ultramicroscopic flash of energy, like a pinpoint of light in the darkness amongst the vast internal constellations which spread and recruit other constellations of neurones. Mental suffering, and the best and worst of which we are capable, arise by means of these neuronal events.

The neurone also enfolds the entire shared genetic legacy of the species in DNA and other protein structures, which replicate themselves unchanged, generation after generation and millennia after millennia. The molecular and ultra-microscopic structure of each individual brain and the inherited species legacy has not changed for a hundred thousand years or more. Each of us has a brain with basic cerebral structures that are still those of our cave-dwelling ice-age ancestors.

Each self is nevertheless unique and an indivisible unit comprising the highly malleable and changing physical brain and its correspondingly changeable mental realm embodied. The self is therefore not the body but the body colonised by the mental realm, the product of thought and prone to change and mutate. Also, for the most part, neuronal activity, thought, is not generated by conscious processes. The eminent neuroscientist, Michael Gazzaniga, tells us that 98% of what the brain does is outside of conscious awareness (Gazzaniga 2000), not governed by the conscious self. Susan Greenfield, the eminent neuroscientist, writes about the lack of progress of neuroscience into the mental realm: 'we have not yet really moved forward at all…the big question that scientists are still ducking is how the actual feel of emotions, raw consciousness no less, is accommodated in the physical mass' (Greenfield 2000), the physical mass being the brain. A similar attitude is voiced by the celebrated neuroscientist, Joseph E. LeDoux who, in the last sentence of an authoritative piece on the neuroscience of the emotions, writes 'we don't know what emotions are and if we don't know what emotions are how can we hope to identify them?' (LeDoux 1995).

Thought may be about things, or it might be the experience itself: the feeling, pain or suffering. This distinction relates to Shattuck's fissure at the heart of our thinking, one side of the fissure being third-person thinking and the other first-person thinking. Thinking about something causes that thing to become objective, whether it is a person, a living thing, or not. By contrast, when we join ourselves to the thing it becomes a first person experience embraced within the space of intimacy and an extension of the 'I'.

The mental experiences of the great Patriarch Abraham and Priam, King of Troy are still potentially part of our day to day lives as we face conflict, turmoil and decision making, relying on the same shared brain reservoirs and capacities. If we look back further to a different cultural source to the Epic of Gilgamesh, we will also find familiar human capacities and actions including suffering in its various forms. If we know nothing of past millennia and live entirely in the present we will nevertheless not escape these experiences as we are bound to them because we are terrestrial social beings. Age-old cellular mechanisms will lead us to live, love and suffer because in the very act of living in the world, the propensities imbedded in the species are inevitably expressed in our day-to-day lives.

About 100 years ago the great Spanish neuroanatomist, Ramón y Cajal, wrote fondly of neurones: 'Like the entomologist in search for highly coloured butterflies, my attention hunted in the garden of the grey matter cells of delicate and elegant form, the mysterious butterflies of the soul' (Cajal 1937). This was written at a time when there seemed no limit to the possibilities of scientific research to advance knowledge and improve the human state. However, despite extraordinary progress of knowledge about the living brain at molecular and ionic levels of precision, the mental realm in general remains problematic territory for neuroscience.

Nobel Laureate Gerald M Edelman also wrote that he was puzzled about the gap between scientific explanations and everyday experiences, including what we consider here. He writes: '…(it) is most curious. In principle, no subject is a priori immune from scientific enquiry. Yet the very ground of our awareness has been left outside the pale' (Edelman 2006). Although many scientists agree with him, others disagree. One, quoted by Edelman, the eminent physicist, Erwin Schrödinger, observed: 'no scientific theory in physics includes sensations and perceptions and to get ahead it must therefore assume these phenomena as being outside of science's grasp' (Edelman 2006).

The celebrated scientist, Noam Chomsky, whose ground-breaking ideas about deep structures in brain reorientated scientific enquiry regarding the origins of language, is another who does not have confidence in the likely success of scientific enquiry in these realms, commenting that we will always learn more about human life and the inner subjective realm 'from novels rather than from psychology' (Chomsky 1988). George Steiner, whilst acknowledging the great achievements of science and technology, remarks in similar vein: 'I mean that they (the natural and mathematical sciences) have added little to our knowledge or governance of human possibility, that there is demonstrably more of insight into the matter of man in Homer, Shakespeare, or Dostoevsky than in the entirety of neurology and statistics', adding 'and it is precisely the 'objectivity', the moral neutrality in which the sciences rejoice and attain their brilliant community of effort, that bar them from final relevance' with regard to the inner world of mental events (Steiner 1990).

The schism at issue here may be partly explained by an astute observation made in 1987 by the celebrated neurobiologist, J. Z. Young, who pointed to two entirely separate modes of enquiry into the brain. There were, he observed, 'those who conduct their enquiries by examining their own subjectivity with their own thoughts and others trained not to do so but trained to think about other peoples' brains using the resources of science'.[4] Here he points to third-person and first-person thinking.

In a celebrated paper, the social scientist Willis Harman, made some crucial observations that are relevant here. He writes: 'When the conscious awareness of the scientist is conditioned by training to look outwards only the present form of science may seem to offer a reasonable world view. But when consciousness turns back upon itself and attention turns inward, not only is another realm of experience added to the picture but a new order of external reality may be seen. The observer is changed in the process' (Harman 1993).

A powerful example of this phenomenon is provided by anthropologist Claude Lévi-Strauss. In the concluding pages of his classic and foundational work *Tristes Tropiques*, he describes how, after working for some years with tribes of Indians in the Brazilian jungles, he found himself suspended between the culture he left in Europe and the Indian culture. He found himself at an 'abyss'—he had been changed. His scientific work required him to make external observations and to record and to measure. However, living within the Indian culture required him to turn consciousness inward, creating another world view. He wrote in the concluding paragraph that the 'scent that can be smelt in the heart of the Lily….(is)….more imbued with learning than all our books…' and, at the end of his time with the Indians

[4] J. Z. Young, quoted in Benson (1994).

he found himself unable to communicate with anyone other than 'perhaps to share a sense of mutual forgiveness....(and)....involuntary understanding....with a cat' (Lévi-Strauss 1992).

The widely acknowledged observations of C. P. Snow regarding the 'two cultures', made in his Reith lecture in Cambridge in 1959, are echoed in the 1987 comment, quoted above, by J. Z. Young. Although the circumstances of Snow's observations at Cambridge more than 50 years ago might be considered to bear little relevance to the day to day experiences of most people today, the insights of neuroscience support his observations. Snow reflected on the divisive effect of training in one mode of thought or another: '...I felt I was moving among two groups—comparable in intelligence, identical in race, not grossly different in social origin, earning about the same incomes who had almost ceased to communicate at all, who in intellectual, moral and psychological climate had so little in common that instead of going from Burlington House or South Kensington to Chelsea, one might have crossed an ocean. In fact, one had travelled much further than across an ocean—because after a few thousand Atlantic miles one found Greenwich Village talking precisely the same language as Chelsea and both having about as much communication with M.I.T. as though the scientist spoke nothing but Tibetan...' (Snow 1993). The scientists were trained as arms-length third-person thinkers, whilst the writers were obliged to turn consciousness inwards towards a first-person mode of thinking and experience.

The achievements of neuroscience provide empirical third-person evidence about the brain and mental realm that suggest that the self is in great part predetermined, not a secure entity directing brain activity with the authority of sound reasoning, but itself the product of the brain, 98% of which is outside of conscious awareness. Thus conscious decision-making is to great degree influenced by impulses and feelings which are not thought through, and the self is changeable and prone to mutations, unexplained and generated from deep within the brain. The self is also divided, incorporating two different and potentially conflicting world-views.

Two simultaneously-existing selves, two consciousnesses in one brain, were demonstrated by the observations of the Nobel Laureate, Roger Sperry, in the 1960's when he performed experiments on patients who had the two hemispheres of their brain separated surgically as treatment for intractable epilepsy (Sperry 1993). Sperry reported that the individuals appeared unchanged with regard to everyday activities and that a routine medical examination did not reveal any abnormality. However special tests showed that each half brain appeared to have largely its own separate cognitive domains with separate private perceptual learning and memory. One patient expressed emotion on only one side of the face and the left hand of one patient attempted to throttle her whilst the other hand came to her aid.

The two simultaneously existing consciousnesses in the one brain may not be in agreement, and the body might become contested territory for each.

His work was expanded by collaborator, Michael Gazzaniga, who described an 'Interpreter' in the left hemisphere, 'the talking hemisphere'. His extensive experiments on many patients led him to several conclusions. He wrote that the Interpreter had an important role: to deceive us by creating 'the impression that our brain works according to our instructions and not the other way around', and also 'we have to learn to lie to ourselves', and that the Interpreter creates our view of ourselves and keeps us believing things, even if they are untrue. He also tells us that the Interpreter is the last step in countless electrical and neuro-chemical exchanges, 'a special device in the left brain, that carries out one more activity upon completion of zillions of automatic brain processes' (Gazzaniga 2000).

This echoes the idea that the self is a product of the brain and constructed by the thinking that precedes, rather than being the originator of the process, an idea presented 120 years ago in William James' landmark book *The Principles of Psychology*. James wrote in its introduction: 'The self….of the individual…no longer has a pre-existing source of representations being reminiscences, perceptions, emotions, volitions, passions, theories and all other furnishings of the individual mind but as their last and most complicated fruit' (James 2007). James conceived of the self being built like a house from stones or bricks. He was, however, also aware that the metaphor of bricks and a house represented a far too rigid concept of the self, and elsewhere he wrote of the 'mutations of the self', and of moments when we become aware of our other simultaneously existing consciousnesses (James 2007).

The body is a crucial part of our conception of self and the image we see reflected back from a shop window is familiar and often reassuring. However, because it is so easily visible and active in the world it can come to be regarded as the 'self' or at least to be synonymous with it. However, the living body is also part of the mental realm, not a separate entity, and in considerable measure a hollow thing which is appropriated by various mutations of self which then may act upon the world through that embodiment. The body is a crucial part of self, but much like a hand puppet at the command of the mental realm.

Up to a point, bodily pain has survival value, and serves to emphasize the bodily aspect of self. We will therefore not touch a biting insect twice, nor will we continue to exert ourselves when we experience angina or other severe muscle pain. Deep pain within the body's surface also serves to draw attention to the site of function threatening or life threatening pathology. However, the body and the mental realm are indivisible and bodily pain also commonly takes its origin entirely from the mental realm. For example, severe phantom pain may occur in a limb which is no longer present after its amputation because the amputation does not change the correlate of the body in the mental realm, a homunculus, which is unchanged by the amputation still with intact limbs. Phantom pain although a mental event, is no less 'real' than the pain induced by physical injury and is sometimes more prone to induce mental suffering because it commonly has a more disturbing quality than bodily pain.

Our physical body, the visible self, is always in some degree contested territory because it can be partially or wholly appropriated by one self and, at other times, by another self. Although the full Jekyll and Hyde phenomenon is rare it is not unusual in lesser degree. Our mental image of our body may also not correspond with the way others see and experience our body. Inner mutations of self result in a group of medical conditions associated with distorted perceptions of self, causing various degrees of suffering.

Emaciated individuals suffering with anorexia nervosa may see themselves as overweight and suffer considerably or even die. There may also be a difference between what one mutation of the self honestly regards the body to be capable of doing, compared with what is regarded to be so for another equally honest mutation of self. Paralysis and other incapacities may unaccountably come and go, or be present and be denied; jobs may be lost; marriages and relationships come apart and lives fall into disarray.

Although the physical self seems immutable and unchanging, it is indivisibly part of the flux of mental events, and therefore all manner of distress might arise from what might be wrongly regarded to be a physical cause.

Almost all feelings and cognitive capacities, in one way or another may contribute to mental suffering. Fear and the power of the imagination are potent common causes, whether related to something happening in the present, something remembered which happened in the past or something wholly imagined.

The powers of the imagination and the emotions have long been likened to great storms at sea which threaten the mariner's craft, while reason is regarded to be the reliable antidote for those internal storms.

This idea grew from a great poem by Lucretius in classical Roman times, *On the Nature of the Universe*, which later brought this Greek notion into Renaissance Europe, and provided a powerful stimulus for the general elevation of reason above feelings—'Can you then doubt that this power rests with reason alone? All life is a struggle in the dark…' (Lucretius 1977) It also provided a powerful stimulus for enquiry into the natural world and for the development of science. Lucretius continued: 'As children in blank darkness tremble and start at everything, so we in broad daylight are oppressed at times by fears as baseless as those horrors which children imagine coming upon them in the dark. This dread and darkness of the mind cannot be dispelled by the sunbeams, the shining shafts of day, but only by an understanding of the outward form and inner workings of nature'.[5] The influence of this way of thinking is still evident in modern times as imagination and strong emotion are still often equated with childhood rather than also being a legitimate and essential part of the mature mind.

Greenfield seems to have this work in mind when she writes about feelings '… When we experience basic and strong emotions our physical brains must in some way be stripped of meaning and memories, that is the brain state of the infant…' (Greenfield 2000).

The elevation of reason and the downgrading of feelings has, however, long attracted dissenting voices, notably the Scottish philosopher David Hume who emphasized the dominance of feelings over reason: moral knowledge arises because of an immediate finer sense, '…….some internal taste or feeling which distinguishes moral good and evil', not by a 'chain of argument and induction….', adding that it is also it is not contrary to reason '….to prefer the destruction of the whole world to the scratching of my little finger…'(Hume 1978, p. 416).

[5] Lucretius (1977), Bk.2, lines 50–62, Bk 1 line 1.

Feelings are also the foundation for our sense of commonality with other humans and unite us when reason alone cannot. Feelings and reason act together naturally because of the way the brain is, in order to create all manner of things and the institutional structures and activities of the species in the world as we know it, from our system of justice to science itself.

Behavioural neuroscience provides support for Hume's opinion, and although feelings and reason may of course in some circumstances be mutually antagonistic, the world view that reason is equated with a mature state of mind and strong feelings and powerful imagination with childhood dangerously distorts the crucial role of their combined action in maturity in the way we think, act and derive meaning from perceptions.

A striking instance of this phenomenon was reported by the neurologist Ramachandran in 1993 (Ramachandran and Blakeslee 1998). He had been consulted by a distressed parent whose son had the delusion that his mother and father were imposters but exact replicas of his real parents. He was not paranoid and reported that they 'meant no harm'. The young man had previously suffered a serious head injury, had apparently made a full recovery and was otherwise normal. Extensive testing revealed no physical or psychiatric abnormality. A single circumscribed abnormality was, however, eventually discovered when the test demonstrated a localised disconnection between the region of the brain responsible for recognising his parents' faces and another region necessary for him to attach meaning to that visual information. The disconnection meant he could no longer experience 'the warm glow' which was a crucial part of his experience when he looked at his parents and because he could not 'feel' that they were his parents he concluded that they were not. His reasoning otherwise on formal testing was normal. However, the proposition that two individuals could be found identical to one's parents in every way, to be generally accepted by others to be who they were, to inhabit their house, and wear their clothes, and yet be impostors, is not remotely possible or plausible. Yet, the absence of a feeling of familiarity was crucial to the cerebral processes that enabled Ramachandran's patient accurately to build meaning. The patient's belief was unreasonable, but absolutely unshakeable.

We may also see the effects of the disconnection of reason and feeling constitutionally in the classical psychopathic personality who is unable to properly comprehend the consequences of actions on others and may do terrible things, and be entirely unmoved by the suffering caused.

Feelings and reason are not competing poles, as suggested by Greenfield, but cognitive capacities that act in concert. People depend on moods, pulses of feeling as influential guides when establishing meaning and making decisions. This was demonstrated in an influential paper entitled 'The Emotional Dog and its Rational Tail' by the psychologist, Haidt (2001). He observed that most thinking occurs automatically outside of consciousness, and found that people could not tell how they reached a judgement. He described participants to have stuttered, laughed and expressed surprise at their inability to find supporting reasons for judgements which they nevertheless persisted in maintaining. Supporting evidence from functional MRI scanning of the brain in the living subject also indicates that flashes of feeling help to explain responses to dilemmas in processing information to determine meaning and decision making. The neurologist, Michael R. Koenigs, has provided case reports showing that feelings are necessary in determining meaning and making judgements about moral[6] dilemmas, about right and wrong (Koenigs et al. 2007).

Cognitive neuroscientist Jorge Moll and his co-workers also produced evidence that feelings are often more important than reason in the way we construct meaning (Moll et al. 2005). They drew attention to groups of feelings necessary in making moral judgements of right and wrong. 'Moral feelings' such as guilt, compassion, regret, anger, shame, pride, contempt and disgust are important in assessing the consequences of decisions and actions on the welfare of others.

Neurological insights indicate that each of these feelings is the consequence of highly dynamic processes involving specific neurological configurations in the brain. The capacity to understand shared feelings with others, empathy, is crucial in the formation of harmonious relationships between individuals and larger groups and its absence facilitates discord or worse. It is likely to have its cellular origin in the Mirror Neurone system described by Rizzolatti and his co-workers (Rizzolatti and Craighead 2004). When we witness something emotionally charged happening in the outside world, perhaps an act of violence or someone in emotional distress, we are able to understand from the inside much more than is circumscribed by the visual content of the experience. Because of it, our brain is activated as though the observer is part of the action. This work has been expanded to include the notion that parts of our cerebral cortex are not private and 'our own', but rather, are 'social' and are the ability to process mental states of others as if they were our own. We are therefore structured by cellular evolution to share the suffering of others. This we can easily acknowledge with family members, friends and those we love and, in some degree, members of our group or tribe but it is not so easy to recognise when we see a competitor, adversary or enemy in trouble when other feelings and thoughts become dominant.

Free will is important in decision making and may lead to actions which will produce or avoid suffering. Relevant observations about the exercise of free will arise from the work of Benjamin Libet. He demonstrated that the conscious self becomes aware of an intended bodily movement only after the brain had already recorded neuronal activity that showed that the intended movement was set in motion at a cellular level before the conscious self had decided to perform the action. Our brain also registers what is happening in the outside world before the conscious self is aware of it. This work has been amply confirmed and extended. It means that the conscious self is the last to know much that goes on in both the outside and inner realm and the inner double has first access to the information.

This points to the disturbing notion that we are in major degree determined by the way the brain works. It is my brain, but, strangely, I am its product.

However we feel we have free will and know we can exercise it for better or worse. Benjamin Libet also happily provided empirical evidence of free will when

---

[6] The *Shorter Oxford Dictionary*: moral—'of or pertaining to the distinction between right and wrong or good and evil in relation to actions, volitions or character'.

he identified a significant measured interval, a crucial delay of between one and two hundred thousandths of a second, small but enough, which is of great significance as it allows time for conscious intervention upon an act already set in motion; something about to be said or done (Libet 1999). This delay provides the conscious mind with the power of veto, provided focussed insight and judgement is actively applied.

Scientific enquiry has provided information which places on an empirical basis things which we recognise as part of our day to day experience. For example, most of us would recognise how easily we are swayed unreasonably by our feelings, how we share the suffering of those close to us and how an involuntary powerful sense of empathy may enhance our closeness to others. Most adults would also recognise the changeable nature of self, how we may change considerably from day to day unaccountably, and how things which might be troubling us may look different when we have simply slept well and nothing else has changed. Self is in flux, a composite of many mutations unconsciously determined by brain activity: those 'zillions' of processes that precede the final step Gazzaniga told us about.

The power of the imagination is different from the brain capacities considered above. It entails the power to conceive of things not and perhaps never present in the senses: a capacity embedded in the brain which seems to allow the exploration of all brain possibilities already partially exposed and of extending thought to an entirely new place, perhaps never before conceived by any individual mind. It is also often associated with strong creative impulses.

The power of imagination generates all sorts of wonderful things in normal day to day life, and activity in science, the humanities and the creative arts. However, like almost all cognitive capacities, imagination also offers opportunities for considerable damaging and distressing possibilities. It varies considerably from individual to individual and is capable of generating such 'reality' in the inner realm as to displace the significance of the world at large and even individual life itself.

The highly regarded psychologist, Mihaly Czikszentmihalyi, who has written about the creative process, pointed to a loosening of connection with the outside world when the imagination is highly active and associated with focused activity. He wrote that 'the roof might fall in and not be noticed when the creative impulse is in full flow' (Czikszentmihalyi 1991). George Steiner also draws attention to the curious phenomenon that made-up characters in a writer's mind might possess a life force greater than that of living creatures. 'A cry in a poem may come to sound louder, more urgent, more real than a cry in the street outside' (Steiner 1990). One of the seminal figures of modernism, Charles Baudelaire, also observed: 'ce qui est crée par l'esprit est plus vivant que la matière'—that which is created by the mind is more living than matter, (Baudelaire 1949) and Poet Laureate, Ted Hughes, bluntly states that the inner world is the place of 'final reality' (Hughes 2008).

The imagination may magnify realities created in the mental realm and also loosen social and environmental connections with lived experience, with a possibility of life enhancing or life impairing consequences.

The extremes of suffering and even the imminence of death itself may be overcome, for a short time. Primo Levi provides direct testimony of this in his now classic *If This is a Man* in which he describes his desperate struggle to piece together a few lines of the Canto of Ulysses as he and another victim of the death camp, Pikolo, trudge through the mud and cold under the smoking chimney at Auschwitz: 'Think of your breed; for brutish ignorance/Your metal was not made; you were made men/To follow after knowledge and excellence'.

Levi writes that when these few lines came to his mind they caused him to feel as if he was hearing the poem for the first time and he likened it to a blast of a trumpet, 'like the voice of God'. He wrote: 'For a moment I forgot who I am and where I was… '. Although desperately short of food he wrote:

'I would give today's soup to know how to connect the fragment 'like on any day' to the last lines. I try to reconstruct it through the rhymes, I close my eyes, I bite my fingers—but it is of no use, the rest is silent. Pikolo begs me to repeat it… how good Pikolo is, he is aware that it is doing me good. I keep Pikolo back, it is vitally necessary and urgent that he listen, that he understand this 'as pleased Another' before it is too late; tomorrow he or I might be dead, or we might never see each other again, I must tell him, I must explain to him about the so human and so necessary, and yet unexpected anachronism, but still more, something gigantic that I myself have only just seen, in a flash of intuition, perhaps the reason for our fate, for our being here today…' (Levi 2006).

Here the lines of a medieval Italian poet written more than 600 years previously have the power to transform for Primo Levi, even briefly, the terrible reality of the death camp.

The power of the imagination may also act to threaten wellbeing and create personal danger, suffering, self-injury and perhaps even suicide.

Thomas Mann remarked insightfully that great art and beauty arise out of mental suffering (Mann 2010). The examples which follow also concern the human mind striving towards realms beyond the mundane, and involvement with the metaphysical realm and exposure to self-inflicted danger.

Let us recall the tragic suicide of Sylvia Plath. Her friend, the critic and poet A. Alvarez, writes that her suicide was an attempt to get herself out of a desperate corner her powerful imagination and creative urge had boxed her into. One of Plath's last poems 'Lady Lazarus' concluded: 'Dying….I do it so it feels real. I guess you could say I've a call' (Plath 2001). The poet here is testing imaginatively the limits of her poetic authenticity to the very end. George Steiner acknowledges this when he remarks about the 'too high cost' of her last 'fiercely honest' poems (Steiner 1990). She here strives towards the realisation of a magnitude of mental authenticity which is all consuming.

There is an increment in the imaginative transaction in the next example as the poet clearly identifies and addresses the inner double. Paul Célan, the most influential European poet of the post World War II period, who also took his own life, wrote these chilling lines: 'To one who stood outside the door …to him I opened my word….to the ugly changeling,….to the misbegotten one—to the brother born in the muddy mercenary's boot, to the twittering homunculus….(and)… to fateful alignments along a line where life faces death' (Célan 2000); and elsewhere: 'I know you: you're the one who's bent so low. You hold me—I am the riddled one—in bondage. What word would burn as witness for us two? You're my reality, I'm your mirage' (Célan 2000).

Here Célan acknowledges the power of the inner double and the imaginative force so great as to cause him to seek a word, so fitting his creative intensity and intended meaning as to burn the very page on which it is inscribed. Célan strives towards an order of poetic realisation beyond human possibility and reveals to us the power of the imagination as the human mind strains against different aspects of itself. The poet addresses the double, in the third person, however the poet remains the self that is embodied.

Although Célan acknowledges that the power of the double reduces the 'I' to a mirage, nevertheless the 'I' colonises the body and controls it: his hand continues to wield the pen. The first-person and the third-person aspect of self remain clearly distinct, and the 'I' has the final say at least in the moment to which we here are witness.

The authority Célan attributes to the inner twin is in keeping with the testament of other poets and also with neurological insights because the double is potentially the equal of its other.

In the examples given, the separation of the third person and the first person is maintained, and although we have witnessed in the words of Plath and Célan the potentially damaging influence of one aspect of self on the other, the inner double has maintained its place on the far side of Shattuck's 'fissure at the heart of thinking'. In what we witness in these works it does not assume the first person role, colonise the body or speak directly to the reader from the page. In the next example, however, we hear its voice directly.

At about the same time that Roger Sperry was investigating the split brain patients, Jorge Luis Borges, celebrated Argentinean author, wrote an extraordinary one-page parable entitled 'Borges and I'. The parable begins 'The other one, the one called Borges …', putting the author firmly into the third-person (Borges 1970).

In Borges' parable, the inner double expresses strong and independent opinions and claims truthfulness greater than that of the author himself, whom it accuses of having a 'perverse custom of falsifying and magnifying things by altering shared likes and preferences and turning them into something false … the attributes of an actor…'. It tells us the 'pages' produced by Borges are of inconsistent quality and 'only some are of value', but that those that are justify its willing role in the process involved in their production. The inner double claims the authority of greater insight. It also tells us of its active involvement in Borges' creative work and that 'little by little' it is 'giving over everything to Borges' and that it even 'goes on living' so that Borges may 'contrive' his literature.

The inner double here is far more than an 'Interpreter', we hear it both as critic and as partner facilitating the creative work. It also claims a privileged place, a special vantage point of perception, putting Borges into a subordinate role with regard to judgement about the authenticity of the work being created.

The emotional tone changes mid-way through the piece, and we hear the inner double become a potential adversary. A sudden increase in tension occurs as it observes it would be an 'exaggeration' to describe it as being 'hostile' to Borges, and also, enigmatically, that 'everything belongs to Borges or to oblivion'; and that it had previously unsuccessfully '... attempted to free itself ...' from the author, and has the intention of doing so again. This seems to suggest that the inner double may choose or refuse to submit to the process undertaken by the author, and that the alternative, oblivion, is associated with successfully freeing itself. It here implies it also has a measure of independent free will.

Oblivion has a vaguely menacing quality bringing to mind finality, void, disappearance, perhaps even death. Here the inner double might be referring to the death of the creative impulse of which it claims a crucial part if it were to successfully free itself from Borges.

However, the importance of the creative process may vary considerably from individual to individual, as does the notion of artistic authenticity. For some, well-being may be considerably threatened by the loss or attenuation of the creative capacity. The intention of the inner double to free itself from Borges may therefore carry an oblique threat, a chilling prospect since the inner double may be only one step away from its enactment. Borges' inner double is strategically situated to know more about the author's mental realm, and to know it before the conscious 'I'. Suicide, accident and premature death sadly, in one form or another, have long been associated with strong creative impulses.

Neuroscience tells us that the 'I' may exercise conscious control, the power of veto, over something already set in motion by the brain in the inner realm. However, we do not know what might facilitate or frustrate the ability to bring to bear the power of will and focused intention in order to exercise the power of veto.

In relation to the parable the part of self which is the 'I' may have been able to exercise that power of veto and thwart any effort of the inner self to 'free itself', or he may have successfully improved his performance and obtained its approval and continued cooperation. We cannot know. In this extraordinary work the embodied self, the one controlling the hand holding the pen, seems to have been the inner twin at the beginning, and not at the end of the piece. Borges also seems to have difficulty differentiating between the two parts of himself. The one-page parable begins 'The other one, the one called Borges' and ends with the admission 'I don't know which of us has written this page'. We seem here to witness a mutation of the self which enabled the inner twin for a time to colonize the body and to inscribe words on a page.

My reading of this parable may seem to some too believing and to attribute too much autonomy to the inner double. That may be so, however there are two possibilities. What we read here might be from deeply within, faithfully representing the transactions in language between two aspects of self and providing a unique testament or, on the other hand, it is possible Borges may be just playing with the reader. Yet if we consider the nature of his writing in general, the first of these possibilities is more likely, especially so as this was written towards the end of his life when his blindness may have pushed him towards greater insightfulness and loosened connection with the visible body.

My comments are also in keeping with the considerable insights provided by his editor, James E. Irby: 'Borges' stories may seem mere formalist games ... but quite the opposite is true. His insistence on knowledge and insight … All his fictional situations, all his characters, are at bottom autobiographical, essential projections of his experiences as a writer …. and human being… ' (Borges 1970).

This remarkable work suggests that far from teaching us to learn to lie to ourselves the inner double in an intact brain may be able to draw upon its privileged position to access the otherwise largely inaccessible inner realm and facilitate the capacity for faithful self-examination, and be a force for inner truthfulness and authentic self realization in what we say and do. Like the 'Interpreter', to use Gazzaniga's description, the double is a device in the brain which carries out one more step after completion of zillions of preceding brain processes but, unlike the Interpreter it is not the product of a damaged, surgically divided brain, but has access to the whole brain and to the whole inner world.

However, the inner world to which it relates is our own personal responsibility, a work of neuronal sculpture or perhaps better imagined as an inner garden of our making. What is found there are the fruits of what we ourselves have planted. However, the garden bed, the ground which nurtures them, is common property across the species, the ground of our humanness, of being human. Truthfulness to oneself, desirable as it may be, does not ensure truthfulness to others nor necessarily that we be good companions, friends or neighbours, or that the truthfulness to self may not lead to actions which are self-destructive, injurious to others and be the origin of considerable suffering for ourselves and others.

Different individuals with their own uniquely constructed inner realms will inevitably have different relationships with their inner double and with their personal mental world. The intensity we witness with Plath and Célan is very different from what we find, for example, in the work of Rimbaud whose experience of his double causes him to remark soberly 'Je est un autre'—I am another (Rimbaud 2002), and Walt Whitman is untroubled by his mutating self and writes: 'Do I contradict myself?….. I am multitudes!', shrugs and moves on (Whitman 1986). Alfred Brendel, one of the most celebrated pianists of our era, listened carefully to a recording of a performance of a work he knew well, took special note of the aspects of the performance of which he disapproved, and when the performance came to an end he discovered to his surprise that he was the performer (Throsby 2010). The first-person experience during the performance entirely excluded the double, while critical third-person appraisal involved the double to the exclusion of first-person awareness.

Memory for distant events is sometimes better than for recent events—the double exists in brain time, not clock time, and events of the distant past don't necessarily recede with time.

In 1987, a little after 10am on a sunny Saturday morning, the concierge of the building where Primo Levi lived with his wife, biophysicist son and mother, heard 'un tonfo'—a thud (Thomson 2003). She opened the door of her apartment and saw his body on the marble floor. She had seen him a few minutes before when he had greeted her, as usual, smilingly and courteously. A few minutes later he projected himself headfirst over the third level railing and into the stairwell.

A survivor of the death camp remarked shortly after, that being a chemist he had access to much more discrete ways of ending his life and 'he would have never exposed his loved ones to such a gruesome sight which he would never have wanted them to see.' Another survivor and friend, Edith Bruck, observed about his books: 'There are no howls of emotion in Primo's writing—all emotion is controlled—but Primo gave such a howl of freedom at his death.'

The title of his great work *If This is a Man* is clearly incomplete—a statement, perhaps to be completed at some future time and in a manner of his choosing. His wife, who was out shopping when the event occurred, remarked of his suicide: '…at the last moment I suppose his self mastery fled him', and the day he died, when he made his 'howl of freedom', the 11th April, was the same date as the day in 1945 when he was liberated from the death camp. Some thought his suicide was related to his prostate problem or depression, however perhaps not.

The Chief Rabbi of Turin, Emanuele Artom, who said the mourner's prayer at 12.10 on the day he died, connected the two events and regarded the act to have been 'not suicide exactly' but 'delayed homicide' (Thomson 2003).

Poets, musicians and writers aside, we acknowledge our transactions with the double by our language in day to day life. When expressing intention with a degree of uncertainty we say 'I tell myself'; in anger 'I am beside myself'; and at times of inner quiet and peace 'I lose myself'.

Notions of wisdom, beauty, goodness, a sense of the possibility of transcendence, of revelation, of vastness and timelessness, and our special relationship with other living things and the natural world are amongst our most valued attributes. Sometimes called spiritual qualities or perhaps attributes of soul, these are inward things, deeply embedded in some form or other in brain structure and seem to be expressed in all races in all places and at all times in some measure in both the spiritual literature, and also surviving powerfully in non-spiritual texts.

These are of the whole brain and therefore within reach of the double, and expressed in different ways in different belief systems and cultural settings. Gazzaniga's expression 'zillions of processes' incorporates these inner things and much else not possible to name within the frames of reference of neurology or neuroscience.

There was for us all in childhood, and also in the evolution of the species, a time of past Innocence, when we had no developed sense of self consciousness, internal duality, and separation from the world; when the inner dialogues of the mature and expanding mind had not begun, and we were in some way inseparably joined and at the center of things. The idea that some ease, some relief to degrees of suffering in our mental world might follow if we achieve oneness, a unity within ourselves, is heard in contemporary times and is a persisting deep desire echoing down the millennia. Here we listen as Plato has Socrates offer a prayer in *Phaedrus*:

> Beloved Pan, and all ye gods who haunt this place, give me beauty in the inward Soul; and may the outward and the inward man be at one. (Hiebel 1948)

Bibliography

Baudelaire, Charles. 1949. Fusées I. In *Journaux Intimes,* eds. Jacques Crépet and Georges Blin. Paris: Librairie José Corti.
Benson, F. D. 1994. *The Neurology of Thinking*. New York: Oxford University Press.
Borges, Jorge Luis. 1970. The house of asteron. In *Labyrinths,* eds. Donald Yates and James E. Erby. London: Penguin Books.
Cajal, Ramón y Santiago. 1937. *Recollections of my Life.* Trans. E.H. Craigie and J. Cano. Cambridge: MIT Press.
Célan, Paul. 2000. *Glottal Stop*. Trans. N. Popov and H. McHugh. Hanover: Wesleyan University Press.
Chomsky, Noam. 1988. *Language and Problems of Knowledge: The Managua Lectures*. Cambridge: MIT Press.
Czikszentmihalyi, M. 1991. *Flow: The psychology of optimal experience*. New York: Harper Collins.
Descartes, René. 1999. *Meditations on First Philosophy.* ed. J. Cottingham. Cambridge: Cambridge University Press.
Edelman, G. M. 2006. *Second Nature*. New Haven: Yale University Press.
Gazzaniga, M. S. 2000. *The Mind's Past*. Berkeley: University of California Press.
Greenfield, Susan. 2000. *The Private Life of the Brain*. London: Penguin Books.
Haidt, J. 2001. The Emotional Dog and its Rational Tail: A social intuitionist approach to moral judgement. *Psychological Review* 108:814–834.
Harman, W. W. 1993. Towards an adequate epistemology for the scientific exploration of consciousness. *Journal of Scientific Exploration* 2 (7): 137.
Hiebel, F. 1948. *The Gospel of Hellas*. New York: Anthrosophic Press.
Homer. 1950. *The Iliad of Homer*. Trans. A. Lang, W. Leaf and E. Myers. New York: The Modern Library.
Hughes, Ted. 2008. *Poetry in the Making*. London: Faber and Faber.
Hume, David. 1978. *A Treatise of Human Nature*, ed. L. A. Selby-Bigg, 2nd ed. Oxford: Clarendon Press.
James, William. 2007. *The Principles of Psychology*. NY: Cosimo Classics.
Koenigs, M., L. Young, R. Adolphs, D. Tranel, F. Cushman, M. Hauser, and A. Damasio. 2007. Damage to the prefrontal cortex increases utilitarian moral judgements. *Nature* 446:908–911.
LeDoux, J. 1995. In search of an emotional system in the brain. In *The cognitive neurosciences,* ed. M.S. Gazzaniga, 1061. Cambridge: MIT Press.
Levi, Primo. 2006. *If this is a man and the truce*. London: Abacus.
Lévi-Strauss, Claude. 1992. *Tristes Tropiques*. Trans. J. Weightman and D. Weightman. New York: Penguin Books.
Libet, B. 1999. Do we have free will? *Journal of Consciousness Studies* 6 (8–9): 47–57.
Lucretius. 1977. *On the Nature of the Universe*. Trans. R.E. Latham. Harmondsworths: Penguin Classics.
Mann, Thomas. 2010. Thomas Mann—banquet speech. Nobelprize.org. http://nobelprize.org/nobel_prizes/literature/laureates/1929/mann-speech.html.org. Accessed 23 Aug 2010.
Moll, Jorge, Roland Zahn, Ricardo de Oliveira-Souza, Frank Krueger, and Jordan Grafman. 2005. The neural basis of human moral cognition. *Nature Review/Neuroscience* 6 (10): 799–809.
Plath, Sylvia. 2001. Lady Lazarus. In *Ariel*. London: Faber and Faber.
Ramachandran, V. S., and S. Blakeslee. 1998. *Phantoms in the Brain*. London: Fourth Estate.
Rimbaud, Arthur. 2002. *Rimbaud Complete,* ed. Wyatt Mason. Trans. W. Mason. New York: The Modern Library.
Rizzolatti, G., and L. Craighead. 2004. The mirror-neuron system. *Annual Review of Neuroscience* 27:169–192.
Shattuck, Roger. 1997. *Forbidden Knowledge*. San Diego: Harcourt Brace (1st Harvest book).
Snow, C. P. 1993. *The Two Cultures*. Cambridge: Cambridge University Press (The Rede lecture).

Sperry, R. W. 1993. Some effects of disconnecting the cerebral hemispheres. (Nobel Lecture, 8 December 1981). In *Nobel lectures, Physiology or Medicine 1981–1990,* eds. T. Frängsmyr and J. Lindsten. Singapore: World Scientific.
Steiner, George. 1990. Humane literacy. In *Language and silence*. London: Faber and Faber.
Thomson, F. 1978. *The Hound of Heaven and other poems*. Boston: Branden Books.
Thomson, I. 2003. *Primo Levi*. London: Vintage.
Throsby, Margaret. 2010. Interview with Sir Neville Marriner. *Mornings with Margaret Throsby,* ABC Classic FM, broadcast Monday 14 June 2010.
Whitman, Walt. 1986. *Leaves of grass.* 1st ed. (1855). New York: Penguin Books.

Index

J. Malpas, N. Lickiss (eds.), Perspectives on Human Suffering,
DOI 10.1007/978-94-007-2795-3, © Springer Science+Business Media B.V. 2012

MIX
Papier aus verantwortungsvollen Quellen
Paper from responsible sources
FSC® C105338

If you have any concerns about our products,
you can contact us on
ProductSafety@springernature.com

In case Publisher is established outside the EU,
the EU authorized representative is:
Springer Nature Customer Service Center GmbH
Europaplatz 3, 69115 Heidelberg, Germany

Printed by Libri Plureos GmbH
in Hamburg, Germany